Philippine Politics and Society in the Twentieth Century

Well over a decade has passed since the dramatic 'People Power Revolution' in Manila, yet until now no book-length study has emerged to examine the manifold changes underway in the Philippines in the post-Marcos era. This book fills that gap. *Philippine Politics and Society in the Twentieth Century* offers historical depth and sophisticated theoretical insight into contemporary life in the archipelago.

Organised as a set of interrelated thematic essays rather than a chronological account, the book addresses key topics which will be of interest to the academic and non-academic reader, such as trends in national-level and local politics, the role of ethnic-Chinese capital in the Philippine economy, nationalism and popular culture, and various forms of political violence and extra-electoral contestation. Drawing on a wide variety of primary and secondary sources, as well as over a decade of research and work in the area, Hedman and Sidel provide an invaluable overview of the contemporary and historical scene of a much misunderstood part of Southeast Asia. This book fills an important gap in the literature for readers interested in understanding the Philippines as well as students of Asian studies, comparative politics, political economy and cultural studies.

Eva-Lotta E. Hedman is Lecturer in Asian-Pacific Politics at the University of Nottingham. **John T. Sidel** is Lecturer in Southeast Asian Politics at the School of Oriental and African Studies, University of London.

Politics in Asia series
Edited by Michael Leifer
London School of Economics

Philippine Politics and Society in the Twentieth Century

Colonial legacies, post-colonial trajectories

Eva-Lotta E. Hedman and
John T. Sidel

London and New York

First published 2000
by Routledge
11 New Fetter Lane, London EC4P 4EE

Simultaneously published in the USA and Canada
by Routledge
29 West 35th Street, New York, NY 10001

Routledge is an imprint of the Taylor & Francis Group

© 2000 Eva-Lotta E. Hedman and John T. Sidel

Typeset in Bembo by
HWA Text and Data Management, Tunbridge Wells
Printed and bound in Great Britain by
TJ International Ltd, Padstow, Cornwall

British Library Cataloguing in Publication Data
A catalogue record for this book is available from the British Library

Library of Congress Cataloging in Publication Data
Hedman, Eva-Lotta E.
   Philippine politics and society in the twentieth century : colonial
  legacies, post-colonial trajectories / Eva-Lotta E. Hedman and
  John T. Sidel.
     p. cm. – (Politics in Asia series)
  Includes bibliographical references and index.
  1. Philippines–Politics and government–20th century.
  2. Philippines–Social conditions–20th century. I. Sidel, John
II. Title. III. Series.
DS685 H43 2000
959.904'7- dc21

                               00-028445

ISBN 0-415-14790-5 (hbk)
ISBN 0-415-14791-3 (pbk)

To our families in Sweden and the United States and to those who took us into their homes in Manila and Cebu.

Contents

Series editor's preface

The study of Philippine politics has tended to take the socio-cultural legacies of a lengthy Spanish rule as its intellectual point of entry. Although the impact of a succeeding American colonialism has not been disregarded, especially in contributing to economic dependency, the overall emphasis of scholarly enquiry has been on political continuity rather than on political change. Indeed, such an emphasis would appear justified with the political reversion attendant on the downfall of the late President Marcos and the restoration of constitutional democracy. This set of interconnected essays by Dr Eva-Lotta Hedman and Dr John Sidel represents a scholarly attempt to redress the balance of analysis in interpreting the nature of Philippine politics during the course of the Twentieth Century and, in particular, during its last two decades. Their declared interest is to highlight the factor of political change during the last century through illuminating the impact of capitalist development on Philippine society. Moreover, they stress the peculiarly American nature of the Philippine state as a consequence of the structures erected and imposed during the course of its colonial era. Instead of just registering the evident resilience of a predatory oligarchy and the way in which democracy has been bent to its will, the authors pay special attention to the centrality of elections and the formative role that this American-bequeathed institution has played in patterns of class and state formation. These engrossing and well-researched essays, which invoke the perspective of comparative historical sociology, stand at the cutting-edge of social science research on the Philippines. The authors, with evident modesty, suggest that this volume is not intended to serve as a definitive work. That may or may not be the case but it is very likely that these highly readable essays will make an important contribution to revising conventional interpretations of Philippine politics. Indeed, it is possible that through their impact, the study of Philippine politics will be obliged to change. For that reason, this volume is to be commended both to country specialists and to students of Comparative Politics.

Michael Leifer

Acknowledgements

This book is the culmination of more than a decade of research and writing on Philippine politics and society, and the debts we have incurred over the years are too numerous to be fully acknowledged here. Taken separately and as a whole, the essays written individually by Hedman (Chapters 2, 3, and 6) and Sidel (Chapters 4, 5, and 7) and co-authored by Hedman and Sidel (Chapters 1 and 8) draw heavily on the influence, insights, and inspiration provided by fellow Philippinists, colleagues, and teachers. In particular, Fenella Cannell, Eric Gutierrez, Ben Kerkvliet, Al McCoy, Resil Mojares, Vince Rafael, and Rosanne Rutten have been a source of inspiration, support and guidance over the period during which this book was written. The influence of our first teachers at Cornell University, Ben Anderson and Sid Tarrow, has been formative and is evident in various chapters and the conceptualisation of the volume as a whole. We would also like to express our gratitude to Michael Leifer and Victoria Smith for their support, encouragement, and patience throughout the long process of writing, editing, and publication. Most of all, the work that went into this book was made both possible and enjoyable by friends and colleagues in the Philippines, whose good company and supportive encouragement we recall with fondness and appreciation. Above all, the Labra clan of Guadalupe, Cebu City and Benitez family of Mariposa, Quezon City took us into their homes and welcomed us into their families, and for this we shall always be grateful.

Abbreviations

AFDC	Aid to Families with Dependent Children
AFP	Armed Forces of the Philippines
ANP	Alliance for New Politics
ARMM	Autonomous Region of Muslim Mindanao
ASEAN	Association of South East Asian Nations
BCC	Basic Christian Communities
BNPP	Barisan Nasional Pembebasan Patani (Patani National Liberation Front)
BOI	Board of Investors
BPI	Bank of the Philippines
BSDU	Barrio Self Defense Units
CAFGU	Civilian Armed Forces Government Unit
CHDF	Civilian Home Defense Forces
CISO	Conference of Inter-island Shipowners and Operators
CNEA	Citizens National Electoral Assembly
COMLEC	Commission on Elections
CP	Charon Pokphand
CPP	Communist Party of the Philippines
CPT	Communist Party of Thailand
DBP	Development Bank of the Philippines
DENR	Department of Environment and Natural Resources
EDSA	Epifanio de los Santos
FACOMA	Farmer's Cooperative Marketing Association
GSIS	Government Service Insurance System
HMB	People's Liberation Army
INC	Iglesia Ni Cristo
INP	Integrated National Police
ISAG	Industrial Security Action Groups
ISAFP	Intelligence Service of the AFP
JUSMAG	Joint United States Military Advisory Group
KBL	Kilusang Babay Lipunan (New Society Movement)
KMP	Kilusang Magbubukid ng Pilipinas (Philippine Peasant Movement)

LM	Lapiang Manggagawa (the Workers' Party)
MASAKA	Malang Samatang Magsaska (the Free Peasant's Movement)
Metrocom	Philippine Constabulary Metropolitan Command
Metrodiscom	Metropolitan District Command
MIM	Muslim Independence Movement
MND	Ministry of National Defense
MNLF	Moro National Liberation Front
MPM	Magsaysay-for-President Movement
NAMFREL	National Citizens' Movement for Free Elections
Napolcom	National Police Commission
NAPOCOR	National Power Corporation
NATU	National Association of Trade Unions
NDF	National Democratic Front
NIE	Newly Industrialising Economics
NISA	National Intelligence Security Agency
NP	Nacionalista Party
NPA	New People's Army
NSFW	Negroes Federation of Sugar Workers
OCW	Overseas Contract Workers
OIC	Officers in Charge
PAFLU	Philippine Association of Free Labor Unions
PC	Philippine Constabulary
PCGG	Presidential Commission on Good Government
PCIB	Philippine Commercial and Industrial Bank
PKM	Pambansang Kaishan ng Mga (National Peasant Union)
PKP	Partido Komunista ng Pilipinas
PMA	Philippine Military Academy
PnB	Partido ng Bayan
PNB	Philippine National Bank
PNP	Philippine National Police
PPA	Philippine Ports Authority
PRRM	Philippine Rural Reconstruction Movement
PSB	Presidential Security Battalion
PSU	Presidential Security Unit
PULO	Patani United Liberation Organisation
PVL	Philippine Veterans Legion
QCCLGG	Quezon city Citizens League for Good Government
RAM	Reform the Armed Forces of the Philippines Movement
ROC	Republic of China
ROTC	Reserve Officers' Training Corps.
RUCs	Regional Unified Commands
SAS	Special Air Service
SGV	Sycip Gorres Velayo
SM	ShoeMart
SPCPD	Southern Philippines Council for Peace and Development

SWPA	Southwest Pacific Area
TFD	Task Force Detainees
TRC	Technology Resource Centre
UNICOM	United Coconut Oil Mills
UNIDO	United Nationalist Democratic Organisation
USAFFE	United States Armed Forces in the Far East
USVA	United States Veterans Administration

1 Introduction

In the mid-1980s, at the height of the Reagan era and the last decade of the Cold War, the Philippines became the focus of considerable international media attention, and news stories tended if not to romanticise the archipelago then at least to imbue it with special geo-political significance. Long-time president Ferdinand Marcos, after twenty years in power, seemed to follow in the footsteps of other brutal and rapacious 'Third World' dictators like Batista, Somoza, and Shah Reza Pahlevi. Newspaper exposés revealed in great detail the extent of the 'ill-gotten wealth' which he and his wife Imelda had accumulated and the extravagance of their lifestyle. Meanwhile, conditions of poverty and social inequality in the Philippines were among the most dramatic in Southeast Asia, as vividly – and repeatedly – described by journalists who visited Manila's vast slum area, Tondo, and interviewed 'scavengers' who earned a livelihood in the infamous garbage dump-site known as Smoky Mountain. Moreover, given the history of American colonial rule in the Philippines, the presence in the archipelago of the two largest US overseas military installations (Subic Naval Base and Clark Air Field) in the world, and Washington's strong support for Marcos, such conditions amply illustrated the harsh injustices of the Cold War, the Reagan Administration's policies in 'The Third World', and US global hegemony in general.

Against this backdrop of dictatorship, destitution, and US imperial design, the Philippines was also the site of well-publicised and somewhat romanticised political struggles at the time. By the mid-1980s, the Communist Party of the Philippines (CPP) had emerged at the forefront of the most potent revolutionary movement in Southeast Asia. With its New People's Army (NPA) guerrillas reportedly present in roughly one-fifth of the villages in the archipelago and church, student, labour and urban poor groups affiliated with the party increasingly active in the seminaries, campuses, factory belts and streets of Manila and other major Philippine cities. Local and foreign journalists alike reported frequently on the growing strength and popularity of the CPP/NPA, celebrated the guerrillas variously as 'Nice People Around' or 'the New Khmers Rouges', and predicted the implosion of the Marcos regime and the victory of revolutionary forces in just a few years' time. Only the candidacy of the 'modest housewife' Corazon C. Aquino, widow of the slain opposition leader Benigno S. Aquino, Jr, in the February 1986 'snap' presidential election brought the foreign correspondents down from the rebels' mountain and jungle hideaways and dramatically concluded the 'Revolution' story with a 'Democratic' dénouement. With US senators and major television network anchors on hand in Manila for the occasion, Marcos proceeded to engineer his own electoral victory on February 7, 1986 through massive fraud, intimidation, and violence, but was ousted a few weeks later by a military rebellion and the mobilisation of more than one million Filipinos in the streets. The success of so-called 'People Power' in Manila provided not only a happy ending of sorts for scores of book-length parachute journalists' accounts,[1] but also a precedent that local democracy activists – and international media commentators – would cite and to some extent follow a few years later, whether in the streets of Prague or, less successfully, Beijing's Tienanmen Square.

By the post-Cold War 1990s, however, the Philippines no longer held special geo-political significance in the gaze of the international media panopticon. In the place of the high drama of the mid-1980s, the Philippines of the 1990s offered only the occasional spectacle of volcanic eruptions, political buffoonery, and seemingly random and rampant violence and criminality. One survey of the *Sydney Morning Herald*'s 1993 coverage of the Philippines, for example, noted the prevalence of stories about natural disasters, 'terrorism', Imelda Marcos, and 'vice and sexual crimes'.[2] Readers of British or American broadsheets in 1999 likewise encountered little more than occasional articles on paedophiles, kidnappings, landslides, Imelda Marcos' notorious shoe collection, and the unseemly antics of the Philippines' new president, popular action-film star Joseph 'Erap' Estrada. If in the 1980s the Philippines produced the signifying chain of Dictatorship, Revolution, and Democracy, today its only claim to international fame seems to be alleged parentage of El Niño, the global meteorological phenomenon ushered in by the 1991 eruption of Mt Pinatubo: if not an entirely empty signifier then certainly one devoid of any discernible political meaning.

In recent years, this tragi-comic image of the Philippines in the media has been echoed and elaborated in lurid detail in fiction, film, and other realms of the global culture industry. Most noteworthy in this regard is probably the Hong Kong-based writer Timothy Mo, whose novels depict a Philippines populated solely by teenage prostitutes, gangsters, and society ladies, who are uniformly duplicitous, grasping, and laughably incompetent and incoherent in their crude pidgin English.[3] Alex Garland's *The Tesseract* also belongs to this genre, as the blurb on the back of the book jacket suggests:

> The sun is setting over Manila. In an abandoned hotel on the wrong side of town, Sean prepares for the arrival of Don Pepe, the mestizo gangster who runs the shipping lanes of the South China Seas. As he kills time, Sean discovers that his bed-sheets are stained with blood, the phone lines to his room are dead, and somebody has screwed a steel plate over the spyhole in his door …
>
> Elsewhere in the city, Rosa, a doctor, waits for her husband to come home. As she puts her children to bed she remembers the coastal village in which

she was raised, and the boy who would meet her on the way to school. Meanwhile, thirteen-year-old Vincente begs from the stream of airconditioned cars on Roxas Boulevard, keeping an eye out for the strange man who lives in the city's most expensive apartment block, and who pays money for street kids' dreams ...[4]

But similarly leering, lecherous portrayals of Filipinos crop up elsewhere as well. The Australian cult movie, *Priscilla, Queen of the Desert*, for example, features a brief scene with a highly flirtatious and scantily clad young Filipina mail-order-bride turned 'entertainer', who performs sexual gymnastics before a rowdy barroom crowd and her obese, aging Australian husband. Even the otherwise sympathetic heroine of Peter Hoeg's best-selling novel, *Miss Smilla's Feeling For Snow*, betrays a similarly casual form of racism:

> In Greenland they say that Filipinos are a nation of lazy little pimps, who are only allowed on ships because they don't ask for more than a dollar an hour, but you have to keep on feeding them vast amounts of steamed rice if you don't want a knife in your back.[5]

Recent trends in scholarship

Meanwhile, the late 1980s and 1990s witnessed a wave of foreign scholarship on Philippine politics and society researched and written in what might be described as an exposé mode. This scholarship was the work of academics writing in large part for a Filipino audience and in self-conscious support of the causes of democratisation, human rights, and social justice in the Philippines. The exemplary figure in this regard is the accomplished historian Alfred W. McCoy, who in the 1970s exposed the links between the US Central Intelligence Agency and the heroin trade in Southeast Asia[6] and who, in late January 1986, on the eve of the 'snap' presidential elections in the Philippines, revealed his discovery of documents which discredited Ferdinand Marcos' claims of anti-Japanese guerrilla leadership and heroism during the Pacific War.[7] In the late 1980s, McCoy did much to draw attention to the glaring social inequalities and injustices in the sugar plantation belt of Negros Occidental and also to document the involvement of the much lionised military 'reformists' (and putschists) in cases of torture and other human rights violations.[8] In the 1990s, moreover, he brought together scholars working on Philippine local history and politics in a collection of essays which underlined the endurance of large landowning families, mafia-style machine politicians and their persistent rent-seeking and criminal activities despite the restoration of formal democracy in the archipelago.[9]

Younger scholars finishing their doctoral research during the Aquino (1986–92) and Ramos (1992–98) administrations likewise tended to write in this exposé mode, combining careful research with a line of inquiry and argumentation designed to debunk the myths of 'People Power' and 'Democratisation' during this period. Political scientists like Mark Thompson and James Putzel, for example, meticulously documented how the opposition politicians who were swept in with Aquino had been utterly opportunistic in their quest for power in the 1980s, and how Aquino and other policy-makers (in Manila and Washington, DC) had systematically blocked efforts to formulate and implement an agrarian reform programme in the late 1980s, thus preserving an extremely high concentration of land and wealth in the hands of a narrow élite.[10] In his careful study of Philippine banking, moreover, political economist Paul Hutchcroft chronicled the political entrenchment of a 'predatory' oligarchy and a history of cronyism and rent-seeking activity which long preceded Marcos and impeded capitalist development in the archipelago.[11] Meanwhile, still other scholars traced the pattern of organisational weakness, ideological myopia, and tactical error which underpinned the decline and division of the Philippine Left in the late 1980s and early 1990s.[12] The authors of the collection of essays in this volume also contributed, however modestly, to this early post-Marcos wave of foreign scholarship on the Philippines, in revisionist studies of the much celebrated mobilisation of 'civil society' for 'free and fair elections' and of the supposedly 'clientelist' basis of local politics in the archipelago.[13]

The foreign Philippinists of this period, it should be noted, wrote with a Filipino audience in mind and in the hope that their work would shed light on the political forces and dynamics which had stolen the promise of 'People Power' and 'Democratisation' in the early post-Marcos period. Yet in tone and substance, these studies sometimes inadvertently echoed the moralising, muckraking accounts that American colonial authors had offered many decades earlier.[14] Compromised by patrimonialism, provincialism, and personalism, Philippine democracy was not fully Democratic, these authors seemed to suggest; Philippine capitalism was not really Capitalist, and even Philippine communism was not properly Marxist or Leninist. Indeed, it is easy to understand how readers critical and suspicious of Orientalism and essentialism might see in these writings a picture not only of the Philippines but also of Filipinos which shared some of the unflattering features of the lurid journalistic and fictional accounts cited above. After all, if the studies of 'patron-client' relations in the Philippines of the quiescent late 1950s and early 1960s depicted Filipinos as essentially deferential and obliging family and community members,[15] and subsequent work in the turbulent 1970s and early 1980s cast Filipinos as courageous rebels and subversives,[16] then much early post-Marcos scholarship tended to portray Filipinos as cynical wheeler-dealers, crass opportunists, and cunning seekers of power and wealth.

Against this prevailing tendency towards disenchantment, debunking, and derogation, another set of contemporary scholars, both Filipino and foreign, has offered an alternative vision of the Philippines and its inhabitants, one much more attentive to the self-understandings and shared aspirations of ordinary Filipinos rather than the country's 'predatory oligarchy' and other oppressors. One direction pursued in this spirit has been historical, with Filipino scholars such as Reynaldo Ileto revisiting the Philippine Revolution of the late nineteenth century, exploring the lives and works of peasant rebels like Apolinario dela Cruz and nationalist intellectuals like José Rizal, and tracing the metaphors and memories of the past in contemporary popular discourse. These scholars' interest in 'subaltern studies' and 'history from below' has worked against the recent efforts of 'official nationalists' to domesticate and defang remembrances and representations of the Revolution in centenniary celebrations, conferences, and coffee-table books.[17] Another line of investigation and inquiry has been ethnographic in nature, concerned with the efforts of ordinary Filipinos to craft identities and lead lives of dignity in the face of considerable material deprivation, exploitative social relations, and political disenfranchisement. Political scientists like Benedict Kerkvliet and Kit Collier,[18] and anthropologists like Fenella Cannell, Thomas Gibson, Mark Johnson, Thomas McKenna, and Michael Pinches were among the pioneers in this wave of ethnographic research on the lived experience of rural and urban poverty in the contemporary Philippines, and contributed nuanced accounts of everyday Filipino life to broader scholarly debates about subaltern consciousness and resistance, the hegemony of dominant ideologies, and the construction of 'culture' and identity.[19] The works of these scholars have helped to rescue Filipinos from both 'the enormous condescension of posterity'[20] and the neglect of contemporary political scientists, whose writings tended to suggest the seamlessness of bossism, patrimonialism, and cacique democracy, on the one hand, and the passivity and powerlessness of the broad mass of the population, on the other.

The book

This volume, by contrast, offers a counterpoint to recent scholarship on the Philippines, not through 'history from below' or ethnography, but through the optic of what might be described as comparative historical sociology. The authors of this book, after all, are neither historians nor anthropologists, and the chapters to follow draw at least as much on the vast secondary literature on Philippine history, politics, and society as on primary documents examined in the archives and personal experiences during many months living and travelling in the Philippines in the late 1980s and 1990s. This collection of essays offers less an effort to restore a sense of historical or cultural depth to our understanding of popular consciousness in the Philippines today, than an attempt to sketch the broad contours of those underlying structures – economic, institutional, social, and geo-political – which have shaped the course of twentieth-century Philippine history and are likely to do so for many years to come. As Perry Anderson noted in another context: 'A "history from above" – of the intricate machinery of class domination – is thus no less essential than a "history from below": indeed, without it, the latter in the end becomes one-sided (if the better side)'.[21]

In this regard, the book departs from the dominant thrust of the scholarly literature on the Philippines in at least three different ways. First, in contrast with recent scholars' emphasis on continuity in Philippine history, politics, and society, this book is explicitly concerned with the question of change, flux, and transformation in the course of the twentieth century in the archipelago. Other authors have stressed the endurance of oligarchy and the persistence of patri-monialism in the Philippines in the twentieth century and bemoaned Filipinos' failure to transform their country into a rapidly growing economy, a thriving democracy, and a vibrant society. These authors describe a country 'constantly failing in its quest for modernity, prosperity and security'.[22] The essays in this volume, by contrast, take as their point of departure an interest in the myriad ways in which capitalist development has transformed Philippine society over the course of the twentieth century. As detailed in the chapters below, industrial-isation and urbanisation have given rise to new circuitries of production and consumption, new social forces, new forms of popular mobilisation, and new patterns of political contestation and containment in the Philippines. Successive chapters examine patterns of change in terms of class and state formation (Chapters 2, 3, and 4), subtle shifts in the structure of local bossism in suburban provinces (Chapter 5), and the transformation of urban social space, public culture, and national consciousness (Chapters 6 and 7), with special attention to the post-Marcos period. The emplotment of these transformations is both dialec-tical and decidedly non-linear, as the pattern of recurring crises of participation and continuismo outlined in Chapter 2 makes abundantly clear.

Colonial legacies: an American state

Second, the essays in this volume take as their point of departure an understanding of the Philippines' distinctiveness that stresses the peculiar – and peculiarly American – nature of the Philippine state. This approach reflects the authors' unease with the notion that Philippine politics and society are shaped by an enduring traditional 'political culture' revolving around notions of personal indebtedness (*utang na loób*), shame (*hiya*), pity (*awa*), and congeniality (*pakikisama*), as well as a putative proclivity for forming instrumental dyadic (patron-client) relationships. Such a notion is not only hopelessly ahistorical and essentialist, but also methodologically dubious and politically pernicious in its assumption that Philippine society today must reflect Filipino 'culture', and its suggestion, however implicit, that Filipinos get the government they want (and thus deserve). However, the authors' stress on the state stems from the suspicion that scholars and other commentators may have exaggerated the impor-tance of the long Spanish colonial era for shaping the nature of modern Philippine society. More than three centuries of Spanish colonial rule did leave the imprint of the Catholic faith among the vast majority of the population of the archipelago, and Spanish policies did encourage the emergence and entrenchment of a pre-dominantly Chinese *mestizo*[23] commercial and landowning class in the course of the nineteenth century. Yet these twin legacies do not in and of themselves explain the distinctive pattern of social and political change in the Philippines over the course of the past one hundred years, and the notion that the Philippines is best understood as a 'Latin' country is deeply misguided.

After all, unlike Spanish colonies in the Americas, *Las Islas Filipinas* were at the periphery of the empire, relatively insignificant, and under much less vigorous royal control. Communications between Manila and the Spanish court, which up until 1768 transpired exclusively via Mexico, normally took two years.[24] The Governor-General of the Philippines remained subject to the viceroy of Nueva España until Mexican independence in 1820.[25] Spanish economic interests in the Philippine archipelago were restricted to the Manila galleon trade with China, mines and landed estates were few, and little native produce was extracted from the colony until the Bourbon reforms of the late eighteenth century.[26] The actual Spanish presence in the Philippines remained minimal throughout much of the colonial era, in sharp contrast with the relatively large settler populations and later the subsequent creole patriots who loomed so large in the Americas.[27] Even in the nineteenth century, the geographical extent of Spanish control remained limited, Catholicised settlement and commercialised agriculture were still patchy, and the opening of Philippine ports facilitated the predominance of non-Spanish (and non-Catholic) European (especially British) merchants and firms in the burgeoning trade with the West.[28] The Philippine Revolution in the late nineteenth century was but a pale shadow of the independence struggles of Simon Bolivar and other American creole patriots during the Napoleonic interlude several decades earlier, and twentieth-century Philippine politics has seen little of the working-class movements, corporatist state policies, military juntas, or populist leaders found in modern Latin America.

Instead, as the chapters below will suggest, the broad contours of recent Philippine history are best understood not against the backdrop of 'traditional' Filipino culture or Hispanicised society, but rather in the context of the state structures erected and imposed in the course of the American colonial era. For even as American troops were still 'pacifying' pro-independence Filipino forces, elections to municipal office, based on highly restricted suffrage, were first held in 1901, followed by those for provincial governors (1902), representatives to the national Philippine Assembly (1907), an American-style bicameral legislature (1916), and the Commonwealth presidency (1935). The timing, phasing, and structural design of 'colonial democracy' left several lasting legacies which have continued to shape Philippine politics long after independence in 1946. For example, the elaboration of a multi-tiered system of elected executive and legislative posts, the staging of first municipal then provincial elections before the national legislative and presidential contests of later years, and the gradual expansion of what was originally a very limited franchise, prefigured a pattern of political competition in which local, particularistic, patronage-based concerns and networks would serve as the building blocks of electoral competition. In addition, the holding of elections prior to the construction of a national bureaucracy and at such an early stage in capitalist development facilitated the emergence of local 'bosses' whose constituencies remained trapped in webs of dependence and insecurity, and whose discretion over state resources, personnel, and regulatory powers provided enormous opportunities for private capital accumulation. Moreover, the inclusion of the previously uncolonised 'pagan' Gran Cordillera in northern Luzon and partially Islamicised Mindanao and Sulu within the boundaries of the Philippine Islands combined with the deferral of local elections in these areas and Manila's imposition of appointed officials to encourage processes of carpetbagging and internal colonisation.[29] Finally, the subordination of the bureaucracy, including the coercive apparatuses of the state, to an American-style multi-tiered hierarchy of elected politicians prevented the autonomy and assertiveness of the military 'as an institution' seen in Latin America and elsewhere in Asia, and instead presaged a long experiment in presidential authoritarianism (1972–86) which, as Chapter 3 makes clear, was profoundly civilian in nature.

Other important legacies of American colonial rule in the Philippines are also worthy of mention. As countless scholars have shown, a pattern of economic dependency on the United States has in myriad ways hindered the process of economic development in the Philippines over the course of the twentieth century. For example, the four decades of American colonial rule witnessed the dramatic transformation of the Philippine landscape, as vast tracts of land were planted with coconut trees in response to the rising demand in the US for soap, margarine, cosmetics, dynamite and other coconut-oil-based products. Up until the 1970s, coconut oil constituted the country's biggest export, and even today, coconut plantations comprise a quarter of the Philippines' agricultural land. As Rigoberto Tiglao has noted, expanding coconut cultivation has been responsible not only for some of the deforestation of the archipelago, but also for the immiseration of its inhabitants. As coconut lands have suffered from declining productivity, the value of coconut oil in the world market has long been in decline, and today 'the poorest of the Philippines' poor are small coconut farmers and rural workers'.[30] Meanwhile, the post-war rise of the Philippines' former coloniser to a position of global hegemony has, through the long presence of US military installations in the archipelago and repeated US interventions, gravely compromised the independence granted in 1946, suggesting that the 'post-colonial' history of the Philippines has been less 'post-' than 'neo-'.

Whilst the chapters to follow are attentive to these economic and geo-political realities, they stress distinctive legacies of the state structures imposed in the American colonial period for shaping the Philippines' post-war experience of incorporation into the world capitalist economy and subordination to US global hegemony. As the chapters below reveal, the nature of the Philippine state and the centrality of elections in Philippine politics have played a crucial role in the patterns of class and state formation, popular mobilisation and repression/re-incorporation, and local and national 'bossism' observed in the more than fifty years of Philippine independence. Indeed, those features of Philippine politics most frequently derided and diagnosed as pathologically 'Filipino' – 'bossism', 'corruption', 'personalism', and 'rampant' criminality and political violence – are best understood as reflections of enduring American colonial legacies.

The Philippines in Asia: regional influences and comparisons

Third and finally, the essays in this volume stress in various ways that the Philippines is best understood in its regional, Southeast Asian, context. Its name, Iberian colonial experience, and Catholic majority notwithstanding, the Philippines is not simply an archipelagic version of Paraguay or Columbia, a set of Hispanicised *islas* which somehow drifted from the west coast of South America, across the Pacific Ocean and into the South China Sea. For example, as emphasised in Chapter 4, the impact of 'Chinese' immigration on Philippine culture, history, and society has long been underestimated (and systematically obscured), and is far more important than the small number of 'Chinese' recorded as residing in the archipelago would suggest. Given the Philippines' proximity to the southern coast of China, its post-war openness to the political influence and economic muscle of neighbouring Taiwan, and its long history of assimilation of Fujianese immigrants, it could hardly be otherwise. Moreover, as noted in Chapter 8, the early inauguration and decentralised nature of Philippine democracy prefigured a style and structure of politics far more reminiscent of pre-colonial Southeast Asia than any other country in the region, including monarchical Brunei and uncolonised Thailand. Thanks to the nature of democratic and decentralised state structures, the Philippine part of the old 'Sulu Zone' has retained its close links with (Indonesian) Sulawesi and (Malaysian) Sabah, and Muslim Filipinos – or 'Moros' – have resisted internal colonisation by Manila more successfully than their counterparts have fought Jakarta and KL.

By situating the Philippines solidly within Southeast Asia, the essays in this volume provide a basis for comparison with other countries in the region. For years, the Philippines has been caricatured as an economic 'basket-case', a political dystopia, and a nation suffering from a weak sense of identity and a 'damaged culture'. Yet the chapters below suggest an alternative view. Chapter 4, for example, highlights the inadequacies of the comparisons drawn between the Philippine and Thai patterns of capitalist development, and suggests that the explanation for differences in long-term growth rates lies not in the 'weakness' of the Philippine state and the 'strength' of its oligarchy, but in the underlying nature of Ferdinand Marcos' authoritarian regime. Chapter 7 likewise rejects the thesis of a Philippine 'identity problem' and argues instead that of all the countries in Southeast Asia, the Philippines boasts the most politically progressive and promising form of popular nationalism. Chapter 8 concludes with a return to the comparison with Thailand and a discussion of the Philippines' advantages in combating the excesses – and transcending the limitations – of local 'bossism' and national 'money politics'.

Chapter outlines

Whilst the broad outlines of this book, the introduction, and the concluding chapter are products of the authors' joint efforts, the next six chapters below represent a division of labour based on differing interests and expertise. Chapter 2, written by Eva-Lotta Hedman, provides an overarching historical frame for understanding post-independence Philippine history, one rooted in an appreciation of the underlying contradictions of Philippine democracy and the recurring crises of participation and *continuismo*[31] which have structured the ebb and flow of politics in the archipelago. Chapter 3, also written by Hedman, examines the organisation and deployment of violence in modern Philippine history, with an eye towards the formation of the state's coercive apparatuses in the American colonial period and the resultant patterns of distinctly civilian authoritarianism on the one hand and peculiarly *para*-military mobilisation on the other.

By contrast, Chapter 4, written by John Sidel, reexamines the pattern of private capital accumulation and bourgeois class formation in the Philippines against the political backdrop sketched in the two preceding chapters and in light of the scholarly literature on 'Chinese', 'landed', and 'crony' capital in the archipelago. Chapter 5, also written by Sidel, traces shifts in the modalities of local bossism in two suburban provinces, Cavite and Cebu, which have seen considerable industrialisation and suburbanisation in the past few decades. Chapter 6, written by Eva-Lotta Hedman, chronicles the transformation of retail marketing and urban social space from the early American period to the 1990s, and discusses the impact of changes in the 'public culture' of Manila and other Philippine cities on popular consciousness and collective action. Chapter 7, written by John Sidel, offers a reassessment of Philippine nationalism and a rejoinder to the notion that Filipinos suffer from a 'damaged culture' and a weak sense of national identity. Chapter 8, co-authored by Hedman and Sidel, concludes the volume with a discussion of the Philippines which situates the archipelago squarely within Southeast Asia and in a paired comparison with Thailand. Whether read separately or together, the essays in this volume provide both a broad overview of twentieth-century Philippine history and a critical reevaluation of the conventional wisdom and academic consensus on the politics and society of the archipelago. The volume is not intended as a definitive work but rather as a contribution which might inspire further debate and discussion among scholars and other interested observers of the Philippines.

Notes

1 See, for example, James Fenton, 'The Snap Revolution', *Granta* 18 (Spring 1986), pp. 33–155; as well as the withering commentary in Benedict Anderson, 'James Fenton's Slideshow', *New Left Review* 158 (July/August 1986), pp. 81–90.

2 Barry Lowe, 'The Demonizing of the Philippines by Western Media', *Pilipinas* 28 (Spring 1997), pp. 14–29.

3 *Brownout on Breadfruit Boulevard* (London: Paddleless Press, 1995); *Renegade, or Halo²* (London: Paddleless Press, 1999).

4 Alex Garland, *The Tesseract* (London: Viking, 1998).

5 Peter Hoeg, *Miss Smilla's Feeling For Snow* (London: The Harvill Press, 1993), p. 261.

6 Alfred W. McCoy, *The Politics of Heroin in Southeast Asia* (New York: Harper & Row, 1972).

7 See: 'Marcos's Wartime Role Discredited in US Files', *New York Times*, 23 January 1986; 'New Doubts on Marcos' War Role', *Washington Post*, 24 January 1986.

8 See, for example, *Priests on Trial* (New York: Penguin Books, 1984); 'The Restoration of Planter Power in La Carlota City', in Benedict J. Kerkvliet and Resil B. Mojares, *From Marcos to Aquino: Local Perspectives on Political Transition in the Philippines* (Quezon City: Ateneo de Manila University Press, 1991), pp. 105–142; and his series of articles on 'RAM Boys', in the 21 September, 28 September, and 12 October 1988 issues of *National Midweek*.

9 Alfred W. McCoy (ed.), *An Anarchy of Families: State and Family in the Philippines* (Madison: University of Wisconsin Center for Southeast Asian Studies, 1993).

10 Mark R. Thompson, *The Anti-Marcos Struggle: Personalistic Rule and Democratic Transition in the Philippines* (New Haven: Yale University Press, 1995); James Putzel, *A Captive Land: The Politics of Agrarian Reform in the Philippines* (Quezon City: Ateneo de Manila University Press, 1992).

11 Paul D. Hutchcroft, *Booty Capitalism: The Politics of Banking in the Philippines* (Ithaca: Cornell University Press, 1998).

12 See, for example, the various essays in Patricio N. Abinales (ed.), *The Revolution Falters: The Left in Philippine Politics After 1986* (Ithaca: Cornell University Southeast Asia Program, 1996).

13 Eva-Lotta E. Hedman, 'In the Name of Civil Society: Contestation and Elections in the Post-Colonial Philippines' (Ph.D. dissertation, Cornell University, 1998); John T. Sidel, 'Coercion, Capital, and the Post-Colonial State: Bossism in the postwar Philippines' (Ph.D. dissertation, Cornell University, 1995).

14 See, for example, Katherine Mayo, *The Isles of Fear: The Truth about the Philippines* (New York: Harcourt, Brace and Company, 1925).

15 See, for example, Mary R. Hollnsteiner, *The Dynamics of Power in a Philippine Municipality* (Quezon City: University of the Philippines Community Development Program, 1963); and Carl H. Landé, *Leaders, Factions, and Parties: The Structure of Philippine Politics* (New Haven: Yale University Southeast Asian Studies, 1964).

16 See, for example, David R. Sturtevant, *Popular Uprisings in the Philippines, 1840–1940* (Ithaca: Cornell University Press, 1976); Reynaldo Clemeña Ileto, *Pasyón and Revolution: Popular Movements in the Philippines, 1840–1910* (Quezon City: Ateneo de Manila University Press, 1979); and Benedict J. Kerkvliet, *The Huk Rebellion: A Study of Peasant Revolt in the Philippines* (Berkeley: University of California Press, 1977).

17 See, for example, Reynaldo C. Ileto, *Filipinos and their Revolution: Event, Discourse, and Historiography* (Quezon City: Ateneo de Manila University Press, 1998).

18 Benedict J. Tria Kerkvliet, *Everyday Politics in the Philippines: Class and Status Relations in a Central Luzon Village* (Berkeley: University of California Press, 1990); Christopher James Collier, 'The Politics of Insurrection in Davao, Philippines' (Ph.D. dissertation, University of Hawai'i, 1997).

19 Fenella Cannell, *Power and Intimacy in the Christian Philippines* (Cambridge: Cambridge University Press, 1999); Thomas Gibson, *Sacrifice and Sharing in the Philippine Highlands: Religion and Society Among the Buid of Mindoro* (London: Athlone Press, 1986); Mark Johnson, *Beauty and Power: Transgendering and Cultural Transformation in the Southern Philippines* (Oxford: Berg, 1997); Thomas McKenna, *Muslim Rulers and Rebels: Everyday Politics and Armed Separatism in the Southern Philippines* (Berkeley: University of California Press, 1998); Michael Pinches, 'Proletarian Ritual: Class Degradation and the Dialectic of Resistance in Manila', *Pilipinas* 19 (Fall 1992), pp. 69–92.

20 E.P. Thompson, *The Making of the English Working Class* (New York: Vintage Books, 1963), p. 12.

21 Perry Anderson, *Lineages of the Absolutist State* (London: Verso, 1974), p. 11.

22 Lowe, 'The Demonizing of the Philippines by Western News Media', p. 27.

23 In the Spanish colonial lexicon, the term mestizo referred to individuals of mixed 'native' and 'Chinese' paentage, in other words, the offspring of native women (indias) and immigrant men from what we now know as China. On the Chinese mestizos in the Spanish Philippines, see: Edgar Wickberg, 'The Chinese Mestizos in Philippine History', *Journal of Southeast Asian History*, Vol. 5, Number 1 (March 1964), pp. 62–100.

24 John Leddy Phelan, *The Hispanization of the Philippines: Spanish Aims and Filipino Responses 1565–1700* (Madison: University of Wisconsin Press, 1959), p. 154.

25 Onofre D. Corpuz, *The Bureaucracy in the Philippines* (Manila: University of the Philippines Institute of Public Administration, 1957), p. 46.

26 Nicholas P. Cushner, *Landed Estates in the Colonial Philippines* (New Haven: Yale University Southeast Asia Studies Monograph Series No. 20, 1976), pp. 23–35.

27   By 1842, there were only 1,500 *peninsulares* and 3,500 *creoles* living in the Philippines, out of a total population of more than five million (Corpuz, *The Bureaucracy*, p. 44).

28   Nicholas Tarling, 'Some Aspects of British Trade in the Philippines in the Nineteenth Century', *Journal of History*, Volume XI, Numbers 3 and 4 (September–December 1963), pp. 287–327.

29   Gerard Anthony Finin, 'Regional Consciousness and Administrative Grids: Understanding the Role of Planning in the Philippines' Gran Cordillera Central' (Ph.D. dissertation, Cornell University, 1991); Patricio Nuñez Abinales, 'State Power and Local Authority in the Southern Philippines' (Ph.D. dissertation, Cornell University, 1997).

30   Rigoberto Tiglao, 'Roots of Poverty', *Far Eastern Economic Review*, 10 June 1999, pp. 63–65.

31   The term *continuismo* is borrowed from Latin American politics and refers to incumbent presidents who retain office beyond their initial term limit, often through extra-constitutional means. See: Linz, *The Failure of Presidential Democracy*, p. 16.

2 *Trasformismo* and Philippine democracy

Introduction

The popular ouster of long-time president Ferdinand Marcos in late February 1986 is often remembered – and celebrated – as a classic example of a 'People Power Revolution' toppling a dictator through non-violent means. Indeed, scholars have drawn the analogy between the 'mobilisation of civil society' on the streets of Manila in February 1986 and other subsequent cases of 'transitions from authoritarian rule'. Filipinos have often drawn such parallels themselves, whether with reference to the events leading up to the Tiananmen Massacre in June 1989 in Beijing or with regard to the more recent – and more successful – campaign for 'Reformasi' and ouster of Suharto in Jakarta in the spring of 1998.

This chapter, by contrast, situates the 'People Power Revolution' in Manila in 1986 within a more historical context and a more structural understanding of Philippine politics. The dramatic events of early 1986, this chapter argues, are best understood as part and parcel of a recurring pattern in the archipelago's post-independence history, wherein underlying tensions in Philippine society crystallised into full-blown political crises – in the early 1950s, the late 1960s, and the mid-1980s. In all three periods, the deteriorating integrative capacity of existing mechanisms for mobilising and channelling popular participation into elections, and the increasing concentration of executive powers in the hands of a reelectionist incumbent president, threatened to undermine the interests of a bloc of dominant social forces in Philippine society: the business class, the Catholic church hierarchy, and the US government.

In 1986, as in 1953, such a crisis was overcome through this dominant bloc's success in generating what Antonio Gramsci has identified as 'transformist' mobilisation.[1] Following Gramsci's distinction between the exercise of power (over and against antagonistic groups) and that of leadership (over and for allied groups) by different political constellations in *Risorgimento* Italy, transformism (*trasformismo*) here refers to 'the parliamentary expression of ... political, moral and political hegemony'.[2] As noted in a recent discussion of Brazilian electoral politics, transformism involves a political process 'whereby radical pressures are gradually absorbed and inverted by conservative forces, until they serve the opposite of their original ends'.[3]

These instances of successful transformist mobilisation occurred against the backdrop of mounting crises stemming from two underlying tensions deeply embedded in the structures of Philippine democracy from its establishment in the 1935 Commonwealth-era Constitution. On the one hand, the absence of formal restrictions on the electoral franchise in the Philippines in the post-independence era allowed for electoral 'mass citizens' participation' whilst political offices remained in the hands of national-level oligarchs and local political bosses. Caught betwixt and between the irreversability of universal mass suffrage and the staying power of narrow oligarchic predominance, Philippine society witnessed recurring participatory crises, in which subaltern classes – peasants, workers, and urban poor folk – supported extra-electoral forms of popular mobilisation.

On the other hand, the political and economic prerogatives of an 'over-developed' executive branch at times threatened to emasculate the interests of the islands' dominant social class, an agro-commercial oligarchy entrenched in both houses of the national legislature. In addition to problems due to the often noted 'zero-sum' nature of presidentialism in general,[4] the executive branch tended to manifest a propensity for 'relative autonomy' common to post-colonial states[5] and perhaps especially marked in cases such as the Philippines where 'there did not occur a clear and violent break from the colonial past and where the colonial [s]tate was substantially carried over into the post-colonial period'.[6]

During three periods in post-war Philippine history, participatory crises combined with a presidential incumbent's excessive muscling of executive powers to threaten to undermine the oligarchy's capacity for capital accumulation and political hegemony. In two of these crises (the early 1950s and mid-1980s), leading elements of the oligarchy, together with allies in the Catholic Church and the US government, succeeded in engineering a transformist (counter-)mobilisation which reaffirmed Philippine democracy against extra-electoral threats from above and below. In the third and intervening crisis (the late 1960s), the weakness and failure of transformist mobilisation left the problems of extra-electoral mobilisation and presidential entrenchment essentially unresolved, thus paving the way for the ('caesarist') declaration of martial law in 1972 and the deepening of these problems over the long years of Ferdinand Marcos' rule.

The remainder of this chapter thus situates the People Power Revolution of February 1986 against the backdrop of these broader patterns in Philippine history. To this end, the chapter first discusses the underlying structural tensions in Philippine democracy. Thereafter, the chapter turns to the crises of participation and executive predominance in the early 1950s, late 1960s, and mid-1980s, and to the variously transformist and caesarist manner of their resolution.

Electoral suffrage and political representation

If the underlying tension between political citizenship and social class has run deep in the post-colonial period, its origins date back to the American colonial era. Less than a decade after the earliest nationalist revolution in Asia ended Spanish colonial rule and the savage Philippine-American war reimposed foreign control, the islands' first national elections saw a recently enfranchised male electorate – some 1.4 per cent of the total population – voting in the National Assembly in 1907.[7] By making suffrage conditional upon literacy, property and language qualifications,[8] the American colonial administration effectively enfranchised an electorate that 'closely approximated the small group of Filipinos who had comprised the *principalias* in the *pueblos* during the Spanish regime'.[9] Over time, however, formal legislation and other dynamics contributed to the expansion of electoral participation (both in absolute and relative terms) under the American colonial regime. For example, this period saw the relaxation and/ or abolition of age, property, and language criteria restricting the franchise, as well as the introduction of female suffrage. In addition, informal practices such as, for example, ballot tampering to 'overcome literacy problems of [clients] in support of their patron's chosen candidates' also contributed to increasing the size of the electorate.[10] However, while expanding beyond the 1.4 per cent of the total population who voted in the first national elections, suffrage remained an exclusive privilege exercised by a mere 14 per cent of all colonial subjects at the close of the American period.[11]

In 1946, however, the transition to formal independence delivered universal adult suffrage to the Philippine Republic. As a result, figures on electoral participation in the years between independence in 1946 and martial law in 1972, for example, show a dramatically expanding electorate – especially when considered in absolute terms[12] and against the relatively static numbers of elected seats in municipal halls, provincial capitols, and the national legislature. Despite this increase in mostly lower and middle class voters alongside widening class cleavages associated with sharpening income inequalities, disintegrating patron–client ties, and nascent urban working-class formation, however, Philippine electoral politics during this period saw neither the transformation of existing elitist parties nor the institutionalisation of alternative third parties. Contrary to the lofty promises of the 'New Society' and the unprecedentedly high 'electoral turnouts' under martial law, moreover, Marcos' 'constitutional authoritarianism' further constrained the options open to Philippine voters in more restricted (and less frequent) contests for local, legislative, and presidential offices between 1972 and 1986.

Overall, universal mass suffrage notwithstanding, Philippine post-colonial electoralism has manifested enduring patterns of narrow class rule already discernible before independence.[13] In fact, throughout the postwar period, a national oligarchy 'essentially recruited from families of long standing economic wealth or political dominance or both'[14] has continued to define the nature and direction of electoral politics as large landowners, commercial magnates, and their scions have filled both houses of Congress as well as the offices of municipal halls and provincial capitols throughout the archipelago. Reflective of the enduring 'Tocquevillean effects' of state institutions and policies,

the existence of a 'national' legislature long before the nation achieved independence and regular congressional elections ... greatly contributed to the creation of a political class that was national in geographic spread and integrated in political outlook.[15]

Significantly, moreover, the colonial lineages of this political class endowed it with control over a combination of clientelist structures, coercive mechanisms and monetary resources which, in turn, facilitated sustained oligarchic predominance in Philippine electoral politics. At the same time, colonial policies introduced discriminatory laws and practices against labour parties and other non-elite political organisations which, buttressed by constitutional provisions for the suppression of 'insurrections', served to further strengthen the institutionalisation of oligarchy-dominated bi-factional electoral politics in the post-war period. Yet, if much of the post-colonial period saw such clientelist, coercive and monetary pressures combine to channel political participation into bi-factional patronage-based parties, the emergence and mobilisation of new social forces during three distinct conjunctures – the early 1950s, late 1960s, and mid-1980s – threatened to unleash participatory crises which threatened the political hegemony of this entrenched oligarchy.

Presidentialism and executive predominance

In addition to resurfacing problems of political participation, the post-colonial Philippines has also encountered recurring crises of presidential *continuismo*. This proclivity for presidential predominance in Philippine politics dates back to the American colonial regime and its constitutional provisions for a strong executive endowed with extraordinary coercive powers and fiscal prerogatives. Whilst the 1935 Philippine Constitution divided powers between executive, legislative and judiciary branches of the government along distinctly American lines, 'the Philippine President was deliberately given a position of predominance not accorded the President of the United States'.[16] For example, in the event of rebellion, invasion or insurrection, 'the [1935] Philippine Constitution categorically states that the power to suspend the writ belongs to the president'.[17] Similarly, constitutional provisions gave the president the authority to declare national emergencies and to assume extraordinary powers.[18] Beyond establishing presidential control over decisions about the suspension of the writ and the assumption of emergency powers, the 1935 Constitution also vested vast powers over matters of national finance and commerce, as well as over government budget appropriations, in the office of the chief executive.[19] As a result of these extensive executive powers granted under the constitution,

> the President could probably make or break many business enterprises, vitally affect the fortunes of any industry, region, or politician in the Philippines, and enormously influence the entire economy of the nation.[20]

In addition to the considerable presidential control over both political and economic policy, the 1935 Commonwealth Constitution also 'established the precedent that an incumbent president can amend the constitution to extend his own term of office'.[21] Finally, the continued significance in the post-colonial period of US economic and military resources, typically channelled through the office of the president, strengthened the propensity for executive 'relative autonomy' from the legislature in the Philippines.

Counterposed against this strong presidency, the 1935 Constitution provided for certain 'checks and balances' by institutionalising a set of mechanisms which allowed the legislature – the primary vehicle for *national* class rule – to exercise power and influence within the executive branch. While its role remained rather circumscribed under a powerful American colonial Governor-General and, after 1935, a Filipino Commonwealth President, the Philippine Congress gained in both legislative importance and political influence *vis-à-vis* the executive branch in the postwar period.[22] In fact, the Philippine legislature's greatest political leverage after independence derived from congressional control over both budget appropriations and government appointments.[23] The Committee on Appropriations and the Commission on Appointments constituted the key instruments of congressional influence over the executive. The former allowed for a 'politics of pork' akin to that in the United States (with the exception of the presidential itemised veto),[24] whereas the latter institutionalised 'personnel patronage' along patterns more peculiar to the Philippines. Thus, for example, through its influence over particularistic legislation allocating public funds and over the 'major vehicle for the distribution of pork',[25] the general Public Works Act, the Philippine Congress controlled vast resources of critical significance for political survival during election years. In addition, due to its legislative authorisation over the 'mad scramble' for positions in various government offices, the Commission on Appointments offered further opportunities for purposes of amassing economic and political capital *vis-à-vis* the executive. Through these institutionalised mechanisms, both the Senate and the House exerted considerable leverage over the executive branch because

> [a]long with legislators, the President, high-ranking executive department officials, and influential private individuals vie in getting these positions for their respective proteges.[26]

In this context, the reelectionist ambitions of incumbent presidents typically ran up against the prerogatives of the Philippine Congress. The Philippine Senate, in particular, has often served as the site of successful congressional counter-mobilisation against presidents seeking re-election. Yet, as detailed in the pages below, on three occasions in postwar Philippine history, *continuista* presidents appeared poised to overcome such institutional and political constraints upon renewed residency in Malacañang Palace.

Postwar conjunctures and critical elections

If post-colonial Philippine electoralism remained susceptible to such dual crises of participation and *continuismo*, the elimination of formal franchise restrictions also rendered election-related fraud and violence particularly significant as political mechanisms for both participatory contestation and containment in the postwar period.[27] Widespread and systematic practices of vote-buying and voter intimidation, for example, translated into *de facto* mass disenfranchisement, thus facilitating the perpetuation of oligarchical rule. Such (coercive) manipulation of the suffrage also presented an obvious challenge to the capacity of elections to represent the 'fictive unity of the nation back onto the masses as if it were their own self-government'.[28]

The candidacy of a reelectionist incumbent with manifest disregard for the 'rule of law' in the presidential elections of 1953, 1969 and 1986 led to anticipations of massive electoral fraud in these elections. While other incumbents also used pork barrel, constabulary intervention, fraud, and other dirty tricks in their bids for reelection, the aggregation of political powers and economic control under President Elpidio Quirino in the late 1940s and early 1950s and President Ferdinand Marcos by the late 1960s signalled qualitative departures from the usual pattern of bi-factional elite contestation under Philippine electoralism.[29] In fact, Quirino's and Marcos' unprecedented efforts at expanding the powers of an already strong executive branch in the years leading up to the 1953 and 1969 elections, respectively, threatened to undermine the political hegemony of the dominant class and the process of capital accumulation. Despite the official lifting of martial law in 1981, moreover, Marcos, backed by his military and business cronies, continued ruling by presidential decree and plundering the Philippine economy up until the 1986 elections.[30]

The rumblings of latent participatory crises in the early 1950s, late 1960s and mid-1980s constituted a perhaps less obvious but equally important backdrop to Quirino's and Marcos' bids for reelection. Each of these elections saw the emergence of previously excluded, unincorporated, or marginal social sectors – peasants, students and workers, and urban middle class elements – acting collectively to press their political demands. Significantly, extra-electoral mobilisation and election-boycott campaigns organised by an underground Left also targeted each of these three presidential contests.

Within the context of escalating participatory and *continuismo* crises, the Philippine presidential contests of 1953, 1969 and 1986 constituted something akin to a Philippine version of 'critical elections',[31] revealing deep-rooted tensions in the polity and important developments in society. More than any other electoral exercises in the postwar Philippines, these were elections

> in which voters [were], at least from impressionistic evidence, unusually deeply concerned, in which the extent of electoral involvement [was] relatively quite high, and in which the decisive results of the voting reveal[ed] a sharp alteration of the pre-existing cleavage within the electorate.[32]

Against the backdrop of significant demographic and economic change in Philippine society, these three elections saw realignments[33] in the electorate that reflected the 'emergent tensions in society which, not adequately controlled by the organisation or outputs of party politics as usual, escalate[d] to a flash point' and eventually manifested themselves as 'issue-oriented phenomena, centrally associated with these tensions and more or less leading to resolution adjustments'.[34] Increasingly centralised electoral fraud – alongside mounting criticisms of executive graft and corruption – surfaced as a prominent political issue in Philippine postwar elections precisely during periods of critical realignments (the early 1950s, late 1960s and mid-1980s) when existing mechanisms of clientelism, coercion and monetary incentives showed signs of declining efficacy.[35]

The presidential elections during these three postwar conjunctures thus signalled both perceived openings and anticipated closures in the structure of institutionalised politics.[36] The greater openness during election campaigns of formal political institutions such as established political parties and the official Commission on Elections[37] offered new opportunities for electorally oriented collective action, while also, paradoxically enough, providing a visible mobilisational target for anti-electoral boycott movements. The looming threat of an executive incumbent clinching reelection by deploying massive political, coercive and monetary resources however, signalled the imminent closure of the window of opportunity offered by these presidential elections. The high stakes of the 1953, 1969 and 1986 presidential elections contributed to exacerbate both the surrounding crises and their immediate resolutions. In fact, the observed 'zero-sum' nature of electoral politics under presidentialism tended to freeze winners and losers for the duration of the presidential mandate, 'a number of years in which there is no hope for shift[ing] alliances [or] broadening of the base of support by national unity or emergency grand coalitions ... that might lead to dissolution and new elections, and so forth'.[38] As a result,

> [t]he losers have to wait four or five years without access to executive power and thereby to a share in the formation of cabinets and without access to patronage. The zero-sum game raises the stakes in a presidential election for winners and losers, and inevitably increases the tension and the polarisation.[39]

Viewed within the context of participatory and *continuismo* crises, the 1953, 1969 and 1986 presidential elections thus constituted a unique combination of opening and closing opportunities which favoured nationwide efforts at counter-mobilisation against the mounting threats to Philippine electoralism from both above and below.

As discussed below, two distinctive shifts in the structure of institutionalised politics surrounding these three critical (presidential) elections in the Philippines further advanced the 1953 and 1986 electoral-reform efforts compared to those of 1969. First, reformist presidential candidates emerged as a 'preferable alternative' to the *continuista* incumbents in 1953 and 1986, and an avowedly non-partisan National Movement for Free Elections (NAMFREL) mobilised to prevent fraud and violence, especially on behalf of the incumbents. As a result, the presidential elections of 1953 and 1986 presented opportunities to link regional and national social networks and political machines behind *transformist* resolutions to the ongoing crises of participation and *continuismo*. Second, the support extended by an influential external ally – the United States government – portended greater visibility for the 1953 and 1986 national election-watch efforts which contributed both to facilitate mobilisation and to discourage repression of these two campaigns. By contrast, neither a reformist opposition presidential candidate nor US endorsements emerged during the more limited mobilisational effort by the Citizens National Electoral Assembly (CNEA) against electoral manipulation, fraud and violence in 1969. The political polarisation of the late 1960s escalated further in the wake of the failed transformist mobilisation in the 1969 presidential elections, with President Ferdinand Marcos declaring martial law in 1972 and extra-electoral mobilisation shifting into an increasingly potent and popular armed insurgency in the late 1970s and early 1980s. The 1953 and 1986 presidential elections, by contrast, provided the occasions for comparatively successful transformist resolutions to the crises of the early 1950s and mid-1980s.

Continuismo **and participatory crises**

The three 'critical elections' of 1953, 1969, and 1986 in the Philippines thus provided unique opportunities for transformist mobilisation to ease, if not resolve, the deep-rooted 'system contradictions' which had crystallised into full-blown political crises in the early 1950s, late 1960s, and mid-1980s, respectively. On the one hand, participatory crises surfaced from the inherent tension between formal democratic institutions based on universal suffrage and protracted elite rule by a national agro-industrial oligarchy and local political bosses. On the ohter hand, presidential *continuismo* threatened to realise to an unprecedented degree the propensity for 'relative autonomy' of the strong executive branch at the expense of the powerful elite-dominated legislature.

The 1953 presidential elections

In the early 1950s, for example, President Elpidio Quirino was widely seen as having won election in 1949[40] through unparalleled electoral fraud and violence which held many parts of the Philippines in a 'virtual reign of terror' at the height of the campaign.[41] Reports of rampant electoral manipulation and blatant voter intimidation led to widespread disaffection with the electoral process as evidenced by several post-election protests, including an armed uprising in a province close to Manila,[42] an unprecedented number of official election protests, and countless complaints of terrorism and fraud.[43] Quirino's subsequent suspension of the elected mayors of Manila, Cebu and Iloilo – then the most important cities in the Philippines – signalled similarly reckless disregard for the existing rules of electoralism.

A series of post-1949 developments in the realms of internal security and economic policy provided further evidence of Quirino's willingness and ability to expand – and abuse – his executive prerogatives. For example, the merger of the Philippine Constabulary (PC) with the Army removed PC forces from the political discretion of provincial governors.[44] Moreover, Quirino's suspension of the writ of *habeas corpus*, essentially implemented to keep alleged Huk sympathisers detained, was decried as 'the hallmark of totalitarian dictatorships and the last resort of corrupt ... governments'.[45] In the sphere of economic policy, the Quirino administration's imposition of exchange controls and involvement in corruption scandals (especially regarding the implementation of such controls and the management of government-owned corporations) triggered criticisms of arbitrary executive interference in the Philippine economy.[46] Such charges of corruption, as well as opposition to expanding government controls and credits in the first place, were identified with the powerful sugar bloc and its politicking to secure continued access to the US market and to the Philippine presidency after the 1953 national elections.[47] Beyond corrupt implementation and partisan jockeying lay the deeper concentration of government power in the realm of economic policy institutionalised with the inauguration of the Central Bank in 1949. As a result, Quirino's presidency was the first under which

> the government, through the Central Bank, exercised enormous powers and discretion in determining who should get import licences and allocations of foreign exchange; in formulating the criteria on goods whose entry should be curtailed or banned; and in determining who should get tax exemptions and other incentives.[48]

This presidential usurpation of powers in the early 1950s coincided with the previously noted problems of popular political participation which the introduction of universal suffrage failed to resolve. In fact, the expansion of the political franchise with formal independence in 1946 took place within a social context characterised by a deepening 'disintegration of the traditional landlord-tenant relationship' in the countryside due primarily to the ongoing commercialisation of agriculture.[49] In addition to market forces, the Second World War also 'temporarily but severely weakened the gravitational pulls of the old Philippine institutional structure' and, as a result, 'pre-war vertical ties between gentry patrons and their peasant clients had become unstuck during the occupation'.[50]

The expansion of formal political participation and the dislodging of traditional patron–client ties presented the Philippine oligarchy with a dilemma stemming from the need to incorporate peasants into political parties while preventing elections from serving as vehicles for popular collective mobilisation. Significantly, after the 1946 congressional elections, six elected candidates closely identified with peasant organisations and guerrilla networks in the densely populated and intensively cultivated rice-bowl region of Central Luzon – and enjoying the support of the Partido Komunista ng Pilipinas (PKP) and the Civil Liberties Union – were barred from taking their respective seats. The massive fraud and rampant violence visited upon Central Luzon during the 1947 local and 1949 national elections were linked to deliberate and concerted efforts at demobilising the most significant counter-hegemonic challenge to locally entrenched oligarchic rule in the Philippines at the time.[51]

In a related development, the extra-electoral mobilisation of armed peasant guerrillas, known as Huks, supported by the PKP after 1948, gained in organisational strength and size between 1946 and 1948 throughout four provinces near Manila that became known as 'Huklandia'.[52] By 1950, the Huks had expanded their areas of control to include all of Central Luzon and large parts of Southern Luzon (i.e. the environs of the national capital) despite failures 'to earn sufficient support from peasants in Bicol, the Visayas, Ilocos, and Northern Luzon regions'.[53] In a reversal of its strategy for legal struggle, the PKP, having declared a 'revolutionary situation' in the aftermath of the 1949 presidential contest, called for a boycott of the 1951 senatorial elections to 'make the masses realise the necessity, the absolute necessity of revolution... [and to] complete the people's disillusionment regarding the elections'.[54]

Against this backdrop of presidential *continuismo* and radical mobilisation, the 1953 elections saw the emergence of a transformist resolution to the emerging crisis. First of all, Quirino found himself confronted by a 'reformist' candidate for the presidency in the person of Ramon Magsaysay, a public figure widely credited with service as a guerrilla leader during the World War II Japanese Occupation and with success in defeating the Huks during his tenure as Quirino's Secretary of Defense. Closely linked with CIA operative Col. Edward Landsdale and strongly backed by the US Embassy, Magsaysay enjoyed enthusiastic American backing in terms of finance and favourable media coverage as well as the nomination of the opposition Nacionalista Party (NP) and the support of segments of the oligarchy fed up with and/or frightened by Quirino's presidency. Second, and in tandem with the Magsaysay-for-President-Movement (MPM), the National Movement for Free Elections (NAMFREL) sounded the battlecry 'protect the ballot and save the nation' in the early 1950s. In the months leading up to the 1953 presidential contest, NAMFREL organised activities ranging from civic-consciousness caucuses and clean-election rallies to voter-registration drives and election-watch efforts.[55] Counting some '60 chapters in the provinces and chartered cities, and about 500 municipal chapters with a total membership of 5,000 members', this NAMFREL campaign enjoyed considerable success in mobilising public support from among so-called 'secondary associations' at home, as well as in focusing media attention from both the international – especially the American – and national press corps.[56] With his votes protected by NAMFREL, Magsaysay succeeded in defeating Quirino by a hefty margin and assuming the presidency in early 1954.

Subsequent years saw the resumption of the pattern of colourless machine politics and oligarchical rule which had preceded Quirino's emergence and entrenchment and the Huks' mobilisation in Central Luzon. The Magsaysay presidency (1954–57) saw the successful demobilisation – and relocation – of the Huk insurgents, some rather tame efforts at reform (including land reform legislation), and, with Magsaysay's untimely death in an airplane accident in 1957, the resumption of regular presidential turnover. Magsaysay's vice-president, Carlos Garcia, was elected to the presidency in November 1957 and served until his defeat at the hands of Diosdado Macapagal in 1961. Macapagal, in turn, failed in his bid for reelection in 1965, losing to Ferdinand Marcos, who assumed the presidency in January 1966.

The 1969 presidential elections

Yet by the late 1960s a broadly *similar* backdrop of simultaneous *continuista* and participatory crises had resurfaced. In the presidential elections of 1969, Marcos, like Quirino before him, ran for reelection after a term during which the prerogatives of the executive branch – in economic, political and military affairs – were greatly strengthened and unprecedented powers were concentrated in his hands.[57] Developments affecting the organisation and deployment of military and police forces during Marcos' first elected term (1966–69) prompted criticisms of 'creeping militarism' from political opponents and other contemporary observers.[58] The creation of ten battalions to form a civic action brigade in 1966, for example, signalled the beginning of an expansion – both in size and role – of the Armed Forces of the Philippines under Marcos.[59] Moreover, the following year saw the organisation of the Philippine Constabulary Metropolitan Command (Metrocom) as a 'centralised, riot-control and internal security force'[60] which served as the 'launching pad' for subsequent integration of police forces under a National Police Commission.[61] In addition to the Manila-based Metrocom, it was also widely assumed that para-military expansion under Marcos included the armed bands terrorising Central Luzon as early as 1967.[62]

Whereas so-called 'pork barrel' had been used by previous presidents to build or destroy individual members of the Senate and House,[63] Marcos moved to circumvent such congressional representatives – by means of other institutionalised channels and/or direct personal intervention – in a more systematic fashion.[64] During his first term, Marcos' skilful manipulation of agencies like the Presidential Arm for Community Development[65] and use of the discretionary Barrio Funds[66] allowed him to strengthen the executive branch *vis-à-vis* the Philippine Congress. In addition to expanding government developmental initiatives – as exemplified by the 1966 Four-Year Economic Program and the 1967 Industrial Investment Act – Marcos reintroduced monetary and fiscal controls in mid-1967. While such state intervention in the economy signalled greater restrictions on private capital, however, they were 'much less stringent than those adopted in the early 1950s'.[67] The destabilising economic policies and unprecedented election-spending nevertheless contributed to plunging the Philippines into a deepening economic crisis in the aftermath of Marcos' 1969 electoral victory, the first instance in which an incumbent had secured a second elected presidential term.

The 1960s had also witnessed continued economic differentiation[68] and rapid urbanisation[69] in the Philippines, with the National Capital Region replacing the northern and southern frontiers as the number one destination of migration.[70] The socio-demographic terrain also changed to include both an increasing segment of 'economically insecure clients' and, in absolute terms, a growing urban middle class.[71] These developments, scholars have argued, signalled an overall decline in the 'integrative capacity of political machines'[72] because of mounting costs of 'particularistic rewards'[73] and weakening client leverage due to the 'specialisation in clientelist structures'.[74]

As existing mechanisms for political incorporation through bifactional party competition appeared increasingly inadequate, embryonic efforts at channelling social mobilisation into alternative institutions with an added extra-electoral agenda emerged in the 1960s, as can be gleaned from the experience of emerging peasant, worker and student collective action during this period. For example, 1963 and 1964 saw the organisation of a workers' party supported by national labour federations,[75] a peasant association backed by former Huks,[76] and a student movement endorsed by radical nationalists,[77] all three of which were identified with prominent Filipino socialists or communists. As the 'increased vocality of a radical intelligentsia in the 1960s helped politicise worker and peasant discontent',[78] these sectors began mobilising demonstrations, launching strikes and battling court cases. Student collective protests[79] similarly added to the tide of non-traditional forms of political action as 'normal channels', participants argued, were 'inadequate and ineffective as instruments for achieving the redress of their grievances or for the institution of the necessary reforms they desired'.[80]

Whilst these attempts at collective mobilisation along sectoral lines essentially remained within the 'rule of law', the late 1960s also saw the addition of organised political action aimed more explicitly against the forces of 'law and order'. The resurgence of the Huks in Central Luzon, the founding of the Communist Party of the Philippines and its New People's Army,[81] and the declaration of the Muslim Independence Movement[82] all signified different extra-parliamentary, counter-hegemonic challenges to the existing parameters of political integration under oligarchy-dominated democracy. In addition to this proliferation of demands for alternative forms of organised political participation, election-related developments also pointed to the weakening hold over Philippine politics of clientelist structures in the late 1960s. For example, scholars have demonstrated that voter participation rates in Philippine national and, especially, local elections correlated negatively with urbanisation in the pre-martial law years.[83] Moreover, while official 1967 and 1969 overall voting turnout showed a slight increase compared to previous elections,[84] the actual decline in the number of registered voters in these elections, contemporary observers claimed, amounted to virtual mass disenfranchisement, especially in certain densely populated cities.[85]

Finally, as the Philippines experienced rising 'violent and mass urban activities, precisely during the period when turnout declined',[86] calls for organised election boycotts emanated from within the country's single most important national institution for higher education, strategically located in the capital city: the University of the Philippines, Diliman. Through the *Philippine Collegian*, the official voice of the U.P. student body, and through reprints in national dailies and weeklies, election boycott advocates on campus articulated their opposition to voting in the 1967 elections:

> Every election is increasingly becoming a farce: what choice do we have
> between candidates espousing the same jaded ideas, harboring the same

greed? What choices lies for the tenant, the worker, the ordinary citizen when they are forced to vote for the candidates of the landlord or the Big Boss, under pain of harassment, exile or even death?[87]

The 1969 presidential elections met with similar criticism as, for example, the boycott argument 'vote wisely – don't vote' appeared in a 'special Tagalog issue of the Collegian intended for distribution among the country's schools and colleges, as well as the masses'.[88] '"Through the boycott", the student paper said … we can make our countrymen aware of the actual conditions around us'.[89]

Some of the same forces mobilised behind Magsaysay and NAMFREL in 1953 rallied behind the Citizen National Electoral Assembly (CNEA) to guard the ballot against threats of fraud and violence in the 1969 presidential elections.[90] Against the calls for boycott, CNEA emphasised that 'all it takes for evil to triumph is for good men to do nothing', and called on people not merely to cast but also to protect their ballots. Whilst this largely Church-supported CNEA crusade was complemented by the business-backed Operation Quick Count (OQC) vote tally in the 1969 election, their combined efforts failed to match the (national) associational support and (international) media publicity of the 1953 NAMFREL campaign. Not only was Marcos' opponent, Liberal Party candidate Sergio ('Serging') Osmeña, Jr, a colourless machine politician completely lacking in 'reformist' credentials, but the US government was also preoccupied with the Vietnam War and inclined to favour caesarist rather than transformist solutions to the participatory crises which seemed to threaten US interests in many parts of the globe in the late 1960s. Without either a credible 'reformist' alternative or US insistence on preventing presidential *continuismo*, Marcos won reelection handily in 1969 and went on to declare martial law in 1972 before the end of his second term. In the absence of a transformist resolution in 1969 the mounting crises of popular participation and presidential *continuismo* continued to deepen in the 1970s and into the 1980s.

The 1986 presidential elections

After the declaration of martial law in September 1972 aborted all efforts to reform Philippine electoralism *writ large,* the next wave of transformist mobilisation emerged in the mid-1980s, precisely as the most acute post-colonial crisis of *continuismo* and participation surfaced in the country. In 1986, after a decade and a half of so-called 'constitutional authoritarianism' and with the New Society Movement[91] – the ruling party machine – well-entrenched throughout the country, few doubted Marcos' willingness and ability to script yet another 'demonstration election'[92] for purposes of perpetuating his presidency. In fact, after abolishing Congress, curtailing civil liberties and replacing the 1935 constitution, Marcos produced 'the highest [turnouts] in recorded Philippine electoral performance'[93] in the first two referenda held under martial law. This new 'era of wholesale fraud in Philippine electoral history'[94] also saw extended military involvement in the carefully orchestrated 'plebiscites' and 'elections' under martial law.[95]

Beyond intervening in elections, moreover, the greatly expanded Armed Forces of the Philippines (AFP) also assumed a more 'extensive role in implementing the policies of the martial law administration'.[96] As scholars have noted, the AFP increasingly found itself working hand-in-glove with, President Marcos:

> Not only did it retain its pre-1972 roles with regard to the promotion of external defense, internal security, law and order, socio-economic activities through its civic action program, among others, but it also acquired judicial, administrative and management and political roles related to activities usually performed by civilian political leaders and private persons. Its management of military-related industries and investment firms meant that it had acquired a niche in the economic sector as well.[97]

By the mid-1980s, the Philippine military had tripled in size compared to the number of pre-martial law troops, with the unit in charge of presidential security swelling first to battalion and then to command strength.[98] In addition, some 65,000 para-military agents – euphemistically known as the Civilan Home Defense Forces[99] – helped to further fortify the Marcos regime, and in 1986, for example, loyalist 'warlord private armies … received 9,000 automatic weapons from [AFP Chief of Staff] Gen. [Fabian] Ver in the weeks before the elections'.[100] By establishing the Integrated National Police and placing it under the command of the Philippine Constabulary Chief, Marcos also increased executive control over the country's police forces.[101]

With Congress suspended and a strengthened AFP under his thumb, the martial-law president successfully established unprecedented autonomy *vis-à-vis* the oligarchy which had previously dominated not merely Philippine politics but also the national economy. In addition to augmenting presidential powers over coercive resources through the expansion and centralisation of military, para-military and police forces, 'Marcos and his cronies [also] exerted a vise over the national economy until it came under their total control or became their private possession'.[102] The notorious 'politics of plunder' under the Marcos regime saw favoured government technocrats milk the public sector while presidential relatives, friends, and cronies shared the spoils from the private economy, including those derived from the systematic raiding of key financial institutions.[103] As a deepening world recession and spiralling domestic financial crisis contributed to the closure of several commercial banks and the tightening of credit in the early 1980s, Marcos' 'crony capitalism' required major bailouts which further eroded the prospects for stable capital accumulation for (non-crony) business in the Philippines in the final years leading up to the 1986 snap-presidential elections.[104]

While martial law served to punctuate the escalating participatory crisis of the 1960s, the abolition of Congress and the installation of 'constitutional authoritarianism' in 1972 had failed to resolve deep-rooted problems of political incorporation.[105] In fact, continuing industrialisation and urbanisation, as well as increasing immiseration[106] in the 1970s contributed to undermining the regime's integrative capacity over time. In the 1980s, as a world recession exposed the limits to 'crony capitalism', Marcos' political coalition began to unravel.[107] Whilst a papal visit in 1981 prompted the official lifting of martial law, Marcos' continued rule by presidential decree failed to accommodate the mounting demands for political representation voiced in the 'parliament of the streets' of the 1980s.

The most organised and sustained extra-electoral opposition to the dictatorship, the Communist Party of the Philippines (CPP)-led New People's Army (NPA) first experienced growth in the hinterlands – especially in sugar, coconut and lumber economies under crony control – before eventually expanding to areas surrounding towns and cities in the early 1980s.[108] During the two final years of the Marcos regime the NPA reportedly doubled its forces and extended its influence to cover an estimated 20 per cent of all Philippine villages.[109] In addition to the guerrilla war, and in part reflective of the CPP's new united front initiative,[110] the Philippines also saw the resurgence of urban mass political action in the 1980s. The formation of a radical inter-university student organisation,[111] a militant labour union federation, and a national democratic peasant alliance,[112] for example, introduced student protests, labour strikes and peasant demonstrations on the scene of Philippine politics once again. Marcos' so-called 'demonstration elections' also met with organised boycotts successfully promoted by the Communist Party of the Philippines in the years leading up to the 1986 presidential contest. In the 1981 presidential election, for example, '[t]he display of unity among all opposition forces, from the old political parties to the Communist Party, in rejecting the election was unprecedented'.[113] In the 1984 elections to the National Assembly, moreover, the CPP-led boycott also succeeded in mobilising the support of more mainstream social groups and political organisations. Finally, as the CPP's Executive Committee ordered an election boycott of the 1986 snap elections, its affiliate labour and student organisations, as well as the united front's national council 'formally approved an active boycott position'.[114]

During the most severe crises of participation and *continuismo* in Philippine history, the mid-1980s witnessed the mobilisation of a dominant bloc of forces behind a transformist solution. Deeply disturbed by the economic crisis and the rapid growth of the CPP/NPA, elements within the business community, the Catholic Church hierarchy, and the US government worked assiduously in the wake of the 21 August 1983 assassination of long-time anti-Marcos opposition leader Benigno S. Aquino, Jr to promote various 'reform' initiatives, including the 'revitalisation of democratic institutions'. As in the early 1950s, it was this bloc of forces that supported the (revived) National Citizens Movement for Free Elections (NAMFREL) and encouraged participation in the Batasang Pambansa (National Assembly) elections of 1984 and the 'snap' presidential polls held in February 1986, against both Marcos' efforts to legitimise his power through fraudulent elections and CPP calls for boycott.[115] Thanks to their support and encouragement, the 'reformist' candidate and widow of the slain opposition leader, Corazon C. Aquino, was able to mount a popular campaign and NAMFREL succeeded in mobilising to counter – or at least to document – massive violence and fraud on the part of the Marcos regime. It was in the wake of this mobilisation for the February 1986 presidential election – and Marcos' much derided claim of victory in its aftermath – that the much celebrated 'People Power Revolution' occurred in Manila, ousting Marcos and ushering in a transformist solution to the most profound crisis of *continuismo* and participation yet seen in Philippine history.

Conclusion

In the early 1950s, late 1960s, and mid-1980s, the ambitious schemes of Elpidio Quirino and Ferdinand Marcos to muscle executive powers against both political opponents and the legislature as an institution threatened to perpetuate the rule of a president whose authoritarian and patrimonial tendencies encroached upon the privileges of the oligarchy and undermined the very process of capital accumulation in the Philippines. Yet whilst the mounting patrimonial and praetorian proclivities of these *continuista* presidential incumbents provided a conspicuous *raison d'être* for 'reformist' presidential candidacies and election-watch movements, these mobilisational campaigns also aimed at mitigating long-term problems of political incorporation and at neutralising short-term extra-electoral challenges 'from below'.

Whilst the participatory crises discussed above manifested important differences in terms of their historical origins and political magnitude, they nevertheless presented challenges of a similar kind in the 1953, 1969 and 1986 elections. The mobilisation of peasants demanding land reform in Central Luzon had already been reversed by 1953, whereas the labour strikes and student-activist campaigns concentrated in Manila were still gaining momentum in 1969, and the NPA's guerilla insurgency was at the peak of its organisational and logistical strength in 1986. The mobilisation of mass support by the Huk peasant guerillas, the *Kabataang Makabayan* (Nationalist Youth), and the National People's Army manifested significant similarities. First, these collective efforts all enjoyed ties to an underground Communist Party intent upon fomenting social revolution in the Philippines. Moreover, these organisations all drew support from previously unincorporated social groups and, by supporting extra-legal forms of collective action and publicy advocating election boycotts, constituted counter-hegemonic challenges to Philippine electoralism and to the interests of the dominant bloc of forces in Philippine society: the oligarchy, the Catholic Church, and the US government.

In sum, transformist mobilisation emerged at the three critical junctures in Philippine post-war history when the extra-electoral mobilisation of previously marginal or unincorporated social groups and the irregular policy interventions of an authoritarian *continuista* president combined to threaten both the political hegemony of the ruling class in Philippine society and the process of capital accumulation itself. These transformist campaigns mobilised not merely in support of democracy but also in opposition to extra-electoral challenges both to the authoritarian regime and to the ruling class. While mobilising in the name of 'civil society', they emerged in a process of political contestation and conflict, and at the expense of more radical demands for social change and democratisation.

Seen in the light of the underlying tensions of Philippine democracy, the pattern of recurring participatory and *continuismo* crises, and the variously 'transformist' and 'caesarist' resolutions of 1953 and 1969, respectively, the 'People Power Revolution' appears as an instance of the phenomenon identified by Gramsci as *trasformismo*. Viewed in this light, the 'People Power Revolution' appears less as an example of the spontaneous resurgence of civil society in the process of transition from authoritarian rule and more as the climax in a cycle of recurring crisis and temporary 'resolution' stemming from deep-rooted tensions in the underlying structures of Philippine democracy that have yet to be resolved. Yet the waves of mobilisation and counter-mobilisation which peaked in the mid-1980s have combined with secular trends of socio-economic transformation to leave complex and significant traces in the realm of national politics and popular consciousness, as the chapters to follow reveal.

Notes

1 See Antonio Gramsci, 'Notes on Italian History', in Quintin Hoare and Geoffrey Nowell Smith (eds. and transls), *Selections from the Prison Notebooks of Antonio Gramsci* (New York: International Publishers, 1971), especially p. 58, fn. 8.

2 Gramsci, 'Notes on Italian History', p. 58.

3 Perry Anderson, 'The Dark Side of Brazilian Conviviality', *London Review of Books*, 24 November 1994, p. 6.

4 See, for example, Juan J. Linz and Arturo Valenzuela (eds), *The Failure of Presidentialism: Comparative Perspectives*, Volume 1 (Baltimore: Johns Hopkins University Press, 1994).

5 Hamza Alavi, 'The State in Post-Colonial Societies: Pakistan and Bangladesh', *New Left Review* 74 (July–August 1972), pp. 59–82.

6 Alex R. Magno, 'Authoritarianism and Underdevelopment: Notes on the Political Order of a Dependent-Capitalist Filipino Mode', in Temario C. Rivera *et al.*, *Feudalism and Capitalism in the Philippines: Trends and Implications* (Quezon City: Foundation for Nationalist Studies, 1982), p. 95. See also: Emiliano P. Bolongaita, 'The Breakdown of Philippine Democracy: A Comparative Institutional Analysis' (Ph.D. dissertation, University of Notre Dame, 1996), especially Chs. 3–4.

7 See, for example, Paredes, 'The Origins of National Politics: Taft and the Partido Federal', in Ruby Paredes (ed.) *Philippine Colonial Democracy* (Quezon City: Ateneo de Manila University Press, 1989), pp. 41–69.

8 See: Jesus M. Manalili, 'Historical Suffrage in the Philippines and its Present Problems', (Ph.D. dissertation, University of Santo Tomas, 1966), p. 75.

9 Joseph Ralston Hayden, *The Philippines: A Study in National Development* (New York: Macmillan Company, 1942), p. 267. The term *principalia* refers to the small local elite of acting and former native village- and town-level officials, the *cabezas de barangay* and *gobernadorcillos*.

10 Arthur Alan Shantz, 'Political Parties: The Changing Foundations of Philippine Democracy' (Ph.D. dissertation, University of Michigan, 1972), p. 287.

11 The Manila press reported registration in the June 18, 1940 Constitutional amendment plebiscite at some 2,270,000 citizens, which translated into about 14 per cent of the Philippine population at that time. See Hayden, *The Philippines*, p. 204.

12 The actual *number* of voters almost doubled between 1951 and 1969 (from 4,391,109 in 1951 to 8,060,465 in 1969). Interestingly, the number of *registered* voters showed an even greater

increase from 4,754,307 in 1951 to 10,300,898 in 1969, which points to a dramatically widening gap between registered and actual voters.

13   See, for example, Dante C. Simbulan, 'A Study of the Socio-Economic Elite in Philippine Politics and Government, 1946–1963' (Ph.D. dissertation, Australian National University, 1965) and Temario Campos Rivera, 'Class, The State and Foreign Capital: The Politics of Philippine Industrialisation, 1950–1986' (Ph.D. dissertation, University of Wisconsin-Madison, 1991).

14   Rivera, 'Class, The State and Foreign Capital', p. 49.

15   Robert B. Stauffer, 'Congress in the Philippine Political System', in Alan Kornsberg and Lloyd D. Musolf (eds), *Legislatures in Developmental Perspective* (Danton, N.C: Duke University Press, 1970), pp. 355.

16   Hayden, *The Philippines*, pp. 74–75.

17   Irene Cortes, *The Philippine Presidency: A Study of Executive Power* (Quezon City: Philippine Legal Studies, College of Law, University of the Philippines, 1966), pp. 170–171.

18   The Emergency Powers bill was introduced into the National Assembly by first Commonwealth president Manuel Quezon on July 15, 1940.

19   Regarding tarrifs, import and export quotas, for example, see the Constitution of the Philippines, Article VI, section 22 (2).

20   Hayden, *The Philippines*, p. 62.

21   Alfred W. McCoy, 'Quezon's Commonwealth: The Emergence of Philippine Authoritarianism' in Paredes (ed.), *Philippine Colonial Democracy*, p. 138. Commonwealth President Manuel Quezon himself admitted that 'the idea of amending the Constitution in this respect was originally conceived and advanced for the only purpose of permitting my reelection'. Cited in Hayden, *The Philippines*, p. 76. The constitutional amendement changing the presidential term from six to four years and introducing a second term of office was passed by national plebiscite on June 18, 1940.

22   See, for example, Jean Grossholtz, *Politics in the Philippines* (Boston, MA: Little, Brown and Company, 1964), pp. 119–124; and Caridad. S. Alfonso, 'Executive-Legislative Relations', in Jose Veloso Abueva and Raul P. de Guzman (eds), *Foundations and Dynamic of Filipino Government and Politics* (Quezon City: Bookmark, 1969), pp. 343–346.

23   Other legislative powers included, for example, the Congressional Electoral Tribunals' sole authority over controversies pertaining to 'the election, returns, and qualifications of all the members of their respective Houses'. See, for example, Gabriel U. Iglesias and Abelardo Tolentino, Jr, 'The Structure and Functions of Congress', in Abueva and de Guzman (eds), *Foundations and Dynamics*, p. 256. In addition, Congress also retained the power to impeach the president of the Philippines, which was vested in the National Assembly under the American period. See Hayden, *The Philippines*, p. 209; 836–837.

24   On pork-barrel politics in the Philippines, see, for example, Ledivina Vidallon-Carino, *The Politics and Administration of the Pork Barrel* (Manila: University of the Philippines, College of Public Administration Local Government Center, 1966).

25   Robert B. Stauffer, *The Philippine Congress: Causes of Structural Change* (London: Sage Publications, 1975), p. 14.

26   Amancia G. Laureta, 'Legislative Authorisation of the Budget', in Abueva and de Guzman, *Foundations and Dynamics*, p. 291. Senate and House members exercised influence within the executive branch through their role in the appointment of high-ranking officials to such key agencies as the Bureau of Customs, the Bureau of Internal Revenue, and the Philippine National Bank.

27   This is, of course, not to deny either the origins or prevalence of such practices under the American colonial regime. See, for example, Benedict R. Anderson, 'Elections and Participation in Three Southeast Asian Countries', in R.H. Taylor (ed.) *The Politics of Elections in Southeast Asia* (Cambridge: Cambridge University Press, 1996), pp. 21–22.

28   Perry Anderson, 'The Antinomies of Antonio Gramsci', *New Left Review* 100 (November 1976 – January 1977), p. 28.

29 On Quirino, see, for example, Jorge R. Coquia, *The Philippine Presidential Election of 1953* (Manila: University Publishing Co., 1955), pp. 100–156; A.V.H. Hartendorp, *History of Industry and Trade of the Philippines* (Manila: American Chamber of Commerce, 1958), pp. 281–290, 297–304; and Frank H. Golay, *The Philippines: Public Policy and National Economic Development* (Ithaca: Cornell University Press, 1961), pp. 58–89. On Marcos, see, for example, Robert B. Stauffer, *The Philippine Congress*, pp. 30–35; and Amando Doronila, *The State, Economic Transformation, and Political Change in the Philippines* (Singapore: Oxford University Press, 1992), pp. 123–149.

30 See, for example, Aurora Javate-de Dios, Petronilo Bn. Daroy, and Lorna Kalaw-Tirol (eds), *Dictatorship and Revolution: Roots of People Power* (Manila: Conspectus, 1988); and Ricardo Manapat, *Some Are Smarter Than Others: The History of Marcos' Crony Capitalism* (New York: Aletheia Publications, 1991).

31 V.O. Key, 'A Theory of Critical Elections', *The Journal of Politics*, 17 (1955), p. 1.

32 *Ibid.*, p. 4.

33 See Hirofumi Ando, 'Elections in the Philippines: Mass-Elite Interaction through the Electoral Process, 1946–1969' (Ph.D. dissertation, University of Michigan, 1971). Ando notes the upset of the two-party balance-of-power in 1953 and 1969 when the Nacionalistas counted 68.9 and 62.1 per cent, respectively, of the presidential votes (see table 3.1, p. 65).

34 Walter Dean Burnham, *Critical Elections and the Mainsprings of American Politics* (New York: W.W. Norton & Company, 1970), p. 10.

35 On clientelism, coercion and money in Philippine politics, see, for example, James C. Scott, 'Corruption, Machine Politics, and Political Change', *American Political Science Review*, Volume 63 (1969), pp. 1142–1158; and Thomas C. Nowak and Kay A. Snyder, 'Clientelist Politics in the Philippines: Integration or Instability?' *American Political Science Review*, Volume 68 (1974), pp. 1147–1170.

36 For a theoretical discussion of the political significance of shifts in the 'structure of political opportunity', see, for example, Sidney Tarrow, 'Struggle, Politics and Reform: Collective Action, Social Movements and Cycles of Protest' (Cornell University: Western Society Paper no. 21, 1989), pp. 32–38; as well as Doug McAdam, *The Political Process and the Development of Black Insurgency* (Chicago: University of Chicago, 1982), pp. 23–35.

37 Initially established by an act of the National Assembly, the Commission on Elections (COMELEC) was given the 'exclusive charge of the enforcement and administration of all laws relative to the conduct of election' according to a constitutional amendment of 1940. See Hayden, *The Philippines*, pp. 455–456; and Cortes, *The Philippine Presidency*, pp. 100–101. For a discussion of COMELEC under Marcos, see Tancangco, *The Anatomy of Electoral Fraud*.

38 Juan J. Linz, 'Presidential or Parliamentary Democracy: Does it Make a Difference?' in Linz and Valenzuela, *The Failure of Presidential Democracy*, p. 19.

39 *Ibid.*

40 Quirino had served as President Manuel Roxas' vice-president since 1946 and ascended to the presidency after Roxas' death in 1948. His campaign thus benefited from all the advantages of incumbency.

41 For contemporary reports of the violence and fraud that marred the 1949 elections, see, for example, the October 3 and November 9, 1949 editions of the *Manila Bulletin*.

42 See, for example, Resil Mojares, *The Man Who Would Be President: Serging Osmena and Philippine Politics* (Cebu City: Maria Cacao, 1986), p. 175.

43 Records from the Senate Electoral Tribunal indicate that 22 per cent of all senatorial ballots were fraudulent in 1949 as compared to 6 per cent in 1946 and 12 per cent in 1947, cited in Jose V. Abueva, *Ramon Magsaysay: A Political Biography* (Manila: Solidaridad Publishing House, 1971), p. 192, fn. 22.

44 Executive Order No. 309, March 30, 1950, cited in Rod B. Gutang, *Pulisya: The Inside Story of the Demilitarisation of the Law Enforcement System in the Philippines* (Quezon City: Daraga Press, 1991), p. 85.

45 *Manila Chronicle*, cited in Hartendorp, *History of Industry and Trade*, p. 301.

46 See, for example, Golay, *The Philippines: Public Policy*, pp. 58–89.

47 See, especially, Coquia, *The Philippine Presidential Election*, pp. 194–214.

48 Doronila, *The State*, p. 54. For a detailed introduction to the Central Bank, see also Golay, *The Philippines: Public Policy*, pp. 217–227.

49 Benedict J. Kerkvliet, *The Huk Rebellion: A Study of Peasant Revolt in the Philippines* (Berkeley: University of California Press, 1977), p. 249.

50 Ronald King Edgerton, 'The Politics of Reconstruction in the Philippines: 1945–48' (Ph.D. dissertation, University of Michigan, 1975), pp. 3 and 19.

51 For a discussion suggestive of the severity of the repression and fraud employed to undermine candidates and supporters associated with peasant organisations in Central Luzon, see, for example, Kerkvliet, *The Huk Rebellion*, pp. 173–174, 205 and 211.

52 For a discussion of this period in the Huk rebellion, see Kerkvliet, *The Huk Rebellion*, p.174–202. The term 'Huk' is short for the Hukbong Bayan Laban sa Hapon, or Hukbalahap [People's Resistance Army against the Japanese], which was changed in 1948 to the Hukbong Magpagpalaya ng Bayan, or HMB [People's Liberation Army].

53 Kerkvliet, *The Huk Rebellion*, p. 235.

54 Cited in Kerkvliet, *The Huk Rebellion*, p. 237. According to Kerkvliet, '[m]any Huk leaders in the field commands and Recos [regional commands] urged boycott, too'.

55 See issues of *The Free Philippines* from September to November 1953 for an overview of NAMFREL's activities.

56 Coquia, *The Philippine Presidential Election*, p. 284.

57 For a general discussion of these developments see, for example, Doronila, *The State*, pp. 126–149. For more on the 1969 presidential elections, see Shantz, 'Political Parties'.

58 See, for example, Benigno Aquino, Jr, *The Garrison State in the Make* (Manila: Benigno S. Aquino, Jr Foundation, 1985). In this period, the Philippine military budget increased as follows: P271.1 million in 1965, P324.2 million in 1966, P366 million in 1967, P415 million in 1968, and P513 million in 1969.

59 Caolina G. Hernandez, 'The Extent of Civilian Control of the Military in the Philippines: 1946–1976' (Ph.D. dissertation State University of New York at Buffalo, 1979); Donald L. Berlin, 'Prelude to Martial Law: An Examination of Pre-1972 Philippine Military-Civilian Relations' (Ph.D. dissertation, University of South Carolina, 1982); and Fact-Finding Commission, *The Final Report* (Manila: Bookmark, 1990), pp. 33–43.

60 Stephen Rosskamm Shalom, *The United States and the Philippines: A Study of Neo-Colonialism* (Quezon City: New Day Publishers, 1986), p. 113.

61 Executive Order No. 120, February 16, 1968 expanded the Metrocom. The martial-law Constitution of 1973 eventually mandated the establishment of an integrated national police. See Gutang, *Pulisya*, pp.88–90. Reportedly, after a 'joint United States-Philippine Government nationwide survey of Philippine law enforcement … in the fall of 1966', USAID police assistance to the Philippines increased from '$62,000 in 1962 … to $618,000 in 1968 [and] $608,000 in 1969', cited in Bonifacio Gillego, 'Our Police Forces As a Tool of American Imperialism', *Ronin*, Volume 1, Number 7 (October 1972), p. 12.

62 See Eduardo Lachica, *Huk: Philippine Agrarian Society in Revolt* (Manila: Solidaridad Publishing House, 1971), pp. 222–229. See also *Manila Times*, October 12 and 13, 1968.

63 Vidallon-Carino, *The Politics and Administration of the Pork Barrel*, p. 10.

64 Stauffer, *The Philippine Congress*, pp. 32-33. For a more recent study which elaborates this argument, see Doronila, *The State*, pp. 123–149.

65 Shantz, 'Political Parties', pp. 153–154. Between 1966 and 1968, for example, the AFP's engineer battalions 'were responsible for P130.1 million worth of public works construction … nearly 21% of the P594.8 million spent'. Quintin R. de Borja, Armando N. Gatmaitan, and Gregorio C. de Castro, 'Notes on the Role of the Military in Socio-Economic Development', *Philippine Journal of Public Administration*, Volume 12, Number 3 (July 1968), p. 279.

66 Josefa Karunungan Cauton, 'Presidential Versus Legislative Control over Disbursement of Public Funds' (M.A. thesis, University of the Philippines, 1971), p. 66.

67 Robert E. Baldwin, *Foreign Trade Regimes and Economic Development: The Philippines* (New York: Columbia University Press, 1975), p. 70.

68 In 1967, for example, the proportion of the Philippine labor force employed in agriculture had decreased to 57 per cent as compared to 72 per cent in 1952. See Vicente B. Valdepeñas, Jr, *The Protection and Development of Philippine Manufacturing* (Manila: Ateneo University Press, 1970), p. 14.

69 Department of International Economic and Social Affairs, *Population Growth and Policies in Mega Cities: Metro Manila* (New York: United Nations publication, Population Policy Paper No.5, 1986), pp. 1 and 3.

70 Ernesto M. Pernia, Cayetano W. Paderanga, Jr, Victoria P. Hermano and assoc., *The Spatial and Urban Dimensions of Development in the Philippines* (Manila: Philippine Institute for Development Studies, 1983), p. 58.

71 Nowak and Snyder, 'Clientelist Politics in the Philippines: Integration or Instability?' *American Political Science Review*, Volume 68, Number 3, (September 1974), p. 1151.

72 *Ibid.*, p. 1165.

73 See Scott, 'Corruption, Machine Politics', p. 1144.

74 Nowak and Snyder, 'Clientelist Politics', p. 1152.

75 *Lapiang Manggagawa* (the Workers' Party) briefly united the National Association of Trade Unions (NATU) with the Philippine Association of Free Labor Unions (PAFLU). Jose Ma. Sison, the future founder and chairman of the Communist Party of the Philippines, was elected vice-president of the LM in 1963. See, for example, Elias T. Ramos, *Philippine Labor Movement in Transition* (Quezon City: New Day Publishers, 1976).

76 *Malayang Samahang Magsasaka* (MASAKA) (the Free Peasants' Union) became one of two major peasant organisations in Central Luzon in the 1960s. Before its split in 1968, it was under the leadership of Felixberto Olalia Sr., a long-time labor organiser with strong ties to the communist party. See: Dante G. Guevarra, Unyonismo sa Pilipinas (Manila: May Akda, 1992), pp. 115-116; and Jose M. Lacaba, 'Felixberto Olalia: Grand Old Man of Philippine Labor', *Mr & Ms*, 12 January 1982, p. 12.

77 *Kabataang Makabayan* (Nationalist Youth) was founded by Jose Ma. Sison in 1964. See, for example, Andres Cristobal Cruz, 'A Natural History of Our Nationalist Demonstrations', *Graphic*, 9 February 1966, pp. 20–21; Ninotchka Rosca, 'The Youth Movement in Retrospect', *Graphic*, 5 March 1969, pp. 6–9; Francisco Nemenzo, 'An Irrepressible Revolution: The Decline and Resurgence of the Philippine Communist Movement' (Australian National University, unpubl. mss., 1984); and William Chapman, *Inside the Philippine Revolution* (New York: W.W. Norton & Company, 1987), pp. 73–75.

78 Thomas C. Nowak and Kay A. Snyder, 'Economic Concentration and Political Change in the Philippines', Benedict J. Kerkvliet (ed.), *Political Change in the Philippines: Studies of Local Politics Preceeding Martial Law* (Honolulu: University of Hawaii Press, 1974), p. 154.

79 Petronilo Bn. Daroy, 'On the Eve of Dictatorship and Revolution', in Javate-de Dios, Daroy, and Kalaw-Tirol, eds., *Dictatorship and Revolution*, pp. 3–5.

80 Special Joint Senate-House Committee on Mass Demonstrations, *Final Report on the Root Causes of Mass Demonstrations* (Manila: House of Representatives, April 16, 1970), p. 133.

81 See, for example, Gregg R. Jones, *Red Revolution: Inside the Philippine Guerilla Movement* (Boulder, CO: Westview Press, 1989), pp. 17–38.

82 On the Muslim Independence Movement (MIM) and the subsequently established Moro National Liberation Front (MNLF), see, for example, T.J.S. George, *Revolt in Mindanao: The Rise of Islam in Philippine Politics* (Kuala Lumpur: Oxford University Press, 1980), pp. 131–142; and W.K. Che Man, *Muslim Separatism: The Moros of Southern Philippines and the Malays of Southern Thailand* (Singapore: Oxford University Press, 1990), pp. 77–81.

83 Nowak and Snyder, 'Clientelist Politics', table 15, p. 1167. For a similar finding, see Ando, 'Elections in the Philippines', pp. 42–43.

84 For a summary of turnout rates in Philippine post-war elections, see Ando, 'Elections in the Philippines', p. 39. Turnout figures measure the ratio of actual votes cast in a given election to the number of registered voters, as indicated by the Commission on Elections' records.

85 Citing both presidential and senate committees, one article estimated that some half million voters were thus disenfranchised in the 1967 elections. See Manuel F. Almario, 'Urgent: A

Change in the Polls', *Graphic*, 11 December 1968, p. 11. Allegations that on election day 'out of 178,000 registered voters in Quezon City, only 58,000 were able to vote' provide further testimony to the failure of urban electoral machine politics. See Teodoro C. Berbano, 'Protests: As Usual Plus Something Else', *Graphic*, 6 December 1967, p. 27.

86 Nowak and Snyder, 'Clientelist Politics', p. 1169.

87 Cited in Yen Makabenta, 'We Will Not Vote', *Graphic*, 15 November 1967, p. 29.

88 Reprinted in 'UP Paper Urges Boycott of Tuesday's Elections', *Manila Bulletin*, 6 November 1969, p. 24.

89 *Ibid*.

90 See, for example, Filemon V. Tutay, 'Policing the Polls: CNEA and OQC 1969 Join Hands with PC to Ensure Clean, Free and Orderly Elections on November 11', *Philippines Free Press*, 1 November 1969, pp. 10–11.

91 *Kilusang Bagong Lipunan* (KBL) in Tagalog.

92 On demonstration elections, see: Edward S. Herman and Frank Brodhead, *Demonstration Elections: US-Staged Elections in the Dominican Republic, Vietnam, and El Salvador* (Boston: South End Press, 1984), p. 202.

93 Raul P. de Guzman, 'Citizen Participation and Decision-Making under Martial Law Administration: A Search for a Viable Political System', *Philippine Journal of Public Administration*, Volume 21, Number 1 (January 1977).

94 Luzviminda G. Tancangco, *The Anatomy of Electoral Fraud*, p. 68. For more general discussions of martial law, see, for example, David E. Rosenberg, ed., *Marcos and Martial Law in the Philippines* (Ithaca: Cornell University Press, 1979); and Gary Hawes, *The Philippine State and the Marcos Regime: The Politics of Export* (Ithaca: Cornell University Press, 1987).

95 For a brief discussion of the Armed Forces of the Philippines' expanded role in elections under martial law, see, for example, Fact-Finding Commission, *The Final Report*, p. 51.

96 Carolina G. Hernandez, 'The Role of the Military in Contemporary Philippine Society', *The Diliman Review*, Volume 32, Number 1 (January–February 1984), p. 21. For a more exhaustive discussion of this topic, see Hernandez, 'The Extent of Civilian Control of the Military'.

97 Hernandez, 'The Role of the Military', p. 21.

98 See, for example, Fact-Finding Commission, *The Final Report*, pp. 46–52.

99 Replaced under President Corazon C. Aquino by the Civilian Armed Forces Government Units (CAFGUs).

100 Alfred W. McCoy, 'The Yellow Revolution' (Adelaide: Flinders University Asian Studies Lecture 17, 1986), p. 13.

101 The Integrated National Police (INP) was organised in 1975 and placed under the Philippine Constabulary, then headed by Gen. Fidel V. Ramos, a second cousin of Marcos who succeed Corazon C. Aquino to the presidency in 1992.

102 Ricardo Manapat, *Some are Smarter than Others*, p. 84.

103 See, for example, Belinda A. Aquino, *Politics of Plunder: The Philippines under Marcos* (Quezon City: Great Books Trading, 1987); Hawes, *The Philippine State and the Marcos Regime*; and Paul D. Hutchcroft, 'Oligarchs and Cronies in the Philippine State: The Politics of Patrimonial Plunder', *World Politics*, Volume 43, Number 3, 1991, pp. 414–450.

104 Emmanuel de Dios, 'A Political Economy of Philippine Policy-Making', in John W. Langford and K. Lorne Brownsey (eds), *Economic Policy-Making in the Asia-Pacific Region* (Halifax: Novia Scotia: Institute for Research on Public Policy, 1990); and Hutchcroft, 'Oligarchs and Cronies', p. 445.

105 See, for example, Rosenberg (ed.), *Marcos and Martial Law*.

106 See, for example, James K. Boyce, *The Philippines: The Political Economy of Growth and Impoverishment in the Marcos Era* (Honolulu: University of Hawaii Press, 1993).

107 See, for example, Hawes, *The Philippine State and the Marcos Regime*.

108 See, especially, Benedict J. Kerkvliet, 'Patterns of Philippine Resistance and Rebellion, 1970–1986', *Pilipinas*, Number 6 (Spring 1986), pp. 35–49.

109 The AFP reportedly estimated 'NPA strength to 24,000–25,000 regulars, half of whom are thought to be armed. The insurgents are thought to be operating in at least 68 out of the

nation's 72 provinces, and to exert significant influence over 20 per cent of the nation's 40,000 villages'. Lawyers Committee for Human Rights, *Vigilantes in the Philippines: A Threat to Democratic Rule* (New York: Lawyers Committee for Human Rights, 1987), p. 3.

110 Jones, *Red Revolution*, p. 146.

111 The League of Filipino Students emerged in the fall 1979 and led student protests in the early 1980s. See Larry A. Niksch and Marjorie Niehaus, 'The Internal Situation in the Philippines: Current Trends and Future Prospects', Congressional Research Service, Report No. 81-21 F, January 1981, pp. 90–91.

112 Formally organised in 1985, *Kilusang Magbubukid ng Pilipinas* (the Philippine Peasant Movement) 'was an alliance of local peasant organisations that had adopted an unambiguous national democratic platform ... clearly the largest organised bloc among the peasantry, since many of the more moderate groups often had only a paper membership. Many veteran peasant leaders were active in the KMP'. James Putzel, *A Captive Land: The Politics of Agrarian Reform in the Philippines* (Quezon City: Ateneo de Manila University Press, 1992), p. 218.

113 Emmanuel S. de Dios, 'The Erosion of the Dictatorship' in Javate-de Dios, Daroy and Kalaw-Tirol (eds), *Dictatorship and Revolution*, p. 81.

114 Jones, *Red Revolution*, p. 158.

115 See: National Citizens Movement for Free Elections, *The NAMFREL Report on the February 7, 1986 Philippine Presidential Elections* (Manila: NAMFREL, 1987). For an enthusiastic account of NAMFREL's 'perils and triumphs', see also Kaa Byington, *Bantayan ng Bayan: Stories from the NAMFREL Crusade 1984–86* (Manila: Bookmark, 1988).

3 Morbid symptoms and political violence in the Philippines

At the military detachment in Oringao, the leader of the Alsa Masa group, Rosendo Mahinay, informed the detachment commander that he had the head of an NPA military commander, and removed the head from the jacket.... The detachment commander, a sergeant, asked the Alsa Masa group the name of the victim; they replied that they did not know. The sergeant instructed the group to take the head to the 7th Infantry Battalion detachment in barangay Bunga.

Accompanied by three soldiers, the group proceeded there.... In Bunga, the head ... was presented to the detachment as the remains of an NPA commander. A sergeant retrieved a stack of photographs of NPA suspects sought by the military, and compared the pictures to [the] head. Finding no 'match' to any of the photographed suspects, the sergeant ordered the group to 'take the head back'. Despite their 'error', the Alsa Masa group was rewarded for their exertions with a sack of rice....

Four members of the Alsa Masa group left the detachment with the head.... They apparently discarded the head; it was found the next day in some bushes near the national road.[1]

Local military detachments. Anti-communist vigilantes. A severed head. Kabankalan, Negros Occidental, Philippines. Sunday, 28 June 1987. Such is the stuff of human rights reports on the Philippines during this period. There were many such reports. And many more victims yet to come.

Within a year of the much-celebrated 'People Power' revolt that ushered in a regime of national reconciliation and democratic restoration in February 1986, the new head of state, President Corazon C. Aquino, declared 'Total War' against the Communist-led New People's Army (NPA) and its supporters. In March 1987, a presidential address to the Philippine Military Academy (PMA) called for 'not social and economic reform but police and military action' to counter the guerrilla movement.[2] In April 1987, the cabinet endorsed 'voluntary and spontaneous [groups] of citizens for self-defense in areas where there was an insurgency'.[3] The same month also saw the Philippine Commission of Human Rights summarily dismissed and replaced with a new one, arguably 'created and staffed by some people who have spent more time defending the military than prosecuting human rights violators'.[4] In May 1987, the first post-Marcos Congressional elections allowed sugar planters in Negros Occidental and their counterparts in other provinces to reassert local political control, to gain legislative leverage *vis-à-vis* the Aquino administration, and, significantly, to ally with regional military commanders in support of counter-insurgency campaigns and para-military groups.[5] This much can be inferred from writings on the rejuvenation of counter-insurgency campaigns and electoral politics in the early post-Marcos Philippines.

Meanwhile, in the years following the ouster of Marcos in February 1986, repeated military efforts to seize power through *coup d'état* marked the transitional regime of Corazon C. Aquino. Between July 1986 and December 1989, so-called 'Marcos loyalists' and/or 'reformists' within the Armed Forces of the Philippines (AFP) engaged in acts of military adventurism which ranged from the 37-hour occupation of the Manila Hotel to the strafing and bombing of Malacañang Presidential Palace.[6]

A decade later, such manifestations of militarisation and military intervention have all but disappeared from the Philippines. Since 1990, there has been no sign of yet another 'season of coups',[7] and the 'day of the vigilante' has likewise drawn to a close.[8] Whilst today government security forces still occasionally confront small bands of Communist revolutionaries and Muslim separatists in armed combat, overall a pattern of demobilisation of military troops and para-military groups across the country has replaced the intense militarisation of the mid-late 1980s.

With the advantage of hindsight, this chapter situates the recent rise and fall of military and para-military mobilisation in broader historical perspective. The chapter reexamines the distinctive patterns of state formation, 'civil-military relations', and para-military mobilisation which have unfolded in the course of the twentieth century. Beyond the consequences of martial law identified in the existing literature, this paper highlights the significance of American colonial legacies and post-colonial Cold War conditions for shaping the organisation – and deployment – of violence in Philippine society. The chapter seeks to provide a historically grounded critique against easy reification of 'civil-military' relations in the Philippines, where both counter-insurgency and election campaigns have tended to blur such distinctions in the past.

Drawing in part on the discrepant histories collected by human-rights activists, journalists and other concerned researchers, this chapter also reexamines the nature and direction of political violence and 'vigilante' mobilisation in the transitional period between exhausted dictatorship and consolidated democracy. This chapter investigates the overt manifestations and underlying dynamics of anti-communism and counter-insurgency in the Philippines during this period, focusing attention on both the symbolic economy and the instrumental politics of vigilantism in the early post-Marcos era. The line of inquiry pursued cuts against the grain of much existing – scholarly, journalistic, and military – treatment of such questions. In lieu of the 'weak' Philippine state posited or assumed in much recent academic literature, for example, the pages below underline the impressive absorptiveness and resilience of this post-colonial state. Against the 'wild' society haunting much media coverage of the late-1980s Philippines, moreover, this chapter highlights the successful interpellation and incorporation of this un-civil society under conditions of intense political contestation and uncertain (re)democratisation. Finally, beyond the 'psywar' preoccupations of security studies, the pages below probe the symbolic representation and circulation of this phantasmagoric violence in the Philippines. This chapter also constitutes an attempt at 'writing against terror' despite the difficulties and pitfalls involved in such an undertaking.[9]

Historical legacies: the American colonial era

Whilst the mobilisation of vigilantes and the mounting of military coups in the late 1980s reflected dynamics peculiar to the 1980s, the pattern of militarisation and demilitarisation during this period was decisively shaped by structures rooted deep in the colonial foundations of the Philippine state. That is, the peculiar coupling of expanded provisions for electoral participation with intensified campaigns aimed at pacification and (re)incorporation of mobilised populations in the 1980s mirrored early critical moments in the history of modern state formation in the Philippines. Furthermore, the enduring structures of 'Philippine colonial democracy'[10] contributed to the marked decentralisation and privatisation of coercive state apparatuses which, in turn, prefigured a recurring pattern of sub-contracted political violence.

Under the official rubric of 'benevolent assimilation' and in the context of an undeclared 'savage war', American incursions into the Philippines at the turn of the century ran up against the first nationalist movement in Asia. Mobilised in 1896 and defeated in 1897, Filipino anti-colonial forces regrouped with the onset of the Spanish-American war in April 1898 and, in but a few weeks' time, revolutionary *supremo* Emilio Aguinaldo declared the first Philippine Republic. The inauguration of a republican constitution and government followed suit in the next few months, but the outbreak of the Philippine-American war interrupted this brief interlude of self-rule in Feburary 1899.

Once rid of Spain, one of the most backward of colonial powers by this period, the so-called 'Philippine Insurrection' found itself confronting the arriviste imperialism of America at the turn of the century. Whilst *conquistadores* imported from the Spanish Americas had laid the groundwork for more than 300 years of friar rule, men and methods drawn from the North American frontier carried the professed 'mission' of the United States in the initial phase of this second coming of colonial conquest to the Philippines. Due to the decentralised nature of the American state and national army, which were still in the midst of a highly contested process of 'patchwork' civil and military institution building at the turn of the century,[11] it is perhaps unsurprising that the United States' first armed adventure in Asia was waged in the spirit and mode of 'Injun Warfare'.[12]

Although administrative reform in the military and electoral considerations among American politicians may have initially deterred US forces from transgressing the boundaries of 'civilised warfare' in the Philippines, such restraint soon gave way to the 'savage war' doctrine which had evolved over the course of the American Civil War and was subsequently invoked from Sand Creek (1864) to Wounded Knee (1890) in the so-called 'Plains campaigns'. This doctrine already reflected the 'lived experience' of many senior as well as junior American officers serving in the Philippines, as a significant number of high-ranking US officers posted to critical positions in the Philippines, such as Generals Elwell S. Otis, Wesley Merritt, Henry W. Lawton, Franklin J. Bell, Jacob Smith and Adna Chaffee, had gained their (s)kills and stars in the American West. Recruited through so-called volunteer regiments of various state militias, the rank and file also earned a certain notoriety for its 'lawless violence', encouraged perhaps no less by individual commanding officers than by the paucity of military training, discipline and experience that characterised these American troops in the Philippines.

Inasmuch as the American 'state of courts and parties' remained in place despite the 'patchwork' reform efforts to expand and rationalise national administrative apparatuses in the late nineteenth century,[13] the new colonial regime in the Philippines also displayed notable affinities with the metropole, as exemplified by the preference for staging local elections rather than building a centralised bureaucracy in the archipelago. Even as military campaigns continued in many parts of the Islands, municipal mayors (1901), provincial governors (1902), and representatives to a national legislature (1907) were elected in the Islands, under conditions of highly restricted suffrage. These elected local officials, in turn, were granted extensive powers over Police/Constabulary forces at both municipal and provincial levels of government under Philippine colonial democracy.[14] Congressmen, moreover, enjoyed significant formal as well as informal influence over the appointments and rotation of Constabulary officers.[15] Finally, at the national level, Nacionalista Senate President (1917–35) and Philippine Commonwealth President (1935–41) Manuel Quezon also exercised considerable, at times decisive, discretion over the Philippine Constabulary (PC) as part and parcel of his marked accumulation of executive powers through skilful manipulation of the government bureaucracy and the constitution, as well as his long-standing intervention in provincial politics.[16]

As noted by other scholars, this pattern reflected – and, in part, reproduced – a peculiarly American experience of state formation, distinguished by the subordination of a weakly insulated bureaucracy (including the police) to elected local and national politicians.[17] Instead of an effectively centralised and insulated colonial bureaucracy, the Philippines thus developed a 'highly decentralised, politicised, and privatised administration of law enforcement' wherein Police/Constabulary appointments, promotions, renumerations, and reassignments became the prerogative of municipal and provincial politicians.[18] Given the Constabulary's centrality to the Armed Forces from the latter's formation in 1936, this pattern characterised 'civil-military' relations as a whole. As a result, the structures of Philippine democracy worked against the emergence of a *military* institution or trajectory beyond the control of elected officials. By the same token, local politicians' discretionary powers over Police and Constabulary forces allowed them to use the coercive apparatuses of the state to staff their private election campaigns and criminal rackets, drawing the institutions of law-enforcement and security in the Philippines well beyond the pale of *civil* society or *civilian* politics as commonly conceived.

Independence and continuing US influence

This subordination of the coercive apparatuses of the Philippine state to elected officials survived the Pacific War and Independence, in a broader context of continuity with post-colonial relations of power in Philippine politics and society, especially when considered in comparative regional perspective. The United States Armed Forces in the Far East (USAFFE), which served to bridge pre-war forces and war-time mobilisation in the Philippines, also provided a launching pad for the new Armed Forces of the Philippines after Liberation.[19] Officially declared 'an umbrella military command' for US and Philippine Army units in July of 1941, the USAFFE emerged through the hurried mass promotion of regular and reserve officers, the mass induction of reserve forces into the USAFFE, and the last-minute attempt at crash-course training in military camps on the eve of Pearl Harbor.[20] Against this backdrop, after the American surrender to Japanese forces in Bataan in April 1942, US-Philippine resistance to Japanese occupation of the archipelago persisted in a highly decentralised form, with guerrilla groups proliferating locally and, to various degree and extent, (re)establishing ties with the SWPA (Southwest Pacific Area Command), especially toward the end of the Japanese occupation.[21]

Whilst resistance against the Japanese occupation was arguably more widespread in the Philippines than elsewhere in Southeast Asia,[22] it also reflected peculiar and enduring patterns of local factional struggles associated with the pattern of electoral politics institutionalised in the American period. With the notable exception of the anti-landlord Huk guerrillas in Central Luzon,[23] the Japanese occupation of the Philippines neither fundamentally displaced 'the paradigm of parochial factional struggles with local rivals'[24] nor effectively encouraged the process of '(nation-) state-building through war-making' observed elsewhere in the region during this period.[25] Instead, with tremendous USAFFE discretion over appointments to municipal and provincial government posts under General MacArthur's liberation regime, the mechanism of official USAFFE guerrilla recognition – promising so-called 'back pay' and pensions denominated in US dollars – helped to jump-start the political careers of many successful veteran claimants (e.g., Ramon Magsaysay and Ferdinand E. Marcos) in the early post-war elections. As official guerrilla status and veteran networks translated into electoral machines and campaigns in the fledgling Philippine Republic, so-called 'new men' and old pre-war politicos alike channelled their considerable energies into local factional politics rather than nationalist movements as seen elsewhere in Southeast Asia.[26]

Consistent with the pattern of conservative electoral rather than radical nationalist mobilisation that linked pre-war Commonwealth to post-war Philippine politics, the USAFFE emerged according to a process of neo-colonial linkage rather than anti-colonial struggle. American rule in the Philippines since the turn of the century, after all, had proved more insulated from the nationalist mobilisation which confronted Dutch, British and French colonial regimes elsewhere in Southeast Asia. With independence (and a small conscript army of regulars with a large reserve force) provided for in the 1935 Commonwealth constitution, and with USAFFE guerrilla veterans filling dozens of seats in the 1946 Congress, the Philippines presented a stark constrast to the war-time emergence of nationalist armies mobilised against colonial troops in other parts of the region. After the landing of liberation forces in Leyte of October 1944, the Philippine Army was officially reconstituted as a section of the USAFFE Headquarters but soon regained its separate status and was awarded organisational autonomy from the US Army within a week of the independent Republic's inauguration – but, importantly, only after the first post-war elections – in 1946.

Beyond USAFFE's significance in the post-war scramble for official guerrilla recognition, backpay and other benefits from the United States Veterans Administration (USVA), the largest such American operation overseas, the terms of Independence also guaranteed a decisive role for the US in shaping the nature and direction of military organisation and para-military mobilisation in the post-colonial Philippines. Through the Military Bases Agreement and the Military Assistance Agreement of 1947, the United States assumed *de facto* responsibility for defending the Philippines against external aggression. There was little domestic impetus for a military build-up of Army, Navy or Air forces after Independence. Instead, internal security remained the primary concern of the coercive apparatuses of the Philippine state in the Republic, as reflected in the formal separation of the Philippine Constabulary (PC) from the Armed Forces of the Philippines (AFP) in 1947 and in the transfer of some 12,000 troops from the AFP to the PC the following year. Reconstituted from the war-time Military Police Command and placed under the Department of Interior, the Constabulary received some additional 8,000 troop transfers in 1948 'to enable that organisation to carry out the restoration of peace and order more effectively'.[27] As the lion's share of Constabulary troops as well as the Joint United States Military Advisory Group (JUSMAG) took internal security as their primary focus,[28] local politics and anti-communist containment were to dominate the nature and direction of police and military forces in the Philippines after Independence as demonstrated during election and counter-insurgency campaigns in subsequent years.

Indeed, against this backdrop, the late 1940s and early 1950s witnessed the launching of the first anti-communist counter-insurgency campaign under US Cold War supervision in the Philippines. As noted in the previous chapter, the electoral franchise had been expanded to universal adult suffrage with Independence, and in this context local and national government measures aimed at the simultaneous demobilisation and (re)incorporation of guerrilla organisations in the aftermath of the Japanese Occupation (1942–1945) and its disruptions to many 'pre-war vertical ties' between landed oligarchy and peasantry.[29] For example, government repression followed the 1946 Congressional election of six Democratic Alliance candidates closely identified with peasant groups and Huk guerrilla networks in the rice-bowl and high-tenancy region of Central Luzon and enjoying the support of the *Partido Komunista ng Pilipinas* (PKP) and the Civil Liberties Union:

> Government authorities, for example, directed police, constabulary soldiers, and civilian guards – who were on the payrolls of landlords and the government – to raid offices of the Democratic Alliance and the PKP, break up political rallies, and beat up peasant leaders and spokesmen.[30]

Yet the unseating of the six Democratic Alliance congressmen, and the subsequent banning of the Huks and the *Pambansang Kaisahan ng mga Magbubukid* (PKM), the National Peasant Union they had organised after the war, did little to undermine the guerrilla movement in Central Luzon during the late 1940s. Instead, abuses by government troops and acts of violence during the elections helped to enhance Huk/PKP organisational strength and revolutionary resolve during this period.[31]

In the aftermath of the Communist victory in China in 1949, the Philippines had assumed increasing geo-strategic and enduring symbolic significance as host to US military installations and as America's 'showcase of democracy', and the pattern of mounting peasant mobilisation in Central Luzon greatly alarmed the Truman Administration in Washington, DC By 1950, a counter-insurgency campaign was launched by the newly appointed Secretary of National Defense, Ramon Magsaysay, with generous American military assistance and cooperation coursed through the Manila-based JUSMAG and its 'special mission' headed by then Lt. Col. Edward G. Lansdale, an intelligence specialist borrowed from the US Air Force. In a Cold War version of the 'Injun Warfare' of several decades earlier, this anti-Huk 'psywar' campaign involved the mobilisation of volunteers into 'hunter-killer' units called the Scout Rangers'.[32] Whilst irregular outfits like the 'Nenita Squad' engaged in such alleged 'savage war' tactics as the vampire-like bloodletting of victims, the regular troops, reorganised into lighter, more mobile and less conventional 'battalion combat teams' by the early 1950s, also recruited among 'all the law-enforcement capability in the area, including municipal police and especially the so-called civil guard, usually a rag-tag group of armed civilians'.[33] Against this onslaught of US-backed 'counter-insurgency' violence, the Huk forces were largely demolished and demobilised by the early–mid 1950s. When Huk remnants reemerged in Central Luzon in the late 1960s, they likewise met with para-military repression at the hands of former Huks and criminals recruited by the PC into the infamous 'Monkees' – 'so-called to distinguish them from Huk liquidation squads commonly known, because of their long hair, as "Beatles"'.[34] With their lumpen formation and their spectacular violence, these para-military groups prefigured the anti-communist vigilantes who were to emerge in the 1980s.[35]

The Marcos era

By the time of Ferdinand Marcos' first presidential inauguration in January 1966, the challenges to 'law and order' arising from fairly rapid socio-economic change already anticipated – and, in some quarters, justified – organisational innovation and role expansion in the coercive apparatuses of the Philippine state. After all, the country's highly decentralised system of local policing and the lack of a nationally coordinated law-enforcement structure appeared out of step with continued economic growth, industrialisation, and urbanisation, most notably in the National Capital Region of Metro Manila, in the 1960s.[36] In response to the increasing conspicuousness and notoriety of organised crime and political violence during this period, Marcos sponsored two major institutional innovations. First, a National Police Commission (Napolcom) was established in 1966, tasked with overall supervision of law-enforcement in the country.[37] Secondly, the Philippine Constabulary Metropolitan Command (Metrocom) was established in 1967 as a 'centralised command with jurisdiction over all riot control and internal security operations'[38] and as the 'launching pad' for the subsequent integration of police forces under Napolcom.[39] In February 1968, an Executive Order further expanded Metrocom into the Metropolitan Area Command.[40]

Beyond questions of criminality, new threats to law and order extended into the realm of 'internal security' during the late 1960s, as noted in Chapter 2 above. In this regard, the resurgence of the Huks in Central Luzon,[41] the founding of the (new) Communist Party of the Philippines (CPP) and its New People's Army (NPA), and the declaration of the Muslim Independence Movement[42] all signified different extra-parliamentary challenges to the existing parameters of political integration and stability. Student demonstrations similarly added to the tide of non-traditional forms of political mobilisation and 'unleashed a torrent of mass protest actions' with the so-called 'First Quarter Storm' of rallies and marches in early 1970. Indeed, this period witnessed an overall escalation of student demonstrations and urban bombings which served as convenient cover for Marcos' increasing imposition of authoritarian controls. Marcos suspended the writ of *habeas corpus* after the grenade attack of the Liberal Party senatorial rally held at Plaza Miranda, Manila, in August 1971, and, on the eve of the alleged assassination attempt upon Defense Secretary Enrile a year later, declared martial law in late September 1972.

Against the backdrop of the rising challenges to 'law and order' in the country, Marcos was especially well positioned to consolidate presidential control over the AFP, thanks to his own professed personal history and his long-standing political involvement in military affairs. Before the 'fake medals' exposé of the mid-1980s, Marcos had enjoyed a reputation as the 'most decorated Filipino soldier' in the Pacific War, thanks to his legendary guerrilla exploits with the 21st Division of the USAFFE and the Maharlika unit in Northern Luzon. More importantly, perhaps, Marcos was named Civil Affairs Officer of the US Army's 14th Infantry Division and subsequently Judge Advocate General of the 2nd Infantry Division of the Philippine Army in the months leading up to formal Independence in July 1946. Moreover, upon his appointment as Manuel Roxas'

Presidential Assistant on Veterans Affairs later that year, Marcos played a role in the organisation and accreditation of guerrilla groups, including the formation of the umbrella federation, the Philippine Veterans Legion (PVL), and the lobbying of the US Congress on veterans' benefits. Thanks to this skilful manipulation of guerrilla war exploits and post-war political networking, upon his first election to the Philippine Congress in 1949, Marcos gained a seat on the House Committee on National Defense (then chaired by Magsaysay) and continued to cultivate close and lasting ties with military officers throughout his career in the House of Representatives (1949–59) and the Senate (1959–65).[43]

Whilst Marcos had developed particularly strong links with the military establishment during his long years in Congress, a set of broader domestic and international trends also contributed to the shifting of greater powers from the legislature to the executive branch in the 1960s.[44] Marcos' election to the presidency in 1965 coincided with the escalation of American military intervention in Vietnam which greatly enhanced the geo-strategic importance of US naval and air force facilities in the Philippines and spelled significant increases in US assistance to the Philippine national government. US foreign assistance supplemented Congressional budget appropriations, facilitating greater centralisation of patronage resources in the hands of the president,[45] and reducing the legislature's leverage over the executive branch. This trend was further strengthened by the Philippine government's increasing reliance on loans from international financial institutions and foreign banks during this period.[46] Meanwhile, the deepening of import-substitution industrialisation and the rising opportunities for buy-outs of US firms divesting corporate assets in anticipation of the 1974 expiration of the Laurel-Langley agreement (which guaranteed *de facto* parity rights to American citizens and corporations in the Philippine economy) increased the reliance of the national oligarchy on the state bank loans and regulatory breaks controlled by the president and his minions.

Thanks to this favourable combination of circumstances, Marcos was able to manipulate military appointments and assert control over the AFP to a far greater degree than any of his predecessors. In 1965, for example, before assuming the presidency, then senator Marcos masterminded a congressional exposé on smuggling which precipitated a dramatic shakeup in the military hierarchy.[47] Within weeks of his arrival in Malacañang in early 1966, Marcos undertook a major reshuffle of the military hierarchy. This reshuffle included 'the forced retirement of fourteen of the military's twenty-five flag officers, including the Chief and the Vice Chief of Staff, the Army Commanding General, the Chief of Constabulary, and all four Constabulary zone commanders. In addition, over one-third of all Constabulary provincial commanders were relieved'.[48] During the first thirteen months of his presidency, moreover, Marcos retained the defence portfolio for himself, thus allowing frequent and direct contacts with the top military brass.[49]

Another key example of Marcos' muscling of presidential prerogative over military assignments was the concentration of tremendous power in the hands of his province-mate, cousin, and personal chauffeur, Fabian C. Ver. Ver had advanced from mere Captain in 1965 to Brigadier General by 1970 despite a rather unimpressive service record,[50] and by the early 1970s he was awarded responsibility for intelligence and presidential security. Under Ver's leadership, a new and enlarged security apparatus, the National Intelligence Security Agency (NISA), emerged. Initially tasked merely with coordinating intelligence gathering and dissemination between the different services of the AFP (a function the Intelligence Service of the AFP (ISAFP) – also headed by Ver – later inherited), NISA was soon placed directly under the Office of the President and, by some accounts, became the most powerful arm of the government. NISA evolved into 'the center of power in the AFP and the repository of all matters regarding "national security".... The AFP, then, appeared as just its operating arm – a frontal violation of the organisation's traditional and regimental set-up'.[51] Thus while Marcos awarded prominent military positions to an older generation of Magsaysay-era 'Amboys' (e.g., José Crisol) and younger 'military professionals' (e.g., Alejandro Melchor, Jr) who enjoyed close links and backing among circles in JUSMAG and in Washington DC, through General Ver he also maintained 'an informal, clandestine, command structure within the armed forces to execute special operations'.[52]

In the Cabinet reshuffle following the student protests of January 1970, Marcos also made two key appointments which also helped to enhance his position against potential military and civilian opposition to the strengthening of presidential powers. First, Marcos named as his executive secretary Alejandro Melchor, Jr, the then undersecretary of defence, an academy-trained navy lieutenant commander, and a man seemingly always eager to promote a greater 'developmental' role for the military-as-institution. This appointment publicly aligned the presidential office with so-called 'technocrat professionals' and their 'apolitical expertise', advertised his close ties to the US government, and endorsed the notion of the 'military as manager' of national development.[53] Second, Marcos consolidated in the hands of Juan Ponce Enrile the two Cabinet posts of justice and defence. By this manoeuvre, Marcos resorted to a practice not attempted since the days of Justice and Defense Secretary Oscar Castelo under Quirino, which seemed designed to '[en]sure that a suspension of the writ of habeas corpus would be supported with legal expertise'.[54] Significantly, Enrile was the very first secretary of defence who had no history of 'guerrilla' activity under the USAFFE and subsequent AFP links of his own. Instead, he remained, at the time, entirely Marcos' man. Operating through a fully acquiescent Enrile, Marcos engineered his 'next major revamp' in January 1972, following the August 1971 suspension of the writ of *habeas corpus* and the November 1971 electoral defeat for the Nacionalista Party.[55]

Martial law appeared a distinct possibility – in political as well as logistical terms. After all, in view of the mounting 'threats from below' posed by radical students, workers, and peasants mobilised in collective action and the declining 'absorptive capacity' of existing mechanisms for political participation and representation, a return to 'law and order' seemed justifiable not merely to Marcos but also to the business community, the US government, and many in the Philippine military establishment. In particular, Marcos' careful cultivation of the military as an institution, and of the commanding officers personally loyal to him, set the stage for senior AFP officers' acquiescence after they were briefed at the infamous 'Rolex Twelve' meeting more than a week before the actual declaration of martial law. In this context, a critical collaborative role in drawing up *de facto* operational plans was also played by lower-ranking officers who commanded the crucial First PC Zone, the Metrocom, and the Rizal PC, who were also accompanied by Defense Secretary Enrile and General Ver, head of the Presidential Security Guard.

The antinomies of constitutional authoritarianism

Yet, as noted by observers, the declaration of martial law did not signal the installation of the military as government but, rather, the enhanced role of the military as institution through the expansion of its powers and resources.[56] The suspension of Congress increased the autonomy of military officers *vis-à-vis* local *politicos*, although to only a limited extent (see below). More generally, rather than militarising the Philippine government *per se*, martial law changed the dynamics and understandings on which 'civil-military relations' were based. An anecdote from the early martial law period illustrates this shifting pattern:

> 'My business is urgent', he said. 'I have to see Enrile at once'. The aide-de-camp protested and said that he had to wait for his turn. The man's face flushed, and he said in a loud voice, 'Don't you know who I am? I am Congressman So-and-So'. 'I'm sorry, sir', the aide-de-camp replied, politely but firmly. 'But we have no more congressmen today. Everybody is equal. We now live in a new society'.[57]

In addition, the creation in 1975 of the Integrated National Police (INP) – 'with the Philippine Constabulary as the nucleus and the local police forces, [and] fire departments and jails as components' – provided the basis for an expansion of the PC/AFP's administrative and operational control down to the municipal level, thus further limiting the opportunities for civilian government officials (i.e. governors and mayors) to sway the loyalties – and shape career paths – of the very men tasked with policing their local bailiwicks.[58] Beyond the revival of para-military groups such as the Barrio Self-Defense Units in Marcos' second term (1970–72), the so-called Civilian Home Defense Forces (CHDF) were founded and placed under PC command by 1976. Thanks to the creation of the INP and the CHDF and their subjugation to PC/AFP control, military officers found themselves well-positioned to dominate various criminal rackets previously run largely by local politicians.[59] In formal terms, the top AFP brass also gained new economic powers, most notably through high-ranking officers' supervisory roles in 'a few strategic private enterprises and public utilities', and the empowerment of military tribunals.[60]

Figures on military troops, budgets and assistance amply attested to the expansion of the PC/AFP under martial law. During the first three years of martial law the military nearly doubled in size,[61] and doubled again over the course of the following decade.[62] Increases in US military assistance funded the dramatic growth in the AFP budget which paid for this pattern of rapid expansion of troop levels in the Philippines. The Philippines' military budget more than tripled in the first five years of martial law, and by 1981, it had doubled again, now totalling $863 million per annum.[63] Calculated on a per capita basis, military expenditures in the Philippines were higher than all other ASEAN states during this period.[64] This military spending boom was fuelled by US military assistance, which more than doubled in the first four years of martial law.[65] Between 1973 and 1984, US military assistance to the Philippines added up to some US $519 million.

Despite this expansion of military spending and personnel, the Marcos regime preserved civilian authority over the military, and the AFP remained weakly insulated from political controls and pressures. Provincial governors with close ties to Marcos enjoyed some influence in the selection of provincial PC commanders,[66] and the twelve Regional Unified Commands (RUCs) introduced under martial law were headed by top officers who typically enjoyed warm relations with the regional chairmen of Marcos' one-party machine *Kilusang Bagong Lipunan* (KBL), like close Marcos cronies Eduardo 'Danding' Cojuangco in Central Luzon (Region III), Roberto Benedicto in the Western Visayas (Region VI), and Antonio Floirendo in Southeastern Mindanao (Region XI). In Manila, moreover, the top AFP brass was selected according to the personal preferences of the president, as exemplified by the promotion of palace pets (and Marcos cousins) General Fabian C. Ver as AFP Chief of Staff and Lt. General Fidel V. Ramos as Chief of the Philippine Constabulary. President Marcos frequently violated the formal chain of command, bypassing Defense Minister Juan Ponce Enrile on a regular basis and allowing favoured 'overstaying' generals to remain on active duty even after they had reached mandatory retirement age. Under Ver, moreover, the Presidential Security Unit (PSU) evolved into a Presidential Security Battalion (PSB) of some 2,000 troops, and later was transformed into an even larger independent command – the Presidential Security Command (PSC).[67] Ver's position as chief of the PSC allowed him to command forces from all four services, plus Metro Manila police forces, and to enjoy authority equivalent to that of the AFP deputy chief of staff,[68] and even after his promotion to AFP Chief of Staff in 1981, Ver essentially retained control over the PSC. As one observer noted: 'When he became the AFP Chief of Staff… Ver relinquished formal command of the PSC to BGen Santiago Barangan. In reality, however, Ver and his sons exercised *de facto* control over PSC. Col Irwin Ver was the PSC's Chief of Staff and Lt Col Rexor Ver was [the] Commander'.[69] Over the course of its dramatic personnel growth and role expansion in the martial law era, the AFP evolved into Marcos's 'praetorian guard' rather than a professional military institution.

The RAM in the 1980s: the myth of 'militarisation'?

Against this backdrop of continuing – if somewhat more centralised – civilian 'political' control over the AFP, the launching of a series of military coup attempts in the 1980s is often traced back to the tendencies of junior officers, especially PMA graduates, to develop close horizontal bonds and a sense of shared purpose under the rubric of 'military professionalism' and 'reform'. The relative small size of classes at the Philippine Military Academy (PMA) and the isolation of cadets quartered in PMA barracks over the course of four years of training worked to promote strong horizontal solidarities among Academy graduates,[70] which were maintained through reunions, networking, and regular communication between former classmates.[71] Indeed, it was a close group of PMA '71 graduates who formed the 'RAM' (Reform the Armed Forces of the Philippines Movement) in the early 1980s. Even more than other PMA 'batches' from the late 1960s and early 1970s, the Class of '71 displayed a marked proclivity for political activism, no doubt due in large part to the formative experiences of 'social ferment in society', open debate at the Academy, and the unprecedented defection to the NPA of PMA '67 graduate and instructor Victor Corpus.[72]

Besides their shared experiences at the Academy, other circumstances also tended to promote a sense of common goals and grievances among PMA graduates from '71 and other years. In the 1970s and 1980s, for example, many recent PMA graduates fought in Mindanao against the Moro National Liberation Front (MNLF) or the New People's Army (NPA), in some cases under conditions of direct combat and counter-insurgency operations. Whilst the troops on field assignments typically lacked in morale as well as equipment, these young officers noted, the generals in Manila were living in considerable comfort and, increasingly, luxury, under the patronage of Marcos and favoured top brass like Fabian Ver.[73] In addition to these combat experiences, it has been argued, some of these young officers developed a certain kind of political consciousness and sense of self-importance through their participation in the interrogation and torture of political prisoners over the same period.[74] While working on the front lines of the Marcos regime's war against its various internal enemies, these officers grew increasingly aware – and resentful – of the growing number of overstaying generals who were clogging up the path to promotion, leaving lower-ranking officers nothing to look forward to but meagre pensions.[75]

By the early-mid 1980s, various members of the PMA Class of '71 cohort had reached the ranks of major and colonel and assumed direct operational control over important commands. Colonel Victor Batac, for example, served as PC Provincial Commander in Albay, and Colonel Jake Malajacan was the Commanding Officer of the 16th Infantry Battalion in Laguna. In short, these middle-ranking 'Young Turks' began to emerge as a group with the greatest proclivity and capacity for some kind of armed mobilisation against the regime. By comparison, those senior AFP officers who commanded significant numbers of troops were hardly inclined to make a move against Marcos because '[t]hey were either too high to be nonpartisan (owing their positions to the powers that be), too comfortable to be interested, or too wealthy to care'.[76]

It was officers from the PMA Class of '71 and other Academy graduates who formed the Reform the Armed Forces Movement (RAM) in the early 1980s, a group which met informally to discuss military reforms and other issues. By May 1985, RAM members had begun to articulate the group's views in the national media, and, secretly, to make plans for the launching of a coup.[77] After 1983, RAM benefited from *de facto* protection of the US government, whose continued support for the Marcos regime in the wake of the Aquino assassination was contingent on the 'professionalisation of the military' as part of a broader strategy for economic and political reform in the Philippines. Whilst RAM's overtures in the summer of 1985 failed to secure US backing for the launching of a coup, American intelligence officials did little to discourage RAM coup-plotting and refrained from revealing RAM's plans to Marcos or Ver at the time. By the time of the 1986 snap presidential election, RAM, while publicly campaigning for 'free elections' and forging ties with prominent businessmen and opposition politicians, was quietly plotting a coup, no doubt in anticipation of Marcos' planned post-election Cabinet reshuffle and internal military purge.[78]

These trends towards the mounting of a *coup d'état* against Marcos reflected not only the gradual coming of age – in terms of solidarities, consciousness, and collective action – of disgruntled young officers in the AFP but also increasing contestation among civilians over the succession to Marcos. RAM, after all, was first formed and assiduously cultivated with the patronage and protection of Defense Minister Juan Ponce Enrile, a prime contender for the presidency in the last years of the Marcos regime. RAM's leader was none other than Col. Gregorio Honasan, Enrile's senior aide-de-camp since 1975, and fellow Class of '71 alumni like Lt. Col. Eduardo E. Kapunan and Col. Oscar B. Legaspi were likewise recruited into the Ministry of National Defense (MND) security unit.[79] In the course of his long tenure as Defense Minister, Enrile had accumulated enormous personal wealth and built up a diversified business empire,[80] and he quietly financed the purchase of sophisticated, expensive high-powered weapons and the hiring of retired British Special Air Service (SAS) instructors to train Honasan, Kapunan, and their men.[81] Yet Enrile's influence had been on the wane for several years, and, as noted above, Marcos frequently bypassed his Defense Minister in favour of direct communications with his trusted AFP Chief of Staff General Ver. In the post-1983 context of rising uncertainty and instability in Manila, Enrile's patronage of RAM promised not only to enhance his reputation among US officials but also to bolster his arsenal for a showdown with Ver in the event of Marcos's sudden death or departure from power. In late February 1986, Enrile and RAM made final preparations for a long-planned coup, whose premature discovery forced them to seize the military headquarters on the Epifanio de los Santos (EDSA) boulevard, thus precipitating the 'People Power' revolt that toppled Marcos and brought Corazon Aquino into office.

It was a clash of (civilian) presidential ambitions, moreover, that lay behind the 'season of coups' against Aquino which followed within but a few months of Marcos' downfall.[82] The first of such attempted *kudeta,* whilst probably the most bizarre, was particularly instructive: the occupation of the Manila Hotel (promptly proclaimed the temporary 'seat of government') by Marcos loyalist politicians and mutinous AFP troops in July 1986.[83] Before the end of the same year, the unravelling of an another putschist plot labelled 'God Save the Queen' once again linked disgruntled 'rebel' officers, this time drawn from RAM, to civilian political ambitions, namely those of RAM patron Enrile, who remained as Aquino's Minister of Defense until his forced resignation in November 1986.[84] Subsequent coup attempts and plots included the occupation of a national television station in Quezon City (the January 1987 'GMA Incident') and the Philippine Army headquarters in Fort Bonifacio (the April 1987 'Black Saturday Incident'), the planned seizure of the country's main international airport (the July 1987 'MIA Takeover Plot') the coordinated moves on the presidential palace, military camps, regional commands, and broadcast networks (in the August 1987 Coup) and, after a lull, the most serious threat to oust the Aquino government by *golpe* in December 1989.[85]

Although these various coup attempts displayed a bewildering diversity of tactics and targets they followed a common pattern. Significantly, all of these various coup attempts were closely linked to political ambitions for *civilian* rule without Aquino, whether through the return of Marcos, the revival of the *Batasang Pambansa* (National Assembly), or the formation of a junta effectively headed by Enrile. Moreover, key *civilian* figures were intimately involved in the planning and execution of the coup attempts and plots listed above. As for internal military backing, the much publicised claims by various media-star 'RAMboys' that they represented the military as an institution did not enjoy widespread support among the junior officer corps as a whole – or for that matter higher up in the chain of command – as seen in the pattern of limited support in the ranks for various failed RAM putsches.

In fact, none of the various coup attempts launched by RAM succeeded in toppling the Aquino government or in creating widespread support for RAM within the AFP. The coup attempts attracted very little in the way of popular support in Manila, and the US government continued to back Aquino against various RAM challenges, most notably during the rebel air strafing of Malcañang Palace on 1 December 1989 when several US Air Force Phantom Jets conducted 'persuasion flights' in the skies above Metro Manila.[86] More embarrassing, perhaps, for RAM's coup-makers were the well-publicised successes of poorly armed police forces, most famously those under the command of General Alfredo Lim, Commander of the Western Police District in Manila, in single-handedly countering and containing the heavy firepower of the military rebels. Within the AFP, moreover, Aquino's position was strengthened *vis-à-vis* RAM by the replacement of Enrile with (Ret.) General Rafael Ileto as Defense Minister in late 1986, and by the emergence of General Fidel V. Ramos as a powerbroker in his own right, first as AFP Chief of Staff, later as Ileto's successor as Defense Secretary, and, in 1992, as Aquino's (anointed) elected – civilian – successor. With the encouragement of Aquino, Ileto, and Ramos, younger officers who openly disagreed with the goals and methods advocated by RAM moved up in the ranks and were promoted to strategically important military commands, with the AFP effectively purged of the putschist 'RAMboys' by the beginning of the 1990s.

The vigilantes in the 1980s

Meanwhile, the late 1980s also saw a wave of anti-communist 'vigilante' mobilisation echoing the earlier counter-insurgency campaign of the late 1940s and early 1950s. Like the Magsaysay-led campaign against the Huks several decades earlier, this effort was strongly supported by the US government and relied heavily on para-military forces rather than large combat operations. Yet the vigilante mobilisation of the late 1980s was distinctive in the unprecedented extent of public spectacle and popular participation entailed.

After a near decade and a half of *de facto* martial law, the Communist Party of the Philippines (CPP) had emerged as the largest revolutionary movement in Asia by the mid-1980s. The CPP-led New People's Army (NPA) claimed strongholds in many provinces, especially in sugar, coconut, and logging areas,[87] and its above-ground affiliates achieved notable success in organising among squatter communities, student leagues and labour unions in the cities. This 'threat from below' was far more serious than the Huks in the late 1940s and 1950s, and required a much more comprehensive response. As the fall of Ferdinand E. Marcos ushered in the restoration of formally democratic procedures and institutions after February 1986, it thus also anticipated the intensified counter-insurgency campaign introduced under Corazon C. Aquino's embattled transitional regime (1986–1992). This campaign in the Philippines also emerged during a period when the Reagan rollback and 'Low-Intensity Conflict' doctrines signalled both renewed commitment and strategic innovation behind US-supported 'contra'-revolutionary warfare.[88]

Perhaps the most remarkable aspect of the counter-insurgency campaign in the Philippines in the late 1980s was the spectacular role played by so-called anti-communist 'vigilantes'.[89] Officially designated as 'civilian volunteer organisations', these vigilante groups also included paramilitary units reportedly recruited from among ill-trained, bolo-equipped young toughs and sometimes even ex-convicts. Overall, the sociological profile of recruits was decidedly lumpen: sometimes led by notorious criminals, including 'police characters with criminal records', vigilante groups were typically composed of youths and, in the words of residents of one vigilante-controlled provincial barrio, 'predominantly illiterate local bullies'.[90]

These vigilantes organised armed neighbourhood patrols and checkpoints, anti-communist radio broadcasts and mass rallies in campaigns of sustained intimidation and spectacular violence, as exemplified in the citation which serves as an epigraph at the beginning of this chapter. As a result, some of the most egregious human rights abuses reported from the counter-insurgency campaign of the late 1980s were linked to vigilante groups.[91] Whilst government officials in Manila typically portrayed such abuses as unfortunate aberrations to otherwise highly institutionalised and professionalised military counter-insurgency operations, this vigilante phenomenon in fact not only emerged against the backdrop of civilian government support as well as military 'holistic' strategy,[92] but also, official disclaimers to the contrary, served to underpin and to propel in significant ways the overall momentum of the counter-insurgency campaign. In all sorts of ways, it is clear that the considerable – instrumental as well as symbolic – powers realised in this form of decentralised and irregular violence decisively shaped the process and outcome of the regime transition in the Philippines of the late 1980s.

As noted above, paramilitary mobilisation and counter-insurgency campaigns trace a long lineage in Philippine history, but the (re)emergence of vigilantes signalled an especially sinister turn in the aftermath of the collapsed ceasefire negotiations between the Aquino government and the insurgent forces (i.e., the CPP/NPA and the so-called National Democratic Front) in early 1987. Indeed, the rise of vigilantism largely coincided with the official return to armed struggle of government and insurgent forces in February 1987. In many parts of the country, moreover, the May 1987 Congressional elections lent additional impetus to the surge of such violence as evidenced by the attacks upon supporters of the new legal left party, the *Partido ng Bayan* (PnB), and its Alliance for New Politics (ANP).[93] Against the backdrop of the 1987 Constitution which stipulated that the notoriously abusive martial-law era paramilitary Civilian Home Defense Forces (CHDF) 'shall be dissolved *or, where appropriate, converted*', vigilante groups also seemed to proliferate locally as the proposed official CHDF successor, the Citizen Armed Force Geographical Unit (CAFGU), met with public criticism in the national media and, eventually, Philippine Congress.[94] By late 1987, more than two hundred different vigilante groups had been identified as operating in the Philippines,[95] and by early 1989, the United States State Department estimated the number of 'Citizens Voluntary Organisations' at 640.[96]

This wave of vigilantism first crashed upon the southern shores of Mindanao with the mobilisation of the notorious *Alsa Masa* ('Masses Arise') in the southern frontier town and 'communist stronghold' of Davao City in 1986, but it eventually reached not only the Visayas and parts of Luzon, but even Metro Manila itself.[97] In particular, vigilantes appeared to emerge in rural, and to a lesser extent urban poor, areas identified as potential NPA/CPP strongholds such as Davao, Negros Occidental and Samar. Actual sites of vigilante violence ranged from street abductions and 'safehouse' tortures to bolo attacks against peasants working in the fields and so-called 'strafing' with automatic weapons fire of entire families in their homes.

Whilst lauded by civilian and military government officials alike for their overall 'effectiveness' in the counter-insurgency effort, vigilantes were implicated by national as well as international human rights organisations in 'a widespread pattern of extra-judicial execution, torture and illegal arrest throughout the Philippines'.[98] The Senate Committee on Justice and Human Rights also reported that vigilantes regularly performed 'police and military activities such as armed patrols, manning of checkpoints, and search and seizure operations'.[99] During this period, vigilantes engaged in a broad range of violent and coercive activities, ranging from routinised threats of force on behalf of the state to the spectacular deployment of violence well beyond the pale of law. Extra-judicial killings and violence by vigilantes were endemic.[100] As one human rights report noted:

[V]ictims ranged from suspected NPA supporters and their families to persons who opposed the formation of vigilante groups in their area. Frequently harassed and attacked were members of social activist groups labeled as NPA sympathisers, including labor and peasant organisers, human rights monitors and church workers.[101]

As often noted in such reports, the practice of so-called 'red-labelling' was widespread at the time and integral to the phenomenon of vigilantism, rendering the 'identification' of victims as 'suspected NPA supporters' something of a foregone conclusion. Under the Negros Occidental PC provincial command of Lt. Col. Miguel Coronel, for example, local chapters of labour, religious, and human rights organisations such as the Negros Federation of Sugar Workers (NFSW), the Basic Christian Communities (BCC), and the Task Force Detainees (TFD) were openly and indiscriminately targeted as 'leading communist fronts'.[102] At the national level, the Aquino government likewise publicly declared an escalation of measures against many above-ground left groups in a heightened drive 'toward the dislodging of these legal fronts'.[103] Besides targetting – actual or alleged – communist guerrillas and sympathisers, vigilantes also directed their violence against 'surrogate victims' of unarmed civilians and family relatives, typically in retaliation for frustrated combat or search efforts.[104]

The vigilante phenomenon of the late 1980s emerged from the continuing revolutionary mobilisation by the New People's Army and National Democratic Front under CPP auspices, and precisely as the staying power of an abusive military and the swift 'return of the oligarchs'[105] in the early post-Marcos period threatened to compromise the very efforts by the Aquino government to promote reinvigorated counter-insurgency campaigns and revived electoral competition. The vigilantes, it must be acknowledged, did show important continuities with Marcos-era paramilitary groups, such as the revived Barrio Self-Defense Units (BSDU) and, eventually, the Civilian Home Defense Forces (CHDF). The notorious CHDF, after all, had included 'members of irregular quasi-military political, religious or criminal groups' since its inception under PC command in 1976.[106] After a papal visit to the Philippines led to the official lifting of martial law in the Philippines in 1981, such groups continued to proliferate and so-called 'cults, fundamentalist sects and fanatic groups' were reportedly 'armed and trained by the military for counter-insurgency purposes [and] involved in massacres, murders, mutilations, cannibalism and torture'.[107] However, it was only with the restoration of formally democratic institutions and procedures under Aquino in the late 1980s that vigilantism emerged as a distinct phenomenon with its own peculiar discourse of 'spontaneous voluntarism'.

As the government declared 'Total War' in February 1987,[108] vigilantism was openly and enthusiastically endorsed by local military commanders and national top brass alike.[109] Upon his posting to Davao City as PC Metrodiscom (Metropolitan District Command) commander in mid-July 1986, for example, Lt. Col. Franco Calida voiced his wholehearted support for the mobilisation of anti-communist vigilantes in this southeastern Mindanao bastion of CPP/NPA strength, most notably the notorious *Alsa Masa*.[110] Calida, the avowed 'God/Father of *Alsa Masa*', also backed the practice of recruiting children as young as eight years of age to serve as lookouts *(pasabilis)* against NPA guerrilla units.[111] In the spring of 1987, moreover, no less than AFP Chief of Staff General Fidel Ramos himself identified the *Alsa Masa* as deserving 'full support and encouragement in dismantling communism' – in Davao and elsewhere.[112] Echoing this sentiment, PC Chief Maj. Gen. Ramon Montano promised vigilante supporters at a *Fuerza Masa* ('Power of the Masses') rally in Leyte province that 'you all deserve the support and protection of your government and the military'.[113] In addition to such public statements, direct military contact and assistance provided 'necessary, if not sufficient' conditions for the emergence of anti-communist vigilantes in various parts of the country. According to Calida, for example, vigilante mobilisation depended on the prior activation of local military detachments to provide the necessary protective cover: '*[K]ung walang* detachment, *hindi mag-aalsa ang mga yan. Kailangan ng proteksyon eh*'.[114] Overall, informal support from civilian and military officials contributed to a widespread pattern of *de facto* authorisation and mobilisation of vigilantism in the Philippines during this period.

To a considerable extent, vigilante mobilisation was driven by the process of regime transition in the Philippines after Marcos, which entailed both the restoration of democratic institutions and procedures and, as noted above, the intensification of counter-insurgency operations in the Philippines. Compared to its martial law predecessor (1972–86), the transitional regime under Aquino (1986–92) encouraged greater revitalisation of *both civil and uncivil society* through the mobilisation of – often overlapping and mutually reinforcing – election and counter-insurgency campaigns. In short, the rise of the peculiar 'voluntarism' and spectacular violence associated with vigilantism coincided with what one author has referred to as the restoration of the pre-Marcos *ancien regime*.[115]

Indeed, the most dramatic manifestations of vigilantism seem to have surfaced when and where the process of regime transition ran up against the martial law legacies of civilian government contraction and armed revolutionary movement expansion. As noted above, the martial law regime was never 'properly' militarised, but it had nonetheless undermined the foundations of local civilian governance in various ways, through the abolition of Congress and the centralisation of power in the presidency initiated in 1972 and the pattern of 'crony capitalism' and 'patrimonial plunder' seen in subsequent years. In this regard, the 'patrimonial' concentration and eventual contraction of the Philippine economy in the early 1980s undermined the willingness – and, in places, the ability – of local officials to govern, as seen in the virtual immobilisation and evacuation of many municipal government offices by the 1980s, especially in so-called NPA 'strongholds'. By the mid-1980s, the NPA had dramatically increased in size and influence, with an estimated 25,000 regulars, in about 20 per cent of the country's barrios, whilst the Armed Forces of the Philippines showed commensurate signs of increasing decay and disrepair. Demoralised by the clogging of military promotions, as well as the concentration of government troops and resources near the presidential palace at considerable cost to those posted elsewhere, countless local AFP commanders reached 'live-and-let-live' arrangements with NPA guerrilla platoons during the last years of the Marcos era.

In this context of eroding government authority and increasing CPP/NPA activism in the provinces, the revival of elected civilian government in 1986–92 encountered distinct challenges in areas with a marked NPA presence. Presidential appointments of (pro-Aquino) municipal and provincial Officers-in-Charge (OIC) paved the way for the national agro-industrial oligarchy and assorted local political bosses to prepare for the 1987 congressional and 1988 local elections; the first set of truly competitive polls since the senatorial and local elections of 1971 before martial law. Areas where the NPA and its supporting networks remained weak saw minimal local manifestations of vigilantism, and the regime transition was achieved largely through elections without counter-insurgency activities. In NPA 'strongholds', by contrast, the transitional Aquino regime and its designated OICs met the challenge of mobilising individual voters *and* demobilising social revolution by encouraging the rise of the vigilantes.[116] In such areas, the support of local military detachments typically constituted a 'necessary, not sufficient' condition for the rise of vigilante groups. That is, the reassertion of a strong military presence and the redeployment of government troops in the previously abandoned hinterlands saw a renewed flow of national resources trickling down and a revived pattern of local groups linking up in many parts of the country. However, the patronage of local politicians and businessmen, plantation families and/or mining companies often helped to shape the nature and direction of individual groups mobilised as vigilantes during the regime transition.

In short, the rise and spread of vigilantism in the late 1980s was part and parcel of the process of regime transition from Marcos to Aquino and from authoritarian rule to restored oligarchical democracy in the Philippines. Of course, the Philippines has a long history of election-related political violence and of predatory para- or pseudo-military formations, but, as suggested above, the rise of the vigilantes after the fall of Marcos was neither spurious coincidence, nor spontaneous contagion. In contrast to Marcos' 'constitutional authoritarianism', the transitional regime under Aquino represented itself as a participatory one and committed itself to the mobilisational processes associated with electoral politics. Whilst this renewed emphasis upon political participation echoed the much-celebrated 'People Power' uprising in Manila of February 1986, it also ran up against the mounting mobilisation of a decidedly more radical, mass-based, and widespread anti-Marcos opposition, led by the CPP and its New People's Army. The laudatory references to vigilantism as 'people power' by Aquino and other high-ranking government officials assumed special significance, inviting comparisons which could not but underscore the very opposite of the celebrated affinity between people power and vigilantism. Sparked by an aborted coup and confined largely to Metro Manila, the February 1986 People Power revolt that ushered in the national transition from authoritarian rule emerged as a peculiarly non-violent, urban upper/middle-class event without organised Left, peasant or urban poor groups present. Vigilantism, by contrast, accompanied more protracted and provincial processes of regime transition through the mobilisation of spectacular violence and lumpen elements in communities where the CPP/NPA and its mass base loomed conspicuously large. The notion of vigilantism as 'People Power' beyond the defining moment and narrow experience of February 1986 thus highlighted the extent to which participatory calls 'from above' inspired mobilisation 'from below' in the name of both civil *and* uncivil society.

Beyond the pattern of vigilantism under conditions of tenuous government – territorial as well as ideological – consolidation in areas of CPP/NPA strength around the archipelago,[117] the nature and direction of mobilisational campaigns in the Philippines of the late 1980s also revealed a peculiar and yet familiar dialectic of sorts. Mobilisation 'in the name of civil society' focused considerable energies on 'free and fair' elections and democratic political representation, most famously and successfully in the form of NAMFREL, the National Citizens' Movement for Free Elections.[118] Mobilisation in the name of uncivil society however, released powerful forces for counter-insurgency and immanent violence. Against the inviolate sanctity of the ballot and the submission to national citizenship, the utter profanation of human life and the sovereignty of fanatic violence were amply suggested in the Alsa Masa checkpoint slogan: *Kill for Democracy!*

The consolidation of the regime transition ushered in with People Power in the late 1980s mobilised volunteers under the telling banner of *Bantay Bayan* (Watchful/Vigilant Nation/People). Insofar as this invocation extended to anti-communist vigilantes by early 1987, it served to transgress and thus to confirm the very boundaries watched over by NAMFREL, with its much publicised calls for a *Bantay (ng) Bayan* campaign still resounding from the snap presidential election of February 1986, revived for the congressional elections of May 1987 and again for the local elections of January 1988. In combination, this mobilisational dynamic of civil *and* uncivil society helped to clinch the subsequent institutionalisation of multi-party elections, the concomitant (re)entrenchment of oligarchic dominance, and the effective marginalisation of organised Left politics in the post-Marcos Philippines.

Conclusion

Whilst existing scholarship on 'civil-military relations' in the Philippines has focused largely on martial law and its consequences for the subsequent transitional period of coup attempts and democratic (re)consolidation under Aquino, this chapter has highlighted the importance of a broader historical context for understanding the distinctive trajectory of military intervention and para-military mobilisation in the early post-Marcos era. To that end, the discussion of the martial law period focused particular attention on patterns of change and continuity with regard to the organisation of violence within the Philippine state and its implications for the early post-Marcos period. However, the pages above underscored that not even the martial law regime was 'properly' militarised in the Philippines and Marcos himself in many ways remained an exceptionally civilian authoritarian ruler, especially when viewed in comparative regional perspective. The various coup attempts launched by the so-called 'RAMboys', moreover, represented less a real threat of seizure of power by the military as an institution, than a high degree of contestation between rival civilian politicians – Aquino, Enrile, and Marcos – over military personnel, policies, and power.

This revisionist reassessment of civil-military relations in the Philippines helps to illuminate the pattern of rapid 'demilitarisation' in the early 1990s. After the high drama of the late 1980s, the presidency of (Ret. Gen.) Fidel V. Ramos (1992–98) provided something of a dénouement, with the restoration of regular competitive elections reestablishing a clearer pattern of civilian authority over military institutions. Besides the former AFP Chief of Staff and Defense Minister himself, the Ramos administration featured dozens of (former) military officers in a broad array of civilian positions, including some key positions. (Ret.) General José Almonte, for example, served as Ramos' National Security Advisor and, more generally, as a major power broker in the regime, and even renegade RAM officers ran for public office with some notable successes, such as Senator Gregorio 'Gringo' Honasan. Yet rather than signalling a new militarist trend in Philippine politics, the prominence of military men in national politics peaked with Ramos, who refrained from extending to his own Defense Secretary (Ret.) Gen. Renato de Villa, the much-coveted presidential endorsement – and associated government resources – which, under Aquino, had helped Ramos win office in the 1992 elections.[119] Instead, the new president, Joseph 'Erap' Estrada chose a Defense Secretary – former senator Orlando Mercado – who had no military background or interest but instead civilian credentials as an anti-Marcos activist and environmentally concerned legislator. On election night 1998, Mercado told journalists that he hoped to deploy troops not in armed combat in the jungle but in the planting of new trees on deforested land.

Indeed, in the aftermath of the Cold War and the demise of the CPP/NPA, the 1990s saw the effective reassertion of civilian elected officials' authority over the military as well as the reorientation of the military to an essentially new role. With the abolition of the Philippine Constabulary and the creation of the Philippine National Police (PNP) under the Department of the Interior and Local Government, police personnel as well as policing functions were removed from the AFP's military chain of command.[120] Thus the AFP itself has now been relegated to a relatively limited role, battling residual pockets of the Maoist and Muslim insurgencies in the remote hinterlands and detaining Chinese fishermen in the remote disputed area of the Spratly Islands in the South China Sea. The provisions of the 1990 Police Act and the 1991 Local Government Code, moreover, reestablished municipal mayors' and provincial governors' discretionary powers over local police appointments, even as the restoration of the national legislature saw the resurrection of the Commission on Appointments and other congressional committees as mechanisms for the exercise of formal and informal political influence over military and police forces alike. Finally, with the end of the Cold War and the Philippine Senate's vote to block the renewal of the Military Bases Agreement in 1991, the US military presence in the archipelago has been substantially diminished if not entirely eliminated, and the AFP has been left with far greater responsibility for external defence than ever before in Philippine history.

Thus, contrary to the hopes of the 'RAMboys' and their supporters in the mid-late 1980s, the Philippines of the late 1990s has seen the supremacy of elected civilian politicians matched by the subordination of a properly military Armed Forces of the Philippines. Whilst former putchists officers, retired military generals and disbanded paramilitaries have resurfaced in second careers in electoral politics, civil administration and, reportedly, criminal racketeering, their prominence seems to have peaked and then subsided in tandem with the rise and fall of the Ramos administration. Today, neither the military as an institution, nor politicised agents within the state coercive apparatus can be found within striking distance of the ruling circles of power in the Philippines. Even the notorious PNP chief Panfilo Lacson (a PMA '71 graduate) and Secretary of the Interior and Local Government Alfredo Lim (a retired Police General) serve at the discretion of President Joseph Estrada and entertain further political ambitions which are decidedly civilian in nature.

Yet the fading prominence of military men in national politics in the late 1990s obscures the crucial role that military intervention and paramilitary mobilisation played in shaping – and restricting – the process and outcome of democratisation in the early post-Marcos Philippines of the mid–late 1980s. This chapter has highlighted the vigilante mobilisation of the late 1980s and located it within the longer history of sub-contracted state violence in the Philippines and the recurring pattern of critical conjunctures of intensified extra-electoral de-mobilisation identified in the previous chapter. In short, the decentralisation and privatisation of coercive state apparatuses encouraged under American auspices remained an enduring and powerful legacy of Philippine colonial democracy even several decades after Independence in 1946. Such legacies served to blur the lines between state/society, civil/military, military/para-military, and legal/illegal, with a variety of peculiar coercive formations – notably so-called 'lost commands', 'private armies' and 'fanatical sects' – operating at the behest of entrenched local 'warlords' and landed oligarchs in the country. In addition, these familiar patterns for managing law enforcement and Philippine elections tended to prefigure a recurring cycle of intensified sub-contracting and political violence during periods of declared 'national emergency', as seen in the late 1940s–early 1950s and, again, in the mid- to late-1980s.

Finally, this chapter has underscored the simultaneous affirmation and disavowal of vigilantism manifested in Philippine and US government support for 'low intensity conflict' with its characteristic 'geographical, epistemological and military-strategic decenteredness'.[121] In the shadow of the structured instrumentalities of vigilantism, there also lurked a grotesque violence haunting common sense and stalking lived experience with the circulation of phantasmagoric rumours and severed heads. Whilst obscuring the future and thus unravelling the present during the regime transition of the late 1980s, such morbid symptoms manifested a terrifying violence, erupting in the final years of the Cold War, that underpinned and propelled the (re)making of state and civil society in the post-Marcos Philippines.

Notes

1 Lawyers Committee for Human Rights, *Vigilantes in the Philippines: A Threat to Democratic Rule* (New York: Lawyers Committee for Human Rights, 1988), pp. 45–46. See also Amnesty International, *Philippines: Unlawful Killings by Military and Paramilitary Forces* (London: Amnesty International, March 1988), pp. 32–33.

2 President Aquino's commencement speech at the PMA, March 23, 1987, cited in Walden Bello, *Creating the Third Force: US-Sponsored Low Intensity Conflict in the Philippines* (San Francisco: Institute for Food and Development Policy, 1987), p. 74.

3 See *Business Day*, April 2, 1987.

4 Joel Rocamora, 'The Philippines under Cory Aquino', in Barry Gills, Joel Rocamora, and Richard Wilson (eds), *Low Intensity Democracy: Political Power in the New World Order* (London: Pluto Press, 1993), p. 201.

5 See Alfred W. McCoy, 'The Restoration of Planter Power in La Carlota City', in Benedict J. Tria Kerkvliet and Resil B. Mojares (eds), *From Marcos to Aquino: Local Perspectives on Political Transition in the Philippines* (Quezon City: Ateneo de Manila University Press, 1991), pp. 126–132.

6 Quotation from President Aquino's commencement speech at the Philippine Military Academy (PMA), March 23, 1987, cited in Walden Bello, *Creating the Third Force: US-Sponsored Low-Intensity Conflict in the Philippines* (San Francisco: Institute for Food and Development Policy, 1987). See also: Hilario Davide *et al.*, *The Final Report of the Fact-Finding Commission (pursuant to R.A. No. 6832)* (Makati: Bookmark, 1990).

7 Francisco Nemenzo, 'A Season of Coups (Reflections on the Military in Politics)', *Kasarinlan* Volume 2, Number 4 (2nd Quarter 1987), pp. 5–14.

8 Justus M. van der Kroef, 'The Philippines: Day of the Vigilantes', *Asian Survey*, Volume 28, Number 6 (June 1988), pp. 630–649.

9 On the problems of such mediation, see especially Michael Taussig, 'Culture of Terror – Space of Death: Roger Casement's Putumayo Report and the Explanation of Torture', in Nicholas B. Dirks (ed.), *Colonialism and Culture* (Ann Arbor: University of Michigan Press, 1992), pp. 135–173.

10 Ruby R. Paredes (ed.), *Philippine Colonial Democracy* (Quezon City: Ateneo de Manila University Press, 1989).

11 Stephen Skowronek, *Building A New American State: The Expansion of National Administrative Capacities, 1877–1920* (Cambridge: Cambridge University Press, 1982).

12 Stuart Creighton Miller, *Benevolent Assimilation: The American Conquest of the Philippines, 1899–1903* (New Haven: Yale University Press, 1982), pp. 196–218.

13 See further Skowronek, *Building A New American State*.

14 On this point, see: Emmanuel A. Baja, *Philippine Police System and Its Problems* (Manila: Pobre's Press, 1933); and Willem Wolters, 'Rise and Fall of Provincial Elites in the Philippines: Nueva Ecija from the 1880s to the Present Day', *Sojourn*, Volume 4, Number 1 (February 1989), pp. 54–74.

15 Cicero C. Campos, 'The Role of the Police in the Philippines: A Case Study from the Third World' (Ph.D. dissertation, Michigan State University, 1983).

16 Alfred W. McCoy, 'Quezon's Commonwealth: The Emergence of Philippine Authoritarianism', in Paredes (ed.), *Philippine Colonial Democracy*, pp. 114–160; Ricardo Trota José, *The Philippine Army 1935–1942* (Quezon City: Ateneo de Manila University Press, 1992).

17　Benedict Anderson, 'Cacique Democracy in the Philippines: Origins and Dreams', *New Left Review* 169 (May/June 1988), pp. 3–31; John T. Sidel, 'Coercion, Capital and the Post-Colonial State: Bossism in the Postwar Philippines' (Ph.D. dissertation, Cornell University, 1995).

18　Sidel, 'Coercion, Capital, and the Post-Colonial State', p. 62.

19　Eva-Lotta E. Hedman, 'Elections in the Early Philippine Republic: Showcase of Democracy in Post-War Southeast Asia', Paper presented at the Annual Meeting of the Association for Asian Studies, Chicago, March 1997.

20　José, *The Philippine Army*, pp. 201–210.

21　Proculo L. Mojica, *Terry's Hunters (The True Story of the Hunters ROTC Guerrillas)* (Manila: Benipayo Press, 1985); Charles A. Willoughby, *The Guerrilla Resistance Movement in the Philippines: 1941–1945* (New York: Vantage Press, 1972).

22　David Wurfel, *Filipino Politics: Development and Decay* (Ithaca: Cornell University Press, 1988), p. 12.

23　Ronald K. Edgerton, 'The Politics of Reconstruction in the Philippines: 1945–48' (Ph.D. dissertation, University of Michigan, 1975); Benedict J. Kerkvliet, *The Huk Rebellion: A Study of Peasant Revolt in the Philippines* (Berkeley: University of California Press, 1977).

24　Alfred W. McCoy, 'Politics By Other Means', in Alfred W. McCoy (ed.), *Southeast Asia Under Japanese Occupation* (New Haven: Yale University Southeast Asia Studies, 1985), p. 158.

25　Charles Tilly, 'War Making and State Making as Organised Crime', in Peter B. Evans, Dietrich Rueschemeyer, and Theda Skocpol (eds), *Bringing the State Back In* (Cambridge: Cambridge University Press, 1985); Charles Tilly, *Coercion, Capital, and European States, AD 990–1992* (Oxford: Blackwell, 1992).

26　Edgerton, 'The Politics of Reconstruction'.

27　A.V.H. Hartendorp, *History of Industry and Trade of the Philippines* (Manila: American Chamber of Commerce of the Philippines, 1958), p. 349.

28　Stephen R. Shalom, *The United States and the Philippines: A Study of Neo-Colonialism* (Quezon City: New Day Publishers, 1986), pp. 74–82.

29　Edgerton, 'The Politics of Reconstruction', p. 19.

30　Kerkvliet, *The Huk Rebellion*, p. 262.

31　*Ibid*.

32　Douglas S. Blaufarb, *The Counter-insurgency Era: US Doctrine and Performance 1950 to the Present* (New York: The Free Press, 1977), p. 28.

33　*Ibid*.

34　Otto D. van den Muijzenberg, 'Political Mobilisation and Violence in Central Luzon (Philippines)', *Modern Asian Studies,* Volume 7, Number 4 (1973), p. 702.

35　See further Rosanne Rutten, '"Mass Surrenders" in Negros Occidental: Ideology, Force and Accommodation in a Counter-insurgency Program', Unpublished Paper presented at the 4th International Philippine Studies Conference, Australian National University, Canberra, July 1992.

36　The USAID sponsored 'Public Safety Program' excerpted from a classified report titled 'Survey of Philippine Law Enforcement' outlines the following recommendations: 'the upgrading, consolidation, and centralisation of the activities of the various law enforcement agencies of the Philippine government'. Cited in Shalom, *The United States and the Philippines*, p. 113.

37　Campos, 'The Role of the Police in the Philippines'.

38　*Ibid*., p. 214.

39　Executive Order No. 120, February 16, 1968 expanded the Metrcom. Reportedly, after the joint survey referred to above, USAID police assistance to the Philippines increased from '$62,000 in 1962... to $618,000 in 1968 [and] $608,000 in 1969', cited in Bonifacio Gillego, 'Our Police Forces as a Tool of American Imperialism', *Ronin* 1:7 (October 1972), p. 12.

40　Rod B. Gutang, *Pulisya: The Inside Story of the Demilitarisation of Law Enforcement in the Philippines* (Quezon City: Daraga Press, 1991), p. 88.

41　Eduardo Lachica, *Huk: Philippine Agrarian Society in Revolt* (Manila: Solidaridad Publishing House, 1971), pp. 13–19.

42　T.J.S. George, *Revolt in Mindanao: The Rise of Islam in the Philippine Politics* (Kuala Lumpur: Oxford University Press, 1980), pp. 131–142.

43 Donald Lane Berlin, 'Prelude to Martial Law: An Examination of Pre-1972 Philippine Civil-Military Relations' (Ph.D. dissertation, University of South Carolina, 1982), p. 181.

44 Arthur Alan Shantz, 'Political Parties: The Changing Foundations of Philippine Democracy' (Ph.D. dissertation, University of Michigan, 1972); Amando Doronila, *The State, Economic Transformation, and Political Change in the Philippines* (Singapore: Oxford University Press, 1985).

45 Doronila, *The State*, p. 115.

46 Robert E. Baldwin, *Foreign Trade Regimes and Economic Development in the Philippines* (New York: Columbia University, 1975), pp. 65–75.

47 John T. Sidel, 'Walking in the Shadow of the Big Man: Justiniano Montano and Failed Dynasty Building in Cavite, 1935–1972', in Alfred W. McCoy (ed.), *An Anarchy of Families: State and Family in the Philippines* (Madison: University of Wisconsin Center for Southeast Asian Studies, 1993), p. 141.

48 Berlin, 'Prelude to Martial Law', p. 187.

49 *Ibid.*, pp. 186–187.

50 Wurfel, *Filipino Politics*, p. 149.

51 Benjamin D. Tesoro, *The Rise and Fall of the Marcos Mafia* (Manila: JB Tesoro Publishing, 1986), p. 97.

52 McCoy, 1993, p. 16.

53 Reportedly, Marcos had first appointed Melchor undersecretary of defense on the basis of the latter's proposal for military role expansion into management, engineering, transportation, and communication. In a curious echo of Samuel Huntington's thesis, Melchor argued that because '[m]ilitary men are trained as managers' they possess expert knowledge as well as social responsibility. Melchor, 'Project Compass', cited in Conrado De Quiros, *Dead Aim: How Marcos Ambushed Philippine Democracy* (Pasig City: Foundation for Worldwide People Power, 1997), p. 367. See also 'The Ascendancy of the Military', *The Philippines Free Press*, 25 April, 1970, pp. 5 and 62.

54 Benigno Aquino, Jr in Nick Joaquin, *The Aquinos of Tarlac*, cited in De Quiros, *Dead Aim*, p. 81. Of course, Enrile was reappointed as secretary of defence after failing to capture a senatorial seat in the November 1971 elections.

55 Berlin, 'Prelude to Martial Law', p. 196. Berlin notes the following change of command: 'the retirement of eighteen Philippine flag officers and the appointment of new commanders of all the military services, Constabulary zones, Army divisions, and separate brigades, as well as a new AFP Chief and Vice Chief of Staff'.

56 Carolina G. Hernandez, 'The Extent of Civilian Control of the Military in the Philippines, 1946–77' (Ph.D. dissertation, State University of New York at Buffalo, 1979).

57 De Quiros, *Dead Aim*, p. 317.

58 Campos, 'The Role of the Police in the Philippines', pp. 218–220.

59 Tesoro, *The Rise and Fall of the Marcos Mafia*; Sidel, 'Coercion, Capital, and the Post-Colonial State'.

60 Hernandez, 'The Extent of Civilian Control', p. 21.

61 Miranda and Ciron put the 1972 manpower figure at 62,715 and that of 1976 at 142,490 See: Felipe Miranda and Ruben F. Ciron, 'The Philippines: Defence Expenditures, Threat Perceptions and the Role of the United States', in Chin Kin Wah (ed.), *Defence Spending in Southeast Asia* (Singapore: Institute of Southeast Asian Studies, 1987), p. 169). Davide *et al.* identify slightly lower figures – 57,100 troops in 1971 and 113,000 in 1976 – amounting to a near doubling (97.89%) of the AFP. [Davide *et al.*, *The Final Report*].

62 Hernandez puts the approximate number of troops as 250,000 in 1984. See: Carolina G. Hernandez, 'The Role of the Military in Contemporary Philippine Society', *The Diliman Review*, January–February 1984, p. 22. An even higher figure – 300,000 – is cited in *Business Day*, 11 March 1983.

63 Hernandez estimates the overall military budget for 1972 at US$136 million, and that of 1977 at US$420 million. *Ibid*. For the 1981 figures, see William Berry, 'The Changing Role of the Philippine Military During Martial Law and Implications for the Future', in Olsen and Jurika (eds), *The Armed Forces in Contemporary Asian Societies* (Boulder, CO: Westview Press, 1986), p. 220.

64   Felipe Miranda, 'The Military', in R.J. May and Francisco Nemenzo (eds), *The Philippines After Marcos* (London: Croom Helm, 1985), p. 95.

65   Walden Bello and Severina Rivera argue that this increase excluded both US weapons sales and unauthorised aid. See Walden Bello and Severina Rivera (eds), *The Logistics of Repression and Other Essays: The Role of US Assistance in Consolidating the Martial Law Regime in the Philippines* (New York: Friends of the Filipino People, 1977), pp. 7–33.

66   G. Carter Bentley, 'Mohamad Ali Dimaporo: A Modern Maranao Datu', and Michael Cullinane, 'Patron as Client: Warlord Politics and the Duranos of Danao', in Alfred W. McCoy (ed.), *An Anarchy of Families: State and Family in the Philippines* (Madison: University of Wisconsin Center for Southeast Asian Studies, 1993), pp. 243–284 and pp. 163–241 respectively.

67   Davide *et al.*, *The Final Report*, p. 52.

68   Wurfel, *Filipino Politics*, p. 149.

69   Tesoro, *The Rise and Fall of the Marcos Mafia*, pp. 94–95.

70   For example, the entire class of '76 refused to sign an official indictment of classmate Victor Corpus upon the latter's abandonment of his teaching assignment at the Academy and defection from the AFP to the New People's Army in December of 1970. Interview with author, Victor Corpus, August 24, 1990, Fort Bonifacio, Pasig, Metro Manila.

71   Alfred W. McCoy, '"Same Banana": Hazing and Honor at the Philippine Military Academy', *Journal of Asian Studies*, Volume 54, Number 3 (August 1995), pp. 689–726.

72   For more on the formative experiences of PMA Class of '71, see Alfred W. McCoy, *Closer Than Brothers: Manhood at the Philippine Military Academy* (New Haven: Yale University Press, 1999), pp. 193–204.

73   Marites Danguilan-Vitug, *Kudeta: The Challenge to Philippine Democracy* (Makati: Philippine Center for Investigative Journalism, 1990), p. 313. Whilst corruption was hardly a novelty, the low rate of rotation at the military top implied that the rewards of such activity were savoured by the same relatively small clique of senior officers over an extended period of time. For example, three 'Ver generals' Maj. Gen. Tomas Dumpit, Brig. Gen. Jaime C. Echevarria, and Maj. Gen. Josephus O. Ramas allegedly amassed a combined total of P13 million under Marcos' patronage. 'PCGG wants wealth of 3 generals forfeited', *Manila Chronicle*, August 2, 1987, p. 1.

74   Alfred W. McCoy, 'RAM Boys: Reformist Officers and the Romance of Violence', *Midweek*, 21 September 1987, pp. 29–33; and 'RAM Boys: The Ethos of Torture in the Theater of Terror', *Midweek*, 28 September 1987, pp. 30–34. See also McCoy, *Closer Than Brothers*, pp. 204–221.

75   Javate de Dios, 'Intervention and Militarism', in Aurora Javate-de Dios, Petronila Bn. Daroy, and Lorna Kalaw-Tirol (eds), *Dictatorship and Revolution: Roots of People's Power* (Metro Manila: Conspectus Foundation, 1988), p. 304.

76   Cecilio T. Arillo, *Breakaway: The Inside Story of the Four-Day Revolution in the Philippines* (Manila: CTA & A Associates, 1986), pp. 186–187.

77   The first such interview, 'Conversations with the Reformists', appeared in *Veritas,* May 12, 1985, p. 14. On the early days of RAM, see further Arillo, *Breakaway*; 'Open Letter to Gringo', *Philippine Star*, 7 September 1987, pp. 1 and 10; and Alfred McCoy's 'RAM Boys Series', published in the February 1990 issues of the *Philippine Daily Enquirer*.

78   On RAM's preparations for a coup, see McCoy, *Closer Than Brothers*, pp. 234–242.

79   Corpus, interview with the author, 1990.

80   Ricardo Manapat, *Some Are Smarter Than Others: The History of Marcos' Crony Capitalism* (New York: Aletheia Books, 1991), pp. 163–205.

81   Arillo, *Breakaway*, p. 137.

82   Francisco Nemenzo, 'A Season of Coups (Reflections on the Military in Politics' *Kasarinlan*, Volume 2, Number 4 (2nd Quarter 1987), pp. 5–14.

83   Davide *et al.*, *The Final Report*, pp. 135–146; McCoy, *Closer Than Brothers*, pp. 266–268.

84   Davide *et al.*, *The Final Report*, pp. 146–158; McCoy, *Closer Than Brothers*, pp. 268–273.

85   Davide *et al.*, *The Final Report*, pp. 221–469; McCoy, *Closer Than Brothers*, pp. 275–298.

86   Davide *et al.*, *The Final Report*, p. 495.

87 Benedict J. Kerkvliet, 'Patterns of Philippine Resistance and Rebellion, 1970–1986', *Pilipinas*, 6 (Spring 1986), pp. 35–49.

88 Walden Bello, *Creating the Third Force: US-Sponsored Low-Intensity Conflict in the Philippines* (San Francisco: Institute for Food and Policy Studies, 1987).

89 See, for example, Justus van der Kroef, 'The Philippines: Day of the Vigilantes', *Asian Survey*, Volume 28 (June 1988), pp. 630–649, and 'The Philippine Vigilantes: Devotion and Disarray', *Contemporary Southeast Asia*, Volume 10, Number 2 (September 1988), pp. 163–181; and Ronald J. May, *Vigilantes in the Philippines: From Fanatical Cults to Citizens' Organisations* (Honolulu: University of Hawaii Center for Philippine Studies, 1992). For further elaboration of the arguments presented below, see also: Eva-Lotta E. Hedman, 'State of Siege: Political Violence and Vigilante Mobilisation in the Philippines', in Bruce Campbell and Arthur Brenner (eds), *Death Squads in Global Perspective: Murder with Deniability* (New York: St Martin's Press, 2000), pp. 125-152.

90 Lawyers Committee for Human Rights, *Vigilantes in the Philippines: A Threat to Democratic Rule* (New York: Lawyers Committee for Human Rights, 1988), p. 50.

91 See, especially, Amnesty International, *Philippines: Unlawful Killings by Military and Paramilitary Forces* (New York: Amnesty International, March 1988); Lawyers Committee for Human Rights, *Vigilantes in the Philippines*; and Sentate Committee on Justice and Human Rights, *Report on Vigilante Groups* (Manila: Republic of the Philippines, 1988).

92 Victor N. Corpus, *Silent War* (Quezon City: VNC Enterprises, 1989), p. 181.

93 Eva-Lotta E. Hedman, 'Beyond Boycott: The Philippine Left and Electoral Politics After 1986', in Patricio N. Abinales (ed.), *The Revolution Falters: The Left in Philippine Politics After 1986* (Ithaca, NY: Cornell University Southeast Asia Program, 1996), pp. 87–89.

94 After the fall of Marcos, the Philippine Congress was only reopened in July of 1987. While initial 'seed money' had reportedly been made available in the amount of approximately 264 million pesos from the president's discretionary fund, a subsequent executive request for CAFGU budget allocations prompted critical senatorial scrutiny and public debate into the legality and funding of this paramilitary organisation. As noted by the Lawyers Committee on Human Rights, '[w]hile Congress approved funding for the CAFGU, the program itself has never been legislated'. Lawyers Committee for Human Rights, *Out of Control: Militia Abuses in the Philippines* (New York: Lawyers Committee for Human Rights, 1990), p. 71.

95 Lawyers Committee, *Vigilantes in the Philippines*, p.xi; Senate Committee, *Report on Vigilante*, p. 10.

96 US Department of State, 'Citizens Self-Defense Groups in the Philippines', 28 April 1989, p. 12.

97 May, *Vigilantes in the Philippines*, p. 29.

98 Lawyers Committee, *Out of Control*, p. 31. See further Lawyers Committee, *Vigilantes in the Philippines* and Amnesty International, *Unlawful Killings*.

99 Senate Committee, *Report on Vigilante*, p. 16.

100 David Kowaleski, 'Vigilante Counter-insurgency and Human Rights in the Philippines: A Statistical Analysis', *Human Rights Quarterly*, Volume 12, Number 2 (1990), p. 257. See further Enrique Delacruz, Aida Jordan and Jorge Emmanuel, *Death Squads in the Philippines* (San Francisco: Alliance for Philippine Concerns, 1987).

101 Lawyers Committee, *Out of Control*, p. 31.

102 Alfred W. McCoy, 'The Restoration of Planter Power in La Carlota City', in Benedict J. Kerkvliet and Resil B. Mojares (eds), *From Marcos to Aquino: Local Perspectives on Political Transition in the Philippines* (Quezon City: Ateneo de Manila University Press, 1991), p. 130.

103 *Manila Chronicle*, 10 November 1988.

104 Lawyers Committee, *Vigilantes in the Philippines*, p. xiv.

105 Institute for Popular Democracy, *Political Clans & Electoral Politics: A Preliminary Research* (Quezon City: Institute for Popular Democracy, 1987), p. 95.

106 Amnesty International, *Report of an Amnesty International Mission to the Republic of the Philippines* (London: Amnesty International, 1982), p. 27.

107 Patricia Startup, M.M. and Eileen Laird, M.M. (eds), *Truth Uncovered: Fact-Finding Mission Report – Cotabato – Zamboanga del Sur May 1985* (Quezon City: Claretian Publications, 1985), p. 15.

108 As noted by Gareth Porter, for example, the counter-insurgency strategy guiding 'Total War' had roots in the martial law period. With intense US lobbying and support, however, the PC/AFP experienced a strengthening of military presence and resources, notably the restructuring of AFP commands in the provinces into Regional Unified Commands (RUCs) and the reactivation of the National Capital Region District Command 'to conduct security operations' in Metro Manila. See Gareth Porter, *The Politics of Counter-insurgency in the Philippines: Military and Political Options* (Honolulu: University of Hawaii Center for Philippine Studies, 1987).

109 See further Bello, *Creating the Third Force*; Corpus, *Silent War*; and Porter, *The Politics of Counter-insurgency*.

110 See, for example, *New York Times*, 4 April 1987; *Manila Chronicle*, 16 March 1988; *Mindanao Daily Bulletin*, 17 July 1989.

111 Lawyers Committee, *Vigilantes in the Philippines*, p. 32.

112 *Asiaweek,* 12 April 1987.

113 *Manila Chronicle*, 6 September 1988.

114 Lt. Col. Franco Calida, cited in Carolyn O. Arguillas, 'The Davao Experiment', *Veritas*, 5–11 March 1987, Special Section, p. 18.

115 Benedict Anderson, 'Cacique Democracy in the Philippines: Origins and Dreams', *New Left Review* 169 (May–June 1988), p. 28.

116 For example, the NPA reportedly issued – for a fee – 'safe-conduct passes in guerrilla-controlled areas' during the 1988 elections. 'Rebs admit bets gave them money', *Malaya*, 15 January 1988, p. 1. Moreover, NPA rebels allegedly campaigned for the new Left party *Partido ng Bayan* in some areas. 'Samar is no longer old politicos turf', *Manila Chronicle*, 17 January 1988, p. 5.

117 See, for example, Jon Rosenbaum and Peter C. Sederberg, (eds), *Vigilante Politics* (Philadelphia: 1976).

118 Eva-Lotta E. Hedman, 'In the Name of Civil Society: Contesting Free Elections in the Post-Colonial Philippines' (Ph.D. dissertation, Cornell University, 1998).

119 James Putzel, 'Democratisation and Clan Politics: The 1992 Philippine Elections', *South East Asia Research*, Volume 3, Number 1 (March 1995), pp. 18–45.

120 Gutang, *Pulisya*.

121 Michael Taussig, *The Nervous System* (London: Routledge, 1992), p. 21.

4 'Forget it, Jake, it's Chinatown'

Introduction: the view from Eddie's log cabin

Eddie's Log Cabin, it is sometimes said, is the real centre of power in Cebu City. On most mornings, the city's 'good old boys' congregate in Eddie's, a modest coffee shop tucked away on a quiet street across from the old customs house (*aduana*) in the port area of this, the Philippine archipelago's hub of inter-island shipping, the country's second city and the Visayas' premier entrepôt. Retired policemen who brood and mutter into their coffee, big-time sugar planters and construction magnates like Horacio 'Dodong' Franco, glad-handing city councillors, and a loud, effusive fellow named Willy who speaks with a strong Hokkien accent and claims to be the city's 'Noodle King': such is the cast of characters assembled at Eddie's on an average morning in Cebu City. But most important and impressive of all is the quiet old gentleman in the wrinkled white shirt, who offers occasional comments in Cebuano, English, and Hokkien (or as he calls it, 'Amoy') amidst the flow of the mid-morning banter.

His name is José Gotianuy, and, his considerable modesty notwithstanding, he is said to own half of Cebu. His business card lists him as Chairman of the Cebu Central College, Benevola de Cebu, Visayan Surety & Insurance Corporation, Alicia Development Corporation, and Pacific Tourist Inn, and as Director of the Cebu Shipyard & Engineering Works, Mactan Electric Company, Chong Hua Hospital, Cebu Liong Tek Fraternity Association, and Cebu Memorial Foundation, Incorporated. The business card of Gotianuy's younger brother, Augusto Go, another regular at Eddie's, lists him as President of the University of Cebu, Chairman of Toyota Cebu City, Cebu Coliseum Complex, Cebu Technical School, AWG Development Corporation, Cebu Central Realty Corporation, and Member of the Board of Directors of Visayan Surety, Cebu Eastern College, Cebu State College, and the National Power Corporation (NAPOCOR).

Beyond Cebu City, moreover, the Go(tianuy) brothers count as members of their extended family two of the wealthiest and most prominent tycoons in the entire Philippines: big-time banker and real-estate mogul Andrew Gotianun and his cousin John Gokongwei, Jr, whose vast diversified conglomerate includes major holdings in agro-business, banking, food processing, media, mining, real estate, telecommunications, and textiles.[1] Gotianun and Gokongwei are often mentioned as examples of Chinese-Filipino business pre-eminence in the 1990s, and both were among the six so-called 'taipans' encouraged by then president Fidel Ramos in 1993 to form Asia's Emerging Dragon Corporation, a consortium created to handle major development projects in the Philippines.[2] The Go(tianuy) brothers recall that their father assisted Gotianun's father, Go Chiong Kang, in winning war damage claims for vessels sunk by US forces during Liberation and helped their young nephew John Gokongwei, Jr. to start up a used clothing business in Cebu City in the early post-war years.[3] It is hard to imagine that Gokongwei's uncles were not similarly instrumental in the series of moves that launched him first into corn and flour milling in the 1950s and 1960s, and then into national orbit with his move to Manila and massive business expansion and diversification drive in the 1970s and 1980s.

The Go(tianuy) brothers themselves, after all, are the grandsons of family patriarch and famous Cebu businessman Pedro Gotiaoco or Go Bon Tiao (1856–1921), a turn-of-the-century immigrant to Cebu from Amoy (today Xiamen), a major southern Chinese coastal port city in Fujian province. Gotiaoco and his brothers, the story goes, arrived penniless but scraped together enough money in due course to start up a small *sari-sari* or dry goods store in the harbour area, not far from where Eddie's Log Cabin stands today. They imported rice from Saigon, bought and sold abaca and copra from nearby Leyte, and eventually established Gotiaoco Hermanos, Inc. (a prominent abaca, rice, and copra-trading firm), the Insular Navigation Company (an inter-island shipping fleet), and the Visayan Surety and Insurance Corporation (an affiliate of a Shanghai-based marine insurance company) in the early years of the twentieth century.[4] In 1918, moreover, Gotiaoco's son Manuel Gotianuy, the father of José and Augusto, founded the Cebu Shipyard and Engineering Works, Inc., together with a group of other ethnic-Chinese businessmen.[5] Today, José Gotianuy sits on the company's board of directors along with executives from major Philippine shipping companies and representatives of controlling shareholder (since 1989) Keppel Philippines Shipyard, a Singapore-based corporation with interests in two other marine repair facilities in the archipelago.[6] Meanwhile, the Gaisano family of contemporary Cebu retail and real-estate fame also traces its roots back to Pedro Gotiaoco via Doña Modesta Singson Gaisano, his daughter by a second wife.[7]

More importantly, perhaps, the Gotianuys today count as their distant – and unofficial – cousins the current generation of Cebu's perennial political dynasty, the Osmeña family. Among Pedro Gotiaoco's 'illegitimate' offspring, it is often said, was Don Sergio Osmeña, Sr, Cebu's pre-eminent pre-war politician and the President of the Philippines in 1944–45. Don Sergio's son Serging subsequently dominated Cebu politics in the post-Independence, pre-martial law period (1946–72), and today his grandchildren include Senator Sergio Osmeña III, Congressman John 'Sonny' Osmeña, former provincial governor Emilio 'Lito' Osmeña, and former city mayor Tommy Osmeña.[8]

This story of José Gotianuy and his extended family casts new light on the political economy of the Philippines in two important ways. First, contrary to the considerable hype surrounding the rapid ascendance and current preeminence of new ethnic-Chinese *'taipans'* in the early post-Marcos era, the above account of Andrew Gotianun and John Gokongwei, Jr's origins suggests that 'Chinese capital' in the Philippines has longer lineages and deeper roots than many commentators have been willing to acknowledge. Indeed, Alfonso Yuchengco, another of today's top *'taipans'*, is the scion of a prominent Binondo (i.e. Manila Chinatown) clan, married into the famous Sycip family, who founded Sycip Gorres Velayo (SGV), Southeast Asia's most successful accounting firm, and counts the Dees of the China Banking Corporation among his in-laws.[9] Second and more fundamentally, moreover, the above thumbnail sketch of the Gotiaco clan's emergence in Cebu and its highly diverse and successful business activities over the years stands in stark contrast to the portrait of the Philippine economy as dominated by landed oligarchs, local political bosses, and presidential cronies. As this chapter suggests, a new and clearer picture of Philippine political economy emerges if instead we treat businessmen like Pedro Gotiaoco, his son Manuel Gotianuy, and his grandsons José Gotianuy and Augusto Go as the *ur-*capitalists of the Philippines.

Oligarchs and cronies revisited: history and 'The Chinese question'

Philippine political economy in the 1980s and 1990s has been understood largely in terms of the predations of a landed oligarchy and a set of politically-connected business cronies.[10] On the one hand, the long years of the Marcos dictatorship saw the emergence and entrenchment of what came to be known as 'crony capitalism'[11] in the archipelago, under which presidential friends and family members accumulated vast fortunes through behest loans from government financial institutions, monopoly concessions, franchises, and contracts offered by the state, and preferential treatment in terms of tariffs, tax holidays, and regulatory breaks. State-backed monopolies and monopsonies were established for the Philippines' two most valuable export crops, sugar and coconuts, and in fields as diverse as the automobile industry, banking, construction, forestry, pharmaceuticals, and telecommunications, Marcos' favourites enjoyed positions of tremendous privilege and profitability.[12] On the other hand, the transitional regime of Corazon C. Aquino (1986–1992), scion of the enormously wealthy Cojuangco clan and part-owner of the vast Hacienda Luisita (a sugar plantation in her home province of Tarlac), dashed hopes for serious land reform efforts in the early post-Marcos era[13] and underscored the staying power of the country's landed oligarchy. Against this backdrop, scholars in the late 1980s began to cite the emergence in the late Spanish colonial era of a class of large landowners and the entrenchment of this plantocracy throughout the twentieth century as key obstacles to sustained capitalist development and industrialisation on the one hand, and social justice and democratic governance on the other. As one noted political scientist concluded:

> The distinctive feature of the Philippines' response to the expanding demand of the world market was the creation of a substantial indigenous land-owning

class. Unlike the other states of Southeast Asia where agricultural export crops were grown on land owned by foreign companies, aristocrat-bureaucrats or small peasants, the commercial revolution in Philippine agriculture gave rise to a new class of commercially oriented landowners who were quite separate from the bureaucracy. It was from the ranks of this class that a new political élite emerged in the late nineteenth century and later, in the twentieth century, a commercial and industrial élite.[14]

Yet in recent years some scholars have also begun to document and delineate the significance of 'Chinese capital' in the Philippines, most notably Temario Rivera, a political scientist based at the University of the Philippines in Diliman, Quezon City. The Philippine bourgeoisie, Rivera's work suggests, has consisted of three class segments: landed capitalists, crony capitalists, and 'Chinese-Filipino' capitalists.[15] At first glance, this trichotomy seems problematic, distinguishing between sub-categories of capital first according to factors of production (land), then by reference to dyadic personal ties (cronies), and finally with regard to ethnic identity ('Chinese'). These sub-categories, moreover, are not only incommensurable but also overlapping: among the most famous of 'cronies' in the Marcos era, for example, were sugar plantation owners like Roberto Benedicto and Eduardo 'Danding' Cojuangco and Chinese-Filipino businessmen like Lucio Tan. Large landowners with recent Chinese ancestry have likewise been in evidence over the years. There are 'Chinese' landed capitalists, 'Chinese' cronies, and landed cronies as well. Finally, 'Chinese' is in itself a highly problematic category. Recent (1997) estimates suggest that the Philippines plays host to some 750–850,000 'ethnic Chinese' (less than 1.5 per cent of the nation's population of 64 million),[16] but many of these 'Chinese Filipinos' have Philippine citizenship, speak better Tagalog or Cebuano than Hokkien or Mandarin, and otherwise identify themselves more closely with the Philippines than with the mainland People's Republic of China, the neighbouring Republic of China (ROC) on Taiwan, or even a broader and looser 'Chinese' diasporic community. More than perhaps any other country in Southeast Asia, with the possible exception of Thailand, the Philippines has assimilated rather than segregated and stigmatised its 'Chinese' immigrant minority, and amongst the country's 'landed' and 'crony' capitalists, 'Chinese' ancestry is commonplace.

Yet these three sub-categories make sense and prove highly illuminating if we think of this trichotomy as representing three different kinds of relationships between state and capital in the context of the enduring structures of twentieth-century Philippine democracy outlined in other chapters of this volume. Viewed in comparative regional perspective, the distinctive feature of capitalist development in the Philippines is that it has proceeded under the auspices of a state which has been controlled by elected politicians (even in the authoritarian Marcos years) since the early years of the American colonial era. As elsewhere, state resources and regulatory powers have played a critical role in facilitating private capital accumulation, and in the Philippines regular, competitive elections have remained the key mechanism for gaining access to and exercising control over state power throughout the twentieth century. The combination of a highly decentralised, presidential, and otherwise American-style state with an impoverished and economically insecure electorate prefigured a system with notoriously weak and fluid political parties and in which clientelist, coercive, and monetary inducements have been critical for winning elections and access to state office and power.

Rivera's trichotomy offers three 'ideal type' of possible relationships between capital and state under Philippine democracy. First, land has provided not only a virtually independant economic base for private capital accumulation, but also a crucial social and political base, as ownership of large rural landholdings has been accompanied by control over tenant farmers, landless labourers, and other dependents who can be mobilised to deliver votes for large landowners and their favoured candidates for office on election day. Over the course of the twentieth century, this control over local blocs of voters has facilitated large landowners' easy access – and ascendancy – to elective office: to municipal mayorships, provincial governorships, and even seats in the national legislature, guaranteeing a privileged position from which to exercise influence over the appointment of government personnel, the dispensing of state patronage, and the nature and direction of public policy formulation and implementation. To this day, and to this end, the owners of large sugar plantations, coconut groves, fish ponds, and rice lands are amply represented in municipal halls and provincial capitols throughout the archipelago and in both houses of the Philippine Congress.[17]

Second, and by way of contrast, the label 'crony' has long been attached to those private capitalists who have accumulated wealth not from a secure and independent economic base but through their preferential access to state resources – loans, land, monopoly franchises, public works contracts – which elected officials can provide. Unlike the landed capitalist, the crony capitalist has offered not (only) a bloc of votes from a secure social and political base but (also) the personal loyalty which guarantees that those profits, market shares, and state resources which might otherwise be mastered by a politician's enemies and mustered against him will remain in friendly hands on election day. Not only Ferdinand Marcos but every town mayor, provincial governor, and congressman in the history of Philippine democracy has had a lazy nephew, golfing buddy, fraternity 'brod'. or townmate to whom a state bank loan, logging concession, illegal gambling franchise, customs brokerage, or construction project could be profitably awarded – but who, through good luck, exceptional business acumen, or proclivity for switching personal allegiances, might eventually survive the demise of his original patron. For every plantation owner-turned politician in the Philippines, there has been at least one machine politician who has made his fortune through such 'privatisation' of state resources, translating 'political capital' into proprietary wealth rather than vice versa.[18]

Third, and finally, those capitalists identified as 'Chinese' by contrast represent neither the direct exercise of political power by those owning large landholdings and commanding local electoral machines, nor the use of state offices for private accumulation of capital by politicians themselves and their cronies, but rather a relationship between state and capital, politician and businessman, mediated almost entirely by money. With vote-buying, machine mobilisation, and the manufacture of fraud so crucial in Philippine elections and Filipino politicians throughout the twentieth century thus so dependent on liquid cash flows, it could hardly be otherwise, and as in any other capitalist democracy, there have always been businessmen willing, ready, and able to pay – for protection from state regulation, and for preferential access to state resources. But these are businessmen who neither aspire to state office themselves nor hope to obtain special favours on the basis of personal loyalty, who neither translate their proprietary wealth into social and political capital nor vice versa. Their relationship to politicians and to the state is based on what James C. Scott has called 'market corruption'. and its sole currency has been money.[19] This is what makes them 'Chinese'.

This identification of 'Chinese' with money pure and simple dates back to the Spanish colonial era, and to the colonial state's policies towards immigrants from the southern coast of the Middle Kingdom who came to the Philippine archipelago in the late-sixteenth, seventeenth, eighteenth, and nineteenth centuries. Mostly small-time merchants from the coastal province of Fujian, attracted by the Spanish galleon trade in Manila and other opportunities for commerce in the archipelago, the early immigrants identified themselves as *sang-li* (Hokkien for 'trader(s)'), and though the Iberian colonisers came to call them *chinos*, the association with commerce persisted. Far more numerous than the Castilian friars, these *chinos* were seen as a threat to the colonial regime and its evangelising mission in the Philippines, and the 'Chinese' community suffered periodic massacres and deportations as well as sustained restrictions on their dress, place of residence, and mobility, as well as higher rates of taxation than the native *indios*.[20] The commitment of the colonial regime to Catholic evangelisation and the racist association of 'Chinese' with commerce in its raw cash form rested on a denial of chino *culture* which has remained a blind spot in the Philippines to this very day.

Indeed, even as scholars have documented the significant number of Hokkien cognates in everyday usage in Tagalog and other Philippine languages, including words for familial relationships and staple dishes of obvious 'Chinese' provenance, this heritage is still systematically ignored.[21] Today, for example, the quaint provincial town of Vigan on Luzon's northwest coast is touted as a promising tourist destination because of its brick-tile 'Antillan' houses, colonial-era horse-and-buggies (*kalesas*), and supposed 'Castillan allure'. even as the town's Hokkien name (meaning 'beautiful shore'), its historic links to the nearby southern coast of China and its collections of Sung and Ming ceramics tell a different tale.[22] As the iconoclastic anthropologist Arnold Molina Azurin has noted, even the *sang-li* ancestry of Vigan's leading families has been subtly obscured, as in the case of the prominent Manila real-estate clan and vaguely Spanish-sounding Syquía family, whose late nineteenth-century progenitor, was a successful *chino* merchant named Sy Quia who enjoyed a monopoly on the distribution and sale of opium in the Ilocos provinces.[23]

But in the Spanish era, unlike in nearby Dutch Java, for example, *chino* merchants like Sy Quia could transform their identity and that of their progeny under the auspices of the Iberian colonial state and the powerful Catholic hierarchy. By marrying an *india* (native woman) in a proper Catholic wedding, taking on a Spanish name perhaps, and having the children born of such 'mixed' parentage baptised by the local priest, *chinos* like Sy Quia became not just Syquías (or Crisologos or Florentinos) but also *mestizos*, an official Spanish category unique in the racialist lexicon of colonial Southeast Asia: one which promised greater mobility, unprecedented freedom of residence, and lower taxation rates than those imposed on *chinos*, as well as the right to own land, participate in native *gremios* (guilds), run for local offices of *cabeza de barangay* (barrio captain) and *gobernadorcillo* (town mayor) in the highly restricted electoral contests overseen by the Spanish authorities. In the course of the nineteenth century, moreover, as the Spaniards opened the Philippine archipelago to foreign trade and spurred the commercialisation of agriculture in the hinterlands of port cities like Cebu, Iloilo, and Manila, the *mestizo* offspring of *chino* merchants emerged as key middlemen, moneylenders, and in due course landowners.[24] Besides the British (and Swiss) trading houses, wealthy Spanish (Basque, and German) merchants like the Aboitizes, Elizaldes, and Zobel de Ayalas, and *chino* merchants like Gotiaoco and Sy Quia, small-time *mestizo* dynasties began to come into their own. By the 1890s, it was a set of wealthy, Spanish-educated, and highly cosmopolitan *mestizos* who had begun to think of themselves as *Filipinos* – a term previously reserved for Philippine-born Spaniards – and to struggle for an independent Philippine nation.[25] Thus scholars writing in the 1980s have focused on the emergence of a predominantly Chinese mestizo 'landed oligarchy' in the late Spanish era and its entrenchment throughout the twentieth century.[26]

Sugar, tobacco, and Marcos: commodity chains, capital accumulation, and democracy

Whilst self-evidently true (if somewhat teleological) in the era of Corazon Cojuangco Aquino, this by now familiar narrative runs the risk of exaggerating the Chinese *mestizo* landowning élite's importance and strength, obfuscating its true origins, and obscuring the historic processes and mechanisms by which it has accumulated and wielded its wealth and power. The image of the rural *hacienda* owner and the location of his wealth in agrarian landholdings, for example, has tended to overshadow the likelihood that his (great-)grandfather was not only a *chino* but a city-based merchant engaged in trade and moneylending – like Pedro Gotiaoco – before venturing into landownership in the hinterlands. The history of Philippine capitalism is not one in which the countryside comes to the city, but rather the colonisation by port cities of their hinterlands, with foreign capital (first European, later American, Japanese and Taiwanese) and a *chino* and *mestizo* domestic bourgeoisie as the conquering force.[27]

Revisionist historical scholarship, moreover, has highlighted the limitations of the Spanish-era landed élite's wealth, landholdings, and geographical distribution, and recast the timing of its emergence as a 'national oligarchy' well into the twentieth century. After all, US colonial government documents estimated that by 1898 only two million hectares, comprising a mere 7 per cent of the colony's total land mass, were privately owned, nearly 10 per cent of which was in the hands of the religious orders.[28] Even the Spanish-era sugar planters of Negros Occidental, who later comprised a major segment of the national oligarchy, claimed modest landholdings in comparison with their latifundist counterparts in Latin America. Revealingly, they called themselves *hacenderos*, a term used in reference to mine workers in Spain, rather than *hacendados*, the proper Spanish appellation for plantation owners.[29] In addition, newly published studies examining the contributions of forest, mineral, and marine resource exploitation – and public land – to the process of capital accumulation in the Philippines have cast considerable doubt on the centrality of private landownership to the generation of wealth in the richly endowed archipelago.[30]

Finally, evidence that the subsequent era of American rule was the crucial period for the acquisition of large landholdings reveals a pattern of private capital accumulation by this 'national oligarchy' in which the institutions of Philippine colonial democracy played a crucial role. It was in fact precisely during this period that wealthy plantation families engaged in significant expansion of their haciendas, bringing large landholdings in early sugar-growing provinces like Negros Occidental and Batangas and new frontier provinces like Tarlac in Luzon and Bukidnon in northern Mindanao to the unprecedented size of several thousand hectares apiece. It was also during this period – in the 1920s and 1930s in particular – that the overwhelming majority of the Philippines' sugar centrals were constructed, a crucial step for those large landowners who were to transform themselves into industrial magnates in the years to come.

With this in mind, it is worth recalling that the large landowners who emerged at the forefront of the national oligarchy were also politicians – provincial governors, congressmen, and senators – and that it was only through their control over elective office and access to state resources that they were able to accumulate so much land and capital. More than 90 per cent of the archipelago, after all, was designated as public land and thus under the jurisdiction of the notoriously corrupt Bureau of Lands, which was staffed by men handpicked by national legislators and their allies. In Nueva Ecija, for example, provincial boss Manuel Tinio, who served as a general during the Revolution against Spain and later as governor of the province, used his influence with the Bureau of Lands and his control over the local government machinery – including police forces, justices of the peace, the Court of First Instance, and the Court of Land Registration – to acquire large landholdings.[31] Meanwhile, in the crucial sugar industry, politically powerful plantation owners used their considerable influence to milk the Philippine National Bank (PNB), a state bank established in 1916, to fund the construction of centrifugal sugar mills to process their cane.[32] There were virtually no sugar centrals constructed during the salad days of the 1920s and 1930s built without PNB funds, except those funded by Hawai'i-based American planters or other foreign interests.[33] As Rivera notes, the vast majority of the 'landed-capitalist' families who are prominent in the manufacturing sector today were (politically connected) PNB-bankrolled sugar mill owners in the 1930s.[34]

Indeed, throughout the twentieth century sugar has been the oligarchy's crop *par excellence*, but a crop whose fate has remained intimately intertwined with that of Philippine democracy. Through the mobilisation of plantation workers and other dependants in elections, after all, landowners from early sugar-growing areas of the Philippines gained mayorships, governorships, and seats in the national legislature. From the vantage point of such elective government positions, moreover, these landowners used their influence over the Bureau of Lands and the Philippine National Bank (PNB) to expand their landholdings and build sugar centrals during the American colonial period. In the post-war era of import-substitution industrialisation, moreover, members of the powerful 'Sugar Bloc' in Congress used their considerable power to obtain the PNB loans, import licences, franchises, tax and tariff deals, and regulatory breaks which would allow them to transform themselves from 'sugar barons' into a key segment of the Philippine's embryonic industrial bourgeoisie.

In this regard, the case of the Lopez dynasty is emblematic, indeed exemplary, as the historian Alfred W. McCoy has so amply demonstrated.[35] The dynasty traces its roots back to Basilio Lopez, a Chinese-*mestizo* timber merchant in the Jaro district of Iloilo City in the mid-nineteenth century, whose many children (ten survived to maturity) were active in commerce, moneylending, and land acquisition in Panay and the frontier province of Negros across the Guimaras Straits from Iloilo. These children acquired large landholdings in Iloilo province and, by the 1860s, vast holdings of sugar land in Negros. Yet as McCoy makes clear, in the early 1900s the family fortune was threatened by a sustained downturn in the price of sugar on the world market, the upheaval of the Philippine Revolution and the American invasion, and the process of fragmentation and dissipation through inheritance.[36] Basilio's grandson Benito (1877–1908) began to overcome these obstacles by asserting the Lopez family's influence in the realm of electoral politics, first through ownership of a local newspaper in Iloilo City and then through election to the Iloilo provincial governorship in 1903. Benito's sons Eugenio (1901–75) and Fernando took up the mantle of family leadership, moving from landownership and provincial publishing to acquisition of a sugar central in the late 1920s, a bus company, an airline, and an inter-island shipping firm in the 1930s and 1940s, and a private commercial bank, a diversified national publishing and media empire, and the Manila Electric Company in the late 1950s and early 1960s.

This process of unsurpassed dynastic accumulation in the realm of business was fairly matched – and significantly facilitated by a parallel process of political ascendancy. Whilst Eugenio ran the family businesses and in the interwar period wielded considerable clout through the family newspaper, *El Tiempo*, Fernando became mayor of Iloilo in 1945, won a Senate seat in 1947, and served as vice-president under Quirino from 1949 to 1953 (when he returned to the Senate), and again under Marcos from 1966 through 1972. Thanks to these political offices, to Lopez leadership of the 'Sugar Bloc' in Congress, and to the family's considerable business interests and political machinery in Iloilo and Negros Occidental, the Lopezes enjoyed enormous political influence in Manila and commensurate access to state resources and special treatment by state regulators, most notably generous financing by state banks for the Lopezes' most important business acquisitions. As McCoy concludes:

> The spectacular postwar climb of the Lopez brothers was based in large part, then, on their masterful manipulation of the state's regulatory and financial powers. Among the Republic's national entrepreneurs, they were the most successful rent seekers, prospering largely because they were skilled in extracting special privileges from a 'state apparatus … choked continually by an anarchy of particularistic demands'. Indeed, at every step, from the founding of their provincial bus company during the 1930s to the formation of corporate conglomerates in the 1960s, the rise of Eugenio and Fernando Lopez relied in some way upon state licenses that restricted access to the market. Since all of their major corporations were in some sense rents, their commercial success involved a commingling of business and politics.[37]

In contrast to the pattern of sugar baron ascendancy exemplified by the Lopezes, the case of tobacco reveals a very different pattern of capital accumulation and political success. In areas where small landholdings predominated, local bosses sometimes emerged and entrenched themselves by using state resources to establish business empires that rested on government contracts, concessions, and monopoly franchises (legal and illegal), rather than accumulating concentrations of land and other forms of proprietary wealth. In the tobacco-producing provinces of northern Luzon, moreover, politicians in the early post-war era also succeeded in using state offices and resources to pioneer a new form of government intervention in the processing and marketing of agricultural commodities and in the protection of an 'infant' cigarette industry in the Philippines. In 1952, under the administration of Ilocano president (and Syquía in-law, as it happens) Elpidio Quirino, legislation was passed mandating high tariffs on the import of foreign cigarettes and promoting local tobacco farmers through a complex scheme involving subsidies and farmers' cooperatives, known as FACOMAs (Farmer's Cooperative Marketing Association). Over the next two decades, gangster-style Ilocano politicians came to play a crucial role in the tobacco industry, not as large landowners or investors in cigarette companies, but through their control and manipulation of the FACOMAs and their establishment of monopolies in the processing of this heavily state-regulated commodity[38]. For example, long-time Ilocos Sur congressman Floro Crisologo and his wife, the governor of the province, came to own the sole tobacco drying plant in Ilocos Sur and set up roadblocks on the sole highway in the province along the borders with Ilocos Norte and La Union (to the south), where farmers and middlemen transporting tobacco beyond Ilocos Sur were forced to pay a punitive tax to the provincial government. Floro Crisologo eventually fell to assassins' bullets while taking communion at the Vigan Cathedral in 1970, but long-time Ilocos Norte congressman Ferdinand Marcos used his own position in the heavily-regulated and subsidised tobacco industry to entrench himself in his district, and from there to rise to the Senate and in due course the presidency (1966–86).

In sum, the pattern of capitalist development under early democratic auspices thus provided a crucial backdrop to the authoritarian regime under Ferdinand Marcos in the 1970s and early 1980s. Indeed, it was no coincidence that by the time of Marcos' declaration of martial law in 1972, his biggest enemies were the Lopezes, leading members of the 'Sugar Bloc' that had been so instrumental for his victories in the presidential elections of 1965 and 1969. With Marcos' unprecedented reelection in 1969 and his rule by decree from 1972 to 1986, the Philippines saw the reversal of the previous pattern of sugar baron hegemony and a protracted period of rule by the nation's premier tobacco-based politician. As noted elsewhere in this volume, a combination of international and domestic circumstances in the late 1960s and early 1970s served to expand the resources and prerogatives of the national state and to strengthen the hand of the presidency vis-à-vis Congress and the national oligarchy it represented, facilitating Marcos' reelection and his proclamation of martial law in 1972.

Thus tobacco trumped sugar, cronies trumped oligarchs, a gangster-politician trumped the plantation owners, and State power trumped that of private capital. The Marcos era, as is well known, saw considerable expansion and innovation in the role of the state in the economy and in the scale of presidential cronyism: behest loans, huge construction contracts, vast logging concessions, and quasi-governmental monopolies/monopsonies in the coconut and sugar industries. Unlike the sugar barons, Marcos was precisely the kind of politician who knew how to avail state resources and prerogatives in order to build and maintain a political machine *without* assuming any proprietary or productive role in the economy. He had developed and perfected this *modus operandi* first as a congressman from Ilocos Norte, then as a senator. It was thus precisely his background as a politician whose base lay in tobacco that shaped the particular brand of 'crony capitalism' that became the hallmark of his long presidency.

'Forget it Jake, it's Chinatown …'

In short, the hallmarks of Philippine political economy – the political entrenchment and private accumulation achieved by a predominantly Chinese *mestizo* 'landed oligarchy'. the 'crony capitalism' pursued by long-time president Marcos – are best understood in the context of a pattern of capitalist development which, unique in Southeast Asia, has proceeded since a very early stage under the auspices of competitive electoral democracy. As suggested above, for the Chinese *mestizo* politicians, two patterns of empire-building and capital accumulation stand out – sugar and tobacco – and capture an important difference between the pre-Marcos and Marcos eras. Both patterns depended heavily on privileged access to state resources and discretion over state prerogatives (regulations, contracts, concessions), and it was through elections and politician's control over the bureaucracy that this access was maintained.

Yet perhaps scholars of 'political economy' run the risk of exaggerating the importance of 'politics' and politicians in the Philippine economy. Indeed, it is possible to argue that the extent of Chinese *mestizo* oligarchical and cronyist control of the economy has been wildly exaggerated if by oligarchy we mean families like the Lopezes and if by cronies we mean the bagmen and business partners of Marcos and perhaps his predecessors and lesser-known local counterparts. After all, aside from sugar, all of the other major agricultural commodities in the Philippines have failed to generate a chain of *mestizo* capital accumulation from landownership to commodity processing and marketing onwards to import-substitution and export-oriented industrial manufacturing. Early restrictions on the use of PNB funds for the coconut industry (imposed by the soybean farmer's lobby in Washington, DC) prevented the emergence of Chinese *mestizo* copra barons and coconut oil mill owners from among the owners of large coconut groves. Thus instead of a 'Coconut Bloc' in Congress, the post-war era saw the emergence and entrenchment of 'Chinese' coconut industry magnates, families like the Lus of Cebu who have maintained a distinctly Chinese identity in the popular imagination (if not in their private lives) and a discreet distance from the realm of politics. Not even the encapsulation and subordination of such 'Chinese' coconut magnates under the Marcos-era United Coconut Oil Mills (UNICOM) dislodged them from a dominant position in the industry.[39]

'Chinese' predominance has likewise been maintained in other key commodity chains. Rice mills and corn mills have long been in mostly 'Chinese' hands, and just as the rice trade in Manila is often said to be in the hands of the 'Big Seven' cartel of Binondo-based traders,[40] so have major Cebu-based corn mill magnates (like John Gokongwei and the Uytengsu family) diversified into bigger food-processing and agro-business ventures.[41] Despite the involvement of politicians like the Crisologos, Chinese-Filipinos have long played a key (and today dominant) role in the domestic tobacco (cigar and cigarette) industry, just as they have figured prominently as sawmill owners, lumber dealers, furniture makers, and, in competition or combination with politicians, as logging concessionaires.[42]

Beyond these commodity chains, Chinese-Filipino businessmen have also predominated in other crucial realms of the economy – industry, commerce, and finance – where and when they have not been outmatched by politicians or foreign capital. Since the 1950s, for example, Chinese-Filipino firms have controlled a preponderance of the textile industry, the classic motor of import-substitution industrialisation.[43] In other early industrial sectors requiring large capital investments, Chinese-Filipino firms have long shared the field with American companies or with local firms owned by families who trace their roots back to European merchants of the late Spanish era, as in the case of breweries and distilleries (e.g. the Sorianos of San Miguel fame) and shipping (e.g. Cebu's Aboitiz and Escaño families).[44] Loans from the Development Bank of the Philippines (DBP) helped Chinese *mestizo* politicians and their business partners build cement plants and flour mills in the 1950s and 1960s, even as sugar barons long indebted to the PNB moved upstream into these and other new urban commercial and industrial ventures. Yet overall, Chinese-Filipino manufacturing firms held their own over several decades of import-substituting and then export-oriented industrialisation. Even Temario Rivera, who views the 'landed-capitalist families' as 'the dominant segment of the postwar local manufacturing class' concedes that as of 1986, the year of Marcos' downfall, 41 leading Chinese-Filipino families controlled 54 (or 45 per cent) of the top 120 local manufacturing firms.[45] By contrast, of the 87 stockholding families and groups controlling the top 120 manufacturing firms, only 23 (or 26 per cent) held substantial land-holdings. As of 1986, these 'big landed capitalist families' controlled only '40 out of the 120 leading manufacturing firms or 33 per cent of the total'.[46] Since 1986, moreover, a recent study of the Philippines' top corporations suggests, the proportion of domestic capital claimed by 'Chinese' businessmen has probably grown. Today, 'Chinese' firms dominate textiles and leather, wood products, paper and publishing, paints, and rubber, plastic, steel, and metal products.[47]

In commerce and finance, Chinese-Filipino predominance has been even more pronounced. As in much of the Spanish colonial era, Chinese Filipinos have operated the key retail networks in the archipelago throughout the twentieth century, and today own the major department store and shopping mall chains in the country.[48] Moreover, of all the private commercial banks established in the 1950s and 1960s, the only major one not owned by Chinese Filipinos, foreign capital, or families of nineteenth-century European vintage was the Lopez-owned Philippine Commercial and Industrial Bank (PCIB). By 1970, the five largest banks, holding almost 50 per cent of all assets in the banking, were (in order of importance): the government-owned Philippine National Bank (PNB), the New York-based Citibank, the China Banking Corporation, Willy Co's Equitable Bank, and the Bank of the Philippine Islands (BPI), whose management the Zobel de Ayalas took over from the Catholic Archdiocese of Manila in 1969.[49] By 1995, Chinese-Filipino banks had captured an even greater share of the financial sector: after the partially privatised PNB, four of the top five banks were controlled or substantially owned by Chinese-Filipino shareholders, with the Ayala's BPI as the sole 'Spanish' exception. If banks with substantial but not controlling Chinese-Filipino shareholders like PCIB and Far East Bank are included, Chinese-Filipino banks claim 48 per cent of all bank assets and over 60 per cent of all those held by private domestic commercial banks.[50]

Conclusions

As the preceding pages have suggested, it is unsurprising that 'Chinese' capital has been so prominent – and, in some sectors, so clearly predominant – in the post-Marcos era.[51] The downfall of the Marcos regime led to the dismantling of the system of centralised, presidential cronyism that had become the hallmark of the martial law era. Quasi-governmental monopolies/monopsonies for sugar and coconuts were abolished, 'crony' companies were sequestered and in some cases returned to their original owners, and state bank loans, contracts and concessions were terminated or rescinded. With the return to competitive elect-oral democracy, the restoration of Congress, and the acceptance of IMF programs mandating privatisation and liberalisation, the late 1980s saw a drastic reduction in the role of the state in the economy. Government financial institutions were privatised and behest loans curtailed, state support for monopolies and cartels in various sectors was withdrawn, and various forms of protection, subsidy, and restrictions on foreign investment and competition were significantly scaled down.[52]

Such changes have combined with economic trends to produce a marked attenuation of the link between business and politics in the Philippines. Taiwanese firms, Hong Kong-based investment houses, New York mutual fund managers, and Manila stockbrokers have channeled considerable funds into the Philippine economy and replaced government financial institutions like the PNB and the DBP and state regulatory bodies like the Board of Investments (BOI) as the key sources and brokers of capital.[53] By the 1990s, the achievement of a truly national market and the elaboration of nation-wide production circuits had converted many mayors, congressmen, and governors into eager facilitators for foreign and Manila-based capital and shifted these local bosses' entrepreneurial energies towards economic ventures outside their bailiwicks and into much more competitive arenas. If in previous decades provincial bosses reaped huge profits on logging concessions or sugar plantations obtained and maintained through political connections, by the 1990s the most lucrative use of state office involved the awarding of construction contracts to, and the manipulation of zoning ordinances for, major firms willing to pay a small percentage 'fee' for such services. At the national level, a similar trend has been visible. Congressmen still use state office to protect and advance their own business interests, in terms of contracts, concessions, franchises, and tax, tarrif, and regulatory breaks. Yet few of the nation's biggest business families are represented directly in the House, and the Senate is filled with celebrities, machine politicians, and corporate lawyers, rather than the Negros-based sugar barons of yesteryear. Today's politicians are the brokers and fixers for 'Big Business'. rather than the biggest businessmen themselves.

The advantages enjoyed by 'landed capitalists' and 'cronies' have been significantly reduced, and a broader path has been cleared for those businessmen whose relationship with politicians and the state has been mediated almost entirely by money – that is, the 'Chinese'. As in any democracy, today's Filipino businessmen pay politicians before, during, and after elections, for the protection and advancement of their business interests through preferential legislation and regulation. Yet the restoration of Congress and the establishment of single presidential terms have produced a pattern of 'market corruption' in which favours are usually dispensed to the highest bidder, and have mediated cronyism through persistent political competition and turnover. Large rural landholdings may still provide the underlying social base for the launching of many a political career but generate far less in profits than many urban commercial and industrial ventures, especially since the collapse in world sugar and coconut prices and the privatisation of the PNB. Today even the sugar refining business is largely in the hands of Chinese-Filipino magnates rather than the sugar barons cum politicians of yesteryear.[54]

If the ascendancy of Chinese-Filipino capital in the post-Marcos era is hardly surprising, it is still often understood as the triumph of 'new' money over 'old'. as the victory of 'Chinese' entrepreneurial talents in a free market now released from the grip of both Marcos' cronies and the notorious landed oligarchy.[55] Yet the preceding pages have suggested otherwise: many of the *taipans* of today are the scions of 'Chinese' dynasties like the Gotiaocos, whose prominence, if not pre-eminence, in the business world dates back many decades. The term 'oligarchy'. in other words, is misleading or mistakenly restricted if taken to mean a landed Chinese-*mestizo* élite exerting direct control over the state through elected political office. Instead, all along, there has been another kind of oligarchy, an oligarchy of 'Chinese' business dynasties far less rooted in rural land ownership than in urban commercial, financial, and industrial activity, and linked to politicians and the state in relationships far more attenuated than families like the Lopezes and the Cojuangcos. Like their 'Spanish' counterparts – the Ayalas, Sorianos, and Aboitizes, for example – these 'Chinese' business families do not have any congressmen or senators in their ranks, nor do they affiliate themselves too closely, exclusively, openly, or persistently with a single politician or political party. Instead, their relationship with the state, with politicians, with 'politics' in all its forms, is mediated through money. This, after all, is what makes them 'Chinese'. It was ever thus.

The significance of this new, broader understanding of the economic base and political role of 'the oligarchy' becomes apparent if we reconsider the scholarly literature which has cast the Philippines in the role of a 'deviant case' among the otherwise spectacular Newly Industrialising Economies (NIEs) of the other countries in the so-called 'ASEAN Four'. namely Indonesia, Malaysia, and Thailand. An early tendency to blame the Philippines' relatively lackluster economic performance over the past three decades on the excesses of Marcos-era crony capitalism was abandoned by the late 1980s against the backdrop of continuing high growth rates in neighbouring Indonesia even as Suharto's children expanded their business activities into realms previously controlled by ethnic-Chinese financiers (*cukong*) close to the Palace.[56] Instead, with the assumption of Corazon Aquino to the Philippine presidency, the resurrection of the Lopez dynasty and the restoration of 'cacique democracy'. blame fell squarely on the shoulders of a 'landed oligarchy'. whose pre-eminence and persistence had impeded the deepening of import-substitution industrialisation and the shift towards export-oriented industrialisation. Major land reform measures had preceded – and jump-started – the economic 'miracles' in neighbouring Taiwan and in South Korea, it was often noted, and of all the 'ASEAN Four' only the Philippines had such a large and influential landholding élite. The conventional wisdom thus used the (Hispanic) Philippines as a confirming case to underline the essential difference between the 'Asian growth model' and the Latin American economies, whose relatively lower growth rates seemed to correlate (inversely) with more substantial and influential *hacienda*-based classes.[57]

Yet, as suggested above, such a stark and simplistic contrast fails to stand up to close and careful scrutiny. Experts on Latin America, after all, have carefully documented the continuing preeminence of large landholding families in Brazil and Chile, two countries whose economies have experienced much more rapid and sustained growth than the Philippines over the past three decades.[58] Nearby Thailand, moreover, achieved double-digit annual economic growth rates in the 1980s and 1990s through a combination of both industrial *and* agricultural export success, with major agro-business conglomerates like the Charoen Pokphand (CP) group representing agricultural interests at least as substantial as those found in the Philippines.[59] Finally, the years of dramatic economic slowdown and decline in the Philippines coincided with the period when the 'landed oligarchy' was by all account at its weakest, with the authoritarian Marcos regime subordinating sugar and coconut planters to quasi-governmental monopolies and monopsonies and otherwise exercising unprecedented 'state autonomy' *vis-à-vis* the landholding class.[60]

The clearest contrast between the Philippines and its more economically successful neighbours is offered in the paired comparison that some scholars have drawn between the archipelago and nearby Thailand. The dramatic difference in growth rates is typically ascribed to the advantages that Thailand's well-insulated 'bureaucratic polity' has offered as against the 'weak state, strong society' configuration in the plantocratic – and less prosperous – Philippines.[61] Yet studies have documented the emergence and entrenchment in the 1950s and 1960s of a close cluster of Sino-Thai bankers, a financial bourgeoisie at least as economically well-endowed (if not as politically empowered) as the Philippines' 'predatory oligarchy'.[62] More importantly perhaps, it is well known that Thailand's 'bureaucratic polity' unravelled in the early 1970s even as the Philippines' oligarchical democracy was replaced by 'constitutional authoritarianism'. with the early October 1973 popular ouster of the Thanom-Praphat military dictatorship in Bangkok following only a year after Marcos' declaration of martial law in Manila in late September 1972. Thailand's 'bureaucratic polity'. moreover, was replaced in the 1980s and 1990s – a period of double-digit annual economic growth – by a system of parliamentary democracy dominated by provincial 'godfathers' (*chao pho*) and Bangkok-based magnates strikingly similar to the post-Marcos Philippines.[63] Even those spheres of economic policy-making once assumed to have remained properly 'insulated' from Thai bosses and the bankers now appear in the light of the 1997–98 economic crisis to have enjoyed little residual protective traces of the 'bureaucratic polity'. Viewed in a properly historicised comparative perspective, the contrast between a Thai 'bureaucratic polity' and Filipino oligarchical democracy is not in fact sustainable.[64]

Somewhat more compelling is Japanese scholar Yoshihara Kunio's stress on the diverging treatment of 'Chinese' capital by Thai and Filipino governments over the years, a difference, which, he concludes, does much to explain the considerable differential in economic growth rates between the two countries.[65] In both Thailand and the Philippines, the period stretching from the 1930s through the early 1950s saw the growth of 'economic nationalism' and the establishment of restrictions on 'Chinese' (and other foreign) business, partly in reaction to the massive surge of immigration from China during this period.

Most notable was the Retail Nationalisation Law enacted in the Philippines in 1954. Such 'anti-Chinese' policies persisted in the Philippines, Yoshihara argues, long after Bangkok's strongman General Sarit had embarked on a liberalisation of the Thai economy, hampering the potential for Chinese-Filipino businessmen to deliver the same levels of investment and growth as their Sino-Thai counterparts. Yet Yoshihara's thesis looks far less persuasive if we consider the ease of assimilation, possibilities for naturalisation, and opportunities for evasion open to Chinese-Filipino businessmen in the 1950s and 1960s, as well as the dramatic easing of restrictions on naturalisation which came under the Marcos regime in tandem with the recognition of the People's Republic of China in 1975. Political office has long been open to the (naturalised) children of Chinese immigrants like the Chiongbian brothers (shipping tycoons and Mindanao politicians) in the pre-martial law era and Alfredo 'Freddy' Lim (Manila Mayor, 1992–98) in more recent memory, and, countless 'Chinese' businessmen have received special privileges thanks to the favour they enjoyed with Filipino presidents, as the case of Lucio Tan during the Marcos and Estrada administration suggests.

Nonetheless, Yoshihara's thesis proves more persuasive if by 'Chinese' we understand him to mean not an essentialised ethnic category but rather a form of private capital whose relationship to the state is mediated neither by the social and political power afforded by landownership, nor by the personal loyalties and advantages of a 'crony', but by money and what James C. Scott calls 'market corruption'. Compared to their Sino-Thai counterparts in the heyday of the Siamese 'bureaucratic polity'. for example, Chinese-Filipino businessmen from early on in the twentieth century often found their capacity for private capital accumulation constrained by elected municipal mayors, provincial governors, congressmen, and senators, who enjoyed privileged access to government loans, contracts, and concessions, and controls over the regulatory levers of the state. 'Chinese' capitalists like the Gotiaocos, in other words, ran up against 'landed capitalists' like the Lopezes, who, as stressed above, doubled (and doubled their fortunes) as politicians, especially in the heyday of colonial democracy and the pre-martial law era. Over the years, (would-be) 'Chinese' owners and operators of ice plants, bus companies, flour mills, cement factories, and private commercial banks in the Philippines often confronted monopolistic and cartel-like practices, stiff competition, and persistent harassment from the rival firms of politicians enjoying non-market-based advantages and effective state subsidies thanks to the perks of elected office. Their Sino-Thai counterparts, by contrast, had to pay off district officers, provincial governors, police colonels, and army generals over the years, but competed on less disadvantageous terms both for state protection and patronage and for market shares and profits. In Siam's 'bureaucratic polity'. there were no Thai landed-capitalists-cum-politicians to stand in their way.

Yoshihara's thesis is further illuminating if we consider the critical decades of the 1970s and 1980s, when the Thai economy 'took off' and the Philippines went into relative and absolute decline. Even as this period saw the increasingly competitive nature of clientist ties between businessmen and bureaucrats in Thailand under conditions of considerable political change and instability,[66] in the Philippines the measure of competition provided by frequent elections and regular presidential turnover in early years was diminished under conditions of martial law and authoritarian rule. Whilst some businessmen of recent Chinese ancestry were among the 'cronies' who benefited handsomely from close ties to Marcos during this period, those businessmen whose access to state patronage and protection depended on money rather than personal connections found their capacity for private capital accumulation increasingly constrained by the mono-polistic privileges enjoyed by those with close ties to the Palace. Just as 'Chinese' capital accumulation was restricted by landed capital in the 1950s and 1960s, so was it constrained by crony capital in the 1970s and 1980s.

The puzzle of economic slowdown and decline in the Philippines can be viewed in a different light. If the political hegemony of the sugar barons impeded the deepening of import substitution industrialisation in the democratic 1950s and 1960s, so did the ascendancy and entrenchment of the country's premier tobacco-based politician undermine export-oriented industrialisation in the authoritarian 1970s and 1980s. Here again the importance of elections as the underlying logic of Philippine political economy is clearly in evidence. For Marcos, unlike most of his authoritarian counterparts elsewhere in Southeast Asia (or Latin America for that matter), was an elected politician who reached the presidency by elections rather than *coup d'état*, and whose experiment with 'constitutional authoritarianism' depended on repeated – if heavily orchestrated – electoral exercises, from the plebiscites of the early martial law years to the National Assembly elections of 1978 and 1984, to the local elections of 1980 and the presidential contests of 1981 and 1986. The zero-sum logic of Philippine democracy had long propelled local politicians to shower state patronage and protection on their loyal supporters and to assemble 'war chests' of liquid campaign funds as insurance against electoral defeat, and Marcos, the seasoned tobacco politician from Ilocos, was no exception. The creation of monopolies/ monopsonies for coconuts and sugar, the awarding of behest loans, huge govern-ment contracts, and special franchises, concessions, and regulatory breaks to presidential cronies followed directly from this logic, as did the avoidance of direct Marcos (or Marcos family) ownership of major Philippine companies (in sharp contrast with the Suhartos in Indonesia), and the accumulation of bank accounts, real-estate holdings, and stock portfolios in the United States and elsewhere around the world. Far from revealing peculiarly irrational tendencies or insufficiently nationalist sentiments, Marcos' strategy of accumulating overseas wealth rested on an appreciation not only of the higher returns of profits to be realised outside the Philippines, but of the greater liquidity and security which such holdings would afford him. Indeed, efforts by successive post-Marcos administrations to confiscate the long-time dictator's 'ill-gotten wealth' have borne little fruit over the years, and today Marcos' wife and children enjoy comfortable lives and successful political careers in Manila largely thanks to the perspicacity of his investment decisions.

Over the course of the late eighteenth and nineteenth centuries, ships from the port of Amoy in coastal Fujian Province brought hundreds of thousands of soon-to-be *chinos* to Philippine shores, immigrants like Pedro Gotiaoco, Juan Co, the progenitor of the Cojuangco family, and the (great-) grandfathers of Ferdinand Marcos and the Lopez brothers. Thanks to their early immersion and experience in the urban cash economy of rapidly commercialising Fujian, unmatched in the relatively 'backward' Philippines, such *chinos* were well placed to occupy crucial middleman or 'compradore' roles as local merchants and moneylenders in a colony which only in the mid-nineteenth century was opened to foreign trade.

Some of these men fathered children destined first to be *mestizos*, later Filipinos, and, in the era of American colonial democracy, *politicos* as well. Where nature – and government nurture – favoured the accumulation of concentrations of proprietary wealth, as in the case of the Lopezes and other lesser dynasties in the sugar belts of Negros, Batangas, and Central Luzon: a distinctly capital-intensive trajectory produced a class of Chinese mestizo landed-capitalists-cum-politicians, whose vast plantations, large blocks of captive vote(r)s, and lockhold on a local bailiwicks and elected offices guaranteed access to state resources which helped transform them into an important segment of the country's industrial bourgeoisie. In other, perhaps less fortunate, regions, where landholdings were neither so large nor so lucrative, a typically more violent, gangster-style pattern prevailed, the *chinos'* progeny became local *politicos* like Ferdinand Marcos, builders of powerful political machines but never of enduring economic empires of their own.

Meanwhile, still other *chinos* fathered children who were destined to remain *sang-li* or *chino*, and later 'Chinamen', *intsik*, 'Chinese-Filipino', *tsinoy*, as would their children and grandchildren, if not in terms of citizenship then at least by their own understanding and that of those who knew (of) them. Instead of amassing the social and political capital that transformed some of their most fortunate *mestizo* cousins into Filipino sugar barons or machine politicians, they focused their ambitions on private capital accumulation and in some cases achieved considerable success in building business dynasties such as the one started by Pedro Gotiaoco, continued by the Go(tianuy) brothers, and now championed by John Gokongwei, Jr and his children. In recent years, such members of a distinctly 'Chinese' oligarchy have emerged from the backrooms of Binondo and from quiet haunts like Eddie's Log Cabin in Cebu City. No longer content to be silent partners or second-place players in the shadow of the sugar barons or the Marcos' entourage, they now openly own the top national newspapers and operate the nation's most famous department store and shopping mall chains. Their beer and ice cream are consumed by millions of Filipinos, and their companies' basketball teams are among the most popular in the country.

Today, at the beginning of the twenty-first century, the eclipse of 'landed' and 'crony' capital and the rise of 'Chinese' capital to its current position of national pre-eminence signal not the end of oligarchy or the triumph of some ethnically-specific form of immigrant entrepreneurialism, but rather a resolution of certain tensions long inherent in Philippine capitalism over the past one hundred years. Perhaps in the wake of the economic crisis in the region, the years to come will reveal that 'Chinese Filipinos' are best viewed not as local representatives of a

Chinese diasporic 'bamboo network'. but rather as special kinds of Filipinos, and that the Philippine economy is best understood not as pathologically deviant, anomalous, or basket-case, but rather as a distinctive variant of Southeast Asian capitalism. In the Philippines, the creative energies and destructive tendencies of capitalism have been decisively shaped by the early imposition, endurance, and transformation of the institutions of American-style presidential democracy in the archipelago. More than the size of the sugar barons' large landholdings, the greed of Ferdinand Marcos and his cronies, or the 'Chinese-ness' of Chinese-Filipino capital, this fact has shaped the pattern of capitalist development in the country over the course of the twentieth century, as it is certain to do in the years to come.

Notes

1   On Gotianun, see: Go Bon Juan, 'Ethnic Chinese in Philippine Banking'. *Tulay*, 4 October 1992, pp. 8–9; and Rigoberto Tiglao, 'Comeback Couple'. *Far Eastern Economic Review*, 28 December 1995–4 January 1996, pp. 112–113. On Gokongwei, see: 'For Gokongwei, success is a journey'. *Business World Anniversary Report 1994* (Manila: Business World 1994), pp. 105–108; and Emmie V. Abadilla, 'From Peanuts to Petrochem'. *Manila Inc.*, May 1994, pp. 24–30.

2   See: Booma Cruz, 'Yuchengco chosen consortium head'. *Manila Chronicle*, 30 April 1993, pp. 1, 6; 'Taipans form P2–B firm'. *Tulay*, 4 October 1993, p. 6. Documents filed at the Securities and Exchange Commission reveal that the taipans contributed one hundred million pesos (close to US$4 million at the time) apiece to the consortium's initial capitalisation but showed little interest thereafter.

3   Interviews with Augusto W. Go and José W. Gotianuy, Eddie's Log Cabin, Cebu City, 17 August 1995.

4   The most complete written account of the Gotiaoco family's early years in the Philippines is to be found in 'She-wu Hua-shang Ching-ying' [Cebu's Outstanding Chinese Businessmen], *Forbes Zibenjia*, March 1992, pp. 64–65. The authors would like to thank Carol Hau and Elizabeth Remick for translating this article into English.

5   Manuel Gotianuy also served as President of the Chinese Chamber of Commerce of Cebu and as honorary consul of the Chinese government in the pre-war period. See: George F. Nellist (ed.), *Men of the Philippines* (Manila: Sugar News, 1931), p. 121.

6   Rigoberto Tiglao, 'Stacked Decks: Philippine shipowners fear Keppel repair monopoly'. *Far Eastern Economic Review*, 25 November 1993, p. 60.

7   'Gaisanos of Cebu: full steam ahead'. *Tulay*, 16 April 1993, p. 4.

8   On the Osmeñas, see: Resil B. Mojares, 'The Dream Goes On and On: Three Generations of the Osmeñas, 1906–1990'. in Alfred W. McCoy (ed.), *An Anarchy of Families: State and Faily in the Philippines* (Madison: University of Wisconsin Center for Southeast Asian Studies, 1993), pp. 311–346. Michael Cullinane has expressed doubt as to the veracity of Gotiaoco's paternal claim. See: Michael Cullinane, 'Playing the Game: The Rise of Sergio Osmeña, 1898–1907'. in Ruby Paredes (ed.), *Philippine Colonial Democracy* (Quezon City: Ateneo de Manila University Press, 1989), pp. 106–107.

9   See: Alfonso T. Yuchengco, 'The Super Smart Billionaire'. *Say*, 5 May 1989, p. 12.

10 Paul D. Hutchcroft, 'Oligarchs and Cronies in the Philippine State: The Politics of Patrimonial Plunder'. *World Politics*, Volume 43, Number 3 (April 1991), pp. 413–450; Paul D. Hutchcroft, *Booty Capitalism: The Politics of Banking in the Philippines* (Ithaca: Cornell University Press, 1998).

11 Belinda Aquino, *Politics of Plunder: The Philippines Under Marcos* (Quezon City: University of the Philippines College of Public Administration, 1987); Ricardo Manapat, *Some Are Smarter Than Others: The History of Marcos' Crony Capitalism* (New York: Aletheia Publications, 1991).

12 See, for example, Gary Hawes, *The Philippine State and the Marcos Regime: The Politics of Export* (Ithaca: Cornell University Press, 1987); and Rigoberto Tiglao, *Looking Into Coconuts: The Philippine Coconut Industry* (Manila: ARC Publications, 1981).

13 James Putzel, *A Captive Land: The Politics of Agrarian Reform in the Philippines* (Quezon City: Ateneo de Manila University Press, 1992).

14 Harold Crouch, *Economic Change, Social Structure and the Political System in Southeast Asia: Philippine Development Compared with the Other ASEAN Countries* (Singapore: Institute of Southeast Asian Studies, 1985), p. 10.

15 Temario Campos Rivera, 'Class, the State and Foreign Capital: The Politics of Philippine Industrialisation 1950–1986' (Ph.D. dissertation, University of Wisconsin at Madison, 1991). This study was subsequently published in revised form as *Landlords and Capitalists: Class, Family, and State in Philippine Manufacturing* (Quezon City: University of the Philippines Center for for Integrative and Development Studies and University of the Philippines Press, 1994).

16 Teresita Ang See, *The Chinese in the Philippines: Problems and Perspectives* (Manila: Kaisa Para Sa kaunlaran, 1997), p. 2.

17 Eric Gutierrez, *The Ties That Bind: A Guide to Family, Business and Other Interests in the Ninth House of Representatives* (Pasig: Philippine Center for Investigative Journalism, 1994).

18 See, for example, Michael Cullinane, 'Patron as Client: Warlord Politics and the Duranos of Danao'. in McCoy (ed.), *An Anarchy of Families*, pp. 163–241.

19 James C. Scott, *Comparative Political Corruption* (Englewood Cliffs: Prentice-Hall, 1972).

20 Edgar Wickberg, *The Chinese in Philippine Life 1850–1898* (New Haven: Yale University Press, 1965).

21 E. Arsenio Manuel, *Chinese Elements in the Tagalog Language* (Manila: Filipiniana Publications, 1948).

22 Arnold Molina Azurin, *Beddeng: Exploring the Ilocano-Igorot Confluence* (Manila: Museo ng Kalinangang Pilipino, Sentrong Pangkultura ng Pilipinas, 1991), pp. 42–43, 57–63.

23 *Ibid.*, pp. 57–63.

24 See, for example, John Larkin, *The Pampangans: Colonial Society in a Philippine Province* (Berkeley: University of California Press, 1972), especially chapters 2, 3, and 4.

25 Edgar Wickberg, 'The Chinese Mestizo in Philippine History'. *Journal of Southeast Asian History*, Volume 5, Number 1 (March 1964), pp. 62–100.

26 See, for example, the influential article by Benedict Anderson, 'Cacique Democracy in the Philippines: Origins and Dreams'. *New Left Review* 169 (May/June 1988), pp. 3–31.

27 See, for example, Ed. C. de Jesus and Alfred W. McCoy (eds), *Philippine Social History: Global Trade and Local Transformations* (Quezon City: Ateneo de Manila University Press, 1982), especially the fine essays by Cullinane and McCoy.

28 On this point, see: Owen J. Lynch, Jr, 'Land Rights, Land Laws and Land Usurpation: The Spanish Era (1565–1898)'. *Philippine Law Journal*, Volume 63, First Quarter (March 1988), p. 84.

29 Filomeno V. Aguilar, Jr, 'Phantoms of Capitalism and Sugar Production Relations in a Colonial Philippine Island' (Ph.D. dissertation, Cornell University, 1992), p. 109.

30 See, for example, Marites Dañguilan-Vitug, *Power From the Forest: The Politics of Logging* (Pasig: Philippine Center for Investigative Journalism, 1993); and Salvador P. Lopez, *Isles of Gold: A History of Mining in the Philippines* (Singapore: Oxford University Press, 1992).

31 Isabelo Tinio Crisostomo, *Governor Eduardo L. Joson: The Gentle Lion of Nueva Ecija* (Quezon City: J. Kriz Publishing Enterprises, 1989), pp. 110–138.

32 On the PNB, see: Venancio Concepcion, *'La Tragedia' del Banco Nacional Filipino* (Manila: 1927); and Peter W. Stanley, *A Nation in the Making: The Philippines and the United States, 1899–1921* (Cambridge: Cambridge University Press, 1974), pp. 238–248.

33 See: Alfred W. McCoy, 'Sugar Barons: Formation of a Native Planter Class in the Colonial Philippines'. *Journal of Peasant Studies*, Volume 19, Numbers 3/4 (April/July 1992), pp. 125–146.

34 Rivera, *Landlords and Capitalists*, p. 32; Yoshihara Kunio, *Philippine Industrialisation: Foreign and Domestic Capital* (Singapore: Oxford University Press, 1985), pp. 134–137. A partial exception

was José Cojuangco, Sr, who founded the relatively modest Paniqui Sugar Mills in 1928 with a large loan from the China Banking Corporation. But his subsequent acquisition of the largest sugar central in the Philippines, the Central Azucarera de Tarlac, was only achieved through public financing and political manipulation. For contrasting accounts, see: Putzel, *A Captive Land*, pp. 93–95; and Marisse Reyes McMurray, *Tide of Time* (Makati City: José Cojuangco and Sons, 1996), pp. 139, 267–280.

35   Alfred W. McCoy, 'Rent-Seeking Families and the Philippine State: A History of the Lopez Family'. in McCoy (ed.), *An Anarchy of Families*, pp. 429–536.

36   *Ibid.*, pp. 441–445.

37   *Ibid.*, p. 435. The citation within this quote is from Hutchcroft, 'Oligarchs and Cronies'. p. 416.

38   Patricia Torres Mejia, *Philippine Virginia Tobacco: 30 Years of Increasing Dependency* (Quezon City: University of the Philippines Third World Studies Center, 1982). See also: Frank Golay, *The Philippines: Public Policy and National Economic Development* (Ithaca: Cornell University Press, 1961), pp. 286–290; and David Wurfel, 'The Bell Report and After: A Study of the Political Problems of Social Reform Stimulated by Foreign Aid' (Ph.D. dissertation, Cornell University Press, 1960), pp. 639–667.

39   On these points, see: Rigoberto Tiglao, *Looking into Coconuts: The Philippine Coconut Industry* (Manila: ARC Publications, 1981), especially pp. 7–9.

40   Eli R. Guieb III, 'The Rice Mafia'. *National Midweek*, 9 May 1990, pp. 3–7; 'An Investigation into the Alleged Existence of a Rice Cartel'. Senate Blue Ribbon Committee Report No. 1075, 2 August 1990; Aurora Alarde-Regalado and Cynthia Hallare-Lara, 'A Profile of the Philippine Rice Industry'. *Rural Development Studies*, Volume 8, Number 3 (July 1992), pp. 1–44; 'Sy Pio Lato and the Rice Cartel'. *Smart File Animal Farm Series* 40 & 41 (1993), pp. 4–28; The Foodwatch Research, *Rice Marketing in Luzon* (Quezon City: Philippine Peasant Institute, 1994).

41   Cynthia Hallare-Lara, 'A Profile of the Philippine Corn Industry'. *Rural Development Studies*, Volume 8, Number 5 (September 1992), pp. 1–51.

42   George H. Weightman, 'The Chinese Community in the Philippines' (M.A. Thesis, University of the Philippines, 1952), p. 70; Nicolas P. Lansigan, 'The Chinese Stranglehold in the Lumber Industry' (M.A. Thesis, Manila Central University, 1949).

43   Laurence Davis Stifel, *The Textile Industry: A Case Study of Industrial Development in the Philippines* (Ithaca: Cornell University Southeast Asia Program Data Papers Number 49, 1963), pp. 76, 93–96; Yoshihara, *Philippine Industrialisation*, pp. 92–93, 151–152.

44   For the broad pattern, see: Yoshihara, *Philippine Industrialisation*.

45   Rivera, *Landlords and Capitalists*, p. 69.

46   *Ibid.*, p. 44.

47   See: Ellen H. Palanca, 'An Analysis of the 1990 Top Corporations in the Philippines: Economic Position and Activities of the Ethnic Chinese, Filipino and Foreign Groups'. *Chinese Studies Journal*, Volume 5 (1995), pp. 47–84.

48   Rigoberto Tiglao, 'Strength in Numbers'. *Far Eastern Economic Review*, 21 July 1994, pp. 60–61; Rigoberto Tiglao, 'Mall Mogul'. *Far Eastern Economic Review*, 31 August 1995, pp. 50–51.

49   Hutchcroft, *Booty Capitalism*, pp. 258–261.

50   Hutchcroft, *Booty Capitalism*, pp. 258–261; Go Bon Juan, 'Ethnic Chinese in Philippine Banking'. *Chinese Studies Journal*, Volume 5 (1995), pp. 85–91.On George Ty's Metrobank, see also: Rigoberto Tiglao, 'Lonely at the Top'. *Far Eastern Economic Review*, 9 November 1995, pp. 60–63.

51   See: Rigoberto Tiglao, 'Gung-ho in Manila'. *Far Eastern Economic Review*, 15 February 1990, pp. 68–71; Leo P. Gonzaga, 'The Taipans'. *Manila Inc.*, March 1994, pp. 24–28; and Temario C. Rivera and Kenji Koike, *The Chinese-Filipino Business Families Under the Ramos Government* (Tokyo: Institute of Developing Economies, 1995).

52   For contrasting accounts of these trends, see: Hutchcroft, *Booty Capitalism*, pp. 170–255; Manuel F. Montes, 'The Politics of Liberalisation: The Aquino Government's 1990 Tariff Reform Initiative'. in David G. Timberman (ed.), *The Politics of Economic Reform in Southeast*

Asia (Makati: Asian Institute of Management, 1992), pp. 91–115; and Emmanuel S. De Dios, 'The Philippine Economy: What's Right, What's Wrong'. *Southeast Asian Affairs 1995* (Singapore: Institute of Southeast Asian Studies, 1996), pp. 273–288; 'Financial Times Survey: The Philippines'. *Financial Times*, 18 September 1996; 'Back on the Road: A Survey of the Philippines'. *The Economist*, 11 May 1996; and Rigoberto Tiglao, 'Boom in Progress'. *Far Eastern Economic Review*, 13 June 1996, pp. 40–49.

53 On Taiwanese investment in particular, see: Wang Heh-Song, 'Philippines: The New Frontier for Foreign Investment from Taiwan'. *Philippine Studies*, Volume 43 (First Quarter 1995), pp. 93–104.

54 On the post-Marcos transformation of the sugar industry, see: Michael S. Billig, '"Syrup in the Wheels of Progress": The Inefficient Organisation of the Philippine Sugar Industry'. *Journal of Southeast Asian Studies*, Volume 24, Number 1 (March 1993), pp. 122–147.

55 See, for example, Amando Doronila, 'Taipans ease out old rich'. *Philippine Daily Inquirer*, 8 January 1995, pp. 1, 2.

56 Adam Schwarz, *A Nation in Waiting: Indonesia in the 1990s* (Sydney: Allen & Unwin, 1994).

57 See, for example, Hutchcroft, *Booty Capitalism*; Rivera, *Landlords and Capitalists*; and Peter Evans, 'Class, State, and Dependence in East Asia: Lessons for Latin America'. in Frederic C. Deyo (ed.), *The Political Economy of the New Asian Industrialism* (Ithaca: Cornell University Press, 1987), pp. 213–215.

58 Frances Hagopian, *Traditional Politics and Regime Change in Brazil* (Cambridge: Cambridge University Press, 1996); Maurice Zeitlin and Richard Earl Ratcliff, *Landlords and Capitalists: The Dominant Class of Chile* (Princeton: Princeton University Press, 1988).

59 Akira Suehiro, 'Capitalist Development in Postwar Thailand: Commercial Bankers, Industrial Elite, and Agribusiness Groups'. in Ruth McVey (ed.), *Southeast Asian Capitalists* (Ithaca: Cornell University Southeast Asia Program, 1992), pp. 35–64.

60 Gary Hawes, *The Philippine State and the Marcos Regime*.

61 Fred Riggs, *Thailand: The Modernisation of a Bureaucratic Polity* (Honolulu: East-West Center Press, 1966).

62 Kevin Hewison, *Bankers and Bureaucrats: Capital and the Role of the State in Thailand* (New Haven: Yale University Southeast Asian Studies, 1989).

63 James Soren Ockey, 'Business Leaders, Gangsters, and the Middle Class: Societal Groups and Civilian Rule in Thailand (Ph.D. dissertation, Cornell University, 1992).

64 But see the more nuanced and empirically grounded arguments in Richard Doner, 'Politics and the Growth of Local Capital in Southeast Asia: Auto Industries in the Philippines and Thailand'. in Ruth McVey (ed.), *Southeast Asian Capitalists* (Ithaca: Cornell University Southeast Asia Program, 1992), pp. 191–218.

65 Yoshihara Kunio, *The Nation and Economic Growth: The Philippines and Thailand* (Kuala Lumpur: Oxford University Press, 1994), especially pp. 15–40.

66 Anek Laothamatas, 'From Clientelism to Partnership: Business-Government Relations in Thailand'. in Andrew MacIntyre (ed.), *Business and Government in Industrialising Asia* (Ithaca: Cornell University Press, 1994), pp. 195–215; Richard F. Doner and Ansil Ramsay, 'Competitive Clientelism and Economic Governance: The Case of Thailand'. in Sylvia Maxfield and Ben Ross Schneider (eds), *Business and the State in Developing Countries* (Ithaca: Cornell University Press, 1997), pp. 237–276.

5 *The Last Hurrah* revisited

In *The Last Hurrah*, his classic 1956 novel, Edwin O'Connor offered the standard story of the American urban political machine's putative demise.[1] The novel, a barely fictionalised account of long-time Boston mayor James Michael Curley, depicted the replacement of the big city bosses by New Deal social welfare programmes which broke their monopoly over the jobs and services provided by the state to urban working-class voters. With the provision of Social Security, Aid to Families with Dependent Children (AFDC), and unemployment compensation, urban voters were no longer dependent upon the machines for assistance, employment, and security.

Whilst O'Connor's novel soon became a bestseller and a Hollywood film starring Spencer Tracy as Mayor Frank Skeffington, *The Last Hurrah* has certainly not had the last word on Curley and the transformation of urban machine politics in the United States. A recent biography, for example, definitively debunks the overly benign (and somewhat nostalgic) portrait of Curley as a glad-handing patron of poor Irish-immigrant Bostonians, providing ample documentation of Curley's ruthlessness against competitors and skill in manipulating the needs and insecurities of his constituents.[2] More importantly, perhaps, *Rainbow's End*, Steven Erie's masterful reassessment of machine politics in American cities, has convincingly challenged both the assumption that machine bosses' emergence and longevity depended upon meeting the demands of (poor, Irish-immigrant) urban voters and the conventional wisdom that all city machines were eliminated by the New Deal. Instead, Erie shows how the emergence, entrenchment, and endurance of machines have rested largely upon the accumulation and manipulation of state resources, and how, in some cities, machine maintenance has been achieved in the post-New Deal era through new forms of state largesse and new mechanisms of voter *de*mobilisation.[3]

Following Erie, this chapter examines not a 'last hurrah', but rather a variegated pattern of change and continuity in the pattern of local bossism found in the Philippines since the mid-1980s. Bossism here refers to a social formation in which local powerbrokers can – and in many instances do – achieve sustained monopolies over coercive and economic resources within geographically defined bailiwicks through the creation of local political machines and economic empires. Bossism, it is argued, has flourished in the Philippines not because of Filipinos' supposed proclivity for personalistic, patron–client relationships or the Philippine capitalist class's concentration of landholdings in the hands of a narrow oligarchy, but because the apparatuses of the state have been subordinated to elected officials at a relatively early stage of capitalist development, one which might loosely be termed 'primitive accumulation'. Under so-called 'primitive accumulation', the broad mass of the population remains economically insecure, divested of access to the means of production and subsistence, susceptible to clientelistic, coercive, and monetary inducements and pressures, while significant economic resources remain under state control. Bosses have emerged and entrenched themselves when and where conditions have allowed them to achieve sustained pre-eminence and predominance within their bailiwick, through some combination of pro-prietary wealth, coercion, and the state-based resources and prerogatives that accompany elected office.

Bossism has assumed a variety of forms in the Philippines. A multi-tiered hierarchy of elected executive and legislative offices encourages the aspirations to boss-hood of municipal mayors, congressmen, and provincial governors but complicates their efforts through overlapping or cross-cutting jurisdictions, resources, and prerogatives. In addition to the separation and division of state powers, the diffusion of economic resources may also impede would-be bosses from accumulating empires and constructing machines in many localities. Hence the intensity of electoral competition and the frequency of office turnover in many municipalities, congressional districts, and provinces in the archipelago. Yet some mayors, congressmen, and governors do succeed in entrenching them-selves as bosses. In some cases, gangster-style bosses have constructed local empires and machines that have endured for decades, but, relying heavily upon violence and state powers, they have proven unable to pass on their mantle to their children. In other cases, by contrast, a dynastic form of bossism has prevailed, one somewhat more paternalistic in style and more solidly based in proprietary wealth and brokerage services to other wealthy local families.

This chapter draws on case studies of small-town, district-level, and provincial bosses in two provinces, Cavite and Cebu, in order to establish broader patterns of continuity and change in local politics in the Philippines in the post-Marcos era. In the first instance, Cavite provides a fine example of state-based, *mafia*-style, single-generation bossism, as small-town gangster-politicians and provincial 'warlords' have held power for decades at a time in Cavite but failed to accumulate stable bases in proprietary wealth or to pass on their empires to successive generations. In the second instance, Cebu provides a contrasting case of capital-intensive, paternalistic, dynastic bossism, as small-town, district-level, and city-based élite families have achieved sustained dynastic rule through a combination of proprietary wealth, state resources, and provision of brokerage services to other members of the local oligarchy.

Since the mid-1980s, moreover, both provinces have experienced rapid and dramatic processes of urban and suburban industrialisation and economic growth. In the case of Cavite, the explosive growth of Manila and the establishment of the Cavite Export Processing Zone as well as major tourist resorts in the province during the Marcos period presaged a massive influx of investment into the province from Manila-based magnates and foreign firms. Today the majority of the population is urban and dependent upon employment in industries and services. The highways linking Cavite to Metro Manila are jammed with commuter buses, jeepneys, commercial vans, and cargo-laden trucks. While industrial estates, residential subdivisions, and golf courses have supplanted rice fields and fishponds in more and more Cavite municipalities, agro-business thrives elsewhere in the province. Thousands of hectares planted to coconut, coffee, and sugarcane link Cavite to nearby mills and processing plants, even as pineapples and peanuts, avocados and ornamental flowers tie entrepreneurs in the province to select Manila markets.[4] Meanwhile, the mid-1980s also saw the emergence of Cebu City, long the Central Visayas' main entrepôt, as a booming modern port, now equipped with a 10,000-container yard and handling over 11 million tons of cargo and more than six million passengers in 1988 alone.[5] With the Mactan Export Processing Zone and other industrial estates in Metro Cebu attracting Manila-based magnates and foreign investors, the province's exports, amounting to hundreds of millions of dollars a year, diversified considerably, today including semiconductors, electronic watches, rattan furniture, frozen shrimps, carrageenan, car stereos, cameras and automobile parts.[6]

Tracing the variegated manifestations of bossism in these two provinces since the fall of long-time president Ferdinand E. Marcos (1966–86) and the restoration of regular, competitive elections in the mid-late 1980s, the remainder of this chapter examines the dynamic of change under way in Philippine bossism. Neither the socio-economic trends experienced since the 1980s nor the local remnants of organised popular mobilisation against the Marcos regime have disrupted the overall pattern of local bossism which has endured in Cavite and Cebu. Nor has the Local Government Code of 1991 significantly affected the structure of opportunities for aspirant and entrenched local bosses in these two provinces. Rather, as argued in the pages below, sustained drives towards suburban industrialisation and new patterns of capital accumulation in the two provinces have stimulated discernible shifts in the nature and exercise of local boss power, trends which may be of some relevance elsewhere in the archipelago.

Cavite: gangster-politicians and suburban industrial growth

In the pre-martial law period, small-town politics in Cavite Province was notorious for high levels of election-related fraud and violence, and for the criminal proclivities of municipal mayors and their henchmen. Today, vote-buying, fraud, and violence still decisively shape elections in Cavite. In the January 1988 local elections, for example, the incumbent mayor of one town sent out teams of armed goons whose intimidation of election inspectors and poll watchers facilitated considerable 'irregularities' in the counting of votes. The mayor's bodyguards and policemen also forcibly drove away an opposing candidate's representative to the Municipal Board of Canvassers and were themselves present for the entire canvassing session.[7] In the 1992 elections, the mayor of another town in the province fielded groups of armed supporters who engaged in widespread vote-buying and intimidation, even as he intrigued to fill the municipal board of canvassers with his sympathisers. Town policemen and the mayor's armed body-guards allegedly harassed voters believed to be sympathetic to an opposing candidate.[8] In a third town, the mayor, more widely feared than loved, ran unopposed in 1988, 1992, and 1995, and thus did not have to engage in such crude electoral tactics. Meanwhile, a number of municipal officials in Cavite have in recent years stood accused of murder,[9] and since 1986 five Cavite mayors and at least two municipal councilors have lost their lives to assassins' bullets.[10]

In terms of these mayors' illegal activities, however, the post-Marcos era has seen a pattern of change, as the increasingly closer integration of Cavite with Metro Manila has drawn the province into the orbit of criminal syndicates operating out of the nation's capital. Instead of running their own local rackets, today's local officials in Cavite take their 'cut' from illegal gambling[11] and narcotics smuggling[12] syndicates based in southern areas of Metro Manila (e.g. Pasay City, Las Piñas), big-time fishing magnates from Navotas (Manila's fishing port) engaged in illegal trawling,[13] and illegal recruiters of overseas contract workers (e.g. female 'hostesses, dancers, and entertainers') with headquarters in Makati, the capital's financial district.[14]

Meanwhile, the ongoing transformation of many Cavite towns into suburban clusters of residential subdivisions, golf courses, and industrial estates has greatly increased the rent-seeking opportunities provided by municipal mayors' regulatory control over local economies. Mayors earn percentages from the awarding of building permits,[15] the passage of municipal zoning ordinances, the use of government-owned land, the allocation of public works,[16] the approval of reclamation projects,[17] and, most importantly, the implementation of agrarian reform. By selectively revising municipal land use plans and applying pressure upon municipal agrarian reform offices and tenant-cultivators (i.e. potential agrarian reform beneficiaries) alike, local officials have facilitated the 'conversion' of land to industrial, commercial, or residential use,[18] exploiting a key loophole in the agrarian reform legislation that exempts non-agricultural land from expropriation and redistribution.[19] With such mechanisms of land-use regulation at their disposal, Cavite's municipal mayors have evolved into the province's leading real-estate agents and brokers.

In addition to discretionary powers over land use, the holders of local political offices have enjoyed considerable regulatory powers over nodal aspects of the local economy through the awarding of petty monopoly franchises and concessions. Licences for fishtraps, market stalls,[20] and cockpits, for example, ultimately depend upon the mayor's patronage or percentage,[21] and special municipal ordinances have facilitated punishment of political rivals through taxes on their businesses. Contracts for the construction of roads, bridges, buildings, and other local government facilities have provided ample opportunities for patronage, pilferage, and profit. Favouritism and kickbacks have guided mayors' awarding of contracts, and many municipal officials own construction companies themselves.

In short, the ongoing economic transformation of Cavite has increased the spoils of local office in the province, with brokerage services for the gate-keepers and facilitators of industrialisation and urbanisation providing ample 'rents' for municipal mayors. As billions of pesos of investment have flooded into Cavite, a massive construction boom has over the past two decades lined the pockets of favoured contractors and local officials alike, much as planned reclamation projects promise to do in years to come. Meanwhile, many Cavite mayors have set up their own businesses – savings banks, recruitment agencies, import-export firms, customs brokerages – in Manila.[22] In particular, the large number of Caviteño employees in the Bureau of Customs has encouraged many politicians from the province to participate in what is often described as 'monkey business' at Manila's notoriously corruption-ridden port area.[23]

In this context, some municipal mayors in Cavite have succeeded in entrenching themselves as small-town bosses in the province. In eight of Cavite's twenty-three municipalities, municipal mayors have served three consecutive terms (i.e. from 1988 to the present), and two of these mayors served previously as mayors in 1980–86 before their temporary replacement by 'Officers-in-Charge' (OICs) under Aquino in 1986–88. While three of these towns – Gen. Aguinaldo, Indang, and Magallanes – are remote upland towns, and a fourth may still serve as a coastal smugglers' haven (i.e. Tanza), the remaining four towns are among the most urbanised and industrialised in the province (Dasmariñas, Gen. Alvarez, Imus, and Kawit). The observable pattern so far appears roughly comparable to the pre-martial law period (1946–72), when eight Cavite mayors – Amadeo, Carmona, Cavite City, Imus, Maragondon, Naic, Silang, and Tagaytay City – served for four or more consecutive terms (curiously enough, in different towns from those in the contemporary period). Small-town bossism, it seems, has adapted – and evolved – in the face of urbanisation and industrialisation in the province. But how have individual small-town bosses in Cavite fared over the past decade?

A small-town boss: Cesar Casal of Carmona

The most relevant case is that of Carmona, the municipality with the longest-lasting small-town boss in the province, long-time mayor (1956–79) and provincial board member (1980 to the present) Cesar Casal. Over the years, Casal used his command over the mayor's office and town police force, discretionary powers over the municipality's three hundred-plus hectares of communal lands, and political connections beyond Carmona to acquire large landholdings and to assume a central role in the agricultural economy of the town.

By the 1970s, however, the construction of the South Expressway, whose four lanes cut right through Carmona, had rendered the suburban municipality a choice site for real estate 'development'.[24] In the early 1980s, for example, José Yao Campos, the Marcos front man and pharmaceuticals magnate, bought up millions of pesos worth of property in Carmona for conversion into a golf course and residential subdivision.[25] Following the ouster of President Marcos in 1986, the Presidential Commission on Good Government (PCGG) sequestered Campos' properties in Carmona and eventually sold them to a Manila-based real-estate firm, the Fil-Estate Realty Corporation. Fil-Estate subsequently began construction in Carmona on the four hundred and thirty hectare Manila South-woods Residential Estates and Golf and Country Club, which by 1993 featured a thirty-six hole Masters and Legends golf course designed by Jack Nicklaus, a residential subdivision, and plans for a commercial centre to be built within the complex. Today Fil-Estate's Manila Southwoods stands as the single largest employer and landowner in the municipality.[26]

In the early 1980s, moreover, at the urging of Cavite Provincial Governor Juanito 'Johnny' Remulla, the Municipality of Carmona redesignated more than one hundred hectares of communal land as the Cavite-Carmona Development Project and sold off plots to various manufacturing concerns for 'industrial development'. The Technology Resource Center (TRC), a government corp-oration under Imelda Marcos' Ministry of Human Settlements, purchased more than fifty hectares for resale or leasing to small- and medium-scale industries. Many of the companies which bought lots were of dubious financial capability and enjoyed close ties to the Marcos family. One company connected to the Enriquez-Panlilio clan, for example, received a six million peso loan from the TRC, as did another company controlled by Governor Remulla's family members and close associates; Marcos crony Ricardo Silverio bought a ten hectare plot. Yet by the late 1980s, Filipino, Japanese, Korean, and Taiwanese companies had invested hundreds of millions of pesos in the Cavite-Carmona Industrial Estate, employing several thousand workers in more than thirty factories. Today, Carmona's once-bucolic landscape stands significantly transformed, with a four-lane highway, a golf course, and an industrial estate as its most visible landmarks.

To a considerable extent, the transformation of Carmona into a suburban 'development' community has eroded Casal's seemingly monolithic control over the town's once largely agricultural economy. Thanks to the South Superexpress-way, many Carmona residents today commute to jobs in Metro Manila and thus support their families outside the realm of Casal's rice and sugar empire in the town. Thanks to the industrial estate and the golf course, moreover, other Carmona residents have found non-agricultural employment in their hometown. Finally, attracted by the profits to be made on Carmona real estate, powerful outsiders like long-time Governor Juanito Remulla (1979–86, 1988–95) and Manila-based real-estate moguls have begun to play active roles in the 'develop-ment' of the municipality.

Faced with these impingements and intrusions upon his fiefdom, Casal has gracefully shifted into semi-retirement while guarding his economic interests in Carmona. In 1979, anticipating the first local elections held since martial law, Casal agreed to step down as municipal mayor in favour of a Remulla-backed candidate and in exchange for inclusion on the Governor's slate for provincial board.[27] In 1980, 1988, 1992, and 1995, Casal won election to the provincial board on the Remulla ticket, while the *engkargado* (overseer) of his sugar plantation secured the vice-mayorship of Carmona.[28]

Considering Casal's options and his advanced age, this form of semi-retirement has distinct advantages for Carmona's former long-time mayor. Born in 1914, Casal is now more than eighty years old and better suited for a back-bench seat on the provincial board rather than for the high-profile mayorship of a busy town. As provincial board member, he has maintained a consistently low profile, avoiding implication in the various controversies which have accompanied Carmona's 'development' over the past decade. When residents protested the sale of Carmona's communal land by building homes on the parcels in question and filing suit against the mayor and the governor,[29] Casal was noticeably silent. When armed goons burned down the homes of these 'squatters' and killed a leading plaintiff in the lawsuit, he remained similarly aloof. In local gossip about the assassination of Mayor Felino Maquinay in 1990, rumours about the 'disappearance' of a local labour activist, and protests against the planned relocation of a Manila dumpsite in Carmona,[30] Casal's name has almost never cropped up. With his *engkargado* as Carmona Vice-Mayor and his own seat on the Cavite Provincial Board, however, Casal has retained a significant measure of influence over local affairs in the municipality.

In effect, Casal's continued involvement in politics serves as a kind of insurance policy for his properties in Carmona. In theory, his extensive landholdings are subject to redistribution as per the Comprehensive Agrarian Reform of 1988, but provincial land use plans and municipal zoning ordinances have conveniently designated his lands as non-agricultural, a ruse that exploits a key loophole in the legislation and effectively exempts the land from land reform coverage. In fact, Casal has sold off some of his properties to the Manila Southwoods (and reportedly bought up condominiums in Quezon City) and may continue to do so as real-estate prices in Carmona rise even higher, but in the meantime his sugarcane plantation remains decidedly agricultural. If Casal were to lose his political clout, however, local Agrarian Reform officials might some day take a more active interest in his extensive properties in Carmona. Thus, just as Casal succeeded in gaining title in the 1950s to landed estates in Carmona expropriated under agrarian reform legislation, today there is considerable (political) uncertainty surrounding the future of his properties. Childless and lacking a political heir apparent (e.g. a favoured niece or nephew), Casal will not be able to protect the security of his estate beyond his lifetime. Upon his death, lawsuits by various claimants to his properties will be more likely to prosper, and the Department of Agrarian Reform may finally take an interest in his considerable landholdings. In short, the transformation of Carmona into a town for golfers, middle-class suburbanites, and industrial estates has neither fatally disrupted Casal's boss rule nor provided him with sufficient resources or opportunities for the establishment of a small-town dynasty. Casal's eventual passing will bear witness to both the continuing possibilities and the enduring limitations of boss rule in Cavite in the era of the province's industrialisation.

A provincial boss: Johnny Remulla of Cavite

Whilst the longevity of small-town bosses in Cavite has varied from municipality to municipality, a distinctive pattern has structured politics in Cavite at the provincial level: a single boss has dominated the province for decades, subordinating town mayors and other local *liders* (vote brokers) to his rule through coercive pressures, seizing control over what might be called the 'commanding heights' of the province's economy, but failing to withstand the hostile intervention of national-level political enemies or to pass on this political and economic pre-eminence to his progeny in 'dynastic' form. Thus revolutionary *caudillo* (strongman) Emilio Aguinaldo sustained a province-wide machine from the onset of American colonial rule to the beginning of the Commonwealth (1901–35), and perennial congressman Justiniano Montano dominated Cavite politics up to the declaration of martial law (1935–72). In recent years, long-time Cavite governor Juanito R. ('Johnny') Remulla (1979–86, 1988–95) has followed in the footsteps of these two earlier 'provincial warlords'.

Remulla's tenure as Cavite Governor clearly entailed as much ruthlessness as his 'warlord' predecessor Montano, as exemplified by his use of violence in elections. In May 1984, for example, Remulla's goons reportedly harassed school-teachers and opposition leaders in the weeks preceding the elections to the Batasang Pambansa (National Assembly), whilst on election day his armed body-guards drove away election observers and opposition representatives from the Provincial Capitol where the election results were canvassed. Scattered election-day reports from various parts of the province detailed massive vote-buying, ballot-stuffing, missing election returns, disenfranchisement through intimidation.[31] When the votes were tabulated, close Remulla associates had won seats in the Assembly. In the February 1986 'snap' presidential elections, Remulla's armed bodyguards once again drove opposition representatives and NAMFREL (the National Citizens Movement for Free Elections) volunteers from the provincial capitol building where the votes for Cavite were canvassed. Reports from around the province spoke of massive vote-buying, flying voters, harassment of opposition and NAMFREL observers by armed goons, policemen, and military officials, and the release of prisoners from Cavite jails on 'special furlough'. Complaints of missing ballot boxes, election returns prepared in advance by local officials, and systematic disenfranchisement were legion.[32] According to NAMFREL's subsequent report:

> In Cavite, armed goons, local officials together with other KBL partisans harassed NAMFREL volunteers all over the province. The NAMFREL was denied entry in 164 precincts and KBL partisans roamed around poll pre-cincts intimidating voters, NAMFREL volunteers, and opposition workers. Flying voters were prolific and vote buying was massive. There were suspicions concerning fake ballots, especially in Trece Martires City. Tampering of election returns may have been rampant, as all election returns had erasures while some did not bear the total number of votes in words and

figures as required. Ghost precincts may have been used as reinforcement as shown by the more than 100 per cent coverage by the Batasan count.[33]

When the votes were published, Remulla's machine had delivered over 240,000 votes for Marcos, handing him an 80,000 margin of victory in a region (Southern Tagalog) which Aquino otherwise carried.

In subsequent elections, Remulla refrained from using such crude tactics, in large part because they were unnecessary. He won election three times to the governorship – 1980, 1988, and 1992 – by margins of over 100,000 votes. In these three contests, the disbursement of enormous sums for vote-buying (enforced with threats of violence), the support of numerous local elected and appointed government officials, and the favourable bloc-voting of the Iglesia Ni Cristo[34] guaranteed Remulla's victory without excessive bloodshed. Yet the threat of violence clearly played a crucial role in the enforcement of vote-buying arrangements and the overall maintenance of the Remulla machine.[35] Five mayors who antagonised Remulla lost their lives to assassins' bullets in the late 1980s and early 1990s.[36]

Once installed in the governorship in 1979, Remulla began to construct a considerable political machine in Cavite. With close allies in the national legislature and in various government agencies, Remulla enjoyed broad discretion over the assignment of officials and distribution of public works in Cavite, as well as the ability to facilitate business for his followers in Manila. For example, Renato Dragon, Remulla's fraternity brother and close associate, who has served as Assemblyman (1984–86) and three-term Congressman from Cavite's Second District (1987–98) in the House of Representatives, has essentially used his seat in the national legislature to advance various business interests inside and outside the province: a controversial savings bank,[37] a recruitment agency for overseas contract workers, various real estate ventures, and a logging concession in Mindanao.[38] To deliver votes to Dragon and other protégés, Remulla had at his disposal generous campaign financing from interested Manila-based *jueteng* operators, construction companies, factory owners, and politicians.[39] In the local elections of 1980, 1988, and 1992, only a handful of Remulla's candidates for mayor failed to win.[40] With his protégés filling municipal positions in various towns, the provincial board, and Cavite's three seats in Congress, by the early 1990s the Governor's political machine appeared even more solid than those of his two predecessors.

Following the downfall of Marcos in 1986 and his reelection to the Cavite governorship in 1988, Remulla established himself as the 'godfather' of the province's industrial revolution through the consistent application of strongarm tactics. In numerous documented cases, he dispatched armed goons, ordered the bulldozing of homes, and engineered the destruction of irrigation canals, so as to expedite the departure of 'squatters' and tenant farmers demanding compensation for their removal from lands designated for sale to Manila-based or foreign companies for 'development' into industrial estates.[41] Though Remulla typically tempered such hardball tactics with offers for a 'settlement', the 'carrot' was never as impressive as the 'stick'. As one peasant leader noted:

If your Barangay Captain, the police, your mayor, your governor make you a request, and if you have not yet acceded to the request, you can expect that next if your carabao does not disappear, or your tools, then maybe you will next disappear yourself; if you don't wind up among the unsolved cases, then for sure you will be ambushed. There's a lot of that here in Cavite but it mostly doesn't come out in the newspapers.[42]

Despite widespread dissatisfaction, Remulla – through municipal and provincial board resolutions and personal lobbying with various government agencies – pushed through the conversion to industrial/residential use of massive tracts of land in Cavite so as to facilitate exemption from agrarian reform.[43] In various Municipal Agrarian Reform Offices in Cavite, log books testify to frequent visits by one of Remulla's sons, and files bulge with local officials' recommendations in favour of land conversion. In Dasmariñas, for example, the Municipal Agrarian Reform Officer processed applications for the conversion of over 2,300 hectares from March 1988 to July 1992.[44] By all estimates, Cavite in the early 1990s became the leading province in land conversion, and Remulla deserved much of the 'credit'.[45] Indeed, various knowledgeable sources in the province estimate that the Governor received a 'fee' of ten pesos for every square metre of land converted to industrial use.

Finally, Remulla evolved into an effective enforcer of the province's semi-official but as yet unchallenged designation as a 'no-strike zone'. A large percentage of jobs in various Cavite-based manufacturing establishments have in practice been 'reserved' for members of the Iglesia Ni Cristo, a church with close ties to Remulla and strictly enforced rules against its followers' entry into labour unions. In general, factories in Cavite have required prospective employees to provide letters of recommendation from the town mayor or the governor attesting to their reliability. Moreover, the Industrial Security Action Group (ISAG), a special police unit directly responsible to the Governor, has made its presence felt at various industrial estates throughout the province. Finally, persistent rumours and stories about the 'salvaging' and 'disappearance' of would-be Cavite labour leaders discouraged even the most powerful labour union federations in the country from attempting to organise workers in the province of 'industrial peace and productivity'.[46] Overall, Remulla's 'industrial relations policies' made Cavite a particularly attractive site for investors, while allowing his political machine to keep pace with the province's ongoing industrialisation.[47] According to some sources, Remulla received millions of pesos a year from factory owners in the province in exchange for his assistance in the suppression of labour unions and strikes.[48]

While servicing big businesses' expanding interests in Cavite, Remulla, like his predecessors, attempted to shore up his position as provincial 'warlord' by amassing proprietary wealth commensurate with his political position. Indeed, the juiciest construction contracts in Cavite were supposedly reserved for companies in which the Governor had a 'special' interest.[49] Moreover, like his predecessors as provincial boss, Remulla had by the 1980s become by far the biggest landowner in Cavite, thanks to the multi-million-peso behest loans he received from various government financial institutions in the Marcos era, the pressures he brought to bear upon landowners reluctant to sell and tenants slow to vacate properties he coveted, and the success he enjoyed in delaying the implementation of agrarian reform on land under his name or those of his dummies.[50] All told, Remulla came to own over one thousand hectares of prime land in various parts of Cavite. The value of his properties shot up dramatically over the years, thanks to Cavite's real estate boom and Remulla's discretionary allocation of new roads and electricity and irrigation facilities.[51] Thus, while depositing various kickbacks, protection payments, and purloined government funds[52] into the war chest of his political machine, Remulla tried to establish a permanent economic base in the province independent of his grip on the state apparatus.

Yet Remulla was destined to go the way of his predecessors, as the results of the 1995 local elections made clear. For while Remulla established close links with major power brokers in the Aquino administration (most notably Jose 'Peping' Cojuangco, Jr, the president's brother) soon after Marcos' downfall, he failed to reach a similar accommodation with her successor, president Fidel Ramos. Indeed, while Remulla won reelection to the governorship in 1992 by an enormous margin and 'carried' numerous protégés into local offices throughout the province, he erred in judging the likely outcome of the presidential contest. Initially throwing his support behind Ramon 'Monching' Mitra, Jr, Remulla ended up hedging his bets, dividing up his machine's Cavite vote between Mitra and rival Eduardo 'Danding' Cojuangco, Jr. After the election, both losing presidential candidates expressed their displeasure with Remulla's 'betrayal' in classic *mafioso* style, sending miniature coffins as gifts on his birthday.[53]

Against this backdrop, the 1995 elections saw the culmination of a determined effort by President Ramos to dislodge Remulla from the governorship of Cavite. Cesar Sarino, a key player in the Ramos' presidential campaign in Cavite,[54] used his position as Chairman of the Government Service Insurance System (GSIS), a notorious milking cow, to amass a substantial anti-Remulla war chest. The owner of the rural bank in Silang, a construction contractor from Kawit, the mayors of Naic, Rosario, and Bacoor, and the Representative of Cavite's Third District in Congress played complementary roles in an evolving anti-Remulla conspiracy. The prominent Campos clan of Dasmariñas was likewise represented in the Department of Defense and the Supreme Court. Early on in the Ramos Administration, moves were already under way by this cabal to install a sympathetic Provincial Police Superintendent, a like-minded Provincial Fiscal, and a set of pliable Regional Trial Court judges in Cavite. Selective 'crackdowns', contracts, and Customs assignments followed shortly thereafter. Moreover, Remulla's properties, previously released from government sequestration through Peping Cojuangco's intercession, were once again placed in the hands of the Presidential Commission On Good Government (PCGG).

By the eve of the May 1995 local elections, Ramos and his allies in Cavite had already recruited key former Remulla backers to help demolish his province-wide machine. Former National Bureau of Investigation (NBI) Director Epimaco Velasco, a native of Tanza, Cavite, was drafted as the Administration's candidate for Governor, while Senator Ramon Revilla, Caviteño action film star and chairman of the powerful Senate Committee on Public Works, fielded his *artista* son 'Bong' as vice-governor on a Ramos-backed slate against Revilla's old cock-fighting chum 'Johnny'. With numerous Cavite town mayors and other key local *liders* around Cavite pressured into switching their loyalties, and generous supplies of money and PNP troops sent from Manila to neutralise the incumbent's monetary and coercive inducements, Velasco beat Remulla easily, removing from Cavite the previously unbeatable 'machine' that had ruled the province since the late 1970s.[55]

Looking back on the shifting pattern of local bossism in Cavite over the past two decades, two interrelated trends are apparent. First of all, the massive inflow of capital into the province has encouraged municipal and provincial officials alike to abandon efforts to achieve and/or maintain economic preeminence through the accumulation of a preponderance of proprietary wealth within their bailiwicks. Instead, aspiring and entrenched bosses in the province have shifted to a strategy of service as brokers, facilitators, and gate-keepers for Manila-based magnates and foreign firms investing in Cavite, using their discretionary powers over government regulations, contracts, concessions, and franchises as the basis for rent-seeking activities, most notably in the realms of real-estate and construction. More than any clear change in the use of coercive, clientelist, and monetary resources and pressures in elections, the shift into a new pattern of capital accumulation – and the subordination of local bosses to national and international capital – is most striking. Second, whilst rapid and dramatic socio-economic change in Cavite has not yet undermined the political machines of municipal and provincial bosses in the province, neither has it enhanced their capacity to withstand supra-local challenges to their rule and to pass on their local empires to successive generations in classic dynasty fashion. The pages below, by contrast, reveal the enduring strength of dynastic bossism in Cebu Province in the era of rapid industrialisation.

Cebu: small-town, district, and provincial dynasties in 'Ceboom'

Whilst small-town electoral politics in Cebu has never been as bloody as in Cavite, vote-buying and fraud (backed up by intimidation and occasional violence) clearly retain an important role in elections in the province, as suggested in the following allegations of 'massive fraud and irregularities' in the 1992 election in the municipality of Ginatilan:

> The ballot boxes were stuffed with manufactured and/or fake ballots…. The ballot boxes were opened by members of the Board of Election Inspectors even after they had been closed and sealed…. There was massive vote buying and intimidation of voters to coerce them to vote for certain candidates…. Votes for the petitioner/ protestant were not counted in his favor. In certain precincts petitioner/protestant's watchers were not allowed to observe the

proceedings of the Board of Election Inspectors…. Election returns were 'doctored' or tampered with to favor the respondent/protestee…. Members of the Board of Canvassers who were highly partisan in favor of respondent/ protestee manipulated the canvass of election returns to favor the respondent/ protestee.[56]

Similarly, while the involvement of Cebu's municipal mayors in illegal rackets has never been as flagrant as in Cavite, their criminal activities do not appear to have declined in recent years. In 1990, for example, the killing of a Constabulary informer brought to light the smuggling network of one municipal mayor in a town located on Cebu's southeast coast.[57] In addition to smuggling, Cebu town mayors' control over municipal police forces has allowed them to engage in selective and extortionary enforcement of laws prohibiting dynamite fishing in their municipal waters. Mayoral involvement in illegal fishing has assumed various forms: imposition of 'protection' payments on local fishermen,[58] intercession on behalf of fishermen apprehended for illegal fishing,[59] and connivance in the marketing of explosive materials used in so-called 'blast-fishing'.[60] In more than a dozen Cebu towns where fishing constitutes a mainstay of the local economy, the use of dynamite by fishermen is a daily occurrence[61] and is estimated to have destroyed eight-six per cent (86 per cent) of the province's original coral reefs.[62]

In addition, Cebu town mayors' discretion over mining[63] and quarry concessions within their municipalities has further strengthened their hold over the local economy, as illustrated in one case in which a town mayor awarded his own brother a permit for the quarrying of sand and gravel in a river in the municipality. While the mayor's brother raked in hundreds of thousands of pesos by selling off the sand and gravel to a local construction company contracted by the provincial government to pave a road through the town, local farmers found their irrigation facilities and farm lands disrupted by the excavation.[64] Moreover, mayoral authority to award (and to terminate) monopoly franchises for ice plants, gasoline stations, and cockpits has provided municipal executives yet another mechanism for control over the local economy.[65] In particular, Cebu's cock-fighting arenas – the least capital-intensive and most lucrative monopoly franchises awarded by municipalities – have served as focal points for small-town political battles and as prizes for the winners of mayoral elections and their local allies.[66] Finally, since the 1980s, the construction of golf courses, residential subdivisions, and industrial estates in the municipalities immediately north and south of Cebu City has, in a pattern reminiscent of Cavite, allowed a number of Cebu's town mayors to regulate and profit from 'real-estate development' through selective dispensing of building permits, passage of municipal zoning ordinances, approval of reclamation projects, and use of government-owned land.

Overall, compared to Cavite, most municipalities in Cebu have been less dramatically, or at least less obviously, transformed by industrial growth and urbanisation. While new opportunities for non-agricultural employment have increased markedly in Metro Cebu since the mid-1980s, new patterns of capital accumulation for local élites families and municipal officials in the small towns of the province have been less discernible. 'Ceboom' has led to a proliferation of real-estate, tourism, handicraft, and tourism ventures in many towns, but without such a Cavite-style shift of control over the 'commanding heights' of local econ-omies into the hands of Manila-based and/or foreign investors. Meanwhile, the success of local élite families in sustaining small-town political machines in Cebu appears to have only slightly diminished during this period of rapid economic growth in the province. Of Cebu's fifty-two municipalities, twenty-three feature mayors who have served three consecutive terms in office since 1988, compared with thirty municipalities with four-term mayors in the pre-martial law period (1946–72). As argued in the pages below, this subtle trend towards greater turn-over in municipal politics in Cebu may reflect a shift towards somewhat greater concentration of power among the province's congressional district- and provincial-level dynasties. First, however, the combination of continuity and change in small-town bossism in Cebu is further explored with regard to the single longest-running dynasty in the province, the Escarios of Bantayan.

A small-town dynasty: the Escarios of Bantayan

Bantayan, a coconut, corn, fishing, and poultry town situated on the island of the same name off the northwest coast of Cebu, is not only one of the most remote municipalities, but also the one with the most enduring dynasty, in the entire province. Since 1937, the Escario family has enjoyed protracted rule over Bantayan, first with patriarch Isidro as mayor (1937–59), followed by his widow Remedios (1959–67), and eventually their son Jesus (1967–86). Following a brief hiatus under an Aquino-appointed 'officer-in-charge' in 1986–88, the family resumed its control over the town, with the mayorship first claimed by son Rex (1988–92), and then reverted to the hands of his aging mother Remedios (1992 to the present), accompanied by daughter Geralyn Escario Cañares as the town's vice-mayor (1992 to the present). While the Escarios have long sponsored illegal rackets and engaged in election-related violence in the town, they have also maintained a reputation as generous patrons and providers to the poor and downtrodden folk of Bantayan, with Mayor 'Ma Mediong' especially beloved for her maternalist streak. Moreover, while the family has used state office and political connections to advance their business interests, they have also shared control over the 'commanding heights' of the Bantayan economy with relatives and allied families in the town.

Well established from the early days of Isidro's rule before World War II, these patterns have persisted to the present day. In the late 1980s and early 1990s, for example, the Escarios have continued to combine their cultivation of clientelist networks of supporters with hardball tactics to win elections, as illustrated by an incident in early 1988 in which Rex Escario and five armed companions barged into the home of an opposition sympathiser (the son of a barangay captain) one night, beat him up, and nearly shot him dead with an M-16.[67] In the midst of the attack, the future mayor of Bantayan is said to have vented his rage against the unreliability of his family's supposed 'clients':

What offences have the Escarios committed that you can say that the Escarios are thieves and hustlers, when you don't even pay rent for your shed on the land we administrate?[68]

After the May 1992 elections, among the most closely contested in the postwar history of Bantayan, opponents claimed that Remedios Escario had won the mayorship through the introduction in many precincts of fake ballots by sympathetic (and/or paid-off) schoolteachers serving as election inspectors, backed up by a campaign of harassment and intimidation perpetrated in part by some eighty 'goons' imported from the nearby provinces of Negros Occidental and Masbate.[69] Members of the Escario family have also been involved in illegal activities in Bantayan and elsewhere in the province, as illustrated by the indictment of Rex Escario (Isidro's son and Bantayan Mayor, 1988–92) for his role in a 1990 bank robbery in Mandaue City.[70]

As for control over Bantayan's economy, the Escario clan has retained its position as *primus inter pares* among the town's élite families. With the Escarios' private port servicing boats laden with San Miguel beer and Coca-Cola twice weekly, the family, according to the records of the Philippine Ports Authority (PPA), earned over three million pesos in *arrastre* (stevedoring) fees in 1991 alone.[71] At the public port in the *poblacion* of Bantayan, meanwhile, the family of Isidro Escario's brother Epifanio holds the lucrative *arrastre* contract, earning hundreds of thousands of pesos in annual fees while, according to PPA officials, pocketing deductions from their poorly paid workers' salaries supposedly handed over to the government Social Security System. In addition, the Escarios engineered the passage of a municipal ordinance in the late 1980s which prohibited the ferry linking Bantayan with nearby Cadiz, Negros Occidental from docking at the pier, ostensibly a precautionary measure taken to avert the dangers to the vessels posed by low tides along Bantayan's shore. Instead, the daily ferry – which services a lively trade in eggs and chicken dung as well as a steady flow of human traffic – was forced to anchor a few hundred meters away from the pier, leaving ferry passengers and cargo alike at the mercy of an Escario-operated dock-to-ferry shuttle service which charged exorbitant rates.[72] Escario cousins have held the franchises to operate the sole ice plant and *sabongan* (cockfighting arena) in Bantayan, in-laws have maintained the only theatre in the town, and the closely allied Mercado clan has operated the sole bus company on the island. However, while the Escarios have also played prominent roles in both the fishing industry and copra trade over the years, they have not achieved commercial monopolies or monopsonies *vis-à-vis* the other owners of large coconut groves and fishing boats in the town. The family has refrained from assuming a role in Bantayan's rural bank or in the electric cooeprative that distributes electricity to the three municipalities of Bantayan island.

Against this backdrop, the Escarios have not seriously impeded Bantayan's local élite families from availing of the new opportunities for profit provided by 'Ceboom'. Encouraged by the extremely hot and arid climate and the low costs of sand and fishmeat on the island, local élite families have begun to invest heavily in poultry farms, which today supply the three Visayan metropoles of Bacolod

City, Ilolio City, and Cebu City with millions of eggs and thousands of bags of chicken dung.[73] While roughly a third of these products are exported via the Escario's private port in Baigad, the bulk of this brisk trade has flowed out through the public ports of Bantayan and Santa Fe, bringing massive profits and commercial linkages to the town's poultry farmers that weaken their dependence upon the Escarios.[74] The rich fishing beds off the coast of Bantayan, moreover, have provided an enormous source of wealth for families owning large fishing vessels (*kubkub* and *basnigan*)[75] and have led to the establishment in the late 1980s of a crab meat processing plant in the town by an American company which buys fresh crabs directly from local fishermen.[76] Similarly, Bantayan island's beautiful white-sand beaches have begun to attract tourists, and a newly constructed small airport in neighbouring Santa Fe may soon service resorts owned by local families (e.g. the decidedly anti-Escario Hubahib/Ybañez clan) with connections to travel agencies and Philippine Tourism Authority offices in Cebu City. Finally, the close connections between Bantayan and Cebu City have allowed members of wealthy families in the town to strike their fortunes in construction, port services, and real estate in the province's booming urban centre or to rise to prominent positions (e.g. a Regional Trial Court judgeship) in the government, even as less fortunate Bantayanons head off to work as factory labourers, itinerant peddlers, domestic servants, construction workers, and seamen in Cebu City, Manila, and such distant destinations as Hong Kong and Saudi Arabia.

All these developments can be seen to work – however gradually and subtly – to undermine the Escario family's once more monolithic control over the 'commanding heights' of the Bantayan economy. Nonetheless, the Escarios remain the masters of Bantayan for the foreseeable future. Through bonds of affinity, consanguinity, and fictive kinship, the family is still central to all political alliances among the town's most prominent families. Through years of control over the mayor's office and key nodal aspects of the economy, moreover, the Escarios retain significant regulatory and proprietary powers in local commerce. Finally, through linkages with powerful patrons in Congress and in the Provincial Capitol, and with a sizeable following of dependants in Bantayan, the clan possesses distinctive advantages over potential political rivals. Although Isidro is dead, his widow Remedios is ailing, and two Escario sons have excused themselves from politics, their daughter – Geralyn Escario Cañares – served as acting mayor for much of the 1990s, and various nephews and cousins are no doubt waiting in the wings to follow in her footsteps. Thus, unlike long-time mayor Cesar Casal of Carmona, Cavite, the Escarios of Bantayan have succeeded in constructing a small-town empire of *dynastic* proportions that has endured for nearly sixty years and, in the face of dramatic economic change, promises to outlive, in some form, its original progenitors.

A district-level dynasty: the Duranos of Danao City

If the Escarios illustrate a pattern of enduring dynastic bossism in Cebu's municipalities, several of the province's eight congressmen exemplify the prevalence of *district-level* boss entrenchment against the backdrop of 'Ceboom'. Of Cebu's eight seats in the House of Representatives, five have been held for three consecutive terms – 1987–92, 1992–95, and 1995–98 – by the same congressmen: Crisologo Abines (2nd District), Celestino E. Martinez, Jr (4th District), Ramon Durano III (5th District), Antonio Cuenco and Raul Del Mar in the two districts representing Cebu City. Four of these five congressmen ran unopposed in 1995, while the fifth (Crisologo Abines) beat his closest opponent by 50,000 votes. In the 3rd District, Pablo Garcia served for two terms and then helped former senator John Osmeña win the seat by a huge 85,000-vote margin in exchange for support in his own gubernatorial bid. This pattern of entrenchment in Cebu's congressional seats compares favorably to the pattern observed in the province in the pre-martial law period, when only four districts saw multiple-term congressmen or dynastic incumbency (Ramon Durano, Sr, 1st District, seven terms; Kintanar family, 4th District, six terms; Cuenco clan, 5th District, five terms, Manuel Zosa, 6th District, four terms).

Of all Cebu's three-term congressmen, today, Ramon Durano III of the 5th District offers the best example of dynastic success in adapting to the new circumstances of the past ten years. Since 1949, seven-term Cebu congressman Ramon Durano Sr had built up his family's empire in Danao City through government behest loans and contracts and the use of elected office (won through notoriously violent and fraudulent means) to promote landgrabbing and various illegal activities.[77] With the overthrow of long-time president Ferdinand Marcos in 1986, the Durano family lost a major source of patronage and protection in Manila, and the arrival of a new – and seemingly hostile – administration threatened to undermine the clan's hold over its bailiwick. Meanwhile, with the death – in testate – of family patriarch Ramon Sr in 1988, the Durano clan appeared poised to dissolve in a dispute over his estate, as suggested by a well-publicised gunfight between two Durano sons.

Yet anointed successor Ramon Durano III succeeded first in reaching a political settlement with the new administration in Manila and then in crafting a family strategy to adjust to the economic problems – and opportunities – of the new era. With Durano joining the new president's political party and winning a congressional seat on the administration's ticket, the family succeeded in salvaging its economic empire, avoiding sequestration of Durano properties by the Presidential Commission on Good Government and retaining ownership of the Durano Sugar Mills. Meanwhile, after the Duranos relinquished control over the heavily indebted Universal Cement Company to government banks in 1986, scions of the prominent Manila-based Araneta and Zobel de Ayala clans teamed up to buy Universal Cement from the Asset Privatisation Trust and reopened the cement plant in Danao City in late 1991.[78] Noting the Durano family's prominence in the town and ownership of the land housing the cement plant, the Aranetas and Ayalas took care to include the Duranos as partners and placed three members of the clan on the new company's seven-member board, including Beatriz Durano, Ramon Sr's widow, as the chair.[79] Moreover, providing plots of land, assurances of 'labour peace', and assistance in securing special tax and tariff 'incentives', the Duranos coaxed the Mitsumi Electric Company of Japan to set up a factory in Danao City in 1988.[80] Today, the Mitsumi plant employs more than three thousand residents of Danao City and neighbouring towns[81] and, together with the Durano Sugar Mills and the reopened cement plant, establishes the Duranos as key partners in Danao's industrial mini-boom.

By 1992, Ramon Durano Sr's favourite son, Congressman Ramon 'Nito' Durano III, had asserted his position as the new family patriarch and consolidated his hold over the 5th Congressional District of Cebu. While, in the absence of a will, the estate of Ramon Durano Sr fell into the hands of his widow,[82] the old man had already transferred control over the sugar mill, titles to numerous properties,[83] and most other valuable assets to Nito before his death in 1988.[84] Though Durano family squabbles may persist,[85] Congressman Nito Durano's supremacy remains beyond dispute. In the 1992 and 1995 elections, with his feuding brothers Jesus ('Don') and Thaddeus ('Deo') winning reelection to the mayorships of Danao City and Sogod respectively, Congressman Durano recaptured the 5th District congressional seat easily, winning by a margin of more than 73,000 votes over his closest rival in 1992 and running unopposed in 1995. With an iron-clad grip over the 5th District, the Durano family has also been able to deliver sizeable margins to favoured candidates for the provincial governorship and the presidency, thus securing ample patronage and protection for the family's empire in Cebu City and Manila.

Meanwhile, in Cebu City, the provincial capitol and the Central Visayas' regional entrepôt, a third generation of the Osmeña family has entrenched itself as Cebu's provincial dynasty. Tomas Osmeña ('Tommy') won two successive terms as Cebu City Mayor (1988–95), while Emilio 'Lito' Osmeña, Jr and John 'Sonny' Osmeña serving as Cebu Provincial Governor (1988–92) and Senator (1988–95) and 3rd District congressman (1995–98), respectively. The family's latest representative on the national political scene, Lito Osmeña, lost a 1992 bid for the vice-presidency of the Republic but, as the former running mate of incumbent president Fidel Ramos, today enjoys considerable access to Malacañang and discretion over the flow of national state patronage to Cebu. With close Osmeña allies installed as Cebu City Mayor and Cebu Provincial Governor, and Tommy's brother Serge occupying a Senate seat since 1995, the family is arguably more powerful than ever, no longer facing serious contenders to its provincial supremacy in Cebu.

Like previous generations of the family dynasty, the current crop of Osmeñas has constructed a political machine based on a combination of state resources and brokerage services to a close-knit local oligarchy of Cebu-based magnates. Despite the expansion of civil service eligibility to more government employees, the passage in 1991 of a new Local Government Code reaffirmed the Cebu City Mayor's control over the urban centre's huge bureaucracy.[86] Thus the Osmeñas' hold over the agencies of the local state apparatus through the Mayor's Office has allowed the family to exercise considerable regulatory powers over the economy of Cebu City. Osmeña influence over the Cebu City Police Department and the City Fiscal's Office has also permitted highly selective enforcement of the law in the metropolis.[87] Clearly, political and pecuniary considerations have often likewise governed the awarding of licences for street vendors and stalls in the public market by a division of the bloated Office of the Mayor.[88] Meanwhile, the Osmeñista City Council has used its manifold prerogatives – in levying taxes, granting business permits, special licences, public works contracts, and monopoly franchises, and enacting ordinances – to wield power over all realms of the local economy. Finally, through the Municipal Board and the Board of Assessment Appeals, as well as the Office of the City Assessor, the Osmeña-controlled City Hall has retained the authority to review and revise business and property tax assessments in accordance with political and economic considerations.[89]

Once entrenched in City Hall, the Osmeñas have used their extensive powers over the local state apparatus to mobilise an elaborate political machine that has mustered majorities for the family and its candidates in local, congressional, and national elections. With thousands of ward *liders*, henchmen, and assorted hangers-on spread throughout populous Cebu City, the Osmeñas have thus been able to carry elections in the metropolis and to deliver large blocs of votes to national-level allies among the candidates for the national Senate and the presidency. In 1992, Mayor Tommy Osmeña won reelection by a margin of more than one hundred thousand votes, garnering a majority in ninety-five per cent of the City's precincts, sweeping in his Vice-Mayor, the two City congress-men, and fifteen of sixteen Osmeñista City councillors, and delivering an impressive bloc of votes to presidential candidate Fidel V. Ramos. In 1995, similar results were mustered for the Osmeñas' stand-in for Tommy, former vice-mayor and family ally Alvin Garcia. Beyond Cebu City, moreover, the Osmeñas have expanded their electoral influence throughout Cebu Province by using family alliances and discretion over national state patronage to build up a network of small-town notables loyal to the City-based clan.

While access to state resources and control over state office have helped to advance the Osmeñas' own real estate interests and other business ventures, the family has largely served as a broker for Cebu City's commercial élite.[90] A large entourage of political lieutenants, lawyers, contractors, fixers, ward *liders* and assorted hangers-on has always surrounded the Osmeña's leading members, linking local law firms, construction companies, and a host of small businesses to the family's political machine. Moreover, a close-knit local oligarchy – compri-sing a handful of merchant dynasties of Chinese, Spanish and *mestizo* lineage – has operated a cartel of shipping companies and agricultural processing centres in the City that has dominated the copra and corn trade throughout the Visayas and Mindanao and the inter-island shipping industry of the entire archipelago for many decades.[91] Over the years, these dynasties – the Gotiaocos, Chiongbians, Lus, Aboitizes, and Escaños – have consistently supported, socialised and occa-sionally intermarried with the Osmeña clan, while refraining from entering Cebu politics themselves. In exchange, the Osmeñas have provided these dynasties – along with urban real-estate and merchant families like the Aznars, Gaisanos, and Lhuillers – access to government financing and contracts and guaranteed friendly regulation of their business operations.

In the early 1990s, the Osmeñas' willingness and ability to service the business interests of Cebu City's leading merchant dynasties have been apparent in the policies of City Mayor Tommy Osmeña and his cousin, former provincial governor (1988–92) Lito Osmeña. While the Cebu City Assessor's Office has allegedly undervalued the real-estate holdings of Osmeña allies, the provincial government has sold off plots of prime urban land to the Gaisano family and to Michel Lhuiller, one of Lito Osmeña's closest associates.[92] Lhuiller, descendant of a former French consul in Cebu and owner of a nation-wide network of pawnshops and jewellery stores, has also been reported to have sponsored the import of the illegal narcotic methamphetamine hydrochloride ('shabu') through the Cebu Port and the Mactan-Cebu International Airport, reportedly with the active assistance of Bureau of Customs[93] and Philippine National Police officials[94] installed by the Osmeñas.[95] In 1992, moreover, Lito Osmeña engineered the appointment of Cebu-based attorney Jesus Garcia, Jr[96] as Secretary of Transportation and Communications in the Ramos Cabinet.

Garcia had previously served as legal counsel to the Conference of Interisland Shipowners and Operators (CISO), the cartel of mostly Cebu-based shipping lines – including the Aboitiz, Chiongbian, and Escaño companies – whose collusion in setting cargo and passenger rates,[97] oligopolistic practices in sharing and dividing inter-island routes,[98] violations of safety and other regulations,[99] and successes in obtaining tax and tariff exemptions[100] came under mounting criticism in the late 1980s and early 1990s.[101] As Transportation Secretary in the first few years of the Ramos Administration, moreover, Garcia served as Chairman of the newly created, autonomous, and powerful Cebu Port Authority[102] and the Mactan-Cebu International Airport Authority.[103] During the same period, moreover, legislation for the deregulation of the inter-island shipping industry in the archipelago was passed and implemented, resulting in increased profits and concentration for the Cebu-based cartel.[104]

Over the past ten years, the Osmeñas have also serviced the interests of Manila-based magnates with investments in Cebu. In his term as Provincial Governor of Cebu (1988–92), Lito Osmeña established a close alliance with the Ayala family, whose Makati-based banking, food processing, and real-estate empire teamed up with the Cebu Provincial Government in a major land development deal and bond issue.[105] In this deal, Cebu Province sold three parcels of land in Cebu City totalling 251 hectares for more than seven hundred million pesos to the Cebu Property Ventures and Development Corporation, a joint venture between the Provincial Government of Cebu and the Ayala Land Corporation.[106] A further tie-up has linked the Ayalas' Cebu interests[107] to mining, publishing, and real-estate mogul Alfredo Ramos,[108] the Soriano family, and the Asia-wide empire of Malaysia-born, Hong Kong-based tycoon Robert Kuok.[109] Meanwhile, the Osmeñas have also reportedly intervened on behalf of major Manila-based companies in biddings for two controversial reclamation[110] and construction[111] contracts. As brokers for the Cebuano oligarchy and facilitators for Manila-based and multinational firms, the Osmeñas have made sure that 'Ceboom' has strengthened, rather than undermined, their City-based but province-wide political machine in Cebu.

Conclusion: 'The last hurrah' revisited in the 1990s Philippines

The decade following the overthrow of the Marcos regime has witnessed not a 'last hurrah' but rather a complex mixture of change and continuity in the pattern of bossism observed in Cavite and Cebu. Overall, the essential pre-conditions for bossism's endurance have remained operative in these two provinces – and in most of the Philippines: the subordination of a poorly insulated state apparatus to a multi-tiered set of elected officials; an impoverished, insecure, and economically dependent electorate susceptible to clientelist, coercive, and monetary inducements and pressures; and an economy in which state resources and regulatory mechanisms remain both available for private appropriation by elected officials and central to local capital accumulation. Neither the Local Government Code of 1991 and subsequent decentralisation efforts nor the pattern of sustained economic growth in the Philippines in the 1990s have seriously undermined the institutional and social foundations of boss rule, it appears, even in the most 'advanced' and prosperous provinces of the archipelago, such as Cavite and Cebu.

Rather, the trends observed in the overall pattern of bossism in Cavite and Cebu in recent years, it has been argued, are best understood in terms of the changing relationship between state and capital in the two provinces. Local bosses in many localities have shifted from efforts to gain monopolistic or oligopolistic control over the 'commanding heights' of local economies to services as brokers, facilitators, and gate-keepers for businesses whose headquarters are located in Manila, Taipei, and Tokyo. Elected office no longer seems to promise much in the way of state *resources* – land, loans, jobs – for private appropriation, at least not when compared with those resources in the hands of private commercial banks, real-estate ventures, and manufacturing firms, domestic and foreign. Rather, elected office offers discretion over state *regulation* – in the realms of law enforcement and land usage, and in the awarding of contracts, concessions, franchises, and monopolies – and thus rent-seeking opportunities whose magnitude depends heavily upon the level of capital invested within boundaries of a given elected official's jurisdiction. Hence the efforts of municipal mayors and provincial governors (and competition between them) to offer the most attractive conditions and concessions for investment within their bailiwicks. The structural logic of capitalism, after all, does tend to shift casinos and construction contracts from gangster to corporate hands.

In the changing relationship between state and capital in Cavite and Cebu, certain subtle trends in the pattern of boss rule in the two provinces seem to be in evidence. In Cavite, *mafia*-style, state-based, and single-generation bosses remain capable of entrenching themselves in eight of the province's twenty-three municipalities, and the passing from the scene of long-time Carmona mayor Cesar Casal and provincial governor Johnny Remulla fits into a broader historical pattern of Cavite boss failure to pass on local empires to successive generations or to withstand the hostile intervention of supra-local political enemies. Three elements of potential change are worthy of further exploration. First, small-town bosses, it appears, are successful in entrenching themselves for multiple terms in municipalities once noted for high rates of turnover, while former municipal boss strongholds – such as Carmona with the passing of Casal – now feature much more competitive elections and perhaps a greater diffusion of power among small-town notables exercising influence via municipal councils. Second, Remulla's eclipse raises doubts as to the possibility of (re)constructing a province-wide political machine and economic empire in Cavite, given both the dramatic changes in Cavite landscape in recent years and the post-Marcos creation of three congressional districts in the province (which may favour a more diffused political configuration reminiscent of, say, suburban Bulacan). Third, the transformation of the province's economy over the past ten years highlights the growing influence of Manila-based and foreign firms over the exercise of political power in the province.

As for Cebu, the province's longstanding pattern of dynastic bossism appears to have endured – indeed, flourished – in the face of the much heralded 'Ceboom'. The entrenchment of small-town dynasties is nearly as prevalent as in the pre-martial law era, and the majority of congressional seats, the provincial capitol, and City Hall are firmly controlled by a set of entrenched political clans. As Cebu's dynasties have long used state office to establish solid bases in proprietary wealth for themselves and their kin and to provide brokerage services to allied members of the local oligarchy, the massive inflow of investment into the province from Manila and abroad appears to have reinforced – and, for the moment, frozen – the existing three-tiered pattern of small-town, district-level, and provincial dynastic bossism in Cebu. If anything, it seems, 'Ceboom' has dampened competition for congressional seats, the provincial governorship, and City Hall, and encouraged a tendency towards greater centralisation of political power in the hands of those enjoying the closest contacts with – and controlling the key local commercial choke-points and administrative bottlenecks for – Manila-based and foreign investors in the province. While the diffusion of wealth and power *within* the bailiwicks of given small-town, congressional, and provincial dynasties – as in the case of three-term 4th District congressman Celestino E. Martinez, Jr, who amply services the district's plantation belt élite – deserves closer scrutiny, the only major threat to continuing dynasticism at the provincial level lies in the rising strength of the labour racketeering bosses of the Associated Labor Unions, long entrenched in the port of Cebu, and growing in numbers and political influence with industrialisation.[112]

In the context of these broad patterns of continuity and transformation observed in Cavite and Cebu, the changes ushered in by the Local Government Code of 1991 appear to be virtually negligible, at least when seen against the more powerful forces unleashed by industrialisation in the two provinces. The long years of authoritarian rule under Marcos did not, for various reasons, generate robust and enduring networks of popular opposition in the two provinces, with the organised Left virtually absent in Cavite and easily crushed in Cebu in the 1980s. Thus the forces which have used the Local Government Code for the empowerment of the dispossessed elsewhere in the Philippines since 1991 have remained considerably weaker in the face of entrenched bossism in these two provinces. All the more reason to examine Cavite and Cebu more closely in upcoming years, and to provide greater support to those beleaguered forces working to challenge the various manifestations of bossism in these two provinces.[113]

Notes

1 Edwin O'Connor, *The Last Hurrah* (New York: Bantam Books, 1956).
2 Jack Beatty, *The Rascal King: The Life and Times of James Michael Curley 1874–1958* (Reading, Massachusetts: Addison-Wesley Publishing Company, 1992).
3 Steven P. Erie, *Rainbow's End: Irish-Americans and the Dilemmas of Urban Machine Politics* (Berkeley: University of California Press, 1988). For a similarly revisionist account of machine politics in a very different setting, see: Judith Chubb, *Patronage, Power, and Poverty in Southern Italy: A Tale of Two Cities* (Cambridge: Cambridge University Press, 1982).
4 See: *Provincial Profile: Cavite* (Manila: Republic of the Philippines National Statistics Office, 1990), especially pp. 14–17, 76–81. See also the excellent study of socio-economic change in Cavite by John P. McAndrew, *Urban Usurpation: From Friar Estates to Industrial Estates in a Philippine Hinterland* (Quezon City: Ateneo de Manila University Press, 1994).
5 Romeo S. Alviso, 'The Port of Cebu', in *Commemorative Magazine: Port of Cebu* (Cebu City: Philippine Ports Authority, 1988), pp. 14–15.
6 See: *Make It Cebu* (Cebu City: Department of Trade and Industry Region VII, 1992), pp. 7, 23; Ma. Olivia R. Caday, 'Cebu's Exports: Where To?', *Data Links*, Volume 1, Number 2 (February 1992), pp. 1–5; 'Semiconductors are now Cebu's No. 1 export', *Philippine Daily Inquirer*, 3 June 1992, p. 19 .
7 'Election Protest', filed March 21, 1988 by Sixto S. Brillantes, Jr and Juanito G. Arcilla, in Election Protest Case No. NC-1, Octavio D. Velasco, Protestant, versus Conrado C. Lindo, Protestee (Naic, Cavite: Republic of the Philippines. Fourth Judicial Region, Regional Trial Court, Branch XV).
8 'Petition' filed May 22, 1992 by Teodorico C. Ramirez, in Election Protest Case No. Nc-2, Teodorico C. Ramirez, Protestant, versus Paulito C. Unas, Protestee (Naic, Cavite: Republic of the Philippines, Regional Trial Court, Fourth Judicial Region, Branch XV).
9 See, for example, Joey Caburnida, 'Plot to kill police officers revealed', *Manila Chronicle*, 11 March 1992.
10 For a complete list of these casualties, see: Carlito Pablo, 'Widows of slain Cavite mayors demand justice', *Philippine Daily Inquirer*, 3 March 1995.
11 See, for example, 'Lawmen raid Pasay gambling lord's "base"', *Manila Standard*, 26 August 1992; 'City gambling lords continue to defy PNP chief's order', *Philippine Star*, 7 September 1992; 'Daily take of Metro gambling lords: P4.5–M', *Manila Standard*, 13 November 1992; 'Sanchez replaced as "jueteng king"', *Philippines Daily Inquirer*, 21 August 1993, p. 6.
12 See, for example, 'Lider ng 14–K Gang nahuli; 300 gramong shabu nakumpiska', *Diyaryo Pilipino*, 22 July 1991; 'Lawyer tagged as drug lord arrested in condo raid', *Philippine Daily Globe*, 15 November 1991; 'Police bust drug ring in S. Tagalog', *Philippine Daily Inquirer*, 27 January 1992.
13 Therese Gladys Hingco and Rebecca Rivera, *The History of Trawling Operations in Manila Bay* (Quezon City: Tambuyog Development Center, 1990); 'End to Cavite illegal fishing seen', *Manila Bulletin*, 6 September 1988; '5 fishermen slain by politician's men', *Philippine Daily Inquirer*, 5 December 1992.
14 Ligorio G.M. Naval, 'Who are behind this syndicate?', *Philippine Daily Globe*, 18 October 1990. See also: David E. Kaplan and Alec Dubro, *Yakuza* (New York: Macmillan Publishing Company, 1986), pp. 139–141, 209–211.
15 Cavite had an average annual growth of 27 per cent in the number of approved building permits for the period 1980–90. In the peak year of 1989, private construction activities in the

province were valued at nearly one billion pesos. See: 'Cavite Tops in Construction in Calabarzon', *Business Star*, 29 October 1991, p. 1B).

16 'DPWH bares 347 Cavite projects', *Manila Bulletin*, 23 July 1991.

17 On the ambitious plans for reclamation along the Cavite coast, see, for example, the 16,000-hectare proposal outlined in *Regal Bay Philippines* (Manila: Regalado Development Corporation, 1992).

18 In various Municipal Agrarian Reform offices in Cavite visited by the author in 1991–92, log books and files bulged with records of local elected officials' visits and letters of recommendation in support of land conversion. In the town of Dasmariñas, the Municipal Agrarian Reform Office processed applications for the conversion of more than 2,300 hectares of land in a period of less than five years. (Municipal Agrarian Reform Office, Dasmariñas, Cavite, 'Dasmariñas Land Use Conversion Status, March 1988 To July 1992'.)

19 John P. McAndrew, 'The Langkaan Syndrome', *Midweek*, 11 April 1990, pp. 6–12; 'Cavite has high rate of illegal land conversions, claim farmers groups', *Business World*, 10 June 1991; 'Southern Tagalog tops agri land conversion list', *Business World*, 31 July 1991; Corinne Canlas, 'Industrializing The Countryside or Undermining Agriculture?: The Calabarzon land conversion project', *Philippine Development Briefing*, Number 4 (1993), pp. 1–15.

20 Ramon Tulfo, 'On Target', *Philippine Daily Inquirer*, 3 June 1992, p. 9.

21 'Municipal Tax Ordinance No. 02–S-92: An Ordinance Imposing Tax On Winnings Of Cockfighting Fronton', in *Excerpts From The Minutes Of The Regular Session Held By The Sangguniang Bayan Of Dasmariñas, Cavite On October 9, 1992* (Dasmariñas, Cavite: Office Of The Sangguniang Bayan, 1992); Civil Case No. 537–91, Arcadio M. De La Cuesta, Plaintiff, versus Inter-Petal Recreational Corporation, Defendant (Imus: Fourth Judicial Region, Regional Trial Court of Cavite, Branch 20).

22 Captain Victor Miranda, one-time mayor of Bacoor, for example, owned shares in a savings bank as well as a recruitment agency that places Filipino merchant marine on international vessels. On the heavily regulated, abuse-ridden, and profitable business of recruiting seamen in the Philippines, see Paul K. Chapman, *Trouble On Board: The Plight of International Seafarers* (Ithaca: ILR Press, 1992), pp. 23–32.

23 Customs and EIIB officials estimate that various forms of 'technical' smuggling amount to billions of dollars a year and involve over one fourth of all Philipine imports. See: Bienvenido Alano, Jr 'Import Smuggling In The Philippines: An Economic Analysis', *Journal of Philippine Development*, Volume XI, Number 2 (1984), pp. 157–190; Economic Intelligence and Investigation Bureau, 'Economic Subversion In The Philippines' (Manila: EIIB, December 1991); Guillermo Parayno, 'Extent Of Smuggling' (unpublished manuscript, 1991).

24 Senior Specialist Angelita R. Legaspi, 'Memorandum For The Director, Examiners And Appraisers Department Re: Southern Heights Land Development Corporation', submitted 15 August 1982, found among documents filed by the Southern Heights Land Development Corporation with the Securities and Exchange Commission.

25 On Campos, see Ricardo Manapat, *Some Are Smarter Than Others: The History of Marcos' Crony Capitalism* (New York: Aletheia Publications, 1991), pp. 353–367.

26 Tracy Posis, 'The Birth Of A New Horizon', *Metro Manila Real Estate Magazine*, September–October 1992, pp. 10–12.

27 Knowledgeable sources in Carmona recall that a lawsuit against Casal for landgrabbing (subsequently dismissed) formed the backdrop to this deal.

28 This *enkargado*, a notoriously unsavoury character, has been named as a prime suspect in the killings of two real estate brokers in a nearby town in January 1992. See: 'Plot to kill police officers revealed', *Manila Chronicle*, 11 March 1992, p. 6.

29 See: 'Complaints', filed 20 October 1988 by Elpidio F. Barzaga, Jr, Counsel for the Plaintiffs, in *RTC-BCV-88049*, Valeriana Cunanan, *et al.*, Plaintiffs, versus Municipality of Carmona, *et al.*, Defendants (Bacoor, Cavite: Regional Trial Court, Fourth Judicial Region, Branch 19).

30 On the dumpsite controversy, see: Guillermo Guerrero, Jr, 'Garbage or Land Reform: The Case of Carmona, Cavite', *Center for Advanced Philippine Studies Monitor Series No. 90–1* (March 1990), pp. 1–19; 'Carmona is not a "basurahan", Caviteños say', *Manila Standard*, 19 December

1990; 'Carmona dumpsite opposed', *Philippine Daily Inquirer*, 16 March 1992; 'Vigil over a landfill', *Business World*, 7 April 1992; 'Cavite folk protest dump site project', *Manila Chronicle*, 30 April 1993; 'Not Here, You Don't', *Philippines Free Press*, 3 July 1993, pp. 12, 26.

31　Oscar F. Reyes, 'Petition', filed January 11, 1986, Annex 'B', Special Action Case No. 73646, United Nationalist Democratic Organisation (UNIDO) And Fernando C. Campos, Petitioners, Versus The Provincial Board Of Canvassers Of Cavite *et al.*, Respondents (Manila: Supreme Court, 1986). See also 'Private armies in Cavite', *Malaya*, 12 April 1984; and 'Cavite KBL bets were turning us to paupers', *Malaya*, 21 May 1984.

32　See Fernando C. Campos, 'Petition', in Special Civil Action Case No. 73646; and '"Historic" Feb. 7 poll fraudulent', *Malaya*, 21 February 1986.

33　*The NAMFREL Report on the February 7, 1986 Philippine Presidential Elections* (Manila: National Citizens Movement for Free Elections, 1986), p. 88.

34　While claiming less than five per cent of the population as its members, the Iglesia Ni Cristo (INC) is an independent church whose strict internal discipline holds certain attractions for politicians like Remulla. Forbidden to join labour unions, INC members received favourable treatment from Governor Remulla in his recommendations to factory owners in search of employees, as has the INC hierarchy in its efforts to build new churches in Cavite. In exchange for these favours, INC clergymen reportedly urged their congregations to support Governor Remulla in his successive bids for reelection.

35　A briefing paper for the 1995 elections in Cavite identified more than sixty members of 'Cavite Gov. Juanito Remulla's Private Armed Group', including bodyguards, jail guards, ex-policemen, and local officials, as well as jueteng operators, drug pushers, and contract killers (with examples of previous victims identified by name).

36　For a list of these victims, see: 'Widows of slain Cavite mayors demand justice', *Philippine Daily Inquirer*, 3 March 1995.

37　According to Dragon's opponents, he milked the Royal Savings Bank before the 1984 National Assembly elections and then allowed his close friend and fellow elected assemblyman from Cavite, Finance Minister Cesar Virata, to arrange a government bail-out for the bank through its sale to the Government Service Insurance System (GSIS). (See: 'Unido urges Batasan probe into Cavite bank closure', *Malaya*, 23 July 1984.) Rumours in early 1994, moreover, suggested that Dragon, now Chairman of the House Committee on Banking, wishes to buy back the bank from the GSIS.

38　A sheaf of documents provided to the author by veteran investigative journalist Marites Dañguilan-Vitug chronicles Dragon's persistent lobbying of the Department of Environment and Natural Resources (DENR) on behalf of Woodland Domain, Inc. (of which he is a major stockholder) accused of various violations forest laws. According to Vitug, the DENR suspended Woodland's licence in 1986 due to non-payment of forest dues, illegal sub-contracting agreements, and logging operations outside Woodland Domain's 72,680-hectare concession in Agusan del Norte. In 1988, however, thanks to Dragon's intercession and influence, the DENR lifted Woodland Domain's suspension. On these developments, see Marites Dañguilan-Vitug, *Power From The Forest: The Politics of Logging* (Manila: Philippine Center for Investigative Journalism, 1993), pp. 97–98.

39　Remulla's opponent in the 1992 election estimated that the Governor spent over P200 million (US$8 million) to guarantee his reelection and that of his protégés in Cavite.

40　Remulla's candidates won 17 of the 22 mayorships in the province in the elections of 1980 and 1988. In 1992, 19 of 23 elected mayors, 16 of 23 vice-mayors, and 129 of 182 municipal councilors were on Remulla's slate.

41　See, for example, 'Comments With Urgent Motion For the Immediate Lifting of the Honorable Supreme Court's Restraining Order Dated September 19, 1991 and To Restrain Petitioner from Further acts of Destruction, Harassment', filed October 2, 1991 by Chairman Mary Concepcion Bautista, Commission on Human Rights, pp. 3–4, in *CHR Case no. 91–1699*, Export Processing Zone Authority, Petitioner, versus The Honorable Commission on Human Rights, Teresita Valles, Loreto Aledia and Pedro Ordones, Respondents.

42 'Kapag ikaw ay pinakiusapan na ng iyong Barangay Captain, mga pulis, ng iyong mayor, ng iyong gobernador, at kapag hindi ka pa nakuha sa pakiusap, maasahan mo na ang susunod ay kung hindi mawala ang iyong mga kalabaw, mga kasangkapan, ay maaaaring ikaw na ang sumunod na mawawala kung hindi man mapasama ka sa unsolved Case ay tiyak na ikaw ay matatambangan. Marami niyan dito sa Cavite nguni't marami rin ang hindi na pupublika sa mga dyaryo'. ('Urgent Motion For Temporary Restraining Order', filed September 15, 1982, by Desales A. Loran in *G.R. No. 57625*, Avelino Pulido *et al.*, Petitioners, versus The Honorable Court Of Appeals, *et al.*, Respondents (Manila: Republic of the Philippines, Supreme Court).

43 On land conversion cases in Cavite, see McAndrew, *Urban Usurpation*, pp. 115–136, 160–179.

44 Municipal Agrarian Reform Office, Dasmariñas, Cavite, 'Dasmariñas Land Use Conversion Status, March 1988 To July 1992'.

45 'Cavite has high rate of illegal land conversions, claim farmers groups', *Business World*, 10 June 1991; 'Southern Tagalog tops agri land conversion list', *Business World*, 31 July 1991.

46 Commentary in Manila newspapers on the state of industrial relations in Cavite is instructive. See, for example, 'The Frankenstein of business', *Philippine Daily Globe*, 8 March 1992; 'Wild, wild Cavite', *Philippine Daily Globe*, 14 March 1992; 'Cavite leaders ban labor militancy', *Philippine Daily Globe*, 19 April 1992; 'Workers Get Raw Deal in Cavite Industries', *Philippine Daily Inquirer*, p. 19; 'Confesor: Growth zones anti-labor', *Manila Chronicle*, 24 February 1995; 'Remulla scored for union busting', *Philippines Daily Inquirer*, 1 May 1995.

47 'Focus: The CALABARZON Project: Possible Glitches: squatters, strikes', *Business World*, 18 October 1990; 'Cavite: Harmonious industrial relations', *Manila Bulletin*, 29 July 1991.

48 A letter to President Fidel V. Ramos dated November 2, 1994 from the 'Concerned Citizens' Group of Cavite' estimated Remulla's annual gains from such arrangements at 162 million pesos per year.

49 Interview by the author with a former Cavite provincial treasurer, 24 July 1991; interview by the author with a former president of the Cavite Contractors' Association, 20 October 1992.

50 See, for example, 'Complaint', filed January 26, 1989 by PCGG Chairman M.A.T. Caparas, in Civil Case No. 0062, PCGG51, Republic of the Philippines, Plantiff, versus Juanito Reyes Remulla, Defendant (Manila: Republic of the Philippines, Sandiganbayan, Third Division).

51 'Complaint' filed January 26, 1989 by PCGG Chairman M.A.T.Caparas, in *Civil Case No. 0062, PCGG51*, Republic of the Philippines, Plaintiff, versus Juanito Reyes Remulla, Defendant (Manila: Republic of the Philippines, Sandiganbayan, Third Division).

52 See, for example, *Annual Audit Report of the Province of Cavite for the Calendar Year 1985* (Quezon City: Commission On Audit, 1986); as well as TBP Case Nos 87–01808 through 87–02029, Fernando C. Campos, *et al.*, Complainant, versus Juanito R. Remulla, *et al.*, Respondents (Manila: Republic of the Philippines, Office of the Ombudsman).

53 No less than Remulla's personal driver has confirmed the veracity of this widely circulated anecdote.

54 As the Acting Secretary of the Department of Interior and Local Government, Sarino played a key role in the distribution of budgetary allocations for local government units. The Aquino Administration was persistently accused of selectively delaying and expediting the release of these funds to local officials throughout the country in order to secure promises of support for Ramos's presidential candidacy. Sarino also handpicked a heavily armed 81man PNP task force that operated in Cavite in the week preceding the May 11, 1992 election.

55 For a thoughtful discussion of Remulla's ouster, see: Amando Doronila, 'FVR intervention won the battle for Velasco', *Philippine Daily Inquirer*, 12 May 1995, p. 5.

56 'Petition', filed 22 May 1992 by Bienvenido R. Sanid, Jr and Vitto A. Kintanar, Counsel for the Petitioners, in S.P. Case No. EC-11, Clarito J. Dinglasa, Petitioner/Protestant, versus Antonio Singco, Respondent/Protestee (Cebu City: Seventh Judicial Region Regional Trial Court Branch 16), pp. 1–2.

57 'Special Report re Illicit Activities of Mayor Daniel Sesaldo of Argao, Cebu', filed 20 August 1990 by PC Major Pedro V. Nicolas, District Commander, Headquarters, 344th Philippine Constabulary Company/INP District II, Sibonga, Cebu, to PC Brig. Gen. Triunfo P. Agustin, Regional Commander/Regional Director, Regional Command 7, Camp Sergio Osmeña, Sr.,

Cebu City; letter of 5 September 1990 from PC Brig. Gen. Triunfo P. Agustin, Regional Commander/Director, INP, Headquarters, Philippine Constabulary Integrated National Police Regional Command 7, Camp Sergio Osmeña, Sr., Cebu City to Director Juliano Z. Barcinas, Regional Director, Department of Local Government, Region VII, Cebu City.

58 PC Lt. Col. Hiram C. Benatiro, 'An Evaluation Of The Government's Campaign Against Illegal Fishing In The Province Of Cebu' (M.A. Thesis, National Defense College Of The Philippines, 1990).

59 See, for example, '"Meddling" of brgy officials in illegal fishing cases noted', *Sun-Star Daily*, 9 July 1991.

60 See, for example, 'Ammonium nitrate released "despite questionable papers"', *Sun-Star Daily*, 3 July 1992.

61 See: Provincial Bantay Dagat Sugbo Council, *1989 Annual Report* (Cebu City: Office of the Vice Governor, Cebu Provincial Capitol, 1990).

62 'Cebu province has smallest coral reef area left', *Sun-Star Daily*, 20 July 1992.

63 A 1992 'Report on Existing Tenements in: Cebu' submitted by the Mines and Geosciences and Development Service (MGDS) of the Department of Environment and Natural Resources (DENR), notes 111 mining concessions in 35 of Cebu Province's 52 municipalities.

64 The Argao quarry case is described in great detail in the following documents: Resolution No. 20, Series of 1990, Argao Irrigators' Service Association, Argao, Cebu; Resolution No. 4, Series of 1991, Argao Irrigators' Service Association, Argao, Cebu; and Letter of 25 April 1991 from Rodolfo C. Orais, Regional Director, Regional Office No. VII, Department of Agriculture to Jeremias Dolino, Regional Executive Director, DENR Region VII, Cebu City. See also: 'NIA report confirms Philrock crusher plant major cause in drying up of Argao irrigation', *Sun-Star Daily*, 13 April 1991; 'Sand-gravel haulers rake in a lot of money', *Sun-Star Daily*, 16 April 1991; and 'Sand-and-gravel scam the worst to hit Argao town in many years', *Sun-Star Daily*, April 19, 1991.

65 As one cockfighting aficionado noted recently after the passage of the 1991 Local Government Code, 'the local government has acquired almost absolute licensing power over cockpits in their respective area of responsibility. The local officials are now in possession of authority to grant licenses or deny the same to operators for cause' (Undo Tabian, 'Cocks & Cockpits: Raising gamefowl as business and hobby', *Sun-Star Daily*, 8 February 1992, p. 17).

66 On this point, see, for example, the documents relating to *Civil Case No. CEBU-4412*, Hee Acusar, Jesus Y. Acusar, and José Y. Acusar, Plaintiffs, versus Mayor Celestino Martinez, Jr, Municipal Mayor of Bogo, Cebu, *et al.*, Defendants (Cebu City: Regional Trial Court, Region VII, Branch VII). See also Tabian, 'Cocks & Cockpits', on mayoral interests in cockpits in the towns of Barili and Balamban.

67 This incident is well documented in 'Information', filed 10 January 1991 by Nancy H. Madarang, Director, Law Department, Commission on Elections, in *Criminal Case No. CBU-20741*, People of the Philippines, Plaintiff, versus Rex A. Escario, Accused (Cebu City: Regional Trial Court Seventh Judicial Region Branch 17). See also the attached Annex 'A': Affidavit of Wilson V. Fernandez of Bantayan, 24 February 1988. This incident is also dicussed in the 'Decision', issued 25 October 1991 by Judge Renato C. Dacudao in *Criminal Case No. CBU-15864*, People of the Philippines, Plaintiff, versus Rex A. Escario, Accused (Cebu City: Regional Trial Court 7th Judicial Region, Branch 14).

68 The original Cebuano text is cited in a Resolution filed 4 October 1989 in the above-mentioned case by Manuel N. Oyson, Jr, Provincial Election Supervisor & Investigating Officer, Commission on Elections (Comelec), Cebu City, p. 9. Translation by the author.

69 The forty 'goons' from Negros Occidental were allegedly provided by Tito Escario (son of Isidro and Remedios), who has married into a wealthy family with large landholdings and a major interest in a sugar mill in the province. The remainder are said to have been supplied by Congressman Celestino E. Martinez, Jr, whose mother's family, the Espinosa clan, has long dominated the political and economic life of Masbate. For newspaper accounts, see, for example, '8 strangers held in Bantayan town, suspected as goons', *Sun-Star Daily*, 12 May 1992; and 'Straight LDP in Bantayan canvassing', *Sun-Star Daily*, 14 May 1992.

70 On Rex Escario's involvement in the 5 October 1990 of the Mandaue City branch of the Far East Bank and Trust Company, which involved the theft of nearly three million pesos and the killing of the bank's chief security guard, see the documents relating to *Criminal Case No. DU-1891*, People of the Philippines, Plaintiff, versus Ruel Ceniza Archua *et al.*, Accused (Mandaue City: Regional Trial Court, 7th Judicial Region, Branch XXVIII).

71 Given Bantayan's extremely hot and dry climate, the three municipalities on the island are said to consume more San Miguel beer than the entire province of Bohol, a point of local pride which San Miguel salesmen are only too happy to confirm.

72 These arrangements are described in considerable detail in a letter of 1 July 1991 from Bantayan Vice Mayor Diosdado Dosdos and Municipal Councilors Vidal Escanuela, Jupiter Pacio, and Arthur Despi to Philippine Ports Authority Team Manager Romeo S. Alviso, Cebu City.

73 The head of a local poultry cooperative told the author in 1992 that more than five hundred thousand eggs are hatched in Bantayan every day.

74 A local Chinese businessman, for example, told the author in 1991 that he might eventually sell off his general store and the gasoline station to raise more capital for his family's already extensive poultry farm operations, which are currently funded in part with small-business loans from the Development Bank of the Philippines and the China Banking Corporation.

75 Several clans of less established lineage in the town (e.g. the Batayolas, Despis, and Montemars) have come to play prominent roles in the local fishing trade.

76 The company supposedly pays out more than five hundred thousand pesos a week in wages and in purchases of fresh crabs. 'Crab fishers' problem: How to get rid of "crabby" habits', *Sun-Star Daily*, 5 September 1992.

77 See: Michael Cullinane, 'Patron as Client: Warlord Politics and the Duranos of Danao', in Alfred W. McCoy (ed.), *An Anarchy of Families: State and Family in the Philippines* (Madison: University of Wisconsin Center for Southeast Asian Studies, 1993), pp. 163–241.

78 'Fortune Cement acquires Universal Cement in bidding', *Sun-Star Daily*, 1 June 1991.

79 'Universal Cement in Danao to reopen; company to hire initial 500 workers', *Sun-Star Daily*, 2 September 1991; 'Universal Cement back in operation by December', *Philippine Daily Globe*, 11 September 1991.

80 'Japanese firm starts operations in Cebu', *Manila Chronicle*, 28 February 1989; 'Cebu Mitsumi plans P75M expansion', *Philippine Daily Globe*, 10 September 1991; 'Mitsumi sets P160M export expansion', *Philippine Daily Globe*, 19 September 1991.

81 'Mitsumi to expand business in Danao', *Sun-Star Daily*, 14 January 1992; 'P67M Japanese electronics project in Cebu up', *Philippine Daily Globe*, 27 April 1992.

82 'Petition', filed 28 December 1988 by Beatriz D. Durano, in *S.P. Proceeding No. 76–SF*, In The Matter of the Settlement of the Estate of the Deceased Ramon M. Durano Sr (Danao City: Regional Trial Court, 7th Judicial District, Branch 25).

83 Documents provided by the provincial office of the Department of Agrarian Reform list more than three hundred hectares of sugar land owned by the RMD Agricultural Development Corporation, a company now controlled by Congressman Durano. *Department of Agrarian Reform 1992 Provincial Master List: Cebu: Landholdings Over 50 Hectares* (Cebu City: Department of Agrarian Reform, 1992).

84 'Supplemental Inventory For Purposes of Collation', filed 29 April 1991 by Gonzalo D. David, Counsel for Paulino Durano, Virginia A. Durano-Aguiling, and Jesusa A. Durano-Macrama, Intervenors, in *S.P. Proceeding No. 76–SF*, In The Matter of the Settlement of the Estate of the Deceased Ramon M. Durano Sr (Danao City: Regional Trial Court, 7th Judicial District, Branch 25).

85 'Duranos are also deeply divided', *Philippine Daily Globe*, 30 March 1992.

86 See: José N. Nolledo, *The Local Government Code Of 1991 Annotated* (Manila: National Book Store, 1992), especially pp. 532–533.

87 See: 'Cebu Central Police to revive campaign v. tong collection', *Sun-Star Daily*, 24 November 1991; 'Cebu city cops extorting tong, traders complain', *Sun-Star Daily*, 2 April 1991; and 'Report says some cops escort smugglers too', *Sun-Star Daily*, 3 April 1991.

88 'City Hall man denies receiving bribes from street vendors', *Sun-Star Daily*, 19 October 1991.

89   For accounts of property tax assessment disputes and scandals in 1991, see: 'Tom seeks relief for real estate taxpayers', *Sun-Star Daily*, 5 April 1991; 'Proposal to lower tax rate for real property heard today', *Sun-Star Daily*, 2 September 1991; 'Plan to reduce rate of realty taxes placed in council freezer', *Sun-Star Daily*, 24 September 1991; and 'Cebu official denies land tax anomaly', *Philippine Daily Globe*, 24–25 December 1991.

90   Adversaries of Emilio 'Lito' Osmeña, Jr in the 1990s have raised similar questions about the real estate properties and profits he garnered in tandem with the various real estate transactions of the provincial government and the construction of the Cebu Trans-Central Highway linking Metro Cebu to the western coast of the island during his term as Cebu Provincial Governor (1988–92).

91   Compare the lists of prominent copra dealers in the early postwar era, ranking Cebuano taxpayers in the mid-1960s, and the richest families in the 1990s in: 'Copra Market Crashes; 6,000,000 People Affected', *Morning Times*, 10 May 1947; 'Who Is The Richest Cebuano?', *Star Monthly*, March 1965; and 'Cebu's Ten Richest Families', *Say*, 11 May 1990, pp. 8–10.

92   '"Friends" tell court province can't sell lots', *Sun-Star Daily*, 14 September 1988; 'PB authorises lease-buy of lots to Lhuillier', *Sun-Star Daily*, 22 December 1991.

93   On these allegations against Lhuiller, see the related articles published in the March 4, 6, and 11 issues of *Newsday*.

94   'Police know 7 to 10 traffickers of shabu but can't nail them', *Sun-Star Daily*, 11 March 1992; 'Ombuds asks Gen. Agustin, 5 others to submit statements', *The Freeman*, 12 June 1992; 'To denounce Agustin, prov'l chief', *The Freeman*, 14 July 1992.

95   'Businessman in gun trade linked to shabu too', *Sun-Star Daily*, 20 December 1991; '5 Cebu businessmen tagged', *Newsday*, 5 March 1992; 'Alvin in an embarassing position', *The Freeman*, 19 August 1992.

96   Garcia's uncle, two-term 3rd District Congressman (1987–1992) and current Cebu Governor Pablo Garcia, is a close ally of Lito Osmeña.

97   Senator Teofisto T. Guingona, Jr, 'The Price Is Wrong', Speech delivered on May 4, 1990, in *Speeches of the Senators* (Manila: Senate, 1990), pp. 130–134.

98   See: '5 William Lines vessels approved for rerouting', *Business World*, 20 December 1991; 'Three shipping lines oppose deployment of more vessels in secondary routes in Cebu', *Business World*, 12 August 1992.

99   See Stella Tirol-Cadiz's series, 'The Perils Of Shipping', published in the 30 September, 1 October, and 2 October 1993 issues of the *Philippine Daily Inquirer*.

100 'BOI approves P350-million expansion of 3 shipping firms', *Business World*, 3 November 1988; 'Domestic shipowners ask for 10-year tax exemption', *Philippine Star*, 26 September 1992.

101 'Manila Orders Opening Of Domestic Shipping', *Asian Wall Street Journal Weekly*, 4 July 1994.

102 For a sense of the considerable autonomy and generous charter of the Cebu Port Authority, see the text of Republic Act No. 7621, 'An Act Creating The Cebu Port Authority, Defining Its Powers And Functions, Providing Appropriation Therefor, And For Other Purposes', approved June 26, 1992 by President Corazon C. Aquino.

103 The author of Republic Act No. 7621, and of Republic Act No. 6958, 'An Act Creating The Mactan-Cebu International Airport Authority', was Cebu City (1st District) Congressman Raul V. Del Mar, a close ally and distant relative of Tommy and Lito Osmeña.

104 See, for example, 'More competition, economic recovery to boost maritime sector this year', *Business World*, 6 February 1995, p. 20; 'Shipping Firms Launch Expansions', *Manila Bulletin*, 24 October 1995, p. B6; 'Local Shipping Industry Navigates into Higher Profits', *Business Daily*, 25 October 1995, p. S1; 'William Lines absorbs Gothong, Aboitiz', *Manila Standard*, 23 November 1995, p. 11; 'WLI, Gothong, Aboitiz Create "Hysteria" in Shipping Circles', *Business Daily*, 24 November 1995, pp. 1, 8; and 'Shipping Industry: Getting Bigger and Better', *Business World*, 7 December 1995, p. 8.

105 *Prospectus: Cebu Equity-Bond Issues* (Cebu City: Province Of Cebu, 1991).

106 'Deed Of Exchange', executed 15 July 1990 by and between The Province of Cebu and Cebu Property Ventures and Development Corporation. The CPVDC's articles of incorporation

(dated 15 June 1990) are found among documents in the Corporation's file at the Securities and Exchange Commission.

107 See the articles of incorporation of Cebu Holdings, Inc. (dated 21 November 1988) and Kuok Philippine Properties Inc. (dated 18 October 1989) on file at the Securities and Exchange Commission.

108 On Ramos' wide-ranging business interests see: Jonathan Friedland, 'Scatter-gun strategist', *Far Eastern Economic Review*, 1 November 1990, pp. 63–65.

109 On Kuok's sprawling empire, which today includes sugar refineries, flour mills, rubber plantations, tin mines, shipping lines, banks, insurance companies, a major international hotel chain, a Hong Kong newspaper, and properties in several Asian countries, see: Sally Cheong, *Corporate Groupings In The KLSE* (Kuala Lumpur: Modern Law Publishers and Distributors, 1990), pp. 121–126; Robert Cottrell, 'The silent empire of the Kuok family', *Far Eastern Economic Review*, 30 October 1986, pp. 59–66; Rigoberto Tiglao, 'More to offer: Kuok Group emerges as a major Manila developer', *Far Eastern Economic Review*, 1 February 1990, p. 49.

110 '3 groups eye Cordova recla project takeover', *The Freeman*, 17 August 1992; 'Decision', promulgated 4 September 1992 by Associate Justice Carolina C. Grino-Aquino in *G.R. No. 101469*, Malayan Integrated Industries Corporation, Petitioner, versus The Hon. Court of Appeals, City of Mandaue, Mayor Alfredo M. Ouano, *et al.*, Respondents (Manila: Supreme Court).

111 'Atlas, Oreta to modernise Mactan airport for P2.5b', *Manila Chronicle*, 22 May 1992; 'House committee questions Mactan airport contract', *Business World*, 18 November 1992.

112 See: John T. Sidel, 'On the Waterfront: Labour Racketeering in the Port of Cebu', *South East Asia Research*, Volume 3, Number 1 (March 1995), pp. 3–17.

113 For further elaboration of the arguments presented in this chapter, see: John T. Sidel, *Capital, Coercion, and Crime: Bossism in the Philippines* (Stanford: Stanford University Press, 1999).

6   Malling Manila
Images of a city, fragments of a century

Nearly a century after the new American colonial regime introduced neo-classicist government buildings outside the Spanish-era walled city of Intramuros in Manila, as the first public architecture to rival the grandeur of its predecessor's great cathedrals, the edifices of church and state no longer dominate this metropolitan landscape in the contemporary Philippines. Instead, spurred on by the construction boom of the post-Marcos era, corporate towers and residential condominiums have come to loom large on urban horizons well beyond the skyline of Makati, Metro Manila's first business and commercial district. Lining the main thoroughfares of metropolitan Manila and provincial cities, moreover, immense malls and commercial complexes have emerged as perhaps the most familiar landmarks and spectacular monuments of urban Philippine society and culture today.

As the malling of Manila and, increasingly, other major Philippine cities proceeds apace, the ever-rising numbers of malls and 'mallers' have already prompted certain discernible 'cultural effects' in the course of the last decade.[1] The practice of 'malling', for example, includes a range of activities such as window-shopping and people-watching, as well as sampling the food courts and going to the movies.[2] The identity of 'mallers', moreover, spans a wide social spectrum from families with children and groups of students, to working professionals and maids on their day off. Malling and mallers also vary considerably across malls, some of which are more deliberately targeting either 'up-' or 'down-' market crowds.[3] Similarly, visiting the mall may be a more or less regular occurrence, with some mallers showing up daily after school and others at least once a week after Sunday Mass.[4] Perhaps unsurprisingly, the mall has also emerged as a site associated with certain contemporary predatory practices (e.g., kidnappings of Filipino-Chinese children) and peculiar 'reformist' discourses (e.g., editorials against air and noise pollution).[5]

Whilst malls and mallers have featured prominently on the business and life-style pages of major Philippine national dailies and news magazine weeklies in the past decade, the 'malling of Manila' viewed as part and parcel of a wider transformation of the city has largely eluded the scrutiny of scholars and chroniclers alike. To date, the most systematic attempt at examining 'Manila's new metropolitan form' instead turns to the so-called 'flyovers' built in recent years to channel private-vehicle traffic onto overpasses across major intersections in this sprawling metropolis, thus allowing middle- and upper-class travellers a transcendent perspective of the city below – arguably 'a space deprived of detail and content and reduced to abstract textures from which one can extract a particular kind of aesthetic pleasure'.[6] Beyond this discussion of the flyover phenomenon, intriguing ruminations in newspaper columns have also explored the production and differentiation of urban space in metropolitan Manila in the first of Philippine parks, the Luneta, and the apparent displacement of 'leisure' from such public outdoor spheres to privatised mall enclosures.[7] Perhaps the most acute sense of the *zeitgeist* molding metropolitan Manila in its image by the 1990s can be glimpsed in writings which identify this period in the Philippines as 'the era of the "mega-malls"'.[8]

This chapter returns to several important questions raised by such writings on flyovers, parks, malls, and, of course, the city writ large. In particular, the chapter probes the relationships between urban space, social relations, collective memory, and political mobilisation. To that end, it situates 'the malling of Manila' in broader historical perspective with an eye to the contested transformations of this urban landscape. Rather than offering grand theory of the mall and the 'postmodern condition', or careful ethnography of malling and 'public culture', the chapter instead takes the 'malling of Manila' as its point of departure for an exploratory excavation of the changing city terrain in the twentieth century. Beyond arguments about ('failed' or 'successful', 'government-led' or 'market-driven') urban development, attention is focused on the reconfiguration of social space and its significance for the lived experience of city dwellers. Inasmuch as any constructed space 'implies, contains and dissimulates social relations',[9] the changing metropolitan map sketched below also provides instructive glimpses of collective solidarities and movements amidst the fragments and ruins of the city beyond the mall.

In order to develop these arguments further, the chapter first sketches the rough contours of the social geography of Manila's retail trade in this century by following its tracks from the exclusive Escolta of the American colonial era and the crowded Plaza Miranda of the postwar period to the massive shopping mall complexes that have become major landmarks of the Philippine urban landscape in both the national capital region and provincial cities during the course of the past decade. Citing the Shoemart (SM) chain of Henry Sy as a leading example, moreover, this chapter also maps in broad outlines the development of department stores and, eventually, shopping malls in the Philippines against the backdrop of changing social demographics and political regimes.

From 'downtown' to 'SM City'

During the American colonial period, the centre of commerce in Manila gradually moved from Calle Rosario and Binondo's 'Chinatown' to the formerly residential parish of Santa Cruz.[10] While the opening of Avenida Rizal at the heart of Santa Cruz provided the inital impetus for this transformation, the addition of the

Santa Cruz Bridge and the trolleycars 'definitely established the city's center in the area bounded by Avenida Rizal, Plaza Goiti, the Escolta and Plaza Santa Cruz – an area that became known as "downtown"'.[11] Considerable activity and diversity characterised this downtown area from around the turn of the century to the Japanese occupation:

> Plaza Goiti was the center of the city's transportation network, meaning the *tranvia*. The Escolta was carriage trade, meaning luxury shop. Plaza Sta. Cruz was entertainment, meaning bar and vaudeville. And Avenida Rizal was Main Street, meaning bazaar, movies, hotel, office, restaurant and bank.[12]

As this brief glimpse suggests, 'downtown' spanned a broad retail market ranging from the myriad bazaars and sidewalk vendors that crowded the Avenida to the awning-decorated department stores and, by the early 1930s, the glass-and-steel Crystal Arcade that lined the Escolta.

The emergence of this diversified downtown area both reflected and reinforced broader changes introduced in the American period. Propelled in part by '[t]he influx of American soldiers, teachers and businessmen', Manila's transformation went beyond the (re)construction of roads, bridges, electricity, transportation and colonial government buildings as '[p]arks, public recreation areas, social clubs, drinking bars and other things to which Americans were accustomed appeared and altered much of the city's landscape'.[13] The new colonial regime also served to expand opportunities for commodity exports, formal education, government and other employment in ways that affected its native subjects across a wide social spectrum in the metropolis, contributing to the ease with which the term 'downtown', with its peculiar American inflection, gained local currency.[14] In the years between 1900 and 1941, one scholar has shown, this 'downtown' area 'attracted many migrants to the city, may well have raised the position of many formerly subsistent urbanites, and at least doubled the pro-portionate size of the dependent middle classes'.[15] Having emerged at the core of a rapidly unfolding 'urban Filipino social structure' in the early century,[16] this 'downtown' then proved more enduring than the American colonial era.

In addition to the expanding domestic market for retail consumption, govern-ment initiatives that ranged from support for vocational sales training and business managerial education to incentives for Filipino-owned enterprises and campaigns promoting local industry and commerce also accompanied the flow of consumer goods and services to and from Manila's downtown area during this period. Beyond the pseudo-scientific officiousness and uninspired 'economic national-ism' of some government efforts at encouraging local industry and commerce, the colonial regime also helped sponsor commercial events of a more spectacular kind in Manila and beyond. As noted in a shopping and sightseeing guide of the early 1930s, for example, '[a] carnival city is built every year in Wallace Field, just east of the old Luneta, and presents a veritable appearance of Fairyland at night, as thousands of electric lights are used for decoration'.[17] This carnival featured an annual industrial exhibit 'participated in by most of the provinces' and 'always crowded with sightseers'. With backing from the Bureau of Commerce, moreover, a Floating Exposition 'displaying every conceivable Philippines-made product' aboard the government cutter *Apo* left Manila harbour for visits to Southern Luzon, Visayas and Mindanao once a year throughout the 1930s.[18] If such cruise expeditions served to bring, in grand style, something of the fashions and flavours of the metropole to the provincial port towns of the Philippines, then the carnival in Manila provided a rather more vaudevillian venue for the display of a wide variety of 'local' specialities such as, for example:

> rice products from Nueva Ecija, Bulacan, Cotabato, the Ilocos provinces and Pangasinan; hemp fiber and hemp products from Davao; coconuts and coconut products from Zamboanga, Laguna, Bohol, Davao, Cotabato, and Lanao; tobacco from the tobacco producing regions; rubber from Zamboanga, Bukidnon, Agusan and Lanao; corn from Bohol, Cotabato, Lanao and Nueva Vizcaya... shells, pearls and mother-of-pearl from Sulu....[19]

As suggested by these glimpses gleaned from contemporary magazines, the exhibition of things at the carnival grounds or aboard a government ship focused greater attention and desire on commodities for consumption and retail in provincial towns as well as in Manila during this period. By the same token, they could not but underscore the relative absence of a 'national' market for consumption and retail in the Philippines of the 1930s. Instead, the displays of the seductive elegance and novelties of the colonial metropole, when juxtaposed with the rich produce and resources of local economies, anticipated the nature and direction of such a market not only by encouraging the circulation and exchange of commodities, but also by drawing men and women into their orbit.

Whilst Chinese shop-owners 'with a centuries-old tradition of commercial network organisation' and American and Japanese distributors 'with superior connections to overseas manufacturers' dominated much of the retail business at the time, the first Filipino-owned department stores, allegedly patterned after Macy's in New York City and advertised as 'Manila's Bon Marché', opened in the area in the 1920s and 1930s in successful competition with the so-called 'Bombay' and other bazaars.[20] In as much as the back alleys, side streets and nearby plazas revealed scores of specialty shops and variety markets for everything from *tsinelas* (rubber sandals) to hats, from toys and import imitations to pastries and sweets, Escolta itself remained exclusive to upscale department stores such as La Puerta del Sol and Estrella del Norte as well as luxury boutiques like Riu Hermanos (Cordovan leather products), Pillicier (French and Spanish fabrics and trimmings), and Rebullida (Swiss clocks and watches). Escolta also first introduced Manila society to the spectacular magic of motion pictures at the two theaters Lyric and Capitol.[21]

The 'Ciudad de Oro'

Manila's finest commercial centre saw its own Escolta Walking Society meet each morning before the stock exchange opened. At the same glassed-in mezzanine coffee shop in Botica Boie, an American drug store, where the Escolta

Walking Society used to congregate during week-days, the city's 'socialites [also] came for merienda and to look down on Manila's well dressed shoppers'.[22] On this short strip comprising 'the city's elite shopping center', Andres Luna de San Pedro y Pardo de Tavera inaugurated his architectural masterpiece, the Crystal Arcade, on June 1, 1932:

> An Escolta landmarks that grows more beautiful with time is the Crystal Arcade which, because it now exists only in the Manilan's memory, is continually embellished with the beadwork of fancy and nostalgia. The Crystal Arcade was literally a crystal building in graceful Art Deco lines, very fancy for Manila of the 1930s. It housed the Manila Stock Exchange and chi-chi shops and people went there as much for the prestige of being seen as for the airconditioning, which was uncommon then.[23]

As the name might suggest, the Crystal Arcade appeared as both magnificent monument to, and spectacular site for, consumption. In something akin to a colonial version of imperial England's 'Great Exhibition of the Industry of All Nations' held at the Crystal Palace built in London for the occasion in 1851, 'the Bureau of Commerce (and Industry) organised the first exposition of Made-in-the-Philippines products at the Crystal Arcade building on the Escolta' in 1932.[24] In a more exclusive rendering of the covered passageways which, with their multitude of specialty shops along the sides, drew consumers and *flâneurs* alike to the nineteenth-century Paris Arcades, for example, the Crystal Arcade emerged as Manila's 'first shopping mall that featured a walk-way leading to the glass-walled shops on the first floor'.[25]

> [It] had a mezzanine on both sides of a central gallery that ran through the length of the building and expanded at the center to form a spacious lobby containing curved stairways.... Stairs, balconies, columns, and skylight combined to create vertical and horizontal movement, as well as a play of light and shadow in the interior.... Art deco bays pierced by a vertical window marked each end of the facade and complemented the tower over the central lobby. Wrought-iron grilles and stucco ornaments were in the art deco style featuring geometric forms, stylised foliage, and diagonal lines and motifs.[26]

At a time when *art decoratif* no longer symbolised high culture and iron and glass had become strongly identified with mass culture constructions elsewhere, Manila's Crystal Arcade, with its art deco lines, 'was considered the most modern structure in the country'.[27] Whilst the Crystal Arcade – both as museum and market of commodities – remained a spectacle of very limited social circulation, it nevertheless anticipated a national culture centered on the commodity. That is, while the Philippine economy had yet to support anything like a mass market, the Crystal Arcade brought into focus the development of a new mode of representation associated with the 'consuming of displays, displays of consuming, [and] consuming of displays of consuming'.[28] Whilst still very much a project of self-definition on the part of the emerging national elite in Manila of the 1930s, the Crystal Arcade also attracted mesmerised gazes from less privileged passersby.[29] In the nostalgic reminiscences of Christmas shopping in Manila during this period, for example, the Escolta with its illuminations and reflections crowned by the Crystal Arcade held particular significance for bringing to the Philippines the cultural forms of consumerism well ahead of a national mass consumer economy:

> Shopping for Christmas was a city-wide operation in pre-supermarket days. Every buy required a separate expedition because certain things could be bought only at certain places – or, at least, *had* to be bought there according to tradition.… Only if you were a millionaire did you go to buy anything at the swank shops of the Escolta … but everybody went window-shopping there on Christmas time to see its ceiling of lights transform the Escolta into a 'Ciudad de Oro'.[30]

The heartbeat of Manila

Whilst the Escolta remained 'the most important business thoroughfare' until the war, the nearby Avenida Rizal also saw rapid continued growth throughout the American colonial era.[31] Located at the centre of Escolta-Avenida-Quiapo, Plaza Miranda gained increasing prominence not only as the site for the weekly *Viernes sa Quiapo* city-wide mass pilgrimages to the Quiapo Church's Black Nazarene, beginning in the 1920s, but also as the hub of retail commerce in pre-war Manila. As *Viernes sa Quiapo* developed into 'the Day of Downtown, when its tills registered the biggest takes of the week – and its traffic, the biggest jams', downtown itself became synonymous with Plaza Miranda in the years preceding the Pacific War.[32]

If Avenida Rizal increasingly captured that new 'urban reality' which, one author claims, 'folk dreamed about when they walked, mesmerised, away from the farm' in the provinces to enter the independent republic's premier city in ever growing numbers, the Escolta never recovered its inter-war status as Manila's most spectacular shopping street.[33] Along with many other inter-war Manila landmarks, for example, the Crystal Arcade itself was destroyed during the war. With the partial exception of Quezon City,[34] the independent Philippine Republic saw little in the way of concerted government efforts at either city planning or reconstruction. Instead, the emergence of post-war Manila with its expanding suburbs and highways, and, eventually, malls and flyovers, proceeded according to 'public works' schemes and 'private development' initiatives informed, for the most part, by the imperatives of electoral and/or business cycles rather than by any discernible overarching vision for urban renewal and/or sustainable development.

The 'trek to the suburbs' began with wealthy Americans and Filipinos building their homes in Forbes Park, 'the first major fully zoned-and-planned subdivision',[35] precisely as the old residential areas of Ermita, Malate, Paco, Santa

Ana, Sampaloc and Tondo grew increasingly crowded with new city migrants in the 1950s. In the case of the Ermita and Malate that (re)emerged from the rubble of the Pacific War (and Liberation), moreover, 'cheap, shabby districts dotted with honky-tonk bars and sleazy brothels' replaced much of the *mestizo*-owned mansions and elite neighbourhoods of the American colonial era.[36] As poor migrants gravitated to the ruins of Intramuros, 'squatting on vacant lots and thus converting the once proud center of Spanish authority and culture into a veritable slum',[37] a peculiarly American 'supermarket-and-country club atmosphere'[38] developed in the enclosed 'villages' which, starting with Forbes Park and, a few years later, San Lorenzo, began to distinguish Manila from other national capitals in Southeast Asia. By the 1960s, when the National Capital Region replaced the northern and southern frontiers as the number one destination of internal migration in the Philippines, the suburbanisation of the city also picked up rapid pace and, as a result, 'Manila's well-heeled shoppers no longer came in droves to Escolta'.

> The affluent moved out of residential Ermita and Malate to Makati, to Mandaluyong, to Quezon City, out where the green country beckoned, and they took with them their shops and their businesses. Within half a decade, Makati was the Big Business center and nothing reflected this more forlornly than Escolta.[39]

Beyond the Makati Shopping Center and the nearby Mile Long Plaza, commercial complexes such as Virra Mall in Mandaluyong-San Juan and Ali Mall and Farmer's Plaza in Cubao, Quezon City also reflected and reinforced this suburban trend.

Whilst the eclipse of Escolta and the flight of the affluent changed the face of downtown Manila, Plaza Miranda retained its throbbing pulse:

> Through this square, and in the cavernous Lacson Underpass beneath, daily flows a vast stream of people. Folk shopping at the Quinta Market, at Carriedo's wilderness of shoes, for ribbons, laces and buttons at Villalobos and in the household utilities-textile stores on Echague; the buyers of dreams at the myriad cinema houses; students, workers, job-seekers, tourists, pimps, lottery ticket vendors, hawkers, beggars, pickpockets, artists – all must pass through this deadcenter point of Manila where all arrivals and departures converge.[40]

Not far from Plaza Miranda where the Quiapo Church's Nazareno continued to attract mass pilgrimages on Friday afternoons, moreover, the Avenida introduced the Philippines to its first Shoemart department store in 1958 and, more generally, featured a 'swirl of shops, moviehouses, restaurants and crowds':

> There are bazaars whose windows displays shirts, dinner plates, ceramic elephants, plastic flowers, thermos flasks and lipstick in unaccountable coziness. Bookstores that sell identical stocks of Penguins, Signets, Mills &

Boones, and overflow with Hallmark greeting cards and stationeries. Shoestores – Alex Shoe Palace, Wellington, ad infinitum.[41]

Outside these commercial establishments, moreover, Avenida's street vendors and job seekers rubbed shoulders with students from the nearby university belt's so-called 'diploma mills'. With nothing to separate them from the crowded sidewalks, street vendors appeared as actual manifestations – instead of spectacular mystifications – of social relations already familiar to their low-income customers and served as reminders of – rather than escapes from – the world of immediate surroundings. And if these sprawling stalls and their customers remained subject to the same beating sun and pouring rain, decaying rubbish and choking pollution that enveloped the downtown area daily, the street vendor market had little to offer in the way of temporary respite or enchanted sanctuary away from everyday lived experience.

As consumption on the Avenida remained intimately embedded within a social context characterised in part by small margins and large sacrifices, the visible presence of those unemployed seeking jobs similarly drew attention to exploitative relations of production. Not only shops and stalls lined the Avenida but also virtual 'employment centers':

> If at the corner of Avenida and certain side streets you see clusters of men standing in attitudes of waiting, those are unofficial employment centers. The men are looking for work and indicate their calling by where they stand. Thus there are the dollar buyer's corner, the bookies', the stage show performers', the musicians', and so forth.[42]

In addition to such prominent evidence of an expanding lumpen proletariat of sorts in the midst of downtown Manila, large numbers of the city's youths from lower- and lower-middle class backgrounds, including working students, also crowded the Avenida during weekdays from the many private colleges and vocational schools in the area. A world apart from the country's leading public and private schools for higher education – like the (secular) University of the Philippines (U.P.) and the (Catholic) Ateneo and La Salle – the so-called 'diploma mills' in the downtown area showed a marked growth in their numbers as well as enrolment figures beginning in the 1960s. As the demand for formal qualifications and accreditation increased on the urban employment market, privately-run specialist colleges and technical institutes packed unprecedented numbers of fee-paying students into overcrowded and sometimes seriously delapidated classrooms and even condemned buildings in downtown Manila. For example, the Philippine College of Commerce counted among its rapidly growing student population 'mostly children of the lowest-income groups – laborers, janitors, carpenters, even laundrywomen'.

> In three places on Lepanto Street in Sampaloc, Manila – between C.M.Recto and the Gota de Leche, between R. Papa and P. Peredes, and behind the old Carbungco restaurant – stand a number of wooden buildings which are

weather-beaten, termite-infested and officially declared fire traps by the Manila Fire Department. These old houses, divided into a total of 147 class-rooms are the school and virtual headquarters of more than 11,000 students of the Philippine College of Commerce, a state college....[43]

Whilst the U.P. Diliman in Quezon City saw the first rumblings of campus-based radical politics with the *Kabataang Makabayan* (Nationalist Youth) in the mid-1960s,[44] it is perhaps not surprising that the 'diploma mills' emerged as the new center of student activism by the end of the decade.[45] As noted by contemporary observers, such activism seemed to intensify and spread beyond individual campuses as school administrations not only failed to respond to demands for the reduction and itemisation of tuition and fees, the abolition of centralised control over student organisations and papers, but also sought to contain such issues by suspending or otherwise punishing individual students for breaking with college rules and regulations.[46] Perhaps the very conditions associated with these 'diploma mills', where children of the labouring classes saw their aspirations to social respectability exploited in the factory-like, profit-driven mass production of college graduates, served to undermine such attempts to single out individual students for disciplinary measures and to invoke absolute administrative discretion over academic issues and campus life alike. In any event, rather than submitting to the terms outlined by college administrations with regard to proper conduct and, ultimately, private property, students challenged them, collectively and publicly, by picketing campuses, marching in the streets of Manila, and demonstrating outside Congress in the late 1960s. Whilst this wave of student activism focused but brief attention on 'dialogue' and 'reform' at the top of college administrations as well as national government, it also left behind a battle-scarred downtown area where buildings with broken and boarded-up windows remained in powerful testimony to the moment of struggle, thus recalling fragments of collective memory from the amnesia of history through lived experience itself:

> Over at Lyceum in Intramuros, many of the windows are patched up with plywood boards, old, dirty, and temporary.... The holes smashed out of the glass by the flying rocks of January are still there, jagged, gaping; the plywood behind every hole only calls attention to the extent of the destruction. At nearby Mapua, where no rocks flew, the glass facade hides behind a plywood curtain. At Feati in Sta. Cruz, the broken windows have been left untouched: it almost seems as if the holes are being preserved as historical relics.[47]

With the mounting political activism that swept Manila campuses during this decade, students increasingly left their classrooms throughout the university belt not only to shop for food, movies or school supplies but to join in the mass demonstrations that filed through or converged upon downtown. As students (and some faculty), workers and peasants alike – and sometimes together – launched new radical organisations and engaged in concerted collective campaigns during the course of the decade, Plaza Miranda – the 'crossroads of the nation' – became a familiar destination not just for Nazareno devotees, downmarket clients and, during election years, political candidates, but also for mass activists – as well as the Metropolitan Anti-Riot squads organised for the occasion.[48]

Demonstrations against the presidential (re)inauguration of Marcos and the opening of Congress gained added momentum with the resumption of classes in January 1970 and ushered in the so-called 'First Quarter Storm' of student activism and mass rallies. During the 'Battle of Mendiola' on January 30, student and other radical protesters fought military and police forces for hours over this bridge separating the area surrounding the presidential palace from the heart of downtown where the battle then continued to rage throughout the night. Whilst government troops had regained control over Mendiola and J.P. Laurel Street by nine o'clock in the evening, according to the foremost contemporary chronicler of the First Quarter Storm, they failed to clear in similar fashion the streets of M. Aguila, Legarda and Claro M. Recto and in Quiapo from demonstrators who 'found doors being opened to them, or people at second-floor windows warning them with gestures about the presence of soldiers in alleys'.[49] Such manifestations of support for the demonstrators from among the broader down-town population stood in sharp contrast to the reactions by many of those living in the walled and guarded enclosures of suburban exclusive so-called 'villages':

> That night, an exodus of privilege made ghost towns of the exlusive villages in the suburbs; the chi-chi crowd, fear in their guts and guilt in their hearts, holed up with their hysteria in the big hotels, driven there by the certainty that Forbes Park and Bel-Air and Dasmariñas and Magallanes would be set afire by an avenging people.[50]

Within less than two weeks of the 'Battle of Mendiola', a large rally held at Plaza Miranda avoided violent confrontations with government forces who refrained from charging this collective claim to the crossroads of the nation as, reportedly, some ten to fifty thousand people 'sat on the streets, leaned against buildings, lolled around the plaza, stood on the other underpass roofs and on the roofs of low buildings nearby, leaned out from the church belfry, hung from the trees in the church patio' for hours while listening to speakers standing outside the Quiapo Church 'denouncing imperialism, feudalism, and fascism'.[51] In the last month of the First Quarter Storm, demonstrators once again took to the streets of the metropole, this time under the banner of the so-called 'People's March'.

> The people's marches inaugurated the strategy of hiking around Manila's populous streets denouncing facsism, feudalism and imperialism through banners, streamers, leaflets and bullhorns. Subsequently, it became a pattern to congregate in different areas of the City, march around the major streets and converge in a common place, usually Plaza Miranda.[52]

In the years leading up to martial law, downtown Manila thus in many ways emerged as both site and target for the escalating political violence that seemed to polarise the nation, as perhaps most fatally testified to by the Battle of Mendiola where government forces killed at least six students in 1970 and the bombing of

Plaza Miranda where several bystanders died as a result of the grenade attack which Marcos perhaps correctly blamed on the CPP-NPA in 1971.[53]

The continued scramble for the suburbs provided but temporary respite for Manila's elite in the 1960s. Perhaps unsurprisingly, the suburban frontiers soon displayed familiar dynamics of contested social space (e.g., growing squatter settlements) and neglected 'non-private' spheres (e.g., decaying public infrastructure).[54] By the late 1950s, for example, ten prominent families backed the initial organisation of the Quezon City Citizens League for Good Government (QCCLGG) to counter pressures associated with a rumoured threat of 'creeping industrialisation' and, significantly, the manifest 'presence of laborers, unemployed migrants from the provinces, as well as squatters and slum dwellers' on this closing suburban frontier.[55] Whilst successfully campaigning for six councillors in the first election to city government in 1959, the QCCLGG enjoyed but a brief and rather lacklustre career, as did its counterparts elsewhere in the early 1960s.[56] Instead of suburban utopias of 'safety, security, and sanitation' governed by 'honest, efficient and responsible city government',[57] these sprawling metropolitan social landscapes remained captive to urban political machines with their 'particularistic rewards' and 'clientelistic structures'.[58]

Whilst these initiatives at reforming the city through electoral politics had largely fizzled out by the early 1960s, as noted above, extra-electoral mobilisation continued to gain momentum from the mid-1960s onwards as student activists took to the streets of Manila armed with radical political discourse, contentious collective action, and expanding protest repertoires developed within the context of the peculiar social spaces of campus enclaves. In this regard, the flagship of Philippine (secular) universities, the U.P. at Diliman in Quezon City, not only emerged as the first such enclave for a new radical politics of the early mid-1960s, but also as the premier site for the realisation of a (sub)urban campus as revolutionary space with the declaration of the 'Diliman Commune' in 1971. After an innovative two-day road blockade to prevent vehicles from entering campus in solidarity with striking jeepney drivers in January 1971 (when the government announced a gasoline price increase), U.P. students seized again on their newly discovered weapon, the 'human barricade', when strike action resumed in February. With Quezon City Police forces and Metrocom troopers entering campus in hot pursuit of student activists, these human barricades were quickly fortified with '[c]hairs, tables, benches, bulletin boards etc'.,[59] while revolutionary poetry and the *Internationale* were broadcast from the occupied radio station DZUP,[60] thus further expanding the repertoire of protest at U.P.

Whilst the 'Diliman Commune' lasted but a week before the negotiated 'voluntary dismantling of the barricades',[61] it signalled a decisive rupture in the contestation over space and hierarchy in the (sub)urban social imagination.

[T]here was an air of romanticism, adventurism, and 'revolutionary fervor' as the barricaders 'liberated' Palma Hall; renamed some buildings on campus after progressive leaders of the Left; set up the 'Diliman commune'; took over DZUP; 'liberated' the UP Press and published *'Bandilang Pula'* [Red

Flag]; splashed the Oblation with red paint; and displayed red flags on 'liberated' buildings.[62]

Such displays of 'revolutionary fervor' could not but underscore the ambiguous position many U.P. students occupied in the city. They typically enjoyed full student privileges at this elite university located on what remained a suburban campus enclave in relative insulation from everyday life in the metropolis. Many students, perhaps especially those provincial high-school graduates 'of middle-class and even working-class and peasant origins' and those commuting from modest boarding houses as far afield as Quiapo,[63] also experienced the growing social stratification and mounting political contestation of the city beyond the university. The rise and fall of the 'Diliman Commune', whilst swift, served as a dramatic subversion of the spatial hierarchy of the city by the 'communards' and their fellow activists. 'After the barricades', one contemporary observer noted, 'protest classes, boycotts, demonstrations became almost a daily spectacle that would beset the University until the declaration of martial law'.[64]

Indeed, as demonstrations targeting government offices and the US Embassy made all too evident, mass actions continued to spill out of the downtown area in the months following the First Quarter Storm and the Diliman Commune. On September 21, 1972, a coalition of more than thirty civic, religious, labour, student, and activist groups mobilised a crowd of 30,000 in a protest rally at Plaza Miranda which received prominent national radio, television, and news-paper coverage.[65] That night, President Marcos declared martial law, finally – and significantly, without much protestation from the elite – putting such a heavy lid on popular mobilisation so as to drive it underground.

Viewed against this backdrop, the peculiar 'beautification projects' sponsored by Imelda R. Marcos, head of the Metro Manila Commission established as a 'supralocal metropolitan government' under martial law,[66] involved not only spectacular displays of presidential patronage and power,[67] but also direct, if inter-mittent, state-sponsored assaults on urban spaces associated with the collective experiences and memories of the metropolitan *masa*, including the waves of popular mobilisation directed against the pre-martial law regime. Imelda Marcos transformed the metropolitan landscape by promoting 'a series of such spectacles as cultural centers, film festivals, landscaped parks, five-star hotels, and glitzy international conferences'.[68] Unsurprisingly, these new construction projects and sporadic 'beautification campaigns' at times required the eviction of urban squatters in large numbers and by coercive means. The old walled city of the Spanish era, later known as Intramuros, was 'cleared' in this fashion so as to pave the way for renovation and 'museumification' of a site now relegated to the 'historical'. In what appeared as a more peculiar approach to promoting urban aesthetics, moreover, 'Madame' also sought to conceal entire squatter settlements by having large walls erected and decorated around squatter settlement areas in anticipation of the 'mobilised gaze' of diplomatic dignitaries, church emissaries, and other international travellers passing through the city.[69] But these cosmetic and episodic efforts to concealing and containing urban poverty proved ephemeral and ineffective, as the slums of Metro Manila continued to grow with every passing year.

Even as the elite turned their backs – and the Marcoses their troops and 'urban developers' – on downtown Manila, moreover, commercial retail continued to expand in the area with new department stores that followed the formula first pioneered by L.R. Aguinaldo in the 1920s and further developed by, among others, Henry Sy in the 1950s. Despite the limited purchasing power and the relative political instability then associated with downtown Manila, future mall-mogul José Go, for example, first realised his 'winning formula' of 'small margins, big volumes' here:

> In 1971 he channeled some of his family's money into building his first store from scratch in downtown Manila. 'Most of my friends in the 1970s were telling me to give up the store', he says, 'as the area was the site of student riots' against President Ferdinand Marcos.[70]

At the same time, street vendors, bazaars and scores of other stores continued lining downtown and endless throngs of people from near and far, city and province, kept traversing these the nation's 'crossroads'. As one of Manila's foremost chroniclers quipped in the late 1970s, 'despite Makati and Cubao, the most famous market in the land is still Divisoria'.[71] If the radical politics and street demonstrations of the 1960s and early 1970s gained much of their momentum from the critical mass of downtown, the swelling crowds of this area also signalled a rapidly growing, already 'vast 'underground' economy' to be tapped right in the heart of Manila.[72] That is, another observer of the 'streets of Manila' has suggested, by the 1970s,

> while Makati has become a ritzy uptown downtown, and rustic Mandaluyong-San Juan had acquired synthetic glass in their shopping centers, and Cubao is forever raw frontier town, Plaza Miranda is still where Manila's pulse beats strongest.[73]

From a downtown shoe store to Mega Mall, EDSA: the Sy story

Against the backdrop of the changing urban social space from the American colonial period through the 1970s, the subsequent rise of the shopping mall to its current prominence can be traced by following the trajectory of a single commercial chain from one small shoe store in downtown Manila to the six-storey, mile-long Shoe Mart (SM) Mega Mall on Epifanio delos Santos (EDSA) Boulevard, and from the metropole to provincial cities. Whilst other Filipino-Chinese magnates like John Gokongwei, José Go and the Gaisano family have also established their own department stores and malls on the rapidly expanding commercial retail market in the past decade, Henry Sy's 'SM' nevertheless holds its own as 'the biggest retailing chain in the Philippines' today.[74] With reported plans to continue building one mall per year in the future, moreover, the Sy family/SM Prime Holding group seems set to deliver on its promise to 'make SM synonymous with Filipino shopping'.[75]

As suggested by the extent to which 'SM' has become a household name, especially in Metro Manila, the story of Henry Sy's successful Shoemart chain in many ways captures the momentum of commercial retail in the post-war period and thus suggestively bridges the previous discussion of downtown's growing 'underground' economy to the malling of the Philippines examined in the pages to follow. The Sy story illustrates the expansion beyond Manila's crowded downtown first to the suburbs and then to the 'highways' that increasingly grid this sprawling cityscape. However, the Shoemart 'case study' below underscores the continued significance of this same downtown in so far as it comprises a key constituency for the rapidly proliferating SM 'Cities'. For example, the company still retains its purchasing and development 'no-frills office' near the location of the now legendary first small shoestore downtown because, in the words of SM president Teresita Sy: '"It's here where I can determine what the mass market wants, what prices are really prevailing"...'.[76] Finally, the expansionary phases of SM's commercial retail business appear to mirror broader patterns within the Philippine economy associated with changing social demographics and political regimes in the post-war period.

An immigrant from Fujian province in China, Henry Sy opened his first store in Carriendo, downtown Manila, in 1945. Soon to be followed by others, this store successfully marketed well-made shoes in sufficiently large quantity and with rapid enough turnover to keep prices down and yet increase profits. In addition to adding new stores, Sy also successively increased his retail business by diversifying into textiles and household goods until, in 1958, the first Shoemart department store opened on Avenida. Within a few years of Shoemart's incorporation in 1960, Sy launched into the first phase of his commercial retail expansion beyond downtown Manila with as many as three new Shoemarts opening in rapid succession in Makati (1962), Cebu (1965) and Cubao (1967). With no new construction undertaken until almost twenty years later, toward the tail end of the long Marcos years, Sy instead focused his management energies and retail cashflows on developing further the existing fleet of four Shoemart department stores until the one located in the Makati Commercial Center emerged as the Philippines' first 'one stop-shopping' complex.

> These were gradually upgraded into ever-larger commercial complexes with Sy funding the growth both through retail cashflow and from the deposits of concessionaries eager to piggyback on his reputation for sound business dealings and good service.[77]

After the construction lull that followed upon Marcos' reelection and subsequent establishment of so-called 'constitutional authoritarianism', the next expansionist Shoemart period started only during the severe political and economic crises of the 1980s when Sy began 'consolidating the basis for his great leap from department-store owner-manager to huge mall magnate'.[78] As the Marcos regime continued devouring entire sectors of the Philippine economy through its 'patrimonial plunder' and the New People's Army kept pressuring business ventures in many parts of the country with its 'revolutionary taxation', a rapid succession of major business-loan defaults, government bailouts, Central Bank foreign-exchange shortages and (selective) national debt moratoria plunged the country into a deepening economic crisis by the early- to mid-1980s.[79] At the same time, moreover, the Philippines secured the unenviable position of most IMF-indebted 'LDC' (lesser-developed country). However, despite the International Monetary Fund and the World Bank 'dramatically restricting badly needed credit', private transnational corporations and banks becoming increasingly wary of investing in the country, and the massive capital flight triggered by Aquino's assassination continuing unabated, Sy nevertheless held his ground, as his harsh reaction to a 1985 strike at Shoemart in Makati amply demonstrated.

> Striking workers of Shoemart, members of the *Sandigan ng Manggagawa sa* Shoemart (SMS), were asking for basic labor rights like vacation and sick leaves. Last March 30 they got their answer: men armed with clubs wildly swinging at picketers lined up in front of the Makati department store.... The labor dispute, which has been festering for more than two weeks, has been wracked with violence twice before, the first one when strikers were dispersed by Makati police.[80]

Sy not only defeated the strike in Makati, but proceeded to inaugurate his own enchanted 'SM City' later that year in the nation's otherwise beleaguered capital, Quezon City.[81] Looking back on the rise of this spectacular 'shopping city' in the midst of a nation in crisis, and with little previous commercial activity save for 'a few beer joints and construction materials stores nearby',[82] a Makati-based business-school professor commended Sy in no uncertain terms: "'He's got guts.... He's probably the only businessman who plunked in so much money when the country seemed to be going to the dogs'".[83] Sy himself offered the following matter-of-fact commentary as if to emphasise the significance of calculated risk and business acumen behind his growing retail empire:

> 'When the economy is down, I buy land, when it's very, very cheap.... That's also when you take over the business left by those who went bankrupt'.[84]

As the pressures for 'structural readjustments' of the economy started bearing down on Marcos and the bailouts of individual companies increasingly dried up for his cronies in the early and mid-1980s, Sy – now widely assumed to be one of the wealthiest men in the Philippines – in many ways helped jump-start the domestic economy by investing and building at a time when much capital continued flowing out of the country. While the details of Sy's land acquisitions, as well as his much-admired retail strategies for centralizing purchasing, cultivating suppliers, and subcontracting concessionaries, lie beyond the scope of this chapter, it is nevertheless noteworthy that within only a few years of SM City's grand opening in 1985, SM Centerpoint also rose in a capital still very much under siege because of the political polarisation and economic paralysis surrounding the regime transition from Marcos to Aquino in 1986. With the subsequent construction of SM South Mall in Las Pinas, SM City-Cebu and Mega Mall, the Sy family continued its commercial expansion even further – both in terms of geographical reach and spectacular scope – as the Philippines began preparing for the 1992 elections and thus its first constitutional transfer of the presidency since Marcos gained reelection in 1969. If SM Prime Holdings, Inc. counted nine department stores and four malls with a heavy concentration on Metro Manila by 1994, its continued expansion by now features monumental shopping malls in provincial cities like Angeles, Bacolod, Cebu, Davao, Iloilo, and Tacloban, scattered around the Philippine archipelago.[85]

Malling Manila

In view of such recent developments in Philippine commercial retail and urban social geography, '[p]erhaps it is not too far fetched to suggest that the latter period of Aquino's regime will be remembered as the era of the "mega-malls"…'.[86] Indeed, as the most spectacular monuments to commodity culture, malls have to a certain extent appeared as a reflection of modern Philippine society itself. If the mall has become an increasingly popular destination, then growing numbers of Filipinos have begun to encounter each other and themselves as consumers of spectacle – whether or not actual purchasing power restricts them largely to window-shopping. In other words, shopping malls have worked to reproduce images of people, or citizens, as mass consumers while at the same time obscuring social class distinctions associated with exploitative relations of production.

As the malling of the Philippines has proceeded apace, social space has undergone a restructuring both within and beyond the confines of the mall's 'wondrous shape'.[87] That is, the malls have tended to create hermetically sealed 'city-within-a-city' utopias remote and removed from traditional Philippine small-town plazas or urbanised 'downtowns' with all their reminders of secular and ecclesiastical power hierarchies, social fragmentation, and political struggles. By the same token, the malls have also increasingly threatened to vacate the old city centres and, as a result, empty notions of national citizenship from the kind of lived experiences without which subaltern historical memory fades and the collective will for political change languishes.

Finally, as social venues that attract visitors from an already broad and continuously expanding spectrum of societal forces, malls have (re)presented a mode of (post-)modern national consolidation. Whereas a certain internal differentiation among malls has tended to reproduce a more socially distinct clientele in upscale Shangri-La Plaza and down-market Gotesco-chain shopping malls, for example, the most successful mall concept to date, 'SM', as well as several of its competitors, have deliberately and successfully drawn large cross-class crowds. Although they also appear less discriminatory than perhaps any other contemporary social institution or practice in the Philippines as far as gender, age, religion, and ethnicity are concerned, moreover, these malls, as suggested above, seem to have afforded common people an unparalleled modicum of 'respect', or, in other words, civility. As enclaves of enchanted convenience and safety, malls thus may most closely approximate something akin to a 'civil society' for the vast majority of the Philippines' urban population who endure daily experiences of routine overcrowding, pollution, logjams, brownouts, floodings, heatwaves, crime and violence in the outside city. Once inside these extraordinarily spacious, clean, smooth, bright, airconditioned, and orderly near 'total' structures, the spectacular display of material abundance and changing styles presents consumers with such a variety of seemingly endless choices and freedoms as to suggest something akin to an elective affinity between mass consumerism and democratic citizenship.

With the flashing images of striking workers at SM's Department Store in posh Makati and leaflet-distributing socialites at Rustan's Supermart in crowded Cubao all but faded from collective consciousness,[88] the malls of the post-Marcos reconstruction period today appear as the 'most enchanted dreamworlds' of the spectacular consumer culture now rising out of the rubble of the past decade's protest politics.[89] Far from both everyday relations and historical memory, these malls seem to yank ever-growing crowds out of not merely present social conditions in residential areas and work places but also away from past lived experiences of political mobilisation and struggle. Like a luminous mirage glimpsed from the smog-filled transit routes traversing metropolitan Manila, the mall beckons invitingly towards passersby caught in the large, congested intersections that increasingly grid this urban landscape. Once inside these 'signature structures' of incomparable grandeur and glamour in the contemporary Philippines, more-over, the spectacle of modern commodity culture appears particularly imposing as nothing larger than the mall itself – not even the weather – interrupts with any unwelcome commercial breaks. As the abundant choices of consumers seem to affirm and confirm the democratic freedoms of citizens, the malling of the Philippines both reflects and reproduces this spellbinding spectacle in something akin to a paramnestic utopia where historical development appears as an endless stream of new arrivals and special events.

Conclusion

Today, local neighbourhood markets and other public spaces in Metro Manila no doubt continue to enjoy a certain vitality in pockets scattered across the urban landscape. In public monuments and common places of greater scale, however, perhaps only the Luneta still draws the large crowds, but then again, more as a site for special and scheduled events – Sunday afternoons booked by the popular religious group El Shaddai, for example – than as a centre of gravity in its own right. The Marcos-era projects like the Cultural Center of the Philippines remain rather desolate spots; but the Left-driven efforts to create oppositional spaces like the Plaza Miranda – and the much fought-over Mendiola Bridge, of course – also appear to have faded from collective memory.

In this regard, the annual 'EDSA' rallies in commemoration of the famed 'People Power' revolt of 1986 continue to serve as a peculiar reminder of this collective paramnesia. The peaceful transition from Marcos to Aquino in February 1986, of course, signalled the beginning of, if not the end of history, at least the end of a particular revolutionary project. In the early to mid-1980s, the so-called moderate opposition to Marcos had donned yellow t-shirts and taken to the streets of Makati within shooting range of local and foreign journalists while the military instead trained its weapons on the Left's red-bannered mass rallies marching on the US Embassy and Malacañang Palace. Whilst places like Plaza Miranda and Welcome Rotunda offered Left activists a broad range of escape routes and hiding places as the military attacked, then the widest urban thoroughfare in the Philippines, Epifanio delos Santos (EDSA), became the spectacular site of the February 1986 'People Power' revolt as mostly middle-class crowds filled this multi-lane highway stretch between the two military camps seized by putschist officers and, 'with the whole world watching', held Marcos' loyal tanks and troops at bay until he backed down and departed for exile.

In the aftermath of 'EDSA', neither the state-led nation-building efforts associated with Marcos, nor the subaltern-led nationalist movement identified with the Left has succeeded in laying hegemonic claims to national public culture and urban social space. Rather than through government policy or movement activity, 'Filipino identity' since the fall of Marcos has been constructed and negotiated largely by market forces and commodity culture, as suggested in Chapter Seven of this volume. The malls – at 'the cutting edge of the construction expansion in metropolitan Manila'[90] – attract ever-growing crowds of Filipinos who, while gazing at the displays of commodities in great abundance and variety, also increasingly encounter each other as consumers of spectacle. If the exclusiveness of Escolta suggested something of a self-definition project on the part of an emerging national elite in the interwar years, then the excess of Mega Mall – or, in the apt Pinoy pun, *Gamol*[91] – perhaps signals a living monument of sorts to the dream of a broader mass market today. Thus representing a commodified public space that serves – however imperfectly – to blur traditional social distinctions and – however fleetingly – to focus modern individual aspirations, the shopping mall reflects and reproduces an image of limited equality that resonates with the promise of democratic citizenship in the contemporary Philippines.

Notes

1 As early as May 1993, for example, Mega Mall had an estimated 200,000 per day by May 1993. 'Shoppers flocking to Ortigas but malls need bigger crowds', *Philippine Daily Inquirer*, 6 May 1993, p. 15. A year later, that figure had reportedly increased to 300,000. Roberto Tiglao, 'Strength in Numbers', *Far Eastern Economic Review*, 21 July 1994, p. 60.

2 See, for example, 'Gokongwei earmarks P1.5B for mall projects', *Philippine Daily Inquirer*, 3 July 1999.

3 For brief glimpses of the 'up-market' Shangri-La Plaza versus the 'down-market' Grand Central Mall see, for example, 'The Art of Shopping', *Philippines Free Press*, November 1991, pp. 41 and 'Mall Mogul', *Far Eastern Economic Review*, 31 August 1995, pp. 50–51.

4 'Answering the call of the mall', *Philippine Daily Inquirer*, 18 August 1994, p. D-2.

5   See, for example, 'Kidnapping of ethnic Chinese rises in the Philippines', *New York Times*, 17 March 1996, p. 3; and 'Sy, Gokongwei should help landscape our malls', *Philippine Daily Inquirer*, 19 June 1999, op-ed page.

6   Neferti Xina M. Tadiar, 'Manila's New Metropolitan Form', *Differences: A Journal of Feminist Cultural Studies*, 5:3 (1993), p. 163 [reprinted in Vincente L. Rafael, *Discrepant Histories: Translocal Essays on Filipino Cultures* (Manila: Anvil Publishing, 1995), pp. 285–314].

7   Ambeth Ocampo, column pieces in *Philippine Daily Inquirer*, early 1990s, personal communications, 1996.

8   Vincente L. Rafael, 'Taglish, or the Phantom Power of the Lingua Franca', *Public Culture*, Volume 8 (1995), p. 118.

9   Henri Lefebvre, *The Production of Space*, trans. Donald Nicholson-Smith (Oxford: Basil Blackwell, 1991), pp. 82–83.

10 For the most systematic study of the city during this period, see Daniel F. Doeppers, *Manila 1900–1941: Social Change in a Late Colonial Metropolis* (Quezon City: Ateneo de Manila University Press, 1984).

11 Nick Joaquin, *Manila My Manila: A History for the Young* (Republic of the Philippines: The City of Manila, 1990), p. 157.

12 Nick Joaquin, *Almanac for Manilenos* (Manila: Mr & Ms Publications, 1979), p. 15.

13 Manuel A. Caoili, *The Origins of Metropolitan Manila: A Political and Social Analysis* (Quezon City: New Day Publishers, 1988), p. 51.

14 On the word 'downtown' entering into local circulation, see Joaquin, *Almanac*, p. 15.

15 Doeppers, *Manila 1900–1941*, p. 137.

16 *Ibid*.

17 American Express, *Manila and the Philippines* (Insular Life Building, Manila: American Express, 1932), p. 33. The caption for pictures of the carnival reads as follows: 'Night Scenes of the Illuminated Carnival City. The Main Entrance, Tower of Jewels, and Search Lights, Stand Out Brilliantly Against the Darkness'. *Ibid.*, p. 35.

18 See, for example, 'Seventh annual Floating Exposition puts out to sea to sell the nation', *Foto News*, 1 May 1938, p. 50. The caption for the pictures read: '[The] byword of the exposition is "Buy Things Philippines"… The entire ship has been transformed into a miniature National Produce Exchange…'.

19 'A riot of fun awaits you at the carnival', *Graphic*, 28 January 1931, p. 34.

20 Citation from Doeppers, *Manila*, p. 8. For more on Leopoldo R. Aguinaldo's department stores, see, for example, the *Manila Times* excerpts cited in Zoilo M. Galang, *Encyclopedia of the Philippines* (Manila: McCullough Printing Company, 1950), Volume 18, p. 213. In addition to having served as the president of the Philippine Chamber of Commerce, L. R. Aguinaldo was also at various points President of Luzon Surety Co., Director of the Manila Railroad Co., member of both the National Economic Protection Committee (NEPA) and, simultaneously, 'an organisation to press for the continuation of reciprocal free trade' with the United States. Citation from Doeppers, *Manila*, p. 30.

21 See, for example, 'Old theatres and new', *Graphic*, 6 May 1931, pp. 12, 49, and 56.

22 De Villa, Jones and Brady (eds), *Manila: The Traveler's Companion* (Manila: Devcon IP Inc., 1987), p. 59.

23 Luning Ira, *Streets of Manila* (Manila: GCF Books, 1977), pp. 60–61. On the Manila Stock Exchange's move to the Escolta, see: Rizal F. Gatica, *Manila Stock Exchange: A Description of its Functions and Operations* (Manila: Manila Stock Exchange, 1964), p. 2.

24 Zoilo M. Galang, *Encyclopedia of the Philippines* (Manila: McCullough Printing Company, 1950), p. 288.

25 Cultural Center of the Philippines, *Encyclopedia of Philippine Art: Volume III Philippine Architecture* (Manila : CCP, 1994), p. 224.

26 *Ibid.*, p. 223.

27 *Ibid*.

28 Citation from Henri Lefebvre, *Everyday Life in the Modern World* (New York: Harper and Row, 1971), p. 108. See further Guy Debord, *The Society of the Spectacle*, translated by Donald Nicholson-Smith (New York: Zone Books, 1995 edn).

29 Magazines from this period provide further instructive glimpses of an emerging national bourgeoisie reinventing, for example, new traditional costumes as part of such a process of self-definition. See, for example, 'Barong Tagalog coming into its own', *Graphic*, 15 April 1931, pp. 6,7, and 17; and 'Ternos and Sayas', *Foto News*, 15 November 1937, p. 51.

30 Joaquin, *Almanac*, p. 311.

31 Zoilo M. Galang, *Encyclopedia of the Philippines* (Manila: McCullogh Printing Company, 1950), Volume 5, p. 271.

32 Joaquin, *Almanac*, pp. 15–16. Joaquin also links 'the rule in the local film industry that a movie must open on a Friday' to *Viernes sa Quiapo*. Ibid., p. 16. For glimpses of pre-war *Viernes sa Quiapo*, see, for example, 'Manila's pious flock to quipo and its Black Nazarene', *Foto News*, 30 November 1937, pp. 24–25.

33 Ira, *Streets of Manila*, p. 100.

34 See, for example, Aprodicio Laquian, 'Manila', in William A. Robson and D.E. Regan (eds), *Great Cities of the World: Their Government, Politics and Planning* (London: Allen & Unwin, 1954), Volume 2, pp. 605–644.

35 Lewis E. Gleeck, Jr, *The Manila Americans (1901–1964)* (Manila: Carmelo & Bauermann, 1975), p. 316.

36 Rafael A.S.G. Ongpin, 'Who turned on the red lights?' *Manila Chronicle*, 22–28 August 1992, p. 8.

37 Caoili, *The Origins of Metropolitan Manila*, p. 71.

38 Gleeck, *The Manila Americans*, p. 316.

39 Ira, *Streets of Manila*, p. 61.

40 Ira, *Streets of Manila*, p. 79.

41 Ira, *Streets of Manila*, p. 100.

42 Ira, *Streets of Manila*, p. 79.

43 'The Philippine College of commerce: A new center of activism', *Sunday Times Magazine*, 2 November 1969, pp. 38–39.

44 See, for example, Andres Cristobal Cruz, 'A natural history of our nationalist demonstrations', *Graphic*, 9 February 1966, pp. 20–21; and Ninotchka Rosca, 'The Youth Movement in Retrospect', *Graphic*, 5 March 1969, pp. 6–9 and 49.

45 For some theoretical foundations for the brief exploration to follow on this wave of student protest, see especially Sidney Tarrow, *Struggle, Politics, and Reform: Collective Action, Social Movements, and Cycles of Reform* (Center for International Studies, Cornell University: Western Societies Program Occasional Paper No. 21, 1989).

46 See, for example, Jose F. Lacaba, 'The Clash of '69', *Philippines Free Press*, 8 February 1969, pp. 2–3, 66–67; and 'Of Dialogue & Demands', *Philippines Free Press*, 15 February 1969, pp. 5, 67.

47 José F. Lacaba, 'Look out Sir! Student power's going to break more windows', *Philippines Free Press*, 9 August 1969, p. 4.

48 See further Chapter 2 above.

49 José F. Lacaba, *Days of Quiet, Nights of Rage: The First Quarter Storm and Related Events* (Manila: Salinlahi Publishing House, 1982), p. 87.

50 Quijano de Manila, 'Foreword', in Lacaba, *Days of Quiet*, p. 19.

51 Lacaba, *Days of Quiet*, p. 93.

52 Oscar L. Evangelista, 'Lopez's Beleaguered Tenure (1969–1975): Barricades on Campus at the Peak of Student Discontent', in Oscar M. Alfonso (ed.), *University of the Philippines: The First 75 Years* (Quezon City: The University of the Philippines, 1985), p. 457.

53 For a discussion of the Plaza Miranda bombing on August 21, 1971, see Gregg R. Jones, *Red Revolution: Inside the Philippine Guerrilla Movement* (Boulder: Westview Press, 1989), pp. 59–69.

54 For an illumination of this notion of 'the public' as the negation of 'the private', rather than something to do with 'the civic', see Sudipta Kaviraj, 'Filth and the Public Sphere', *Public Culture*, Volume 10, Number 1 (1997), pp. 83–113.

55 Jose V. Abueva, 'The Citizens League and the 1959 Local Elections', in Raul de Guzman (ed.), *Patterns in Decision Making: Case Studies in Philippine Public Administration* (Honolulu: East-West Center Press, 1963), pp. 506 and 513.

56   See, for example, 'Pasay league's defeat analysed', *Manila Chronicle,* 15 November 1963, p. 16; and 'QC citizens league, off politics', *Manila Times,* 21 November, 1963, p. 24. By 1963, one study also identified such citizens leagues in Pasay City, Makati, Malabon, Mandaluyong, and Manila. See Aprodicio A. Laquian, 'The City in Nation-Building: Politics in Metro Manila' (Ph.D. dissertation, Massachusetts Institute of Technology, 1965).

57   Abueva, 'The Citizens League', pp. 513, 518.

58   For analyses of money and clientelism – and coercion – in Philippine politics during this period, see James C. Scott, 'Corruption, Machine Politics, and Political Change', *American Political Science Review,* Volume 63 (1969), pp. 1142–1158; and Thomas C. Nowak and Kay A. Snyder, 'Clientelist Politics in the Philippines: Integration or Instability?' *American Political Science Review,* Volume 68 (1974), pp. 1147–1170.

59   Evangelista, 'Lopez's Beleaguered Tenure', p. 462.

60   Elmer A. Ordoñez, 'Diliman: The Fifties to the First Quarter Storm', in Belinda A. Aquino (ed.), *The University Experience: Essays in the 82nd Anniversary of the U.P.* (Quezon City: University of the Philippines Press, 1991), p. 53. This author also mentions the infamous broadcast of the so-called 'Dovie Beams tape' with Marcos crooning to his starlet mistress.

61   Elmer A. Ordoñez, 'Diliman: The Fifties to the First Quarter Storm', in Belinda A. Aquino (ed.), *The University Experience: Essays in the 82nd Anniversary of the U.P.* (Quezon City: University of the Philippines Press, 1991), p. 53.

62   Evangelista, 'Lopez's Beleaguered Tenure', p. 463.

63   Luis V. Teodoro, 'UP in the Sixties: Life in the "Diliman Republic"', in Aquino (ed.), *The University Experience,* p. 59.

64   Evangelista, 'Lopez's Beleaguered Tenure', p. 464.

65   See, for example, David A. Rosenberg, 'Liberty versus Loyalty', in David Rosenberg (ed.), *Marcos and Martial Law in the Philippines* (Ithaca: Cornell University Press, 1979), p. 159.

66   See, for example, Jurgen Ruland, 'Metropolitan Government under Martial Law: The Metro Manila Commission Experiment', *Philippine Journal of Public Administration,* Volume 29, Number 1 (1985), pp. 27–41. Created by presidential decree, the MMC spanned four cities and thirteen municipalities at the outset in November 1975.

67   Vicente L. Rafael, 'Patronage and Pornography: Ideology and Spectatorship in the Early Marcos Years', *Comparative Studies in Society and History,* Volume 32, Number 2 (April 1990), pp. 282–304.

68   *Ibid.,* p. 295.

69   See, for example, Stephen Shalom, The United States and the Philippines: A Study of Neocolonialism (Quezon City: New Day Publishers, 1986), p. 176.

70   Rigoberto Tiglao, 'Mall Mogul', *Far Eastern Economic Review,* p. 51.

71   Joaquin, *Almanac,* p. 270.

72   Henry Sy cited in Rigoberto Tiglao, 'Strength in Numbers', *Far Eastern Economic Review,* 21 July 21 1994, p. 60.

73   Ira, *Streets of Manila,* p. 79.

74   See Temario C. Rivera and Kenji Koike, *The Chinese-Filipino Business Families under the Ramos Government* (Tokyo: Institute of Developing Economies Joint Research Program Series, No. 114, 1995), p. 48. The summary below draws heavily on Rivera and Koike's discussion on pp. 46–52. This work also examines questions of ownership, management and development up until the establishment of SM Prime Holdings by the Sy family in 1994.

75   Teresita Sy, cited in Rigoberto Tiglao, 'Strength in Numbers', *Far Eastern Economic Review,* 21 July 1994, p. 60. After over 20 years in the family business, Teresita Sy, an Assumption Convent graduate, is presently president of Shoemart and Banco de Oro as well as executive vice president of SMPH. Rivera and Koike, *Chinese-Filipino,* pp. 51–52.

76   Rigoberto Tiglao, 'Strength in numbers', p. 61.

77   Jonathan Friedland, 'Manila store wars', *Far Eastern Economic Review,* 22 December 1988, pp. 50–52.

78   Rivera and Koike, *Chinese-Filipino,* p. 46.

79 For detailed accounts of the graft and corruption under Marcos, see Belinda A. Aquino, *Politics of Plunder: The Philippines under Marcos* (Quezon City: Great Books Trading, 1987); Ricardo Manapat, *Some are Smarter than Others: The History of Marcos' Crony Capitalism* (New York: Aletheia Publications, 1991); and Paul David Hutchcroft, 'Predatory Oligarchy, Patrimonial State: The Politics of Private Commercial Banking in the Philippines' (Ph.D. dissertation, Yale University, New Haven, 1993). In a meeting on 'insurgency and the business community' called by the Harvard Business School Association of the Philippines, moreover, some '500 barong-clad corporate executives and their associates' heard Benguet Corporation President Jaime V. Ongpin speak on the revolutionary taxation of the country's largest mining company. Cited in *Veritas*, 30 June 1985, p. 4.

80 'At Shoemart, they've done it all', *Veritas*, 7 April 1985, p. 10.

81 Citation from Robin Broad, *Unequal Alliance: The World Bank, the International Fund, and the Philippines* (Berkeley: University of California Press, 1988), p. 219.

82 Angel I. Irlandez, 'The Shopping City', *Philippines Free Press*, 30 April 1988, p. 26.

83 Danilo Antonio, professor at the Asian Institute of Management, Makati, cited in Tiglao, 'Strength in numbers', p. 61.

84 Henry Sy, cited in Tiglao, 'Strength in numbers', p. 61.

85 Four of these nine SM Deparment Stores are located in SM's own Malls, and four of the remaining five such stores can be found in metropolitan Manila. Rivera and Koike, *Chinese-Filipino*, p. 48.

86 Rafael, 'Taglish', pp. 117–118.

87 The expression is from Roland Barthes, 'The New Citroen', *Mythologies* (New York: Hill and Wang, 1972 translation, 1995 edition), pp. 88–91.

88 For a glimpse of such an event featuring (future Congressional representative of first the House, then the Senate) Nikki Coseteng, see 'A Taste of a Bit of Freedom', *Mr & Ms*, 4 November 1983, p. 11.

89 For an illuminating discussion of Walter Benjamin's notion of the 'dream world of mass culture', see Susan Buck-Morss, *The Dialectics of Seeing: Walter Benjamin and the Arcades Project*, esp. pp. 253–286.

90 Notably, the rapid construction expansion of malls in Metro Manila has proceeded at a time when '[g]overment infrastructure projects have not – relatively – seen the spectacular growth rate of the private sector'. See Tiglao, 'Unexpected boom just keeps going', *Far Eastern Economic Review*, 4 May 1989, p. 55.

91 Cited in, for example, Jason Sulit Inocencio, 'Hangouts, tambayans, and places to eat', *Mr & Ms*, 27 April 1993, pp. 60–61. *Gamol* refers to something in excess, too much (almost vulgar).

7 From Pugad Lawin to Pugad Baboy

The making of the 'new native'

The lost continent: a search for origins

In San Juan, Metro Manila, not far from where the authors lived for many months in the early 1990s, there lies an area known as Pinaglabanan, a Tagalog word meaning 'battlefield'. Indeed, the name commemorates the outbreak of armed conflict in this part of San Juan in 1899 between Filipino defenders of the newly (and briefly) independent Malolos Republic and recently arrived American occupational forces. There is also a monument in the area, known as the Pinaglabanan Monument, which, if memory serves, consists essentially of a crescent-like saber rising out of a stone fulcrum at the end of a long plaza. But the Pinaglabanan Monument is hardly a well attended, or well tended, monument to Philippine nationalism: it is covered with graffiti and otherwise neglected by the authorities. More revealingly, perhaps, the monument is also surrounded by the homes of more than one hundred 'squatter' families. The plaza is used as a makeshift basketball court, and residents let visitors know that they are not particularly welcome.

Just around a bend in the road, however, lies a strikingly attractive square, filled with Spanish-style homes, many of which are occupied by the descendants of very well-to-do Revolution-era families (and also by the action film star, former mayor of San Juan, and current president, Joseph 'Erap' Estrada). Among the homes along this square is one which used to be owned by a certain Agnes Arellano, scion of a family whose progenitor, Cayetano Arellano, played a prominent role in events at the turn of the century. She converted this house and its grounds into an art gallery, the 'Pinaglabanan Gallery', a salon for Manileño artists and a very hip place in the 1980s.

In July 1989, the Pinaglabanan Gallery sponsored a highly intriguing and aesthetically impressive exhibit, 'Lemuria'. The artists responsible included avant-garde filmmaker Eric de Guia, better known by his nickname 'Kidlat Tahimik' (Quiet Lightning), painter and psychologist Katrin De Guia, and musician Shant Verdun.[1] The theme for this curious multi-media exhibit was the rediscovery and celebration of Lemuria, an ancient continent said to have once extended east from the Philippine archipelago far across what today comprises the Pacific Ocean. Through paintings, sculptures, video installations, and a bamboo contraption identified as a 'Lemurian Unidentified Floating Object Sight-Seeing Station', the artists colourfully represented this virtual lost city of Atlantis as an ancient civilisation of great sophistication and complexity. A 'great civilisation' which could, no doubt, be drawn upon for Philippine culture. Yet the guiding spirit of the exhibit was neither sanctimonious nor didactic, but rather imaginative and experimental. As Lemuria's creators explained:

> We are not out to prove that Lemuria existed.... But then again, we are not saying that Lemuria did not exist. Perhaps science should set out to prove its existence, but we are not scientists. We are just artists inspired by the myth of Lemuria and we have attempted to present Lemuria in our own artistic interpretations. We want to show the beauty of Lemuria, not whether it is real or not.[2]

The artists' notion of an ancient Lemurian civilisation as the basis for Philippine culture, it is worth noting, stood in stark contrast with the standard official account of history and 'pre-history' in the Philippines, which has left a curious blank spot when it comes to the 'origins' of the archipelago and of those identified today as Filipinos. As asserted in a key elementary school textbook published two years prior to the opening of the Lemuria exhibit:

> The Aetas or Negritos were the first to come to the Philippines. Aetas were short people. They had black skin. Their hair was short and kinky. They had small flat noses. Their lips were thick. Their hands and feet were short. They used bows and arrows to hunt for their food.
>
> Indonesians came to the Philippines. They were taller than the Negritoes. They had wider bodies. They had wide foreheads. They wore better clothes.
>
> Malays were brown in color. They were not so short and not so tall. They had black hair and eyes. They had small bodies. Like the Negritoes, they had small and flat noses, too.[3]

Subsequent passages credit Spain with bringing Christianity to the Philippines civilising and enlightening the population, and finally the Americans with teaching the Filipinos the art of self-government. 'We are forever indebted to her for our democratic system of government and laws'.[4] From a virtual *tabula rasa*, this narrative shows the emergence – and evolution – of the Philippines through the 'inevitable retreat of darker skinned, more savage inhabitants in the face of advancing groups of lighter skinned, more civilised and physically superior conquerors'.[5] As the elementary school textbook concludes this lesson, knowledge of these origins should ensure 'that every Filipino shall become conscious and aware of his roots and feel proud about it'.[6]

But the real lesson of this textbook is one of absence, the absence of origins, the revealed 'pre-historic' emptiness of the Philippine archipelago, the notable absence of a pre-colonial, indigenous civilisation as the basis for what is presented as an inherently problematic 'Filipino identity'. 'To be Filipino is not good enough', the anthropologist Niels Mulder concludes:

He [the Filipino] stands naked and in need of being dressed in foreign gear. Even for qualities that he most certainly had before alleged or actual culture contact took place, he must feel dependent, indebted, and grateful to others. To the Chinese for close family ties, to the Hindus for being superstitious, to the Spaniards for Christian virtues, and to the Americans for learning to take care of his own affairs. Everybody brought things to the Philippines and nobody is apparently interested in the idea that the pre-Spanish Filipinos sailed the South China Sea in all directions, trading with the Moluccas, Malacca, Champa, and southern China, and that they might have discovered and developed things for and by themselves.[7]

This standard account of Philippine 'origins', of course, bears obvious traces of a discourse established under colonial rule. Beginning in the sixteenth century, the Iberian colonists, in their post-Reconquista zeal to evangelise in the archipelago, attacked Islamic influences and suppressed those imported by immigrants from the southern coast of China. In terms of language and religion, Castilian Catholicism was imposed as a common 'Great Tradition' above the plurality of 'little traditions' found among the native inhabitants of the archipelago. As Vicente Rafael has noted:

It was as if the Tagalogs, along with the majority of other linguistic groups in the Philippines, had remained outside of history – that is, history as it was known to the West. What the Spaniards saw was a mass of ritual practices that did not seem to be attached to any identifiable 'civilisation'. Hence the project of evangelisation involved the alignment of this cultural mass with the laws of Spanish-Catholic civilisation.[8]

Subsequently, in the first four decades of the twentieth century, the American colonial regime, which in its first census (1903) categorised the population in terms of black, brown, and yellow, 'civilized' and 'wild', accentuated the racist dimension of this long-standing tendency to relegate 'native culture' to the categories of primitive, backward, and parochial. Those classified as 'civilized' owed this distinction to Catholicism and other effects of Spanish rule, whereas the 'wild' Muslims or pagans who had resisted or otherwise escaped earlier efforts at colonisation (and evangelisation) were portrayed as living in 'stages between almost complete savagery and dawning civilisation'.[9] As the anthropologist Benito Vergara, Jr. has argued, the plurality of 'non-Christian tribes' designated by the American census underlined that the Filipinos 'were not merely incapable of self-government; they were not even a "people".'[10] Filipinos' 'seeming inability to achieve some sort of national cohesion' served, Vergara notes, 'as a clear sign of inferiority, and a rationale for colonisation'.[11]

This pattern of Spanish and American colonial disregard and dismissiveness of indigenous Philippine culture(s) stood in stark contrast with the well documented efforts towards the 'invention of tradition' pursued in the other colonies of Southeast Asia. In Java, for example, the Dutch encouraged the subjugated local aristocracy to develop 'Javanese' court culture in accordance with Dutch Javanologists' advice and authority,[12] whilst in the Federated Malay States, British residents inspired the sultans to codify and regulate Islamic law and *adat* (local custom).[13] Even in French Indochine, French lycée lessons in Cambodge sang the praises of Angkor's abundant architectural splendour and its (exaggerated) agricultural productivity, chastising the 'Khmers' for the decline of 'their' once-great empire.[14] In all of these cases, 'traditions' were invented, continuities conjured up, and (lost) civilisations celebrated. In the Philippines, by contrast, a deafening silence reigned: with no pre-colonial temple tablets to pore over, no native aristocrats to pamper and preoccupy, the colonial representation of 'civilisation' in the archipelago centred unequivocally around the Catholic Church and a rather Hispanicised élite.

In short, the backdrop to the Lemuria exhibit is a well established, officially propagated notion that the Philippine archipelago was essentially *empty* centuries ago, until various *foreigners* showed up, blessing it with their presence, their blood, their heritage, until something like 'a Filipino' emerged as a by-product of this process. Thus there is no real point of origins at all, no notion of a pre-colonial 'usable past', but rather a residual sense of 'Filipino culture' as that which explains deviations from the Great Traditions that have left such marked traces on the archipelago and its inhabitants.

The creators of Lemuria can perhaps be seen as engaged in a somewhat belated quest for the lost origins of the Philippines, in the service not of colonialism but of what might be described as a nationalist project. Indeed, members of the so-called Propaganda Movement, which emerged among wealthy, educated Filipinos in the late nineteenth century and in some key ways contributed to the Philippine Revolution of 1896–98, showed great interest in the exploration – and exaggeration – of pre-colonial Tagalog society and the native aristocratic élite of the archipelago.[15] More recently, of course, long-time president (1966–86) Ferdinand E. Marcos had promoted the recuperation of pre-Spanish 'culture', now deployed in a half-hearted official nationalism and state-building project that included the renaming of sub-municipal *barrios* as *barangay* and an (ill-fated) plan to change the name of the Philippines to Maharlika in commemoration of the pre-colonial village 'nobility' of Tagalog areas.[16]

Yet the creators of Lemuria offered their Lost Continent not as an authoritative source of national origins, but as something far more ambiguous, elusive, ethereal, and ultimately unavailable as the foundation for an essentialised notion of Philippine authenticity. The Lost Continent, as the artists themselves made clear, stood as testimony to the creativity of Filipinos today in representing themselves, their past and future, their hopes and dreams.

Yet perhaps the Lost Continent, for all its evocative beauty and nationalist potential, is a lost cause of sorts. After all, the Pinaglabanan Gallery enjoyed a very exclusive clientele in the 1980s and eventually closed in the 1990s, its avant-garde exhibits unlikely to have made much of an impact upon the broader population at large. The kids playing basketball across the road in front of the Pinaglabanan Monument, if they happened to make it through grade school, were more likely to have read the official textbook account of Philippine origins than to have entered the art gallery physically nearby but socially many, many miles away. The explanatory signs accompanying the exhibit, moreover, were in English, the sometimes wistful, sometimes tongue-in-cheek captions addressed not to the Tagalog-speaking street kids down the road, but to well-educated, English-speaking readers.

Looking beyond Lemuria and the Pinaglabanan Gallery, the remainder of this chapter examines other instances in which Filipinos, in recent years, have come to represent themselves, in new and creative ways, to a broader audience. These varied manifestations of a vibrant nationalist consciousness, it is argued, rely neither on notions of a recuperable pre-colonial past, nor on glorification of historical heroes, nor on an essentialised conception of an authentic *ur*-Filipino. Maintaining a healthy distance from the half-baked state-sponsored 'official nationalism' typified by the elementary school textbooks cited above, the popular nationalism in evidence today draws on the shared lived experiences of millions of Filipinos as they have struggled, since the 1970s, in the face of dramatic economic, social, and political change. Against the grain of arguments that Filipinos suffer from neo-colonial consciousness,[17] a weak sense of national identity,[18] and a 'damaged culture',[19] this chapter shows Filipino nationalist consciousness and sentiment today to be far more vibrant, more inclusively gendered, and more politically promising than the official nationalisms promoted elsewhere in Southeast Asia.

History: a question of heroes?

A fine example of this flourishing Filipino nationalism can be found today in the extraordinary popularity of a contemporary historian, Ambeth Ocampo. Ocampo, a favourite student of the late nationalist historian (and author of official textbooks) Teodoro Agoncillo and now himself the occupant of a prestigious chair in Philippine History at the City University of Manila, is a novice in the Benedictine Order who combines the monkhood with teaching and extensive historical research and writing. Ocampo writes regular columns titled 'Looking Back' in the *Philippine Daily Inquirer*, the leading Manila broadsheet, and sometimes pens additional columns for other papers under a variety of thinly disguised *noms de plume*. He has published more than a dozen books, mostly compilations of his newspaper columns, which have won numerous prizes and sold tens of thousands of copies over the past decade. Extraordinarily popular and influential, widely read and appreciated, Ocampo has done more than any single author in recent years to inspire interest in and enthusiasm for Philippine history among a broad Filipino audience.

Without a pre-colonial 'civilisation' to anchor some notion of authentic Philippine origins, it could be argued, interest in and celebration of Philippine history – and the heroic struggle for Philippine independence – may offer an alternative source for the promotion of nationalism today. Indeed, in tandem with the centennial anniversary of the Philippine Revolution, the government has sponsored a variety of commemorative activities, events, and spectacles. Yet these state-sponsored history lessons have clearly failed to generate much interest among a broad Filipino audience. The televised version of José Rizal's classic late nineteenth-century novel *Noli Me Tangere* elicited little in the way of comment or enthusiasm, and director Raymond Red's two Revolution-era films, 'Bayani' and 'Sakay', found faint praise among those who attended the very limited, exclusive screenings, with critics bewailing the overly stiff and sanctimonious tones of the scripts. The government-sponsored conference on the Philippine Revolution, held in the posh Manila Hotel in August 1996, gave centre stage to Philippine politicians and foreign dignitaries (e.g. Malaysian Deputy Prime Minister Anwar Ibrahim), generating little public interest and leaving serious historians of the Revolution with minor, supportive roles or, in the case of Ambeth Ocampo, effectively excluded.

Ocampo's newspaper columns, now translated into Tagalog for reprinting in Manila's tabloids, continue to attract a broad audience, reflecting the popularity which his distinctive style and subject matter have earned among readers. Like many other historians, Ocampo evinces considerable interest in such luminaries of late nineteenth-century Philippine history as José Rizal, Apolinario Mabini, Andres Bonifacio, and Emilio Aguinaldo. Yet Ocampo's columns do not simply reaffirm these nationalist icons' heroic contributions to the struggle against the Spanish colonial regime. Instead, he brings these characters to life through vignettes uncovered through his relentless trawlings in the National Archives and his own personal library. Rizal's undergarments, adolescent crushes, and favourite breakfast dishes, Aguinaldo's shopping list in exile in Hong Kong, Bonifacio's bolo – such are the topics of many Ocampo columns. Instead of a narrative of exemplary heroes, Philippine nationalism is shown to be embedded in a distinctly local context, one whose recovery serves not to elevate the heroes to mythical status, but to render their lives more accessible to a broader audience of Filipinos today. Instead of heroic 'great men', Ocampo highlights an emerging Filipino culture; instead of the grand narrative of Nationalist Struggle, he portrays the struggles of everyday life. Nationalism, Ocampo seems to stress, is not just for exemplary, élite individuals – it is for all. As he concludes in a 1989 column, 'our heroes have been so glorified that people cannot imagine them eating, drinking, womanizing, or having plain human emotions like you and me'.[20]

Moreover, Ocampo frequently calls attention to the political uses to which Philippine History has been subjected, even as he chips away at the fossilising effects of an official nationalism that has domesticated the memory of its National Heroes. As Ocampo notes in the preface to his aptly titled *Rizal Without the Overcoat*:

> Rizal is so much a part of everyday life Filipinos have taken him for granted. At most he is remembered annually on 19 June and 30 December when politicians use him as an excuse to bore people with their sophomoric speeches. I would have ended up like everyone else if my father had not brought me to Luneta as a boy and asked why Rizal always wore his heavy

winter coat even in the tropics. *Ang init-init dito naka*-overcoat! [It's really hot here to be wearing an overcoat!] From then on I started thinking, what would Rizal be without his overcoat![21]

Against the Rizal whose profile marks Philippine pesos, whose statue graces every town plaza in the archipelago, and whose name adorns countless streets, parks, and companies, Ocampo revisits the Rizal celebrated by Rizalista cult members as a living force on Mount Banahaw, near his hometown of Calamba, Laguna. Against the Rizal whose life, poetry, and novels are mandatory reading for thousands of (resentful, bored) university students, Ocampo recalls the controversy surrounding the passage of the Rizal Bill in 1956, when members of the Catholic Church hierarchy vehemently opposed the legislated compulsory inclusion of Rizal's novels – deemed offensively anti-clerical in countless passages – in the national university curriculum. Against the fixity of José Rizal, National Hero, Ocampo celebrates the multiplicity of Rizals in popular myth and memory; against the authority of History, he offers colourful – but critical – historiography.

More importantly, perhaps, Ocampo writes with considerable admiration and enthusiasm for the José Rizal he finds 'without the overcoat'. Drawing upon diaries and correspondence, Ocampo shares with us the acerbic comments about American tourists in Europe he discovers among Rizal's journal entries, passages of prurient interest he savours in Rizal's novels, and humorous drawings sketched by Rizal in Germany and during his exile in Dapitan. Here we find not the solemnly silent Rizal of town plaza statues, nor the Rizal whose novels, as Benedict Anderson has shown, have been translated and reproduced (in *komiks* and film) in a peculiarly demodernised, bowdlerised, delocalised, and anachronistic fashion for the sanctimoniously 'educational' purposes of Philippine official nationalism.[22] Instead, we find the Rizal whose uncomfortable features have elsewhere been systematically effaced, the Rizal whose biting wit and social commentary have been erased by translators from the pages of the Noli: the popular nationalist whom Anderson describes as 'a socially radical, iconoclastic, satirical, earthy, moralising Rizal'.[23] Thus 'our *Lolo* (Grandpa) José' affectionately invoked (and effectively evoked) by Ocampo is not a stern, moralising old schoolmaster but a witty, worldly, brilliant satirist, an endearingly hopeless romantic, and a lovable old duffer to be sure.

Egged on by the amiable spectre of Lolo José, Ocampo has proceeded in the spirit of mirthful irreverence. Ruminating about Rizal's psychic powers in late October 1987, Ocampo bows out, mischievously, with 'Happy Halloween'. Speculating about the origins of syphilis or the history of sodomy in the archipelago, or pondering the question 'What's the National Smell?', Ocampo has not only contributed to what has been described as 'the unlearning' of 'the inherited dominative mode', he has wrested History from Authority and let loose countless histories with which to thumb one's nose at the contemporary status quo.[24]

No doubt inspired by Ocampo's example, a group of fellow-travellers, self-described as 'Los Enemigos', in 1993 published an hilarious spoof on Rizal's movingly patriotic poem 'Mi Ultimo Adios', accompanied by a caveat – 'with all due respect and apologies to Dr. José Rizal, ex-future Secretary of Health' – and a gas mask superimposed over the photographed face of Lolo José.[25] The Los Enemigos version combined the love of country expressed in Rizal's original with amply justified dismay at the environmental condition of the contemporary Philippines. 'Adiós, Pátria adorada…', they begin, echoing Rizal, but then Rizal's 'Perla del mar de oriente, nuestro perdido Edén' (Pearl of the eastern sea, our lost Eden) becomes 'Perla del mar de trapiko, nuestro perdido tambutso' (Pearl of the sea of traffic, our lost exhaust pipes). After many more such verses, in which Tagalog punch-lines and contemporary reference points substitute for Rizal's solemn Spanish, Los Enemigos reach their final stanza. Compare Rizal's last lines:

> Adiós, padres y hermanos, trozos del alma mia,
> Amigos de la infancia, en el perdido hogar;
> Dad gracias que descanso del fatigoso día;
> Adiós, dulce extranjera, mi amiga, mi alegría,
> Adiós, querido séres, morir es descansar.

> [Farewell, fathers and brothers, pieces torn from my soul,
> Childhood friends, in ruined homes,
> Give thanks that I now rest from the tiring day;
> Farewell, sweet stranger, my friend, my joy;
> Farewell to all my loved ones, to die is to rest.]

And the spoof version of Los Enemigos:

> Adios erpats, mga utol, troso ng mga logger
> At ikaw na law enforcer, arestuhin mga smoke-belcher
> Dad gracias de descanso, People Power! People Power!
> Adios Edsa, Bayang Sawi, how dirty the Pasig River
> Adios Baha, Adios Lahar, morir es respirar.

> [Farewell pops, bruthers, loggers' logs
> And you, law enforcer, arrest the smoke-belchers
> Give thanks for rest, People Power! People Power!
> Farewell Edsa, unfortunate nation, how dirty the Pasig River
> Farewell floods, farewell mud-slides, to die is to breathe.][26]

Authenticity: the new native

Alongside the resurgence of interest in Philippine history exemplified by Ambeth Ocampo, recent years have also witnessed a renaissance in the representation – or, in the words of the iconoclastic anthropologist Arnold Azurin, the reinvention – of The Filipino.[27] In some cases, this trend has assumed the form of a renewed search for a timeless, essentialised Filipino, with discussions of Filipino

Personality, Filipino Identity, and Filipino Culture circulating more broadly than ever. In the academe, for example, Philippine scholars have initiated a critical reexamination of the 'Filipino values' – *utang na loób* (eternal debt of gratitude), *awa* (pity), *hiya* (shame), *pakikisama* (mutual cooperation), and 'smooth interpersonal relations' (SIR) – posited by sociologists at the exclusive, Jesuit-run Ateneo de Manila University's Institute of Philippine Culture in the 1960s and early 1970s.[28]

Whilst these prior treatments of 'Filipino values' presented a composite image of the Filipino as a 'smiling, peace-loving, religious, deferential, hard-working, family-bound and hospitable native',[29] subsequent scholarship has drawn less conservative conclusions. Already in the 1970s, for example, Reynaldo Ileto, in his classic *Pasyon and Revolution*, linked these 'values' to a rich and long-standing tradition of peasant rebellion and popular religion, whilst Vicente Rafael in the early 1980s suggested their centrality in shaping (as well as subverting) what he described, in his path-breaking work *Contracting Colonialism*, as the 'translation' of Iberian Catholicism into terms comprehensible and compelling to the members of Tagalog society. Inspired by the nationalist force and counter-hegemonic thrust of such studies, other Filipino scholars by the late 1980s were writing – now often in Tagalog rather than English – on indigenous religious beliefs and practices and other similar topics with considerable intensity and insight.

Whilst this trend has remained largely confined to a narrow academic audience and begun to fossilise into the self-importance and pseudo-science of 'Pilipinolohiya', the interest in Filipino-ness today appears to be circulating more widely (and more freely) outside the university classroom. Take, for example, an article which appeared in the newsletter *Ang Tambuli* in December 1995, titled 'Are You Really a Filipino??? 115 Ways to Make Sure'.[30] The test has six sections: Mannerisms and Personality Traits, Vocabulary, Home Furnishings, Automobiles, Family, and Food. Sample questions provide a sense of the notion of The (Real) Filipino promoted by the test:

1   You point with your lips.
18   You play pusoy and mah jong.
28   You consistently arrive 30 minutes late for all events.
29   You always offer food to all your visitors.
30   You say 'comfort room' instead of 'bathroom'.
35   You refer to the refrigerator as the 'ref' or 'pridyider'.
38   You say 'Ha?' instead of 'What?'.
55   You own a *karaoke* system.
59   You have two to three pairs of *tsinelas* (sandals) at your doorstep.
62   You display a big laughing Buddha for good luck.
63   You have a shrine to the Santo Niño in your living room.
84   You have aunts and uncles named 'Baby', 'Girlie', or 'Boy'.
89   Your parents call each other 'mommy' and 'daddy'.
106   You use your fingers to measure the water when cooking rice.
111   You eat purple yam-flavoured ice cream.
114   You think half-hatched duck eggs are a delicacy.

Originally designed for Filipino immigrants in California, the test instructs test-takers to give themselves three points for each item and then to tabulate their score, with those over 259 told 'There's no doubt what your ethnic identity is! You're Filipino, through and through', whilst those garnering below 172 points receive a mixed message: 'You have OFT (OBVIOUS FILIPINO TENDEN-CIES). Go with the flow to reach full Filipino potential. Prepare for assimilation; resistance is futile'.

As this ambivalent advice suggests, the notion of Filipino-ness in the 'test' is decidedly open-ended. Instead of a set of 'core values', Filipino identity is shown to revolve around a cluster of everyday practices. Rather than a sanctimonious, ivory-tower 'Sikolohiyang Pilipino', the test invites Filipinos both to celebrate and to chuckle at the myriad qualities and habits that mark them as Filipinos, even as the sheer diversity, comic effect, and contradictory nature of the one hundred and fifteen 'ways to make sure' suggest both the possibility of virtually anyone being – or at least becoming – Filipino, and the impossibility of stabilising 'Filipino' in a single, timeless essence. As the self-mockingly named Pidrofile (as in Pedro-phile) t-shirts sold in Manila's shopping malls proudly proclaim, 'Pilipino Ako' (I am a Filipino), and then, sheepishly, below, 'Walang Pangit Sa Dilim' (No one's Ugly in the Dark). The real message on Filipino identity, it appears, is that it should be seen, shared, and savoured through a light, affectionately self-deprecatory joke, a joke that perhaps only other Filipinos can truly appreciate.

Today's rising interest in forms of indigenous ethnic identity, seen as virtually uncorrupted by foreign influences of Christianity, colonialism, and consumerism, also appears to follow the same guiding spirit. The romanticisation of the un-Christianised and 'tribal' peoples of Northern Luzon's Gran Cordillera (often referred to collectively as 'Igorots') and Mindanao's interior (similarly glossed as 'lumad', meaning 'native' in Tagalog) is evident in the scenery of numerous recent films, the proliferation of stores selling 'ethnic' jewellery and fabrics to foreign tourists and urban Filipinos alike, and the collections of textiles, furniture and other 'tribal objects' assembled in the homes of wealthy Manileños. As Ramon Villegas, a Manila-based antiques and jewellery dealer, told a visiting correspondent from the American magazine *House & Garden*, 'The tribal people are being integrated. I wanted something left here so the next generation would know about their heritage'.[31]

Yet for a broader Filipino audience, the celebration of 'indigenous' culture shows greater evidence of honesty – and humour – with regard to the nature of claims to a common, *ur*-Filipino 'heritage'. One case in point is a recently published book of magical spells, whose purposes vary from stimulating sexual attraction to inducing invisibility, bringing luck to homes, and obtaining business assistance from white dwarven spirits. The book, which promises readers that anyone can use such benign witchcraft (and without spending more than twenty minutes on a given spell), provides a complete list of the ingredients to be used in each instance. Alongside candles, sugar, water, sand, and local fruits, the spells typically rely on common household ingredients: 12 White Rabbit candies, Scotch tape, red giftwrapping ribbon, a plastic bag from National Book Store, 7 pages of the Philippine Daily Inquirer, spoonfuls of Pride powder detergent. As the author notes in the introduction: 'Anyone can pray, likewise anyone can also cast spells. Like me. Like You. Make magic!'[32]

Another case in point is the folk music group Bagong Lumad (New Native), founded by composer and lead singer Joey Ayala and a group of other musicians based in Davao City. In recordings and performances, Bagong Lumad relies heavily on a decidedly 'ethnic' set of instruments, including a T'boli lute, gongs, and various bamboo string and percussion devices drawn from other musical traditions in their native Mindanao. Yet persistent memories of the Tasaday hoax in the early 1970s, when the Marcos government (as well as a number of local and foreign anthropologists and journalists) claimed to have discovered a rainforest-dwelling, 'stone-age tribe' in the Cotabato region of Mindanao, may have helped to shape Bagong Lumad's claim to represent a New Native form of music.[33] Even as Ayala and his fellow band members dress in distinctively 'ethnic' costume, sing songs (mostly in Tagalog, but sometimes in the Cebuano prevalent in southeastern Mindanao) of an expressedly environmentalist nature, and strum or thump instruments of T'boli, Manobo, or Bagobo provenance, they make sure not to be seen to take themselves too seriously. In concert performances and in interviews, Ayala is quick to note that he grew up not in the bucolic backhills of Mindanao, but in the concrete jungles of Cubao, Quezon City; onstage, once he has explained the ethnic origins and musical functions of various instruments, he turns to the audience and, with eyebrows arched and a sly grin emerging, points out what he describes as his equally Traditional, Native electric guitar.[34]

Mimicry: imitation and subversion

Whilst Joey Ayala and Bagong Lumad have certainly remained 'alternative' (in Ayala's words, 'alter-native'), their concerts and recordings appealing to a very narrow, if deeply committed, set of fans, the broader phenomenon of Pinoy Rock has in recent years enjoyed growing popularity among a much larger audience. Drawing eclectically from various foreign blues, folk, rap, rock, reggae and ska traditions, Pinoy (i.e. Filipino) Rock groups play to full houses in the nightclubs of Manila and several other major Philippine cities. On boats, buses and jeepneys, in homes, factories, and offices throughout the archipelago, the sound of Pinoy Rock is blaring today with great intensity.[35]

Tagalog lyrics aside, Pinoy Rock, it could easily be argued, sounds much like a localised version of music heard all over the world in this age of digital reproduction. Pinoy Rock groups have names reminiscent of American or British bands, like The Jerks, The Eraserheads, Color It Red; they sing covers of classic rock tunes by the Beatles, the Rolling Stones, and The Who. Even their own songs often revolve around the predictable themes of modern pop music: unrequited loves, frustrated ambitions, psychedelic experiences, the troubles of the world. Pinoy Rock, it could be said, is nothing more – or less – than Rock Music in the Philippines, its forms (and its popularity) ample testimony to the global reach of American culture and the subjugation of the Philippines to what some have derided as 'Coca-Colanisation'.

Yet the practitioners of Pinoy Rock have also proven to be particularly adept and creative in what deserves to be called the art of appropriation, their mockery of mimicry slyly subverting the hierarchy of mimesis assumed by most observers. Take Parokya ni Edgar, for example, a Pinoy Rock band whose poignant rhapsody of friendship, alcoholism, and suicide, 'Buloy', became a top radio hit in 1996. The band's first album fades in with space-age tones and an equally ethereal female voice (titled 'Galactic Lady Intro') announcing, in evenly enunciated, amply Americanised syllables: 'Welcome to the Parokya ni Edgar Experience.... Dim the Lights, Take a Deep Breath, Close Your Eyes, and Count to Four...'. Seconds later, a raucous chorus of several male voices, with heavily exaggerated Filipino accents, responds: 'Wan, Too, Tree, Por!' and the fun begins, inaugurated by a bauble of voices and a rousing set of heavily wah-pedalled guitar riffs.

A variety of songs follow, all in Tagalog, many commending themselves for a distinctive blend of musical virtuosity and comic appeal, but two songs in particular are relevant for the present discussion. The first, on Side A, offers a fast, electric version of Bob Dylan's 'Knocking on Heaven's Door', crooned as mournfully as in the original version. Yet the Tagalog lyrics substituted by Parokya ni Edgar combine the pathos of the Dylan tune with an alternative setting: instead of Bob Dylan wailing 'Kno-kno-knocking on Heaven's Door', we hear the Parokya's lead singer moan 'Na-na-nakaw ang wallet ko!' – My wallet was stolen! – and listen as he begs for assistance on the street with this line as his refrain. After a few original Tagalog tunes, the band turns, on Side B, to a very tongue-in-cheek rendition of another classic rock love song, but this one restyled to capture the singer's love for the Special Siopao (a very doughy kind of meat bun) at a nearby Chinese restaurant:

> Whenever I'm at Shaolin House, I blow all my money
> On order after order of meat balls and pork stew
> Whatever flavour, cat or dog
> So long as it's the Special Siopao, it's so very special....
> This is the trip, this is what I want
> That's why I'm always here, 'Cause I do belong here....
>
> I think I've gotten indigestion on this siopao
> I've eaten more than eighteen of them
> I want you to know that The Special Siopao
> Is really my favourite, it's so very special....
>
> [Pag Nasa Shaolin House, naubos ang pera ko
> Sa aking kakaorder ng bola-bola't asado
> Kahit anong flavour, pusa man o aso
> Basta siopao na special, it's so very special....
> Ito ang trip, ito ang gusto ko
> That's why I'm always here, 'Cause I do belong here....

> Sa siopao na ito, na empacho yata ako
> Ang aking nakain ay lampas labing walo
> I want you to know that paborito ko talaga
> Ang siopao na special, it's so very special....]

The next song is a cover of The Clash's classic 'Should I Stay or Should I Go?', equally tortured, but now reworked in Tagalog as 'Bakit Ang Pangit-Pangit Mo?' – Why Are You So Ugly?

Overall, even as Parokya ni Edgar mimics these American and British rock classics, it seems, the group reverses whatever submissiveness might be suggested by the act of mimesis, by mocking the songs, the mimicry, and themselves. But the quality of the music and the jokes, the sheer force of the band's evident talents, belies the mockery itself, in yet another ironic twist. Even the very name of the band itself suggests slippage in this direction: Parokya ni Edgar (Edgar's Parish) sounds like Parodya ni Edgar (Edgar's Parody or The Parody of Edgar).

Such sly mockery of mimicry is also evident in yet another powerful medium in the contemporary Philippines: Tagalog films. Recent years, in fact, have seen the production of several movies whose comic plot and substance relies heavily on this same kind of humour, movies with names like 'Starzan', 'Elvis and James', and 'Michael and Madonna'. 'Michael and Madonna', for example, depicts a budding romance between a motor-tricycle driver (Michael) and a hot dog-stand attendant (Madonna). The tricycle driver, played by the half-toothless, bulgy-eyed, scraggly-haired comedian Rene Requiestas, is, the audience soon learns, seemingly obsessed with the idea that he is – or at least that he wants to be – the pop super-star Michael Jackson, as he reminds us by wearing a black leather jacket, making extravagant gestures reminiscent of Michael Jackson videos, and issuing proclamations based on Michael Jackson song lyrics but reiterated in an exaggeratedly heavy Filipino accent. Requiestas' delivery is perfect, tongue-in-cheek somehow mixed in with 'Michael's' solemnity, as is his (and Madonna's) footwork in the dance in the final scene, and he virtually beams with self-satisfaction throughout the film. As he proclaims after examining himself approvingly in the mirror, grinning almost toothlessly, in the small shack where he lives: 'Ang ganda mong lalaki. Hayop ka talaga!' – You handsome dude. You animal!

This recurring mockery of mimicry in Philippine popular music and films seems to resonate with practices of everyday life engaged in by ordinary Filipinos throughout the archipelago. The anthropologist Fenella Cannell, for example, in her account of life in a poor rural barangay in the Bicol Peninsula, writes eloquently of her friend Ilar singing an English song in the rice fields where she works:

> There is a particular elan about carrying off well a song in this foreign language, especially solo. It is, it appears, a small act of triumph; a small act of possession of this culture which largely excludes the poor. At the same time, there is a kind of nostalgia which attaches to it when sung in this context;

not the nostalgia for an autumn leaf in a place on the other side of the world which evades the imagination, but a nostalgia for the fragility of this act of possession, perhaps of any acts of possession; the difficulty of appropriating fragments of this culture as your own.

Combined with this nostalgia, though, is the sense of daring which comes from performing the song; the taking part in a shared joke. Ilar and all her friends know she is not American, not a glamorous singer or film star or even a local chanteuse for a dance band, but a poor farmer with T.B. and old clothes even at a wedding. The performance is therefore partly a conspiratorial joke, a sending-up by both audience and performer of the incongruity between the standards of American stardom and the circumstances of life in the barangay. It is this kind of joke which figures constantly in daily conversation; the ironic references to typhoon damage as 'air-conditioning'....[36]

Reflecting on such practices, Cannell argues that imitation in the Philippines must not be confused with 'mere derivativeness'; in Bicol, she concludes, 'imitation of content can constitute a self-transformative process which is itself part of Bicol culture and its historical continuity'.[37]

Thus the quest for a 'Filipino identity' may lead beyond a celebration of the 'indigenous' and towards a form of discovery which takes place through the appropriation of the foreign. A fine example of this process revealed by Cannell is found in a scene in Pugad Baboy, the popular *komiks* strip regularly featured in the *Philippine Daily Inquirer*. One of the main characters, a member of the leftist New People's Army named Ka (Comrade) Noli, leads a group of his neighbours from Manila on a tour of the Ilocos provinces. Wandering through the remote hills of the area, they stumble upon an old farmer, Ka Kwate, a man of great simplicity and self-evident 'folk wisdom' and a comrade of Ka Noli in the struggle.

The city-dwellers (accompanied by the talking dog Polgas) find themselves in a series of wacky adventures with Ka Kwate, including a local land dispute with none other than Ka Damuseyn, the spitting image of the Iraqi dictator. The series concludes with Ka Noli and his gang taking their leave of Ka Kwate, with the two comrades first exchanging solemn farewells in Ilocano, followed by a similarly serious parting scene in Tagalog between Ka Kwate and another of his visitors from Manila. Finally, Polgas and Ka Kwate exchange meaningful glances, and then the talking dog raises his paw high in the air saying 'Ibigay mo "tol" – a literal Tagalog translation of "Give it to me, bro"'. Responding appropriately with a quick 'high five', the wisened old Ilocano farmer shouts back the punchline: 'Rayt-on Bebe!'

Language and representation: the Filipino experience

As this example suggests, cartoon strips like Pugad Baboy offer an ideal medium for the representation of Filipinos and the Philippines, for what Benedict Anderson has memorably described as nationalist 'imaginings'.[38] Published regularly in Manila's best daily broadsheet, the *Philippine Daily Inquirer*, Pugad Baboy has earned the loyalties of thousands upon thousands of readers, as seen in the publication of numerous Pugad Baboy compilations and the sale in Manila's shopping malls of t-shirts depicting the various characters in the cartoon strip. In its subject matter and its sensibility, Pugad Baboy provides readers, quite literally, an 'imagined community' of fellow-Filipinos, whose everyday encounters and extraneous excursions are – humorously or otherwise – familiar to many residents of the Philippines.

The cartoon strip conjures up an imaginary neighbourhood somewhere in Metro Manila, Pugad Baboy or, literally translated, Pigs' Nest. Significantly, in striking contrast with virtually all previous (and even contemporary) cartoon strips, Pugad Baboy depicts not classic Western comic-book characters who look unmistakably like Europeans and North Americans,[39] but instead noticeably plump, and in some cases distinctly porcine, Filipinos who live in this appropriately named urban community. As an imaginary community, Pugad Baboy is one which, by metonymy rather than metaphor, appears decidedly national and inclusive in its scope and composition. The motley cast of characters includes a Constabulary sergeant and a member of the Communist Party-led New People's Army, the family of an overseas contract worker in Saudi Arabia (complete with Visayan housemaid), a corrupt politician, an aging hippy, and a Chinese immigrant with a transvestite son.

These characters' daily lives and wacky adventures provide the basis for both the hilarious humour of Pugad Baboy and the cartoon strip's capacity for representing the Filipino condition today. Many of the scenes depicted in Pugad Baboy are familiar ones to any resident of Manila: the insides of crowded jeepneys and buses, boulevards where car drivers encounter extortionist traffic cops or street-corner beggars, road-side beer-houses and *carinderias*, elementary school classrooms and doctor's offices, and the makeshift basketball courts and laundry-filled windows of countless Manila neighbourhoods. Other scenarios take the cast of cartoon characters farther afield: to the construction sites of Saudi Arabia or the remote jungles of Northern Luzon, where they encounter everything from a foreign paedophile syndicate (operating a military-protected illegal airstrip) to an 'ethnic tribe' (in need of repairs for a broken video cassette recorder).

Throughout Pugad Baboy, the twin messages of humour and humanity are skilfully interwoven. In many instances, the joke revolves around Pugad Baboy residents' commentaries on current events, or their dealings with various predators – e.g. corrupt policemen and politicians, surly Arab bosses, local swindlers and drug-pushers, Japanese gangsters – and pompous prigs – e.g. holier-than-thou schoolteachers, snotty *balikbayan* (returning emigré visitors) on holiday in Manila. The extortionist or intruder shows him/herself to be a fool or a fraud, whilst the Pugad Baboy resident counters with a deft riposte or a wry aside, exposing exploitation and subverting relations of hierarchy in the process. Other jokes come at the expense of the Pugad Baboy regulars themselves, centring on their evident obesity, crass materialism, narrow-mindedness, and various prejudices. But here the humour is affectionately self-deprecatory: readers of Pugad

Baboy are clearly laughing at themselves for failings and foibles that are distinct-ively, forgivably, even lovably 'Filipino'.

Moreover, as in the popular music and movies cited above, this cartoon strip is careful to turn the humour back on itself. Whenever the portrait of Pugad Baboy threatens to become too sappy and sentimental, whenever the claims of 'community' appear too sanctimonious and self-congratulatory, the joke comes at the expense of nationalism itself. After the neighbourhood's resident NPA cadre and Constabulary sergeant conclude a beer-house debate on communism and capitalism with a water-pistol gunfight, their friend Mang Dagul intercedes with an earnest plea:

> I'm not siding with either one of you, but I hope that you can come to an understanding. In any case, we're living cheek-by-jowl here in Pugad Baboy. Christian or Muslim or Iglesia Ni Kristo, capitalist or communist, we're still Filipinos! I don't know, when will we open our eyes? When will our nation wake up...?
>
> [Wala akong pinapanigan sa inyong dalawa, pero sana naman ay magkasundo na kayo. Tutal e magkapit-kural naman tayo dito sa Pugad Baboy. Kristiano man o Muslim o INK, kapitalista o komunista, Pinoy pa rin tayo! Ewan ko ba kung kailan tayo mamumulat! Kung kailan magigising ang ating bayan...]

At this moment, to the evident horror of all three Pugad Baboy residents, the spectral figure of once-popular folk singer Freddy Aguilar appears, strumming his guitar and wailing a line from his early 1980s nationalist classic 'Bayan Ko' (My Country/People). Likewise, when, after the Constabulary sergeant thanks his NPA cadre neighbour for donating blood to save his life, the Communist begins to delivers a soliloquy on national unity and reconciliation from his adjoin-ing hospital bed, the talking dog Polgas starts up a solemn violin solo to accompany the speech. Acknowledging the excess of sentimentality of the scene, the soldier turns immediately to the 'comrade' and, disgusted, asks, 'Do you have a gun, mate?' [Me baril ka ba d'yan, mate?]

Whilst Pugad Baboy's portrait of plump, porcine *Filipinos* represents a dramatic departure from previous cartoons, similar developments in the realm of Philip-pine literature likewise suggest a shift or rupture that goes beyond the merely aesthetic. Indeed, scholars have long linked patterns of innovation in literary form to changing forms of historical consciousness, and, more recently, Benedict Anderson has aligned the emergence of the novel (and the newspaper) with the dawning of nationalism. Like the newspaper, Anderson argues, the novel both reveals and promotes a distinctly modern understanding of 'empty, homogeneous time' not presented, for example, in poetry or drama, and offers a portrayal of characters and events against a backdrop that is typically national in its demar-cations.[40]

In addition, the novel offers a depiction of human activity, interaction, senti-ment, and thinking in a language which, thanks to the modalities of print capitalism, can lay the bases for nationalist consciousness by creating 'unified fields of exchange and communication'.[41] Thus, in Europe since the sixteenth century, readers of novels and newspapers have participated in the emergence of 'national print languages':

> In the process, they gradually became aware of the hundreds of thousands, even millions, of people in their particular language-field, and at the same time that only those hundreds of thousands, or millions, so belonged. These fellow-readers, to whom they were connected through print, formed, in their secular, particular, visible invisibility, the embryo of the nationally imagined community.[42]

In this vein, the resurgence of Tagalog literature since the 1980s represents a noteworthy development in the history of the Filipino novel. After all, the great nationalist novel of the late Spanish colonial era, José Rizal's *Noli Me Tangere*, was written in Spanish, and, as Ambeth Ocampo has shown, Rizal's efforts to write a novel in Tagalog ended in failure.[43] In the aftermath of the Revolution and with the imposition of American colonial rule at the turn of the century, the Tagalog novel (and, it is worth noting, its Cebuano counterpart) emerged and even flourished, with more than four hundred examples of the genre published (often in serialised form in Tagalog magazines) over the course of succeeding decades.[44] Yet, as Resil Mojares has noted, these novels, which suffered from excessive didacticism, formalism, and sentimentality, soon fell out of favour with authors and audiences alike.[45] By the 1920s, Mojares notes, readers had grown tired of this 'trite, repetitious fiction' serialised in Tagalog magazines, and, with the growth of English-language periodicals like the *Philippines Free Press*, writers of the American colonial era began to pen novels in English.[46] This trend persisted after independence in the post-war era, with the Philippines' most celebrated novelists writing in English, whilst Tagalog novelist Amado V. Hernandez languished in jail for his involvement in the Communist Party and its labour organising efforts in the 1950s.[47]

Yet several decades of increasingly popular Tagalog *komiks*, movies, radio, tabloids, and television generated both readers and writers eminently capable of 'imagining' the Philippines in a 'national' language other than English. Indeed, just as Amado Hernandez worked as a columnist for various Tagalog tabloids in his day, so is Lualhati Bautista, the premier Tagalog novelist of the 1980s and 1990s, a writer of Tagalog movie and television screenplays. Born, like Hernandez, in modest circumstances in the populous Manila district of Tondo (today counted as one of Asia's largest slums), Bautista has written novels which rely not on the highly formalised 'Pilipino' promoted by official nationalists since the Marcos era, but rather on a Tagalog which is very casual, syncretic, and 'street'.[48] Her novels won prizes in the early-mid 1980s and, in ample testimony to her popularity, remain available in many bookstores in the Philippines today.

Bautista's novels are definitely 'nationalist' novels, not just allegorically, as some scholars might lead us to expect,[49] but in the sense that the main characters are 'coming of age' – coming to terms with personal conflicts, fighting for personal goals – even as a broader Filipino nation seems to crystallise in the background. In her two prize-winning (1982–84) novels, *Dekada '70* and *Bata, Bata, Paano Ka Ginawa?* for example, this parallel is evident both in the regular news-flashes and other historical events that punctuate the narrative, and in the activities of the narrators and other major characters. In the first novel, one of the narrator's sons joins the Communist Party of the Philippines, whilst another is 'salvaged' (i.e. extra-judicially murdered) by the police. A third joins the wave of emigration by moving to California to work for the US Navy. In the second novel, the main character is a member of a human rights group that joins up with various other 'cause-oriented groups' in the wave of popular mobilisation which followed the 1983 assassination of anti-Marcos opposition leader Ninoy Aquino.

Significantly, the narrator and central character in both these novels – like the author herself – is a woman. Here the surprise of authorship, narrative voice, and hero(ine) is evident when compared to the gendering of other nationalist novels. In Rizal's *Noli*, for example, the nationalist hero has lost his parents, is prevented from marrying his beloved (who turns out to be the daughter of a Spanish friar), and instead remains free to join in a nationalist 'brotherhood' of men. In the United States, it has been shown, classic nationalist novels have typically constructed narratives that centre around two men, single, unattached, one white, the other non-white, whose adventures and intimacies offer the possibility of redemption in a land of violent conquest and slavery.[50] Even the nineteenth-century novels enshrined in various national canons in Latin America are, in the words of one scholar, 'almost inevitably stories of star-crossed lovers who represent particular regions, races, parties, economic interests, and the like. Their passion for conjugal and sexual union spills over to a sentimental readership in a move that hopes to win partisan minds along with hearts'.[51]

By contrast, Lualhati Bautista's Filipino novels of the 1980s offer nationalist narratives that are very differently gendered, with a middle-class 'Mom' as the central character. In the first novel about the 1970s, 'Mom' is stuck at home, but through the activities and experiences of her sons – in the Communist Party, in the US Navy, and at the hands of the police – she becomes more aware of 'the Philippines' even as she begins to articulate her own desires, needs, and prerogatives *vis-à-vis* her husband.[52] By the end of the novel, she and her husband have reestablished a level of intimacy that had faded over the long years of parenthood, and she faces the impending prospect of an 'empty nest' with a self-confidence fortified by her emerging commitment to the radical Left anti-Marcos struggle.

In the second novel, about the 1980s, the main character and occasional narrator, Lea Bustamante, is a much more independent woman, one who earns her own salary, engages actively in radical Left anti-Marcos politics, and experiences something of a sexual 'liberation'. (She has left her husband and had a child (out of wedlock) with another man, and during the course of the novel she contemplates (but does not consummate) an affair with a third.) The end of the novel finds her alone, single parent of two children (of two different fathers), but feeling gratitude rather than regret, and fully engaged in an active role in society and politics. The final scenes show her first at a political rally (where she bids farewell to her former husband, now bound for the United States), and then at a school graduation ceremony for her son Ojie, where, despite the once scandalously plural paternity of her two children, she is invited to deliver an 'inspirational talk'. Her impromptu speech, addressing the question raised in the book's title, 'Child, child, how were you made?', ends the novel on a determinedly hopeful note, encouraging the graduating students to continue to ask questions, to interrogate authority, and to fight for what they believe to be the answers.

In Bautista's novels, it is clear, women do not constitute dangerous distractions from the 'real' business of forging a nation, nor do they represent vessels for cross-racial/class impregnation and the consummation of national unity. Instead, women in these novels, through their activities, their thoughts, their feelings, and, vicariously, their children, are themselves shown to undertake a decidedly nationalist project themselves. Yet to understand why the most celebrated nationalist novels of the 1980s in the Philippines have been women's novels, it is necessary to step back and examine the historical circumstances which have combined to generate the various manifestations of artistic creativity and nationalist consciousness in the Philippines since the 1980s discussed in the preceding pages.

The Filipino laughs last: nationalism and humour

Through examples drawn from popular newspaper columns, music, movies, *komiks*, and novels, this chapter has provided glimpses of a veritable renaissance in the creative arts and of a vibrant nationalist consciousness today in the Philippines. As the previous pages have shown, this nationalist consciousness has proven decidedly ambivalent about idealised (or self-abnegatory) myths of Filipino origins, irreverent towards the Great Men of Philippine History, non-essentialist in its treatment of Filipino identity, and artfully critical (and slyly self-critical) in its appropriation of foreign influences. Curiously, as noted in the discussion above, this nationalist consciousness has found expression in forms that appear more inclusively (and less hierarchically) gendered than seen in many other 'nationalist imaginings', whether elsewhere in the world or in the Philippines in previous epochs. As the preceding analysis has suggested, the vibrant nationalist consciousness and sentiment in evidence today appear to have crystallised not around a strong attachment to 'The Philippines' as a geographical entity or as a nation-*State*, but rather through the creative construction and self-conscious celebration of what it means to be 'Filipino', not in terms of some innate essence, but in terms of shared lived experience.

To understand how this structure of feeling has emerged and flourished in recent years, it is necessary to draw attention to a conjuncture of three important social and political trends under way in the Philippines since the early 1970s. First of all, President Marcos' declaration of martial law and introduction of so-called 'constitutional authoritarianism' in 1972 (steps taken under the twin banners of 'nation-building' and 'state-building') inaugurated a set of policies to create a truly *national* state and promote a half-hearted (and often curiously self-abnegatory) form of 'official nationalism'.[53] If the highly decentralised and weakly insulated Philippine state of the pre-1972 *ancien régime* was poorly suited to this task, Marcos' own Bonapartist efforts were likewise compromised (as suggested elsewhere in this volume) by his own background and *modus operandi* as an elected politician, his close relations with the United States, and his patrimonial, predatory tendencies. Without an indigenous aristocracy of pre-colonial heritage, a heroic revolutionary Independence struggle of recent vintage, or an effectively absolutising central state to draw upon, 'official nationalism' in the Philippines was doomed to be an unsuccessful enterprise, especially in the clumsy, greedy, and blood-stained hands of Ferdinand and Imelda Marcos.[54]

Second, it was precisely in the shadow of – and in the struggle against – this 'US-Marcos dictatorship' that a new form of *popular* nationalism emerged and grew in the 1970s and early 1980s. Already in the late 1960s, a lively student movement of distinctly nationalist orientation had surfaced and spread among the universities of Metro Manila and other Philippine cities, protesting, *inter alia*, the ongoing use of US military bases in the Philippines for the prosecution of the war in Indochina.[55] Pushed underground and further radicalised by martial law, such student activists revived the moribund Communist Party of the Philippines and built up the New People's Army (NPA) in the 1970s, and organised a number of closely affiliated 'cause-oriented groups' which by the early 1980s had mobilised thousands of peasants, workers, and urban poor folk against a common *national* target – the Marcos regime.[56] By the mid-1980s, through strikes, street demonstrations, semi-clandestine meetings, and protest literature, and under the rubric of such organisations as the Kilusang Mayo Uno (May First Movement), the Kilusang Magbubukid ng Pilipinas (Peasant Movement of the Philippines), and the Bagong Alyansang Makabayan (New Nationalist Alliance), this movement had swelled in tandem with the growth of the New People's Army in many provinces, creating a nation-wide, popular-nationalist, counter-hegemonic language and culture of protest – largely in Tagalog – which posed a grave threat not only to the Marcos regime but to the interests of the US government and the Philippine business class. As argued elsewhere in this book, it was only through a subsequent wave of counter-mobilisation, first in the guise of 'civil society' (i.e. NAMFREL and the February 1986 'People Power Revolution') and later under the rubric of a (notably *un*civil) 'counter-insurgency' programme, that conservative business, Catholic Church, and US interests succeeded in beating back the rising tide of radical popular nationalism.

This pattern of sustained popular nationalist mobilisation (and counter-mobilisation) in the 1980s, unparalleled in its breadth, depth, and duration elsewhere in Asia during the same period, has left in its wake a set of lasting legacies which have yet to be seriously studied and understood. Yet, the shared lived experience of sustained struggle for a national(ist) cause has clearly expanded the audience, in some instances supplied the authors, and often provided the material for new modes of representing Filipinos and the Philippines which have been decidedly distant from – and slyly subversive of – the 'official nationalism' promoted (however feebly) by Marcos and his successors. Many of today's artists and authors, such as Joey Ayala and Lualhati Bautista, discussed above, were themselves involved in various ways in the popular nationalist politics of the 1970s and 1980s, as suggested by the style and substance of their songs, novels, and movie screenplays. Perhaps, too, the participation of thousands of *Filipinas*, in many cases, quite prominently – in Church[57] and 'cause-oriented' groups, demonstrations, strikes, and indeed in armed struggle[58] during this period – helps to situate the role of women in Tagalog nationalist novels such as those treated above, and in Philippine nationalist consciousness today more broadly. Thus, for example, Lina Brocka's film 'Sister Stella L.', one of the best cinematic depictions of the period, stars the actress Vilma Santos as a young nun drawn into social activism and radical politics by her involvement in a strike.

Finally, whilst state-promoted 'official nationalism' has proved unappealing, and even as the popular nationalist struggle peaked and subsided in the 1980s, the circulation of commodities, especially through national media and the international flows of Filipino labour power, has continued to shape and to enhance the 'nationalist imaginings' discussed in the bulk of this chapter. At least by the 1970s, the expanding circuitries of the national media industry had, through Tagalog movies and television shows, succeeded – where Marcos' 'official nationalism' failed – in connecting millions of Filipinos to a common 'imagined community' (in Tagalog) reinforced by analogous trends in the production and distribution of consumer goods for a truly *national* market.[59] Thus the variegated creative modes of representing Filipinos discussed in this chapter – songs, movies, newspaper items, books, t-shirts – have, by and large, appeared in *commodity* form, rendering participation in 'nationalist imaginings' an act of consumption, and, it must be noted, restricting participation to those Filipinos who can afford to pay the price.

The increasing circulation of Filipino labourers, both within the Philippines and internationally, has also worked both to enhance and to define the representation and celebration of the Filipino experience treated in the preceding pages. Aside from complex patterns of internal migration in the archipelago, the growing numbers of Filipino overseas contract workers (OCWs) – working as construction labourers, domestic servants, merchant marine, nurses, prostitutes, and in a variety of other occupations in Asia, Australia, Europe, the Middle East, and North America – have helped to promote a new kind of 'long-distance nationalism' that stretches far beyond the map of the Philippine islands.[60] With more than 4.5 million OCWs (and nearly 2 million emigrants residing permanently abroad, mostly in the United States) clustering in *Filipino* labour niches and enclaves and sending billions of pesos a year *home* to their loved ones in the Philippines, it could hardly be otherwise.[61] Thus the cartoonist Pol Medina Jr. first began to sketch his Pugad Baboy scenes while doing contract work for an oil company in Iraq, described by a friend as 'that period of sun-drenched, sand-blasted madness, in between spells of extreme homesickness, melancholia and unbelievable boredom'.[62]

Moreover, as tragi-comically portrayed by Medina in his depiction of Pugad Baboy native-son 'Kules' as a construction worker in Saudi Arabia, the shared hardships of OCWS from the Philippines have worked to generate new solidarities and forms of consciousness among Filipinos. On construction sites in Saudi Arabia or Japan, at housemaids' day-off meeting places in Abu Dhabi, Hong Kong, Rome, and Singapore, in the basements of hotels and hospitals in London and New York, and on the lower decks of ocean-going freighters, Filipinos regularly congregate, eat, swap stories, and share news from the Philippines. In such venues, and increasingly among concerned friends and relatives back home, the shared lived experience of Filipino OCWs is understood as that of subalterns, as overworked and underpaid, as exploited and ill-treated *Filipinos*,[63] such that the 1991 murder of Maricris Sioson, a 'Japayuki' in Tokyo, the 1995 execution of Flor Contemplacion, a maid in Singapore, and the imprisonment in the same year of the 16-year-old maid Sarah Balabagan in Abu Dhabi led to widespread *nationalist* outrage, as seen in countless newspaper articles, television shows, and demonstrations in front of embassies in Manila.[64] Today comprising roughly half of all overseas labourers from the Philippines, women OCWs have – now in movies on Maricris Sioson, Flor Contemplacion, and Sarah Balabagan – emerged in recent years as new nationalist icons, representatives of the shared hardships of all Filipinos.[65] For the estimated two million Filipinos working overseas illegally, moreover, this sense of vulnerability and subalternity *vis-à-vis* a hostile state has been all the more acute, sometimes compared to life in the Communist 'underground' in the Philippines during the Marcos era by some who survived both experiences. Recalling his days on the docks of the Tokyo harbour, Rey Ventura, a former activist, thus describes himself as 'a strange kind of outlaw'. He notes: 'The bananas I had been unloading had been grown by Filipinos in Mindanao, transported on ships with Filipino crews, and handled by Filipinos in the docks of Yokohama. The only thing we didn't do with these outsize[d], uniform, intensely cultivated, tasteless fruit[s] was eat them. We despised them. We used to mock the Japanese for eating them...'.[66]

In short, the experience of anti-Marcos struggle in the 1980s, enjoyment of Philippine movies, television and pop music, and everyday struggles of Filipino OCWs have combined to provide a sociological basis – in both authorship and audience – for new modes of representing Filipinos and imagining a Philippine nation. As seen in the songs, movies, and writings discussed in this chapter, the past two decades have witnessed a cultural renaissance and a resurgence of nationalist consciousness and sentiment stimulated not, as elsewhere in South East Asia, by 'official nationalism', but by the creative energies of Filipinos labouring outside – and often against – the Philippine state. Contrary to the conventional wisdom that Filipinos suffer from 'a weak sense of national identity', a 'damaged culture', and a 'neo-colonial consciousness', the examples provided above have, through a variety of creative media, shown broad and deep attachment to an 'imagined community' of Filipinos. In contrast with the official nationalisms found elsewhere in the region, today's popular nationalism in the Philippines does not involve reference to and reverence for mythologised Origins, Great Man History, essentialised Identity, 'othering' of The West, or the promotion of a narrowly, patriarchically gendered form of nationalist 'brotherhood'. In lieu of the sanctimoniousness of (invented) Tradition, rather than domestication of the desires and identities unleashed by modernity through the stabilisation of a national hierarchy,[67] a mirthful irreverence and a 'playful diasporic intimacy' seem to reign among Filipinos today.[68]

By way of concluding, it is probably worth reemphasising a recurring, if unstated, theme of this chapter: the recent expressions of Filipino nationalist consciousness and sentiment voiced in recent years have been, above all else, consistently, *funny*. Here, if we consider the dangers of 'nationalism' being deployed in the service of domination, or in ways that are exclusionary or oppressive, the ironic, self-deprecatory humour with which Filipinos have begun to represent themselves might be seen as boding well for the future. As Mikhail Bakhtin aptly noted with reference to late medieval Europe:

> The serious aspects of class culture are official and authoritarian; they are combined with violence, prohibitions, limitations and always contain an element of fear and of intimidation…. Laughter, on the contrary, overcomes fear, for it knows no inhibitions, no limitations. Its idiom is never used by violence and authority.[69]

Notes

1   For descriptions of the exhibit, see: Jaime T. Licauco, 'An exhibit explores connection between Philippines and Lemuria', *Philippine Daily Inquirer*, 13 July 1989, p. 19; 'Remembering Lemuria', *Woman's Home Companion*, 26 July 1989, p. 18; and Nerissa S. Balce, 'Lemuria Revisited', *Philippine Daily Globe* Guide, 30 July 1989, pp. 12, 10. These sources were very kindly provided to the authors by Agnes Arellano.

2   Balce, 'Lemuria Revisited', p. 10.

3   N. Carmona-Potenciano and T. T. Battad, *Our Country and Its People 1* (Manila: Bookmark, 1987), pp. 3–5, cited in Niels Mulder, 'Philippine Textbooks and the National Self-Image', *Philippine Studies*, 38 (1990), p. 88.

4   Mulder, 'Philippine Textbooks', p. 90.

5   Vicente Rafael, 'White Love: Surveillance and Nationalist Resistance in the US Colonisation of the Philippines', in Amy Kaplan and Donald E. Pease (eds), *Cultures of United States Imperialism* (Durham: Duke University Press, 1993), pp. 185–218.

6   Mulder, 'Philippine Textbooks', p. 89.

7   *Ibid.*, p. 91.

8   Vicente L. Rafael, *Contracting Colonialism: Translation and Christian Conversion in Tagalog Society under Early Spanish Rule* (Quezon City: Ateneo de Manila University Press, 1988), pp. 106–107.

9   Rafael, 'White Love', p. 196. Rafael draws the passage quoted above from the 1903 Census.

10 Benito M. Vergara, Jr, *Displaying Filipinos: Photography and Colonialism in Early 20th Century Philippines* (Quezon City: University of the Philippines Press, 1995), p. 50.

11 *Ibid.*, p. 67.

12 See: John Pemberton, *On the Subject of 'Java'* (Ithaca: Cornell University Press, 1994), pp. 28–147; and Kenji Tsuchiya, 'Javanology and the Age of Ranggawarsita: An Introduction to Nineteenth-Century Javanese Culture', in *Reading Southeast Asia* (Ithaca: Cornell University Southeast Asia Program, 1990), pp. 75–108.

13 Moshe Yegar, *Islam and Islamic Institutions in British Malaya: Polices and Implementation* (Jerusalem: The Magues Press, 1979; William R. Roff, *The Origins of Malay Nationalism* (New Haven: Yale University Press, 1967), pp. 69–74.

14 Anthony Barnett, '"Cambodia Will Never Disappear"', *New Left Review*, 180 (March/April 1990), pp. 101–125.

15 See: John N. Schumacher, S.J., 'The Propagandists' Reconstruction of the Philippine Past', in Anthony Reid and David Marr (eds), *Perceptions of the Past in Southeast Asia* (Singapore: Heinemann Educational Books, 1979), pp. 264–280.

16 See: Reuben R. Canoy, *The Counterfeit Revolution: The Philippines from Martial Law to the Aquino Assassination* (Manila: Philippine Editions, 1981), pp. 158–165, 231–237.

17 Renato Constantino, *Neocolonial Identity and Counter-Consciousness: Essays on Cultural Decolonisation* (London: Merlin Press, 1978).

18 See, for example, the Senate report commissioned by Senator Leticia Ramos-Shahani (sister of Fidel V. Ramos), titled 'A Moral Recovery Program: Building a People – Building a Nation', issued in May 1988.

19 James Fallows, 'A Damaged Culture', *Atlantic Monthly*, November 1987, pp. 49–57. For a sense of how influential Fallows' formulation has become among Filipino intellectuals, see the long essay by novelist and commentator F. Sionil José, 'Let's Repair Our "Damaged Culture"', *Business World*, 12 June 1986.

20 'Demythologizing Rizal', in Ambeth Ocampo, *Rizal Without the Overcoat* (Pasig: Anvil Publishing, 1990), p. 127.

21 Ambeth R. Ocampo, *Rizal Without The Overcoat* (Pasig: Anvil Publishing, 1990).

22 See: Benedict Anderson, 'Hard To Imagine: A Puzzle in the History of Philippine Nationalism', in Raul Pertierra and Eduardo F. Ugarte (eds), *Cultures and Texts: Representations of Philippine Society* (Quezon City: Ateneo de Manila University Press, 1994), pp. 81–117, especially pp. 85–96.

23 *Ibid.*, p. 103.

24 Raymond Williams, *Culture and Society* (London: Hogarth Press, 1982), p. 336.

25 Los Enemigos, 'Mi Ultimo Adios', *Sunday Chronicle*, 2 May 1993, p. 15.

26 All translations by the authors. *Erpats*: Tagalog slang for father(s); *smoke-belcher*: term often (and aptly) used with reference to cars and buses; *Edsa*: the Manila boulevard where the 1986 'People Power Revolution' took place; *'how dirty the Pasig River'*: imitation of Taglish, with Tagalog grammar structuring English vocabulary; *Lahar*: massive mudflow caused by the volcanic eruption of Mt. Pinatubo.

27 Arnold Molina Azurin, *Reinventing the Filipino: Sense of Being and Becoming: Critical Analyses of the Orthodox Views in Anthropology, History, Folklore and Letters* (Quezon City: CSSP Publications, 1993).

28 See, for example, Frank Lynch and Alfonso de Guzman II (eds), *Four Readings on Philippine Values* (Quezon City: Ateneo de Manila University Institute of Philippine Culture, 1962).

29 Reynaldo Clemeña Ileto, *Pasyon and Revolution: Popular Movements in the Philippines, 1840–1910* (Quezon City: Ateneo de Manila University Press, 1979), p. 9.

30 Many thanks to Wigan Salazar for providing a copy of this test, which appears to have circulated far and wide among Filipino communities in the United States and Europe, as well as the Philippines.

31 Suzanne Slesin, 'Pacific Theater', *House & Garden*, June 1997, p. 112.

32 Translation by the authors. In the original Tagalog: 'Ang sinumang tao na maaaring magdasal, kung gayon, ay maaari ring mangkulam. Katulad ko. Katulad mo. Kaya't… mangkulam!'. Tony Perez, *Mga Panibagong Kulam* (Pasig City: Anvil Publishing, 1996), p. x. The title means something akin to 'New Spells'. Many thanks to Rosary Benitez for the gift of this book.

33 On the Tasaday controversy, see: Gerald D. Berreman, 'The Incredible "Tasaday": Deconstructing the Myth of a "Stone-Age" People, *Cultural Survival Quarterly*, Volume 15, Number 1 (1991), pp. 3–44; Jean Paul Dumont, 'The Tasaday, Which and Whose? Toward the Political Economy of an Ethnographic Sign', *Cultural Anthropology*, Volume 3, Number 3 (1988), pp. 261–275; and Aram A. Yengoyan, 'Shaping and Reshaping the Tasaday: A Question of Cultural Identity – A Review Article', *Journal of Asian Studies*, Volume 50, Number 3 (1991), pp. 565–573.

34 On Ayala and Bagong Lumad, see: Eric S. Caruncho, 'Joey Ayala at ang Bagong Lumad: Forging Filipino', and 'Who the Hell is Joey Ayala? And Why Are They Saying All Those Wonderful Things About Him?', in *Punks, Poets, Poseurs: Reportage on Pinoy Rock & Roll* (Pasig City: Anvil Publishing, 1996), pp. 55–60, 83–90. See also: Eric S. Caruncho, 'Joey Ayala: Into the Mystic', *Sunday Inquirer Magazine*, 7 August 1994, pp. 10–11.

35 See the various fine essays in Caruncho, *Punks, Poets, Poseurs*.

36 Fenella Cannell, 'Catholicism, Spirit Mediums and the Ideal of Beauty in a Bicolano Community, Philippines' (Ph.D. dissertation, London School of Economics, 1991).

37 *Ibid.*, pp. 340–341.

38 Benedict Anderson, *Imagined Communities: Reflections on the Origin and Spread of Nationalism* (London: Verso, 1983). All subsequent citations from this book are drawn from the revised edition (1991).

39 See: Cynthia Roxas and Joaquin Arevalo, Jr, *A History of Komiks of the Philippines and Other Countries* (Manila: Islas Filipinas Publishing Company, 1985).

40 *Ibid.*, pp. 22–36.

41 *Ibid.*, p. 44.

42 *Ibid.*, p. 44.

43 Ambeth R. Ocampo, *Makamisa: The Search for Rizal's Third Novel* (Pasig: Anvil Publishing, 1992).

44 See: Resil B. Mojares, *Origins and Rise of the Filipino Novel: A Generic Study of the Novel Until 1940* (Manila: Islas Filipinas Publishing Company, 1985), pp. 192–193.

45 *Ibid.*, pp. 256–301. A perfect example of the use of literature as an instrument for moral and social reform was Lope K. Santos' lengthy (and supposedly quite tedious) socialist-realist novel *Banaag at Sikat*, which, according to Mojares, sold 4,000 copies when it was published in 1905 (*Ibid.*, p. 193).

46 *Ibid.*, pp. 336–352. In the 1939 census, more than 4.25 million Filipinos, representing over 26% of the total population of the archipelago, claimed proficiency in English. See: Andrew B. Gonzalez, *Language and Nationalism: The Philippine Experience Thus Far* (Quezon City: Ateneo de Manila University Press, 1980), p. 26.

47 Mina Roces, 'Filipino Identity in Fiction, 1945–1972', *Modern Asian Studies*, Volume 28, Number 2 (1994), pp. 287–293.

48 For a brief, lucid discussion of the language issue, see: Rosario E. Maminta, 'The National Language: Filipino or Tagalog with a New Label?', *Sunday Inquirer Magazine*, 7 August 1994, pp. 3–4.

49 'All third-world texts are necessarily', Fredric Jameson has argued, 'allegorical, and in a very specific way: they are to be read as what I will call national allegories…. [T]he story of the private individual destiny is always an allegory of the embattled situation of the public third-world culture and society'. ('Third-World Literature in the Era of Multinational Capitalism', *Social Text*, 15 (Fall 1986), p. 69.)

50 Leslie Fiedler, *Love and Death in the American Novel* (New York: Stein and Day, 1966).

51 Doris Sommer, *Foundational Fictions: The National Romances of Latin America* (Berkeley: University of California Press, 1991), p. 5.

52 For an acutely sensitive analysis of this novel which raises questions of gender and class, see: Jacqueline Siapno, 'Alternative Filipina Heroines: Contested Tropes in Leftist Feminisms', in Aihwa Ong and Michael G. Peletz (eds), *Bewitching Women, Pious Men: Gender and Body Politics in Southeast Asia* (Berkeley: University of California Press, 1995), pp. 216–243.

53 Following Benedict Anderson, official nationalism here refers to 'the form of nationalism which surfaces as an emanation and armature of the state. It manifests itself, not merely in official ceremonies of commemoration, but in a systematic program, directed primarily, if not exclusively, through the state's school system, to create and disseminate an official nationalist history, an official nationalist culture, through the ranks of its younger, incipient citizens – naturally, in the state's own interests. These interests are first and foremost in instilling faith in, reverence for, and obedience to, its very self.' (Anderson, 'Hard To Imagine', p. 103.)

54   See, for example, Vicente L. Rafael, 'Patronage and Pornography: Ideology and Spectatorship in the Early Marcos Years', *Comparative Studies in Society and History*, Volume 32, Number 2 (April 1990), pp. 282–304.

55   On this phenomenon, see, for example, José F. Lacaba, *Days of Disquiet, Nights of Rage: The First Quarter Storm and Related Events* (Manila: Asphodel Books, 1986).

56   On this process, see, for example, Gregg R. Jones, *Red Revolution: Inside the Philippine Guerrilla Movement* (Boulder: Westview Press, 1989); and Benjamin Pimentel Jr., *Edjop: The Unusual Journey of Edgar Jopson* (Quezon City: KEN, 1989).

57   On the radicalisation and mobilisation of Filipina nuns during the Marcos period, see: Coeli M. Barry, 'Transformations of Politics and Religious Culture Inside the Philippine Catholic Church (1965–1990)' (Ph.D. dissertation, Cornell University, 1996), especially pp. 212–267.

58   Anne-Marie Hilsdon, *Madonnas and Martyrs: Militarism and Violence in the Philippines* (St Leonards: Allen & Unwin, 1995).

59   On the enormously popular Philippine film industry, see, for example, Rafael Maria Guerrero (ed.), *Readings in Philippine Cinema* (Manila: Experimental Cinema of the Philippines, 1983); J. Eddie Infante, *Inside Philippine Movies 1970–1990: Essays for Students of Philippine Cinema* (Quezon City: Ateneo de Manila University Press, 1991); and Emmanuel Reyes, *Notes on Philippine Cinema* (Manila: De La Salle University Press, 1989). For an amply illuminating historical overview of the advertising industry in the Philippines, see: Visitacion R. de la Torre, *Advertising in the Philippines (Its Historical, Cultural and Social Dimensions)* (Manila: Tower Book House, 1989).

60   See: Benedict Anderson, *Long-Distance Nationalism: World Capitalism and the Rise of Identity Politics* (Amsterdam: Centre for Asian Studies Amsterdam, 1992).

61   These figures are drawn from Joy G. Perez, 'On Overseas Filipino', *Philippine News Agency*, 13 September 1996 and Jonathan Karp, 'A New Kind of Hero', *Far Eastern Economic Review*, 30 March 1995, pp. 42–45. For broader analyses, see: Graziano Battistella and Anthony Paganoni (eds), *Philippine Labor Migration: Impact and Policy* (Quezon City: Scalabrini Migration Center, 1992); The *Labour Trade: Filipino Migrant Workers Around the World* (London: Catholic Institute for International Relations, 1987); and the special issue on 'Filipino Labor Overseas' in *Solidarity*, Nos. 141–142 (January – June 1994), pp. 5–96.

62   See the remarks of Frank Aldana in his preface to Pol Medina Jr's 1989 collection, *The Very Best of Pugad Baboy* Manila: Pol Medina Jr.

63   On Filipino seamen, for example, see: Paul K. Chapman, *Trouble On Board: The Plight of International Seafarers* (Ithaca: Institute of Labor Relations Press, 1992), pp. 22–33, 45–51; and Scott L. Malcomson, 'A Reporter at Large: The Unquiet Ship', *The New Yorker*, 20 January 1997, pp. 72–81.

64   See, for example, the profusion of articles about Sarah Balabagan in Manila newspapers in September 1995.

65   On women OCWs, see, for example, Rochelle E. Ball, 'The Process of International Contract Labour Migration from the Philippines: The Case of Filipino Nurses' (Ph.D. dissertation, University of Sydney, 1990); Ma. Rosario P. Ballescas, *Filipino Entertainers in Japan: An Introduction* (Quezon City: Foundation for Nationalist Studies, 1992); and Mary Ruby Palma Beltran and Aurora Javate De Dios (eds), *Filipino Women Overseas Contract Workers: At What Cost?* (Manila: Goodwill Trading Company, 1992).

66   Rey Ventura, *Underground in Japan* (London: Jonathan Cape, 1992), p. 123. See also the discussion of his experiences as a member of the 'underground' Left back home (pp. 64–73).

67   On Indonesia, for example, see: John Pemberton, *On The Subject of 'Java'* (Ithaca: Cornell University Press, 1994); and James T. Siegel, *Fetish, Recognition, Revolution* (Princeton: Princeton University Press, 1997).

68   Paul Gilroy, *The Black Atlantic: Modernity and Double Consciousness* (London: Verso, 1993), p. 16.

69   Mikhail Bakhtin, *Rabelais and His World* (Bloomington: Indiana University Press, 1984), pp. 90–91.

8 The Sulu zone revisited

The Philippines in Southeast Asia

Seventeen kilometers from Zamboanga City, along the coast of the Zamboanga Peninsula in western Mindanao, stands the Philippines' most prominent and historically significant mosque, located in the barangay of Taluksangay amidst a cluster of makeshift seaside dwellings and at the heart of the Nuño family's local bailiwick. The Nuños own considerable landholdings in Taluksangay, control the trade in *agar-agar* (seaweed) and other products from the mangrove swamps along the coast, serve as partners (and providers of security) to a Japanese pearl farm venture in nearby waters, and have been active in the barter trade between Zamboanga City and the port city of Labuan in the Malaysian state of Sabah on Borneo. In recent years, various Nuños have served as barangay captain and municipal councillor for Taluksangay, headed the Zamboanga Electric Cooperative, the local branches of the Philippine Amanah Bank, the Philippine Charity Sweepstakes Office, represented the community (or at least the family's considerable interests therein) on the Zamboanga City Council, and earned such political clout that a succession of candidates for the Philippine presidency have paid their respects to the family while on campaign visits to Zamboanga. Indeed, it was no doubt in large part thanks to the intercession of Margarita 'Tingting' Cojuangco, sister-in-law of then president Corazon C. Aquino and a long-time friend and business associate of the Nuños, that in late February 1992, just a few short months before the national elections in early May of that year, the National Historical Institute installed a plaque on the mosque, acknowledging the central role of the family's forefather, Hadji Abdullah Maas Nuño, in its founding.[1]

Indeed, if existing historical sources are to be believed, not only do the mosque and the entire community owe their existence to Hadji Abdullah Maas Nuño, but this legendary progenitor of the Nuño clan links Taluksangay to the rise and fall of the Sulu Sultanate in the late eighteenth and nineteenth centuries.[2] For Nuño, the story goes, was the son of Panglima Taupan, the local ruler or *datu* of a Samal settlement on the island of Balangingi in the (predominantly Taosug) Sulu Archipelago, which served as the 'most important island ... dwelling place and organisational centre of the major slave-retailing group for the Sulu Sultanate in the first half of the nineteenth century'.[3] As the historian James Warren has shown, shifts in international trade patterns, most notably between England and China, gave rise in the late eighteenth century to a loosely structured port polity centred around the Sulu Sultanate and extending as far as northern Celebes (Sulawesi), northeastern Borneo (Sabah), and the central and western territories of Mindanao. This polity, which Warren memorably dubbed the 'Sulu Zone', was based on trade with English merchants eager for marine and jungle products – such as bird's nests, pearl, mother of pearl, and *tripang* (beche de mer or sea slug) – and, crucially, on the mobilisation of labour to obtain them. As Warren explains:

> The rate of growth of the Sultanate's population had not kept pace with its expanding commercial economy. The Western traders' insatiable demands for produce acceptable in Chinese markets promoted the intensification of Taosug-sponsored Iranun-Samal raiding expeditions to obtain captives. It would be Visayan, Minahassan, and Buginese captives as well as flotillas of nomadic Samal Bajau laut that would gather the *tripang*, mother of pearl, and tortoise shell for the European traders to take to China. The gunpowder and firearms supplied by the traders allowed the coastal dwelling Taosug to promote raiding on a large scale and keep the zone free of intruders and competitors until 1840.[4]

The Samal community based on the island of Balangingi played a crucial role in this system of labour mobilisation and exploitation. As Warren notes:

> It was the Balangingi Samal – slave raiders from May to November and fishermen and manufacturers of salt during the west monsoon – who annually brought several thousand captive people to Sulu to be trained to work alongside the Samal Bajau Laut in the *tripang* and mother of pearl fisheries. It can be roughly estimated from trade statistics that some 68,000 fishermen must have engaged in diving for mother of pearl and fishing for *tripang* by hundreds of Taosug *datus* and Samal headmen during the 1830s.[5]

Yet by the late 1840s, Spanish efforts to extend control over previously uncolonised areas of Mindanao and the Sulu Archipelago culminated in a bloody attack by Spanish steam-powered gunboats on the Samal settlement on Balangingi. At the time of the attack in 1848, the Samal *datu* Panglima Taupan was reportedly elsewhere in the Sulu Archipelago or in Borneo, and he returned to find the settlement destroyed – dwellings burnt to the ground, and the local population taken captive by the Spaniards. Amongst the Samal Balangingi taken away by the Spaniards was Panglima Taupan's ten-year-old son, who, like the rest of the prisoners, was transported to the Spanish naval station in Cavite just south of Manila Bay and forced to convert to Christianity. Shortly thereafter, the Spanish government entered into a contract with the Compania Tabacalera for the trans-shipment of the Samal Balangingi to the company's hacienda in the Cagayan Valley in northeastern Luzon, in what today is the province of Isabela. Legend has it that Panglima Taupun managed to contact his son, now known as Antonio Nuño, in Isabela, and that they subsequently met in Vigan, Ilocos Sur, whereupon the father died and the son moved back to Cavite and served there as a sacristan or altar boy in a Catholic church for several years. Yet by 1880, at the age of 31, this same Nuño had obtained the permission of the Spanish Governor-General to return to Balangingi, or at least to Basilan, with other Samal refugees, and, subsequently, to establish a new settlement on a patch of land less than twenty kilometers from Zamboanga City which was given the name of Taluksangay. Shortly thereafter, Nuño made the pilgrimage to Mecca and returned, now known as Hadji Abdullah Maas Nuño, to establish the mosque in Taluksangay in 1885.

From this point on, the Nuño family story is one of dynastic entrenchment in Taluksangay. Recognised early on by the US military authorities as a local worthy, Hadji Maas Abdullah was deployed in the 'pacification' campaigns of the early American colonial years and travelled as far afield as Dipolog and Dapitan in Zamboanga del Norte to spread 'peace and the gospel of Islam'. By the time of his death in 1918, Nuño had installed his (adopted) son in the municipal mayor's office and convinced his friend the American governor of Zamboanga to accede to the enlistment of a Turkish *imam* at the mosque. Yet he also entreated the authorities to make arrangements for an American-style education for his two grandsons, who were, as once source noted, 'destined by reason of the prestige of their grandfathers and earlier ancestors to be when they become men, leaders of much infuence among the Mohammedans of Mindanao and of considerable influence in Sulu'.[6]

The history of the Nuño family and the Samal community in Taluksangay thus links contemporary politics in the southern Philippines to the Sulu Zone of the late eighteenth and nineteenth centuries. For the slave-raiding expeditions of the Samal Balangingi were crucial, not only for the enrichment and extension of authority of the Sulu Sultanate, but also for establishing an enduring negative stereotype of Muslim Filipinos in the eyes of the Christian majority.[7] As countless scholars have noted, political power in sparsely populated pre-colonial Southeast Asia revolved around the control of men rather than land, and local rulers (*datus*) throughout the Philippine archipelago led frequent raids on other communities, known as *mangayaw* or *pangayaw*, whose main object was the taking of captives. As William Henry Scott has noted, these 'slave raiders' from the Philippine archipelago 'ranged as far afield as Ternate [in the Moluccan islands of eastern Indonesia], and sold or ransomed off their captives, some of whom wound up in their master's grave or had warships launched over their prostrate bodies'.[8] Beginning in the sixteenth century, however, the process of Spanish colonisation saw the disarming of *datus* and the discontinuation of their *mangayaw* raids in the 'pacified' and evangelised areas of the archipelago, stretching from northern Luzon down through the Visayas and as far south as the coasts of Mindanao, even as periodic Spanish attacks on the Islamicised settlements of Maguindanao, Sulu, Borneo, Celebes and the Moluccas 'stirred up a hornet's nest of raids which were the only method of waging interisland warfare known in Southeast Asia'.[9] Moreover, as noted above, the continuing practice of 'slave-raiding' and 'piracy', if these are in fact the appropriate terms, combined with rising Anglo-Chinese trade in the late eighteenth century to propel the growth of the Sulu Sultanate at the core of a major regional trading entrepôt and port polity. Thus Muslims from the unhispanicised, uncolonised areas of the southern Philippine archipelago, most notably the Samal Balangingi, held 'slaves' and raided Christianised settlements under Spanish rule – and analogous communities in the Dutch East Indies and British-run parts of Borneo – not because they were Muslim, but because they had yet to be subordinated to colonial authority.

The demise of the Samal settlement on Balangingi, the disruption of Samal 'slave raiding' practices, and the deportation of the young son of Panglima Taupun to Cavite and then Isabela thus marked the end of an era for the Sulu Zone. By the 1850s, the Sulu Sultanate had begun to submit to Spanish authority, and by the 1870s, Spanish troops occupied Jolo; among the Muslim sultans and datus of central Mindanao, a similar process was simultaneously under way.[10] As with similar and roughly contemporaneous efforts in French Indochina, British Malaya, Chakri Siam and the Dutch East Indies, this 'Forward Movement' represented an attempt to extend the authority of the modern Spanish colonial state to the furthest territorial extremities of the Philippine archipelago, and to subordinate 'indirectly ruled' areas more fully to central colonial administration. Yet, as elsewhere in Southeast Asia, the Spanish 'Forward Movement' met with local resistance. As Warren notes:

> These dispersed Balangingi, who were known in the European records as 'Tawi-Tawi pirates', were able to assemble between 60 and 100 prahus by joining forces with kindred groups in Jolo, and the Iranun of Tunku. By the mid-1850s the Samal had renewed their attacks on the Philippines archipelago and the Moluccas, and their expeditions now preyed on Taosug trade between Borneo and Sulu as well.[11]

Indeed, Samal Balangingi 'piracy' and 'slave-raiding' in the Sulu Zone continued until at least the end of the Spanish era.

Hadji Maas Abdullah Nuño's collaboration with the US military authorities in the first decades of this century and the installment of successive Nuños in local office in Taluksangay and Zamboanga City exemplifed the ways in which the Islamicised areas of Mindanao and the Sulu Archipelago were incorporated into the Philippines in the American period. As noted by specialists on the southern Philippines,[12] and as suggested elsewhere in this volume, the key mechanism of 'national integration' was elections, and the opportunities elections afforded such *datus* as Hadji Maas Abdullah Nuño to reinvent themselves as local political bosses, first under American 'colonial democracy' and then under the auspices of the independent Republic. Thus like their Catholic counterparts in municipalities elsewhere in the Philippines, the Nuños evolved into a local political clan or dynasty through a combination of landownership, local commercial monopolies, marriage alliances with other elite families (e.g. the Loongs of Sulu), joint ventures with Manila-based and foreign capital, and close connections with provincial and national-level politicians.

Yet the Nuños of Taluksangay distinguished themselves from prominent local families elsewhere in the Philippines not only by virtue of their religious faith, but also by the very nature of their transnational connections beyond the archipelago. Like Panglima Taupan and his son Hadji Maas Abdullah Nuño one hundred years earlier, the Nuños of the late twentieth century have seen themselves as part of a broader Islamic community stretching far beyond the southern Philippines, and, through the barter trade and other commercial ventures, they have maintained economic links to nearby Southeast Asian ports like Labuan in Sabah. In the 1980s, even as the Nuños were cultivating ties with Manila-based political figures like Tingting Cojuangco, so were they also playing host to the likes of Nur Misuari, the head of the armed separatist Moro National Liberation Front (MNLF), who is said to be distantly related to the family by marriage.

Indeed, we can only understand the recent political history of armed separatist rebellion and regional autonomous government in the southern Philippines if we understand how the distinctly American pattern of decentralised democracy has preserved certain elements of the Sulu Zone over the course of the twentieth century. The importance of regular competitive elections and the subordination of local agencies of the state to elected municipal mayors and provincial governors has guaranteed that the accumulation and mobilisation of local personal followings would, as in pre-colonial Southeast Asia, remain a key source of political power in the modern Philippines. With Philippine independence in 1946 and the onset of import-substitution industrialisation in the early 1950s, moreover, the existing commercial links between Mindanao and Sulu on the one hand, and Indonesian Sulawesi and Malaysian Sabah on the other hand, now became profitable precisely because of the different protectionist restrictions on trade across the modern state boundaries of the old Sulu Zone. Thus the early postwar era saw the emergence and growth of a vast illegal economy in the southern Philippines, with local politicians in the Muslim provinces (and elsewhere) evolving into 'smuggling lords' thanks to their control over law enforcement.[13] Against this backdrop, then president Ferdinand Marcos's declaration of martial law in 1972, the confiscation of 'loose firearms' and disbanding of 'private armies', the centralisation of law-enforcement in the hands of an Integrated National Police (INP) attached to the Philippine Constabulary (PC) and subordinated to the Armed Forces of the Philippines (AFP), and the awarding of control over the 'barter trade' to the Southern Command (Southcom) of the AFP echoed the Spanish 'Forward Movement' of the late nineteenth century and was met with similar resistance. In the late 1960s, Liberal politicians from the predominantly Muslim provinces of Cotabato and Lanao Muslim politicians had already begun to sponsor a Muslim Independence Movement (MIM) and to arm and train Muslim guerrilla fighters as part of a defensive strategy in the face of 'an increasingly aggressive national president who was actively strengthening (with money and arms) their Nacionalista Muslim rivals in their home provinces'.[14] With the declaration of martial law, moreover, local resistance to Manila's 'Forward Movement' began to coalesce around the Moro National Liberation Front (MNLF), led by Nur Misuari, a Taosug from Sulu who had become a radical student leader and later a professor of political science at the University of the Philippines' main campus in Diliman, Quezon City, and who had trained with other Muslim guerrilla fighters in the late 1960s.

From its inception, the MNLF drew strength from the broader world of Islamic community bonds and Southeast Asian commercial links which stretched far beyond the southern Philippines and dated back at least to the days of the Sulu Zone. As is well known, alongside Manila-educated activists like Misuari were dozens of Muslim Filipinos who had studied at the Al Azhar university in Cairo, and Islamic countries in the Middle East, most notably Qaddafi's Libya, offered considerable diplomatic, financial, and logistical backing to the budding armed separatist movement beginning in the early-mid 1970s. Tun Mustapha, the chief minister and political boss of Sabah during this period, enjoyed close ties with Muslim politicians from Mindanao and the Sulu Archipelago, and had from the early days of the MIM provided money, arms, and a base for the Muslim guerrillas.[15] Generally, over the course of the 1970s and 1980s, the MNLF (and a splinter group, the Moro Islamic Liberation Front or MILF under Hashim Salamat) drew sustenance from the density of remaining cultural, economic, and political linkages across the Sulu Zone. Smuggling and the government-sanctioned 'barter trade' between southern Philippine ports and Labuan provided a regular 'predatory income' for rebel commanders through protection rents, piracy, and shareholder profit,[16] and the thousands of Muslim Filipinos working (illegally) in Malaysian Sabah or on fishing boats in the tuna-rich Indonesian waters off North Sulawesi served as a network for arms, training, and guerrilla recruitment.[17] One knowledgeable observer estimated in the mid-1990s that as many as 75% of the MNLF rank and file had spent time as overseas labourers in Sabah.[18]

Yet with the revival of competitive electoral politics and the re-decentralisation of law-enforcement in the late 1980s and early 1990s, the southern Philippines has witnessed a process of MNLF domestication and incorporation vaguely reminiscent of the US pacification drive of the early decades of this century. The local elections of 1988, 1992 and 1995, for example, saw the election of numerous MNLF and MILF activists and allies to local government positions, revealing and reinforcing the close linkages between the rival guerrilla groups, on the one hand, and local and national electoral politics, on the other.[19] It was in the context of both formal peace talks and informal political alliances that in 1996 Nur Misuari agreed to a cessation of armed struggle in exchange for government backing of his subsequent (successful) bid for the governorship of the Autonomous Region of Muslim Mindanao (ARMM) and a key role in the Southern Philippines Council for Peace and Development (SPCPD).[20] Today, after the incorporation of hundreds of MNLF guerrillas into the Philippine National Police (PNP) and the AFP, the avowedly more militant MILF in principle rejects autonomy in favour of independence, but in practice exercises its influence through elected officials like Magindanao Governor Zacarias Candao and countless municipal mayors in MILF stronghold towns in central Mindanao and the Sulu Archipelago.[21]

The Philippines in Southeast Asia: a comparison with Thailand

As illustrated by the case of the Nuño family, the recent history of Muslim Mindanao and the Sulu Archipelago thus suggests two ways in which Philippine politics and society can only be understood within the regional context of Southeast Asia. First, a complex economy of barter trade, smuggling, large-scale fishing, and labour migration has continued to link the southern Philippines to nearby Indonesian Sulawesi and Malaysian Sabah, in a new Sulu Zone not yet fully subjugated to national capitals through internal colonisation. Second, the emergence and entrenchment of armed 'guerilla' groups in the southern Philippines since the early 1970s represented not simply the strength of 'Moro' separatist sentiment, but also the distinctive features of state formation in the the archipelago. Whilst the 'iron cage' of Jakarta and Kuala Lumpur's centralising, bureaucratising authoritarianism had closed in on local officials in North Sulawesi and Sabah by the late 1970s, in the Philippines the contemporaneous thrust of this 'Forward Movement' ran aground against the enduring logic of electoralism. After all, as in pre-colonial Southeast Asia, political power in the twentieth-century Philippines continued to rest on control over men rather than control over territory, no less in local elections in Ilocos Norte than on the high seas of the latter-day Sulu Zone, with both locally and nationally elected politicians measuring their authority in terms of votes rather than the enforcement of territorial sovereignty. President Ferdinand Marcos quite willingly abandoned his fledgling 'Forward Movement' with the signing of the Tripoli accords in 1976, which signalled if not the establishment of an effective regional autonomous government then at least the cessation of hostilities, the prevalence of live-and-let-live arrangements between the AFP and the MNLF, and the co-optation of 'rebel surrenderees' as local mayors and governors in Muslim Mindanao and the Sulu Archipelago. By the 1990s, moreover, the restoration of competitive elections, the (re-)devolution of substantial powers to local elected officials, and the elaboration of a regional autonomous government in the southern Philippines had served to further blur the distinctions between rebel movements, smuggling rackets, and electoral factions in the southern Philippines, helping to preserve the prominent role of local 'men of prowess' in the late twentieth-century's Sulu Zone.[22]

If in descriptive terms the contemporary Philippines is thus arguably the most 'Southeast Asian' country in the region, in analytical terms the broad contours of the political configuration in the archipelago today can perhaps best be understood in regional comparative perspective, especially in contrast with Thailand. Thailand, for example, has also had a history of southern Muslim armed separatist organisation and activity, yet one which petered out by the 1980s without anything approaching the concessions (e.g. regional autonomous government) won by the MNLF or the continuing MILF presence in the southern Philippines today. In his broad comparative study of the Philippines and Thailand, *The Nation and Economic Growth*, Yoshihara Kunio explains this difference in terms of a Philippine failure to 'maintain peace and order' – also evident in terms of criminality and the Communist 'insurgency' – which ultimately stems from the absence of a pre-colonial Filipino kingdom and of other sources of national integration, in stark contrast with the supposedly more historically rooted, uncolonised, and ethnically homogeneous case of the Thai nation-state.[23] By Yoshihara's account, in twentieth-century Thailand 'government authority was more acceptable to the people, and the bureaucracy was more effective (particularly in maintaining peace and order). This may be related to the fact that Thailand had an established tradition of governing'.[24] Thanks to a stronger national consciousness, Thailand thus had a stronger, more meritocratic, and less corrupt military than the Philippines and 'its government leaders paid a lot of attention to national interests'.[25] Yoshihara notes:

> There were no Thai leaders like Marcos, who borrowed from abroad almost irrationally, leaving a legacy of debt to the country. The Thai military leaders who ran the country in the 1960s – Sarit Thanarat, Thanom Kittikachorn, Prapart Charustien, and Narong Kittikachorn – are said to have been corrupt. Sarit amassed about $150 million, and the last three (sometimes called the three tyrants) $70 million. These sums are 'peanuts' compared with the $5–10 billion Marcos is alleged to have stolen from the country. Besides, the economy of Thailand kept growing several per cent per annum during their regimes, unlike that of the Philippines which was badly scarred by Marcos.[26]

The Philippines' failure to match Thailand's impressive record of rapid, sustained industrial growth and rising prosperity in recent decades, moreover, is likewise attributed to Thailand's more receptive treatment of 'Chinese' and foreign capital and more effective government intervention in the economy (e.g. financial sector regulation, state enterprises, agricultural monopolies, trade barriers, and price controls), which in turn are linked to national integration and nationalist sentiment in the Thai case and the lack thereof in the Philippine case.[27] Yoshihara thus concludes: 'In summary, it is tempting to say that the Thai economy performed better than the Philippine economy because Thailand was more of an *echt* nation than the Philippines was'.[28]

As the discussion of the Philippines in the preceding pages and chapters of this volume has suggested, however, an alternative basis for comparison with Thailand lies not in these two societies or 'cultures', but rather in the strikingly different patterns of state formation – and democratisation – in the two cases. Despite a number of obvious and oft-noted ostensible differences between Thailand (Buddhist Kingdom, 'bureaucratic polity') and the Philippines ('damaged culture', 'cacique democracy'), the two countries in fact share a set of important commonalities that mark these two countries as distinctive in the Southeast Asian context and make a 'paired comparison' more plausible and promising. First, in the era of high colonialism (c. 1850–1940), while ethnically segmented 'plural societies' crystallised elsewhere in the region, Siam and the

Philippines provided unparalleled opportunities and incentives for the assimilation and upward social mobility of Chinese immigrants and their Sino-Thai/ Chinese *mestizo* offspring.[29] Second, in the postwar era of capitalist industrialisation, Thailand and the Philippines have thus provided a sharp contrast with Indonesia and Malaysia in the cultural, economic, *and* political ascendance of predominantly Chinese and Sino-Thai/Chinese *mestizo* business élites relatively unconstrained by 'pariah entrepreneur' status and the predations of 'indigenous' (*pribumi/bumiputra*) military officers, politicians, and their children and cronies. Third, only in Thailand and the Philippines have such self-conscious and self-confident business élites succeeded in institutionalising the trappings of bourgeois democracy: a state apparatus firmly subordinated to elected officials, a schedule of regular and competitive elections, a familiar set of recognised civil liberties, and a free and lively press. Fourth, in the absence of 'popular nationalist' struggles for independence in the early postwar period, and after the withdrawal of both US military facilities and US support for authoritarian regimes in both countries, democratic institutions in Thailand in the Philippines do not appear to have encouraged the emergence of major political parties or social movements fighting for radical social change. Rather, fifth and finally, in both Thailand and the Philippines the (re)establishment of democratic institutions since the mid-1980s has given rise to comparable forms of money politics and local bossism.[30] In short, in all of Southeast Asia there are no two other countries so socially and politically alike as the Philippines and Thailand.

The salient differences between the two countries can be seen more clearly as the product of distinctly diverging patterns of state formation and democratisation. In striking contrast with the decentralised, American-style 'colonial democracy' in the early twentieth-century Philippines described in previous chapters of this volume, the same period saw the emergence of a centralised bureaucracy in independent Siam virtually unencumbered by concessions to localised forces of socio-linguistic diversity and residual aristocratic privilege. With the *fin-de-siècle* creation of a Ministry of the Interior and a Ministry of Finance, the famously 'modernising' monarch Chulalongkorn (Rama V) succeeded in subordinating various principalities on the fringes of the realm to the exertions and exactions of policing and revenue-collecting agents dispatched from Bangkok and, with a rapidly achieved regularity, rotated from district to district and province to province.[31] Moreover, following the *coup d'état* of 1932, control over this apparatus of provincial administration shifted from the hands of absolutising monarchs to, in the post-war era, avowedly anti-communist and 'development'-orientated military officers, in what came to be known as a well-insulated (if internally factionalised) 'bureaucratic polity'.[32] It was Southeast Asia's most ruthlessly centralised state apparatus which oversaw the ethno-linguistic consolidation of the 'Thai' nation and the first few decades of industrial growth in Thailand in the postwar period,[33] and it was only after many years of this 'bureaucratic polity' that the state apparatuses were subordinated to elected officials thanks to democratisation. As the preceding chapters have made clear, the contrast with the Philippine path to (presidential) democracy could not be starker: early bureaucratisation and centralisation in Siam, and early democratisation and decentralisation in the Philippines.

Against the arguments of Yoshihara and other scholars who stress the salience of societal and cultural differences between the two countries, this volume's persistent emphasis on the distinctiveness of Philippine state formation suggests an alternative explanation for a wide range of differences – in economic growth rates over the past several decades, in the fate of southern Muslim separatist 'insurgencies' since the 1970s, and in the state of democracy today – between the Philippines and Thailand. As noted in Chapter Four, for example, Thailand's much greater success in maintaining high rates of industrial growth since the 1970s and the Philippines' contemporaneous experience of relative economic stagnation and decline must be situated within the context of the strikingly different state structures and political trends in the two countries. In Thailand, economic 'take-off' was achieved against the backdrop of the breakdown of the 'bureaucratic polity' in the 1970s and the shift towards parliamentary democracy in the 1980s, processes which subjected governments to greater public scrutiny and bankers and businessmen to greater competitive pressures, even as policy-makers and bureaucrats retained a measure of insulation from 'politics' thanks to the rather late and somewhat halting pattern of democratisation.[34] In the Philippines, industrial slow-down and increasing immiseration proceeded under the aegis of Marcos' martial law regime, which centralised power in the hands of a highly unaccountable president whose background as an elected politician – and concern for future elections – prefigured the concentration of monopoly rents in the hands of a close circle of cronies and the accumulation of enormous liquid, secure assets outside the country. In short, early American-style democratisation (and, arguably, Cold War-era US support) rendered the Philippines' experiment with authoritarianism in the 1970s and 1980s a much less effective rubric for economic growth than Thailand's fading 'bureaucratic polity' and fledgling democracy in the same period.

Differences in state structures also help to explain the varying strength of southern Muslim armed separatist movements and other threats to 'peace and order' in the Philippines and Thailand. As noted above, Yoshihara views this question through the prism of 'national integration', and other comparative studies of the MNLF in the Philippines and its counterparts – PULO (Patani United Liberation Organisation) and BNPP (Barisan Nasional Pembebasan Patani [Patani National Liberation Front]) – in southern Thailand have attributed great causal significance to variation in state repression, non-Muslim migration and violence, charismatic Muslim leaders, economic deprivation, and foreign support.[35] Yet what is most strikingly different in the two cases is the timing of armed Muslim separatist mobilisation relative to state formation and democratisation. In the case of southern Thailand, where a ruthlessly centralising state had subordinated the former sultanate Patani to the Ministry of the Interior in Bangkok in the late nineteenth century and provided no official footholds for local Muslim leaders in subsequent decades, it was only during periods of heightened political contestation and uncertainty in the national capital – the brief Pridi interlude in 1945–47, the democratic opening of 1973–76 – that demands for Muslim autonomy or independence were voiced with any vigour.[36] Due to the centralisation and autonomy of Thailand's police and military institutions, moreover, suppression of the small-scale insurgency of the 1970s was not complicated by the kinds of local accommodations and alliances so crucial in the southern Philippine case as noted above. There were no Thai counterparts to the Muslim Filipino mayors, governors, and congressmen who aided and abetted the MNLF against the centralising drive of Marcos in the late 1960s and early 1970s, and the Thai generals in Bangkok did not share the same willingness to entertain the schemes for 'regional autonomy' and local live-and-let-live arrangements which came so easily to the (civilian, elected) Philippine president in the late 1970s and early 1980s. Hence the continuing strength of the MNLF in Muslim Mindanao and the Sulu Archipelago well into the 1990s, the Ramos government's deal with Misuari in 1996, and the remaining armed presence of the MILF in the southern Philippines today, two decades after the Thai Muslims of Pat(t)ani fell off the radar screen of the generals in Bangkok. A parallel of sorts is evident in the scattered 'areas of influence' still held today by the Communist Party of the Philippines (CPP) and its New People's Army (NPA), whose early organising efforts in the 1970s owed much to the assistance they enjoyed from anti-Marcos politicians (including Benigno S. Aquino, Jr.),[37] and whose subsequent growth in the early-mid 1980s was concentrated in the sugar, coconut, and logging areas most rapaciously plundered by Marcos and his cronies.[38] The Communist Party of Thailand (CPT), by contrast, enjoyed a much more limited period of armed mobilisation in the immediate aftermath of the 1973–76 democratic interlude, and claimed a much more restricted area of influence (the impoverished Northeast along the border with Laos) before complete demobilisation and dissolution in the early 1980s.[39]

As for the state of democracy today in the Philippines and Thailand, significant differences between the two countries likewise reflect contrasting patterns of state formation and democratisation. In both the Philippines and Thailand, vote-buying, fraud, and violence have continued to play an important role in elections, and the vast majority of elected officials in the two democracies are machine politicians, wealthy businessmen, or gangsters. Yet compared to the manifestations of money politics and local bossism observed in the Philippines, the contemporary Thai variant is distinctive in two key respects. First, the transfer of effective control over the state apparatus to *elected* officials came *relatively late vis-à-vis* the process of capitalist development, with enormous Bangkok-based financial, agro-business, and industrial conglomerates and up-country magnates with province- or region-wide empires already entrenched and equipped with ample resources for electoral competition. Thus prominent Bangkok bankers and industrialists have themselves assumed political party leadership posts or otherwise engineered alliances with regional clusters of local bosses (known as 'godfathers' or *chao pho*), and provincial businessmen have in some cases exercised *chao pho*-like influence over multiple constituencies or even provinces.[40] This Thai pattern contrasts with the much more attenuated relationship between the owners of major business conglomerates and politicians in the Philippines and the tendency for the economic empires of local bosses in the archipelago to be confined to their own municipalities or provinces. Today, none of the top business magnates in the Philippines has a seat in the Senate or even a nephew or son-in-law in the House of Representatives, and in the provinces there is no sign of bosses or businessmen with significant region-wide influence.

Second, in Thailand the subordination of the state apparatus to a parliament drawn from multiple-seat constituencies and without proportional representation has encouraged a highly fluid system of political parties held together largely by patronage networks (regional and national) and personal ties and coalition governments stitched together through multi-party Cabinets. Thus *chao pho* exercising control over several constituencies have found it relatively easy to install themselves or their stooges in Cabinet and thereby to wield considerable influence over the internal affairs of key central ministries and their local agents. With poor rural constituencies still outweighing the urban middle-class vote mustered in Bangkok, the only institutional checks on the upward mobility of provincial Thai bosses thus seem to lie in the residual prerogatives of the military and the King, who represent the vestiges of the 'bureaucratic polity'.[41] The distinctiveness of this configuration in contemporary Thailand again stands in stark contrast with the Philippines, thanks to important institutional differences between the two democracies. The Philippines' directly elected presidency and the peculiar institution of a nationally elected Senate, for example, appear to offer far greater opportunities for reformist and populist challenges to the politics of money and machinery than those provided by the parliamentary system and prime ministerial office in Thailand. Thus the 1992 presidential elections saw the narrow – and perhaps fraudulent – defeat of anti-corruption crusader Miriam Defensor Santiago, and the 1998 race saw popular action film star Joseph 'Erap' Estrada capture the presidency by a large margin; the Senate now features Santiago and fellow 'reformist' Raul Roco (a 1998 presidential also-ran).[42] In Thailand, by contrast, the 1990s saw the eclipse of former Bangkok Governor Chamlong Srimuang, a once popular reform zealot, and the takeover of his Palang Dharma party by a major business magnate cum machine politician.[43]

Finally, in the realm of civil society, the differential patterns of state formation and democratisation in the two countries likewise prefigure the much greater challenges to – or at least constraints on – machine and money politics in the Philippines as compared with Thailand. In Thailand, after all, the process of absolutist state centralisation under successive Chakri monarchs gave rise to a 'bureaucratic polity' famously inhospitable to autonomous associational activity in society, as exemplified by the consolidation and retention of state control over the ecclesiastical institutions of Theravada Buddhism (the sangha) in the late nineteenth century and for many decades thereafter.[44] Moreover, given the relatively slow and easy pattern of commercialisation of agriculture in the Central Thai Plain and the insulation of Thailand from the disruptions which facilitated revolutionary mobilisation elsewhere in Southeast Asia during World War II and its immediate aftermath, the CPT (and Thai radicalism more generally) enjoyed only a brief period of influence in the 1970s and was easily defeated before power was shifted from the military to parliament in the 1980s and 1990s.[45] Thai democracy today is characterised by the relative weakness of established civic associations on the one hand, and the relative paucity of 'residues' (e.g. labour unions, peasant associations, NGOs, environmental or human rights groups) from the era of radical mobilisation in the 1970s, on the other.[46] Indeed, one author has gone so far as to argue that it was precisely this 'dearth of social capital' in Thailand which facilitated the country's protracted period of export-oriented industrial growth.[47]

In the Philippines, by contrast, the early imposition of a highly decentralised form of (colonial) democracy – and the separation of Church and State – during the American period favoured the emergence and entrenchment of a broad range of voluntary associations and other manifestations of a relatively vibrant 'civil society'. Thus the Philippines has long played host to 'civic associations' like the Rotary Club and the Jaycees, professional organisations, Church groups, and philanthropic foundations, and as early as the 1950s, the country saw the emergence of labour federations, the Philippine Rural Reconstruction Movement (PRRM), and the National Citizens' Movement for Free Elections (NAMFREL).[48] Moreover, as noted in Chapter 2 of this book the restoration of democracy in the Philippines in the late 1980s proceeded against the backdrop of widespread extra-electoral popular mobilisation – by student associations, human rights activists, labour unions, peasant organisations, urban poor groups, and Basic Christian Communities – championed by the Left, and counter-mobilisation led by business groups and conservative elements in the Catholic Church hierarchy. In the Philippine politics of the 1990s, the legacies of this pattern of democratisation and contestation have been evident in a relatively strong union movement and in a broad range of non-govermental organisations (NGOs) working on issues of poverty, human rights abuses, environmental degradation, land reform, and the rights of women and children, and with variously 'Progressive', 'Church-y', or Business affiliations and orientations.[49]

The authors' evident 'Philippinist' sympathies notwithstanding, this paired comparison is not intended to cast aspersions on Thai democracy or to promote a rose-tinted view of contemporary Philippine politics and society, as the arguments made in various other chapters of this volume should make clear. Instead, the parallels and contrasts between the Philippines and Thailand drawn in the preceding paragraphs highlight the manifold insights afforded by a comparative regional perspective and suggest that not all of the oft-noted 'peculiarities' of the Philippines condemn the archipelago to immutable 'basket-case' status. Indeed, in the wake of the recent Asian economic crisis, some scholars have even suggested that the Philippine political system is better equipped than its neighbours to adjust to fluctuations in the global economy and to implement economic reform,[50] and as democratisation proceeds in Indonesia and possibly even Malaysia in the years to come, the achievements of 'people power', election-watch movements, and NGOs in the Philippines will likely continue to be admired – and emulated – elsewhere in Southeast Asia.

In contrast to the stereotypes argued against from the very first pages of the introductory chapter, this book has articulated an understanding of the Philippines based not on notions of an essentialised Filipino 'political culture' or an immutable Filipino social structure, but on an appreciation of the enduring distinctiveness of the Philippine state. Against the backdrop of this decentralised, electoralised institutional 'grid', successive chapters have charted the twentieth-century transformation of Philippine society motored by (dependent) capitalist 'development', chronicling catastrophe and 'progress', and tracing change in the realms of capital accumulation, class formation and contestation, popular mobilisation and electoral (re-)incorporation, urban social space and national consciousness over the past several decades.

Notes

1 The original Tagalog text reads: 'The sole mosque on the Zamboanga Peninsula, established by Hadji Abdullah Maas Nuño in 1885. This is the only Islamic centre [in the Philippines] known internationally and in such countries as Turkey, Saudi Arabia, India, Malaysia, Indonesia and Borneo. Here the teaching of Islamic precepts, practices, and jurisprudence flourished and rapidly spread Islam on the Zamboanga Peninsula, Basilan, and the Sulu Archipelago'. Translation by the authors.

2 The paragraphs below draw heavily on the following sources: Margarita de los Reyes-Cojuangco, 'The Samal Balangingis: An Experiment in Colonial Diaspora' (M.A. Thesis, University of Santo Thomas, 1986), pp. 132–137; Helen N. Mendoza, 'The Moro Tapestry', in Antonio E. Orendain II (ed.), *Zamboanga Hermosa: Memories of the Old Town* (Manila: Vera Reyes, 1984), pp. 229–250; and Hadji Jainuddin Nuño, 'Additional Historical Facts of Taluksangay Mosque', attachment to letter of 13 February 1991 from Hadji Jainuddin Nuño to Dr. Serafin Quiason, Chairman, National Historical Institute, Manila.

3 James Francis Warren, 'Trade, Slave Raiding and State Formation in the Sulu Sultanate in the Nineteenth Century', in Jeyamalar Kathirithimby-Wells and John Villiers (eds), *The Southeast Asian Port and Polity: Rise and Demise* (Singapore: Singapore University Press, 1990), p. 188.

4 James Francis Warren, *The Sulu Zone 1768–1898: The Dynamics of External Trade, Slavery, and Ethnicity in the Transformation of a Southeast Asian Maritime State* (Quezon City: New Day Publishers, 1985), p. 53.

5 *Ibid.*, p. 74.

6 Letter of 1 June 1918 from F.W. Carpenter, Office of the Governor, Zamboanga, Philippine Islands, Government of the Philippine Islands, Department of Mindanao and Sulu, to Carl M. Moore, Esq., Department Superintendent of Schools, Zamboanga, filed in the 1918 correspondence files of the Manuel L. Quezon presidential papers, Filipiniana Division, National Library, T.M. Kalaw Avenue, Manila.

7 See, for example, Eduardo Ugarte, 'Muslims and Madness in the Southern Philippines', *Pilipinas*, 19 (Fall 1992), pp. 1–23.

8 William Henry Scott, *Slavery in the Spanish Philippines* (Manila: De La Salle University Press, 1991), p. 3.

9 *Ibid.*, p. 54.

10 See: Warren, The Sulu Zone, pp. 104–125; Reynaldo C. Ileto, *Magindanao: 1860–1888: The Career of Datu Uto of Buayan* (Ithaca: Cornell University Southeast Asia Program Data Paper No. 82, 1971).

11 Warren, *The Sulu Zone*, p. 195.

12 See: Patricio N. Abinales, 'State Authority and Local Power in Southern Philippines' (Ph.D. dissertation, Cornell University, 1997), pp. 385–396; Jeremy Beckett, 'The Defiant and the Compliant: The Datus of Magindanao under Colonial Rule', in Alfred W. McCoy and Ed. C.

de Jesus (eds), *Philippine Social History: Global Trade and Local Transformations* (Quezon City: Ateneo de Manila University Press, 1982), pp. 391–414; and Thomas M. McKenna, *Muslim Rulers and Rebels: Everyday Politics and Armed Separatism in the Southern Philippines* (Berkeley: University of California Press, 1998), pp. 86–112.

13　On local politics in the southern Philippines during this period, see: Wilfredo F. Arce, *Before the Secessionist Storm: Muslim-Christian Politics in Jolo, Sulu, Philippines 1961–62* (Singapore: Maruzen Asia, 1983), pp. 30–31; Jeremy Beckett, 'Political Families and Family Politics among the Muslim Maguindanaoan of Cotabato', in Alfred W. McCoy (ed.), *An Anarchy of Families: State and Family in the Philippines* (Madison: University of Wisconsin Center for Southeast Asian Studies, 1993), pp. 285–309.

14　Thomas M. McKenna, 'The Sources of Muslim Separatism in Cotabato', *Pilipinas*, 21 (Fall 1993), p. 11. At the same time, (Christian) Liberal politicians in Central Luzon such as Senator Benigno S. Aquino, Jr. were similarly engaged in collaboration with the revived Communist Party of the Philippines (CPP) and its fledgling New People's Army (NPA).

15　On the local, national, regional, and international dimensions of the armed separatist movement, see: T.J.S. George, *Revolt in Mindanao: The Rise of Islam in Philippine Politics* (Kuala Lumpur: Oxford University Press, 1980); McKenna, *Muslim Rulers and Rebels*, pp. 138–169; and Lela G. Noble, 'The Moro National Liberation Front in the Philippines', *Pacific Affairs*, Volume 49, Number 3 (1976), pp. 405–424.

16　On the barter trade, see: 'Presidential Decree No. 93, "Establishing Guidelines for Liberalizing Traditional Trade for the Sulu Archipelago and Adjacent Areas"', 9 January 1973; 'Letter of Instruction No. 1409', 9 May 1984; 'Rules and Regulations Governing Barter Trade', Pursuant to Memorandum Order No. 24, 24 July 1986; 'The South's barter trade days are numbered', *Manila Chronicle*, 29 September 1988, pp. 1, 7; 'Barter trading is alive and well', *Manila Chronicle*, 21 May 1989, p. 5

17　On the links between Tawi-Tawi and Sabah, for example, see: Marites Dañguilan-Vitug and Criselda Yabes, *Jalan-Jalan: A Journey Through EAGA* (Pasig City: Anvil Publishing, 1998), pp. 128–141.

18　Katamsi Ginano, Interview, September 1996, Manado.

19　Thomas M. McKenna, 'Martial Law, Moro Nationalism, and Traditional Leadership in Cotabato', *Pilipinas*, 18 (Spring 1992), pp. 1–17; Eric Gutierrez, 'In the Battlefields of the Warlords', in José F. Lacaba (ed.), *Boss: 5 Case Studies of Local Politics in the Philippines* (Pasig: Philippine Center for Investigative Journalism, 1995), pp. 127–167.

20　Patricio P. Diaz, *To Tripoli and Back: A Discussion of Issues Involved in the Demand of Autonomy by the Moro National Liberation Front under the Tripoli Agreement of 1976* (Cotabato City: 1995); Eric Gutierrez, 'The Problems of Peace: A Troubled Transition Imperils the Peace Accord in Moroland but its Leaders Remain Confident', *Work in Progress Occasional Paper* (Quezon City: Institute for Popular Democracy, 1997); 'Compromising on Autonomy: Mindanao in Transition', *Accord: An International Review of Peace Initiatives*, 6 (1999).

21　For assessments of the MILF, see: 'Hidden Strength', *Far Eastern Economic Review*, 23 February 1995, pp. 22–28; 'To Fight or Not to Fight', *Far Eastern Economic Review*, 9 March 1995, p. 21; 'MILF shadow government up', *Today*, 5 September 1996; 'The Fire Next Time', *Far Eastern Economic Review*, 28 March 1996, pp. 26–30; and 'MILF: Force to be reckoned with', *Philippine Reporter*, 15 October 1996.

22　On 'men of prowess' in pre-colonial Southeast Asia, see: O.W. Wolters, *History, Culture, and Region in Southeast Asian Perspectives: Revised Edition* (Ithaca: Cornell University Southeast Asia Program, 1999), pp. 18–26.

23　Yoshihara Kunio, *The Nation and Economic Growth: The Philippines and Thailand* (Kuala Lumpur: Oxford University Press, 1994), pp. 211–253.

24　*Ibid.*, p. 220.

25　*Ibid.*, p. 128.

26　*Ibid.*, p. 128.

27　*Ibid.*, pp. 15–126.

28　*Ibid.*, p. 241.

29   G. William Skinner, *Chinese Society in Thailand: An Analytical History* (Ithaca: Cornell University Press, 1957).

30   On this point, see: John T. Sidel, 'Siam and its Twin?: Democratisation and Bossism in Contemporary Thailand and the Philippines', *IDS Bulletin*, Volume 27, Number 2 (April 1996), pp. 56–63.

31   Tej Bunnag, *The Provincial Administration of Siam 1892–1915: The Ministry of the Interior Under Prince Damrong Rajanubhab* (Kuala Lumpur: Oxford University Press, 1977).

32   Fred W. Riggs, *Thailand: The Modernization of a Bureaucratic Polity* (Honolulu: East-West Center Press, 1966).

33   Thongchai Winichakul, *Siam Mapped: A History of the Geo-Body of a Nation* (Honolulu: University of Hawaii Press, 1994).

34   Anek Laothamatas, 'From Clientelism to Partnership: Business-Government Relations in Thailand', in Andrew MacIntyre (ed.), *Business and Government in Industrialising Asia* (Ithaca: Cornell University Press, 1994), pp. 195–215; Richard F. Doner and Ansil Ramsay, 'Competitive Clientelism and Economic Governance: The Case of Thailand', in Sylvia Maxfield and Ben Ross Schneider (eds), *Business and the State in Developing Countries* (Ithaca: Cornell University Press, 1997), pp. 237–276.

35   See, for example, W.K. Che Man, *Muslim Separatism: The Moros of Southern Philippines and the Malays of Southern Thailand* (Quezon City: Ateneo de Manila University Press, 1990); and Syed Serajul Islam, 'The Islamic Independence Movements in Patani in Thailand and Mindanao of the Philippines', *Asian Survey*, Volume 38, Number 5 (May 1998), pp. 441–456.

36   On this point and more generally, see: Ruth McVey, 'Identity and Rebellion Among Southern Thai Muslims', in Andrew D.W. Forbes (ed.), *The Muslims of Thailand: Volume 2: Politics of the Malay-Speaking South* (Gaya: Centre for South East Asian Studies, 1989), pp. 33–52.

37   See, for example, Gregg R. Jones, *Red Revolution: Inside the Philippine Guerrilla Movement* (Boulder: Westview Press, 1989), pp. 27–57.

38   Benedict Kerkvliet, 'Patterns of Philippine Resistance and Rebellion, 1970–1986', *Pilipinas* 6 (Spring 1986), pp. 35–49.

39   See: Benedict Anderson, 'Radicalism after Communism in Thailand and Indonesia', *New Left Review*, 202 (November–December 1993), pp. 3–14.

40   On the *chao pho* phenomenon and the broad patterns of provincial bossism in Thailand, see: James Soren Ockey, 'Business Leaders, Gangsters, and the Middle Class: Societal Groups and Civilian Rule in Thailand' (Ph.D. dissertation, Cornell University, 1992).

41   *Ibid.*

42   John T. Sidel, 'Take the Money and Run?: "Personality" Politics in the Post-Marcos Era', Public Policy, Volume II, Number 3 (July/September 1998), pp. 27–38.

43   See: Duncan McCargo, *Chamlong Srimuang and the New Thai Politics* (London: C. Hurst & Company, 1997).

44   See, for example, Stanley Tambiah, *World Conqueror and World Renouncer: A Study of Buddhism and Polity in Thailand Against a Historical Background* (Cambridge: Cambridge University Press, 1976).

45   On this point, and on the comparison between civil society's counter-hegemonic potential more generally in Thailand and the Philippines, see: Eva-Lotta E. Hedman, 'In Search of Oppositions: South East Asia in Focus', *Government and Opposition*, Volume 32, Number 4 (Autumn 1997), pp. 578–597.

46   See, for example, Kevin F.F. Quigley, 'Towards Consolidating Democracy: The Role of Civil Society Organisations in Thailand' (Ph.D. dissertation, Georgetown University, 1995); and the essays by Andrew Brown, Philip Hirsch, Prudhisan Jumbala and Maneerat Mitprasat, Thitinan Pongsudhirak, and Scott Bamber in Kevin Hewison (ed.), *Political Change in Thailand: Democracy and Participation* (London: Routledge, 1997), pp. 163–250.

47   Danny Unger, *Building Social Capital in Thailand: Fibers, Finance, and Infrastructure* (Cambridge: Cambridge University Press, 1998).

48   See: Eva-Lotta Elisabet Hedman, 'In the Name of Civil Society: Contesting Free Elections in the Post-Colonial Philippines' (Ph.D dissertation, Cornell University, 1998). On the 1950s

in particular, see: ibid., pp. 11–176; and on the PRRM, see: Gerard Clarke, *The Politics of NGOs in South-East Asia: Participation and Protest in the Philippines* (London: Routledge, 1998).

49 See, for example, Masataka Kimura, 'Philippine Peasant and Labor Organisations in Electoral Politics: Players of Transitional Politics', *Pilipinas*, 14 (Spring 1990), pp. 29–78; Patricio N. Abinales (ed.), The Revolution Falters: The Left in Philippine Politics After 1986 (Ithaca: Cornell University Southeast Asia Program, 1996); G. Sidney Silliman and Lela Garner Noble (eds), *Organizing for Democracy: NGOs, Civil Society, and the Philippine State* (Honolulu: University of Hawaii Press, 1998); and Clarke, *The Politics of NGOs in South-East Asia*.

50 Andrew MacIntyre, 'Institutions and Investors: The Politics of the Financial Crisis in Southeast Asia', paper presented at the annual meeting of the American Political Science Association, Atlanta, Georgia, 25 September 1999. The authors are grateful to Professor MacIntyre for making available a copy of this interesting unpublished paper.

Bibliography

Abinales, Patricio. 'State Power and Local Authority in the Southern Philippines'. Ph.D. dissertation, Cornell University, 1997.

Abinales, Patricio N. (ed.). *The Revolution Falters: The Left in Philippine Politics After 1986*. Ithaca: Cornell University Southeast Asia Program, 1996.

Abueva, José V. *Ramon Magsaysay: A Political Biography*. Manila: Solidaridad Publishing House, 1971.

Abueva, José V. 'The Citizens League and the 1959 Local Elections'. In Raul de Guzman (ed.), *Patterns in Decision-Making: Case Studies in Philippine Public Administration*. Honolulu: East-West Center Press, 1963.

Abueva, José Veloso and de Guzman, Raul P. (eds). *Foundations and Dynamics of Filipino Government and Politics*. Quezon City: Bookmark, 1969.

Aguilar, Filomeno V., Jr. 'Phantoms of Capitalism and Sugar Production Relations in a Colonial Philippine Island'. Ph.D. dissertation, Cornell University, 1992.

Alano, Bienvenido Jr. 'Import Smuggling in the Philippines: An Economic Analysis'. *Journal of Philippine Development*, Volume XI, Number 2 (1984): 157–190.

Alarde-Regalado, Aurora and Hallare-Lara, Cynthia. 'A Profile of the Philippine Rice Industry'. *Rural Development Studies*, Volume 8, Number 3 (July 1992): 1–44.

Alavi, Hamza. 'The State in Post-Colonial Societies: Pakistan and Bangladesh'. *New Left Review*, 74 (July–August 1972): 59–82.

Alfonso, Caridad S. 'Executive-Legislative Relations'. In José Veloso Abueva and Raul P. de Guzman (eds) *Foundations and Dynamics of Filipino Government and Politics*. Quezon City: Bookmark, 1969.

Amnesty International. *Philippines: Unlawful Killings by Military and Paramilitary Forces*. London: Amnesty International, March 1988.

Amnesty International. *Report of an Amnesty International Mission to the Republic of the Philippines*. London: Amnesty International, 1982.

Anderson, Benedict. 'Elections and Participation in Three Southeast Asian Countries'. In Robert H. Taylor (ed.), *The Politics of Elections in Southeast Asia*. Cambridge: Cambridge University Press, 1996.

Anderson, Benedict. 'Hard To Imagine: A Puzzle in the History of Philippine Nationalism'. In Raul Pertierra and Eduardo F. Ugarte (eds), *Cultures and Texts: Representations of Philippine Society*. Quezon City: Ateneo de Manila University Press, 1994.

Anderson, Benedict. 'Radicalism after Communism in Thailand and Indonesia'. *New Left Review*, 202 (November–December 1993): 3–14.

Anderson, Benedict. 'Long-Distance Nationalism: World Capitalism and the Rise of Identity Politics'. Amsterdam: Centre for Asian Studies Amsterdam, 1992.

Anderson, Benedict. *Imagined Communities: Reflection on the Origin and Spread of Nationalism*. Revised Edition. London: Verso, 1991.

Anderson, Benedict. 'Murder and Progress in Modern Siam'. *New Left Review*, 181 (May/June 1990): 33–48.

Anderson, Benedict. 'Cacique Democracy in the Philippines: Origins and Dreams'. *New Left Review*, 169 (May/June 1988): 3–31.

Anderson, Benedict. 'James Fenton's Slideshow', *New Left Review*, 158 (July/August 1986): 81–90.

Anderson, Benedict. 'Studies of the Thai State: The State of Thai Studies'. In Eliezer B. Ayal (ed.), *The Study of Thailand: Analyses of Knowledge, Approaches, and Prospects in Anthropology, Art History, Economics, History, and Political Science*. Athens: Ohio University Southeast Asia Series No. 54, 1978.

Anderson, Perry. 'The Antinomies of Antonio Gramsci'. *New Left Review*, 100 (November 1976–January 1977): 5–80.

Anderson, Perry. *Lineages of the Absolutist State*. London: Verso, 1974.

Ando, Hirofumi. 'Elections in the Philippines: Mass-Elite Interaction through the Electoral Process, 1946–1969'. Ph.D. dissertation, University of Michigan, 1971.

Aquino, Belinda. *The Politics of Plunder: The Philippines Under Marcos* Quezon City: Great Books Trading, 1987.

Aquino, Belinda (ed.). *The University Experience: Essays in the 82nd Anniversary of the U.P.* Quezon City: University of the Philippines Press, 1991.

Arce, Wilfredo F. *Before the Secessionist Storm: Muslim-Christian Politics in Jolo, Sulu, Philippines 1961–62*. Singapore: Maruzen Asia, 1983.

Arillo, Cecilio T. *Breakaway: The Inside Story of the Four-Day Revolution in the Philippines*. Manila: CTA & A Associates, 1986.

Azurin, Arnold Molina. *Reinventing the Filipino: Sense of Being and Becoming: Critical Analyses of the Orthodox Views in Anthropology, History, Folklore and Letters*. Quezon City: CSSP Publications, 1993.

Azurin, Arnold Molina. *Beddeng: Exploring the Ilocano-Igorot Confluence*. Manila: Museo ng Kalinangang Pilipino, Sentrong Pangkultura ng Pilipinas, 1991.

Baja, PC Major Emmanuel A. *Philippine Police System and its Problems*. Manila: Pobre's Press, 1933.

Bakhtin, Mikhail. *Rabelais and His World*. Bloomington: Indiana University Press, 1984.

Baldwin, Robert E. *Foreign Trade Regimes and Economic Development: The Philippines*. New York: Columbia University Press, 1975.

Ball, Rochelle E. 'The Process of International Contract Labour Migration from the Philippines: The Case of Filipino Nurses'. Ph.D dissertation, University of Sydney, 1990.

Ballescas, Ma. Rosario P. *Filipino Entertainers in Japan: An Introduction*. Quezon City: Foundation for Nationalist Studies, 1992.

Barnett, Anthony. '"Cambodia Will Never Disappear"'. *New Left Review*, 180 (March/April 1990): 101–125.

Barry, Coeli M. 'Transformations of Politics and Religious Culture Inside the Philippine Catholic Church (1965–1990)'. Ph.D dissertation, Cornell University, 1996.

Barthes, Roland. *Mythologies*. New York: Hill and Wang, 1972.

Battistella, Graziano and Paganoni, Anthony (eds). *Philippine Labor Migration: Impact and Policy*. Quezon City: Scalabrini Migration Center, 1992.

Beatty, Jack. *The Rascal King: The Life and Times of James Michael Curley 1874–1958*. Reading, Massachusetts: Addison-Wesley Publishing Company, 1992.

Beckett, Jeremy. 'The Defiant and the Compliant: The Datus of Magindanao under Colonial Rule'. In Alfred W. McCoy and Ed. C. de Jesus (eds), *Philippine Social History: Global Trade and Local Transformations*. Quezon City: Ateneo de Manila University Press, 1982.

Bello, Walden. *Creating the Third Force: US-Sponsored Low Intensity Conflict in the Philippines*. San Francisco: Institute for Food and Development Policy, 1987.

Bello, Walden and Rivera, Severino (eds). *The Logistics of Repression and Other Essays: The Role of U.S. Assistance in Consolidating the Martial Law Regime in the Philippines*. New York: Friends of the Filipino People, 1977.

Beltran, Mary Ruby Palma and Javate-De Dios, Aurora (eds). *Filipino Women Overseas Contract Workers: At What Cost?* Manila: Goodwill Trading Company, 1992.

Benatiro, PC Lt. Col. Hiram C. 'An Evaluation of the Government's Campaign Against Illegal Fishing in the Province of Cebu'. M.A. Thesis, National Defense College of the Philippines, 1990.

Bentley, G. Carter. 'Mohamad Ali Dimaporo: A Modern Maranao Datu'. In Alfred W. McCoy (ed.), *An Anarchy of Families: State and Family in the Philippines*. Madison: University of Wisconsin Center for Southeast Asian Studies, 1993.

Berlin, Donald Lane. 'Prelude to Martial Law: An Examination of Pre-1972 Philippine Civil-Military Relations'. Ph.D. dissertation, University of South Carolina, 1982.

Berreman, Gerald D. 'The Incredible "Tasaday": Deconstructing the Myth of a "Stone-Age" People'. *Cultural Survival Quarterly*, Volume 15, Number 1 (1991): 3–44.

Berry, William. 'The Changing Role of the Philippine Military During Martial Law and Implications for the Future'. In Edward A. Olsen and Stephen J. Jurika, Jr. (eds), *The Armed Forces in Contemporary Asian Societies*. Boulder: Westview Press, 1986.

Billig, Michael S. '"Syrup in the Wheels of Progress": The Inefficient Organization of the Philippine Sugar Industry'. *Journal of Southeast Asian Studies*, Volume 24, Number 1 (March 1993): 122–147.

Blaufarb, Douglas. *The Counterinsurgency Era: U.S. Doctrine and Performance 1950 to the Present*. New York: The Free Press, 1977.

Bolongaita, Emiliano P. 'The Breakdown of Philippine Democracy: A Comparative Institutional Analysis'. Ph.D. dissertation, University of Notre Dame, 1996.

Bonner, Raymond. *Waltzing with a Dictator: The Marcoses and the Making of American Policy*. New York: Times Books, 1987.

Boyce, James K. *The Philippines: The Political Economy of Growth and Impoverishment in the Marcos Era*. Honolulu: University of Hawaii Press, 1993.

Broad, Robin. *Unequal Alliance: The World Bank, the International Monetary Fund, and the Philippines*. Berkeley: University of California Press, 1988.

Buck-Morss, Susan. *The Dialectics of Seeing: Walter Benjamin and the Arcades Project*. Cambridge: MIT Press, 1989.

Bunnag, Tej. *The Provincial Administration of Siam 1892–1915: The Ministry of the Interior Under Prince Damrong Rajanubhab*. Kuala Lumpur: Oxford University Press, 1977.

Burnham, Walter Dean. *Critical Elections and the Mainsprings of American Politics*. New York: W.W. Norton & Company, 1970.

Byington, Kaa. *Bantay ng Bayan: Stories from the NAMFREL Crusade 1984–86*. Manila: Bookmark, 1988.

Campos, Cicero C. 'The Role of the Police in the Philippines: A Case Study from the Third World'. Ph.D. dissertation, Michigan State University, 1983.

Cannell, Fenella. 'Catholicism, Spirit Mediums and the Ideal of Beauty in a Bicolano Community, Philippines'. Ph.D. dissertation, London School of Economics, 1991.

Canoy, Reuben R. *The Counterfeit Revolution: The Philippines from Martial Law to the Aquino Assassination*. Manila: Philippine Editions, 1981.

Caoili, Manuel A. *The Origins of Metropolitan Manila: A Political and Social Analysis*. Quezon City: New Day Publishers, 1988.

Caruncho, Eric S. *Punks, Poets, Poseurs: Reportage on Pinoy Rock & Roll*. Pasig City: Anvil Publishing, 1996.

Cauton, Josefa Karunungan. 'Presidential Versus Legislative Control over Disbursement of Public Funds. M.A. thesis, University of the Philippines, 1971.

Chaloemtiarana, Thak. *Thailand: The Politics of Despotic Paternalism*. Bangkok: Social Science Association of Thailand, 1979.

Chapman, Paul K. *Trouble On Board: The Plight of International Seafarers*. Ithaca: ILR Press, 1992.

Chapman, William. *Inside the Philippine Revolution*. New York: W.W. Norton & Company, 1987.

Cheong, Sally. *Corporate Groupings in the KLSE*. Kuala Lumpur: Modern Law Publishers and Distributors, 1990.

Chubb, Judith. *Patronage, Power, and Poverty in Southern Italy: A Tale of Two Cities*. Cambridge: Cambridge University Press, 1982.

Clarke, Gerard. *The Politics of NGOs in South-East Asia: Participation and Protest in the Philippines*. London: Routledge, 1998.

Collier, Christopher James. 'The Politics of Insurrection in Davao, Philippines'. Ph.D. dissertation, University of Hawai'i, 1997.

Concepcion, Venancio. *'La Tragedia' del Banco Nacional Filipino*. Manila: 1927.

Constantino, Renato. *Neocolonial Identity and Counter-Consciousness: Essays on Cultural Decolonization*. London: Merlin Press, 1978.

Coquia, Jorge R. *The Philippine Presidential Election of 1953*. Manila: University Publishing Company, 1955.

Corpus, Victor N. *Silent War*. Quezon City: VNC Enterprises, 1989.

Corpuz, Onofre D. *The Bureaucracy in the Philippines*. Manila: University of the Philippines Institute of Public Administration, Studies in Public Administration No. 4, 1957.

Corpuz, Onofre D. *The Roots of the Filipino Nation*. Volumes I and II. Quezon City: Aklahi Foundation, 1989.

Cortes, Irene. *The Philippine Presidency: A Study of Executive Power*. Quezon City: Philippine Legal Studies, College of Law, University of the Philippines, 1966.

Crisostomo, Isabelo Tinio. *Governor Eduardo L. Joson: The Gentle Lion of Nueva Ecija*. Quezon City: J. Kriz Publishing Enterprises, 1989.

Crouch, Harold. *Economic Change, Social Structure and the Political System in Southeast Asia: Philippine Development Compared with the Other ASEAN Countries*. Singapore: Institute of Southeast Asian Studies, 1985.

Cullinane, Michael. 'The Changing Nature of the Cebu Urban Elite in the 19th Century'. In Alfred W. McCoy and Ed. C. de Jesus (eds), *Philippine Social History: Global Trade and Local Transformations*. Quezon City: Ateneo de Manila University Press, 1982.

Cullinane, Michael. 'Patron as Client: Warlord Politics and the Duranos of Danao'. In Alfred W. McCoy (ed.), *An Anarchy of Families: State and Family in the Philippines*. Madison: University of Wisconsin Center for Southeast Asian Studies, 1993.

Cullinane, Michael. *'Ilustrado* Politics: The Response of the Filipino Educated Elite to American Colonial Rule, 1898–1907'. Ph.D. dissertation, University of Michigan, 1989.

Cullinane, Michael. 'Playing the Game: The Rise of Sergio Osmeña, 1898–1907'. In Ruby Paredes (ed.), *Philippine Colonial Democracy*. Quezon City: Ateneo de Manila University Press, 1989.

Cultural Center of the Philippines. *Encyclopedia of Philippine Art: Volume III Philippine Architecture*. Manila: Cultural Center of the Philippines, 1994.

Cushner, Nicholas. *Landed Estates in the Colonial Philippines*. New Haven: Yale University Southeast Asia Studies Monograph Series No. 20, 1976.

Danguilan-Vitug, Marites. *Power From The Forest: The Politics of Logging*. Pasig: Philippine Center for Investigative Journalism, 1993.

Danguilan-Vitug, Marites. *Kudeta: The Challenge to Philippine Democracy*. Makati: Philippine Center for Investigative Journalism, 1990.

Danguilan-Vitug, Marites and Yabes, Criselda. *Jalan-Jalan: A Journey Through EAGA*. Pasig City: Anvil Publishing, 1998.

Daroy, Petronilo Bn. 'On the Eve of Dictatorship and Revolution'. In Aurora Javate-de Dios, Petronilo Bn. Daroy and Lorna Kalaw-Tirol (eds), *Dictatorship and Revolution: Roots of People Power*. Manila: Conspectus, 1988.

Davide, Hilario *et al. The Final Report of the Fact-Finding Commission (pursuant to R.A. No. 6832)*. Makati: Bookmark, 1990.

De Dios, Emmanuel. 'The Philippine Economy: What's Right, What's Wrong'. In *Southeast Asian Affairs 1995*. Singapore: Institute of Southeast Asian Studies, 1996.

De Dios, Emmanuel. 'A Political Economy of Philippine Policy-Making'. In John W. Langford and K. Lorne Brownsey (eds), *Economic Policy-Making in the Asia-Pacific Region*. Halifax: Novia Scotia: Institute for Research on Public Policy, 1990.

De Dios, Emmanuel. 'The Erosion of the Dictatorship'. In Aurora Javate-de Dios, Petronilo Bn. Daroy and Lorna Kalaw-Tirol (eds), *Dictatorship and Revolution: Roots of People Power*. Manila: Conspectus, 1988.

De Dios, Emmanuel. *An Analysis of the Philippine Economic Crisis*. Quezon City: University of the Philippines, 1984.

De la Torre, Visitacion R. *Advertising in the Philippines (Its Historical, Cultural and Social Dimensions)*. Manila: Tower Book House, 1989.

de los Reyes Conjuanco, M. 'The Samal Balangingis: An Experiment in Colonial Diaspora' (M.A. Thesis, University of Santo Thomas, 1986), pp. 132–137.

De Quiros, Conrado. *Dead Aim: How Marcos Ambushed Philippine Democracy*. Pasig City: Foundation for Worldwide People Power, 1997.

Debord, Guy. *The Society of the Spectacle*. New York: Zone Books, 1995.

Delacruz, Enrique, Jordan, Aida and Emmanuel, Jorge. *Death Squads in the Philippines*. San Francisco: Alliance for Philippine Concerns, 1987.

Department of International Economic and Social Affairs. *Population Growth and Policies in Mega Cities: Metro Manila*. New York: United Nations Population Policy Paper No. 5, 1986.

Diaz, P.P. *To Tripoli and Back: A Discussion of Issues Involved in the Demand of Autonomy by the Moro National Liberation Front under the Tripoli Agreement of 1976* (Cotabato City: 1995).

Doeppers, Daniel F. *Manila 1900–1941: Social Change in a Late Colonial Metropolis*. Quezon City: Ateneo de Manila University Press, 1984.

Doner, Richard. 'Politics and the Growth of Local Capital in Southeast Asia: Auto Industries in the Philippines and Thailand'. In Ruth McVey (ed.), *Southeast Asian Capitalists*. Ithaca: Cornell University Southeast Asia Program, 1992.

Doner, Richard and Ramsay, Ansil. 'Competitive Clientelism and Economic Governance: The Case of Thailand'. In Sylvia Maxfield and Ben Ross Schneider (eds), *Business and the State in Developing Countries*. Ithaca: Cornell University Press, 1997.

Doronila, Amando. *The State, Economic Transformation, and Political Change in the Philippines, 1946–1972*. Singapore: Oxford University Press, 1992.

Doronila, Amando. 'The Transformation of Patron-Client Relations and Its Political Consequences in Postwar Philippines'. *Journal of Southeast Asian Studies*, Volume 16, Number 1 (March 1985): 99–116.

Dumont, Jean Paul. 'The Tasaday, Which and Whose? Toward the Political Economy of an Ethnographic Sign'. *Cultural Anthropology*, Volume 3, Number 3 (1988): 261–275.

Edgerton, Ronald King. 'The Politics of Reconstruction in the Philippines: 1945–48'. Ph.D. dissertation, University of Michigan, 1975.

Erie, Steven P. *Rainbow's End: Irish-Americans and the Dilemmas of Urban Machine Politics*. Berkeley: University of California Press, 1988.

Evangelista, Oscar L. 'Lopez's Beleaguered Tenure (1969–1975): Barricades on Campus at the Peak of Student Discontent'. In Oscar M. Alfonso (ed.), *University of the Philippines: The First 75 Years*. Quezon City: University of the Philippines, 1985.

Evans, Peter. 'Class, State, and Dependence in East Asia: Lessons for Latin America'. In Frederic C. Deyo (ed.), *The Political Economy of the New Asian Industrialism*. Ithaca: Cornell University Press, 1987.

Fenton, James. 'The Snap Revolution'. *Granta* 18 (Spring 1986): 33–155.

Fiedler, Leslie. *Love and Death in the American Novel*. New York: Stein and Day, 1966.

Finin, Gerard Anthony. 'Regional Consciousness and Administrative Grids: Understanding the Role of Planning in the Philippines' Gran Cordillera Central'. Ph.D. dissertation, Cornell University, 1991.

Friedland, Jonathan 'Manila store wars', *Far Eastern Economic Review*, 22 December 1988, pp. 50–52.

Galang, Zoilo M. *Encyclopedia of the Philippines*. Manila: McCullough Printing Company, 1950.

Garland, Alex. *The Tesseract*. London: Viking, 1998.

Gatica, Rizal F. *Manila Stock Exchange: A Description of its Functions and Operations*. Manila: Manila Stock Exchange, 1964.

George, T.J.S. *Revolt in Mindanao: The Rise of Islam in Philippine Politics*. Kuala Lumpur: Oxford University Press, 1980.

Gilroy, Paul. *The Black Atlantic: Modernity and Double Consciousness*. London: Verso, 1993.

Gleeck, Lewis E., Jr. *The Manila Americans (1901–1964)*. Manila: Carmelo & Bauermann, 1975.

Golay, Frank H. *The Philippines: Public Policy and National Economic Development*. Ithaca: Cornell University Press, 1961.

Gonzalez, Andrew B. *Language and Nationalism: The Philippine Experience Thus Far*. Quezon City: Ateneo de Manila University Press, 1980.

Gramsci, Antonio. 'Notes on Italian History'. In Quintin Hoare and Geoffrey Nowell Smith (eds and transls), *Selections from the Prison Notebooks of Antonio Gramsci*. New York: International Publishers, 1971.

Grossholtz, Jean. *Politics in the Philippines*. Boston MA: Little, Brown and Company, 1964.

Guerrero, Rafael Maria (ed.). *Readings in Philippine Cinema*. Manila: Experimental Cinema of the Philippines, 1983.

Gutang, Rod B. *Pulisya: The Inside Story of the Demilitarization of Law Enforcement in the Philippines*. Quezon City: Daraga Press, 1991.

Gutierrez, Eric. 'The Problems of Peace: A Troubled Transition Imperils the Peace Accord in Moroland but its Leaders Remain Confident'. *Work in Progress Occasional Paper.* Quezon City: Institute for Popular Democracy, 1997.

Gutierrez, Eric. 'In the Battlefields of the Warlords'. In José F. Lacaba (ed.), *Boss: Case Studies of Local Politics in the Philippines.* Pasig: Philippine Center for Investigative Journalism, 1995.

Gutierrez, Eric. *The Ties That Bind: A Guide to Family, Business and Other Interests in the Ninth House of Representatives.* Pasig: Philippine Center for Investigative Journalism, 1994.

Gutierrez, Eric, Torrente, Ildefonso C. and Narca, Noli G. *All in the Family: A Study of Elites and Power Relations in the Philippines.* Quezon City: Institute of Popular Democracy, 1992.

Hagopian, Frances. *Traditional Politics and Regime Change in Brazil.* Cambridge: Cambridge University Press, 1996.

Hallare-Lara, Cynthia. 'A Profile of the Philippine Corn Industry'. *Rural Development Studies*, Volume 8, Number 5 (September 1992): 1–51.

Hartendorp, A.V.H. *History of Industry and Trade of the Philippines.* Manila: American Chamber of Commerce, 1958.

Hawes, Gary. *The Philippine State and the Marcos Regime: The Politics of Export.* Ithaca: Cornell University Press, 1987.

Hayden, Joseph Ralston. *The Philippines: A Study in National Development.* New York: Macmillan Company, 1947.

Hedman, Eva-Lotta E. 'State of Siege: Political Violence and Vigilante Mobilization in the Philippines'. In Bruce Campbell and Arthur Brenner (eds), *Death Squads in Global Perspective: Murder with Deniability.* New York: St Martin's Press, 2000.

Hedman, Eva-Lotta E. 'In the Name of Civil Society: Contesting Free Elections in the Post-Colonial Philippines'. Ph.D. dissertation, Cornell University, 1998.

Hedman, Eva-Lotta E. 'In Search of Oppositions: South East Asia in Focus'. *Government and Opposition*, Volume 32, Number 4 (Autumn 1997): 578–597.

Hedman, Eva-Lotta E. 'Elections in the Early Philippine Republic: Showcase of Democracy in Post-War Southeast Asia'. Paper presented at the Annual Meeting of the Association for Asian Studies, Chicago, March 1997.

Hedman, Eva-Lotta E. 'Beyond Boycott: The Philippine Left and Electoral Politics After 1986'. In Patricio N. Abinales (ed.), *The Revolution Falters: The Left in Philippine Politics After 1986.* Ithaca: Cornell University Southeast Asia Program, 1996.

Heh-song, Wang. 'Philippines: The New Frontier for Foreign Investment from Taiwan'. *Philippine Studies*, Volume 43 (First Quarter 1995): 93–104.

Herman, Edward S. and Brodhead, Frank. *Demonstration Elections: U.S.-Staged Elections in the Dominican Republic, Vietnam, and El Salvador.* Boston: South End Press, 1984.

Hernandez, Carolina G. 'The Extent of Civilian Control of the Military in the Philippines: 1946–1976'. Ph.D. dissertation, State University of New York at Buffalo, 1979.

Hewison, Kevin. *Bankers and Bureaucrats: Capital and the Role of the State in Thailand.* New Haven: Yale University Southeast Asian Studies, 1989.

Hewison, Kevin (ed.). *Political Change in Thailand: Democracy and Participation.* London: Routledge, 1997.

Hilsdon, Anne-Marie. *Madonnas and Martyrs: Militarism and Violence in the Philippines.* St. Leonards: Allen & Unwin, 1995.

Hingco, Tehrese Gladys and Rivera, Rebecca. *The History of Trawling Operations in Manila Bay.* Quezon City: Tambuyog Development Center, 1990.

Høeg, Peter. *Miss Smilla's Feeling For Snow*. London: Harvill Press, 1993.

Hollnsteiner, Mary R. *The Dynamics of Power in a Philippine Municipality*. Quezon City: University of the Philippines, Community Development Research Council, 1963.

Hutchcroft, Paul D. *Booty Capitalism: The Politics of Banking in the Philippines*. Ithaca: Cornell University Press, 1998.

Hutchcroft, Paul D. 'Predatory Oligarchy, Patrimonial State: The Politics of Private Domestic Banking in the Philippines'. Ph.D. dissertation Yale University, 1993.

Hutchcroft, Paul D. 'Oligarchs and Cronies in the Philippine State: The Politics of Patrimonial Plunder'. *World Politics*, Volume 43, Number 3 (April 1991): 413–450.

Iglesias, Gabriel U. and Tolentino, Abelardo Jr. 'The Structure and Functions of Congress'. In José Veloso Abueva and Raul P. de Guzman (eds). *Foundations and Dynamics of Filipino Government and Politics*. Quezon City: Bookmark, 1969.

Ileto, Reynaldo C. *Filipinos and their Revolution: Event, Discourse, and Historiography*. Quezon City: Ateneo de Manila University Press, 1998.

Ileto, Reynaldo C. *Pasyón and Revolution: Popular Movements in the Philippines, 1840–1910*. Quezon City: Ateneo de Manila University Press, 1979.

Ileto, Reynaldo C. *Magindanao: 1860–1888: The Career of Datu Uto of Buayan*. Ithaca: Cornell University Southeast Asia Program Data Paper No. 82, 1971.

Infante, J. Eddie. *Inside Philippine Movies 1970–1990: Essays for Students of Philippine Cinema*. Quezon City: Ateneo de Manila University Press, 1991.

Ira, Luning. *Streets of Manila*. Manila: GCF Books, 1977.

Javate-de Dios, Aurora, Daroy, Petronilo Bn. and Kalaw-Tirol, Lorna (eds). *Dictatorship and Revolution: Roots of People Power*. Manila: Conspectus, 1988.

Joaquin, Nick. *Manila My Manila: A History for the Young*. Manila: Republic of the Philippines, 1990.

Joaquin, Nick. *Almanac for Manileños*. Manila: Mr & Ms Publications, 1979.

Jones, Gregg R. *Red Revolution: Inside the Philippine Guerrilla Movement*. Boulder: Westview Press, 1989.

José, Ricardo Trota. *The Philippine Army 1935–1942*. Quezon City: Ateneo de Manila University Press, 1992.

Juan, Go Bon. 'Ethnic Chinese in Philippine Banking'. *Tulay*, 4 October 1992, pp. 8–9.

Kaplan, David E. and Dubro, Alec. *Yakuza*. New York: Macmillan, 1986.

Kaviraj, Sudipta. 'Filth and the Public Sphere'. *Public Culture*, Volume 10, Number 1 (1997): 83–113.

Kerkvliet, Benedict J. Tria. *Everyday Politics in the Philippines: Class and Status Relations in a Central Luzon Village*. Berkeley: University of California Press, 1990.

Kerkvliet, Benedict J. 'Patterns of Philippine Resistance and Rebellion, 1970–1986'. *Pilipinas*, 6 (Spring 1986): 35–49.

Kerkvliet, Benedict J. *The Huk Rebellion: A Study of Peasant Revolt in the Philippines*. Berkeley: University of California Press, 1977.

Kerkvliet, Benedict J. and Mojares, Resil B. (eds). *From Marcos to Aquino: Local Perspectives on Political Transition in the Philippines*. Quezon City: Ateneo de Manila University Press, 1991.

Kimura, Masataka. 'Philippine Peasant and Labor Organizations in Electoral Politics: Players of Transitional Politics'. *Pilipinas*, 14 (Spring 1990): 29–78.

Kowaleski, David. 'Vigilante Counterinsurgency and Human Rights in the Philippines: A Statistical Analysis'. *Human Rights Quarterly*, Volume 12, Number 2 (1990): 246–264.

Lacaba, José F. *Days of Quiet, Nights of Rage: The First Quarter Storm and Related Events*. Manila: Salinlahi Publishing House, 1982.

Lachica, Eduardo. *Huk: Agrarian Society in Revolt*. Manila: Solidaridad Publishing House, 1971.

Landé, Carl H. *Leaders, Factions, and Parties: The Structure of Philippine Politics*. New Haven: Yale University Southeast Asia Studies, 1964.

Lansigan, Nicolas P. 'The Chinese Stranglehold in the Lumber Industry'. M.A. Thesis, Manila Central University, 1949.

Laquian, Aprodicio. 'The City in Nation-Building: Politics in Metro Manila'. Ph.D. dissertation, Massachusetts Institute of Technology, 1965.

Laquian, Aprodicio. 'Manila'. In William A. Dobson and D.E. Regan (eds), *Great Cities of the World: Their Government, Politics and Planning*. London: Allen & Unwin, 1954.

Larkin, John. *The Pampangans: Colonial Society in a Philippine Province*. Berkeley: University of California Press, 1972.

Laothamatas, Anek. 'From Clientelism to Partnership: Business-Government relations in Thailand'. In Andrew MacIntyre (ed.), *Business and Government in Industrialising Asia*. Ithaca: Cornell University Press, 1994.

Laureta, Amancia G. 'Legislative Authorization of the Budget'. In José Veloso Abueva and Raul P. de Guzman (eds), *Foundations and Dynamics of Filipino Government and Politics*. Quezon City: Bookmark, 1969.

Lawyers Committee for Human Rights. *Vigilantes in the Philippines: A Threat to Democratic Rule*. New York: Lawyers Committee for Human Rights, 1987.

Lefebvre, Henri. *The Production of Space*. Oxford: Basil Blackwell, 1991.

Linz, Juan J. and Valenzuela, Arturo (eds). *The Failure of Presidential Democracy: Comparative Perspectives*. Baltimore: Johns Hopkins University Press, 1994.

Lopez, Salvador P. *Isles of Gold: A History of Mining in the Philippines*. Singapore: Oxford University Press, 1992.

Lowe, Barry. 'The Demonizing of the Philippines by Western Media'. *Pilipinas*, 28 (Spring 1997): 14–29.

Lynch, Frank and de Guzman, Alfonso II (eds). *Four Readings on Filipino Values*. Quezon City: Ateneo de Manila University, Institute of Philippine Culture, 1973.

Lynch, Owen J., Jr. 'Land Rights, Land Laws and Land Usurpation: The Spanish Era (1565–1898)'. *Philippine Law Journal*, Volume 63, First Quarter (March 1988): 82–111.

MacIntyre, Andrew. 'Institutions and Investors: The Politics of the Financial Crisis in Southeast Asia'. Paper presented at the Annual Meeting of the American Political Science Association, Atlanta, Georgia, 25 September 1999.

Magno, Alex R. 'Authoritarianism and Underdevelopment: Notes on the Political Order of a Dependent-Capitalist Filipino Mode'. In Temario C. Rivera (ed.), *Feudalism and Capitalism in the Philippines: Trends and Implications*. Quezon City: Foundation for Nationalist Studies, 1982.

Man, W.K. Che. *Muslim Separatism: The Moros of Southern Philippines and the Malays of Southern Thailand*. Singapore: Oxford University Press, 1990.

Manalili, Jesus M. 'Historical Suffrage in the Philippines and its Present Problems'. Ph.D. dissertation, University of Santo Tomas, 1966.

Manapat, Ricardo. *Some Are Smarter Than Others: The History of Marcos' Crony Capitalism*. New York: Aletheia Publications, 1991.

Manuel, E. Arsenio. *Chinese Elements in the Tagalog Language*. Manila: Filipiniana Publications, 1948.

May, Glenn, A. *Battle for Batangas: A Philippine Province at War*. New Haven: Yale University Press, 1991.

May, Ronald J. *Vigilantes in the Philippines: From Fanatical Cults to Citizens' Organizations*. Honolulu: University of Hawaii Center for Philippine Studies, 1992.

Mayo, Katherine. *The Isles of Fear: The Truth About the Philippines*. New York: Harcourt, Brace and Company, 1925.

McAdam. *The Political Process and the Development of Black Insurgency*. Chicago: University of Chicago, 1982.

McAndrew, John P. *Urban Usurpation: From Friar Estates to Industrial Estates in a Philippine Hinterland*. Quezon City: Ateneo de Manila University Press, 1994.

McCargo, Duncan. *Chamlong Srimuang and the New Thai Politics*. London: C. Hurst & Company, 1997.

McCoy, Alfred W. *Closer Than Brothers: Manhood at the Philippine Military Academy*. New Haven: Yale University Press, 1999.

McCoy, Alfred W. '"Same Banana": Hazing and Honor at the Philippine Military Academy'. *Journal of Asian Studies*, Volume 54, Number 3 (August 1995): 689–726.

McCoy, Alfred W. (ed.). *An Anarchy of Families: State and Family in the Philippines*. Madison: University of Wisconsin Center for Southeast Asian Studies, 1993.

McCoy, Alfred W. 'Rent-Seeking Families and the Philippine State: A History of the Lopez Family'. In Alfred W. McCoy (ed.), *An Anarchy of Families: State and Family in the Philippines*. Madison: University of Wisconsin Center for Southeast Asian Studies, 1993.

McCoy, Alfred W. 'Sugar Barons: Formation of a Native Planter Class in the Colonial Philippines', *Journal of Peasant Studies*, Volume 19, Numbers 3/4 (April/July 1992): 106–141.

McCoy, Alfred W. 'The Restoration of Planter Power in La Carlota City'. In Benedict J. Kerkvliet and Resil B. Mojares, *From Marcos to Aquino: Local Perspectives on Political Transition in the Philippines*. Quezon City: Ateneo de Manila University Press, 1991.

McCoy, Alfred W. (ed.). 'Quezon's Commonwealth: The Emergence of Philippine Authoritarianism'. In Ruby R. Paredes (ed.), *Philippine Colonial Democracy*. Quezon City: Ateneo de Manila University Press, 1989.

McCoy, Alfred W. *The Yellow Revolution*. Adelaide: Flinders University Asian Studies Lecture 17, 1986.

McCoy, Alfred W. '"Politics By Other Means': World War II in the Western Visayas, Philippines'. In Alfred W. McCoy (ed.), *Southeast Asia Under Japanese Occupation*. New Haven: Yale University Southeast Asia Studies Monograph Series Number 22, 1985.

McCoy, Alfred W. *Priests On Trial*. New York: Penguin Books, 1984.

McCoy, Alfred W. and de Jesus, Ed. C. (eds). *Philippine Social History: Global Trade and Local Transformations*. Quezon City: Ateneo de Manila University Press, 1982.

McCoy, Alfred. *The Politics of Heroin in Southeast Asia*. New York: Harper & Row, 1972.

McKenna, Thomas M. *Muslim Rulers and Rebels: Everyday Politics and Armed Separatism in the Southern Philippines*. Berkeley: University of California Press, 1998.

McKenna, Thomas M. 'The Sources of Muslim Separatism in Cotabato'. *Pilipinas*, 21 (Fall 1993).

McKenna, Thomas M. 'Martial Law, Moro Nationalism, and Traditional Leadership in Cotabato'. *Pilipinas*, 18 (Spring 1992): 1–17.

McMurray, Marisse Reyes. *Tide of Time*. Makati City: José Cojuangco and Sons, 1996.

McVey, Ruth. 'Identity and Rebellion Among Southern Thai Muslims'. In Andrew D.W. Forbes (ed.), *The Muslims of Thailanad: Volume 2: Politics of the Malay-Speaking South*. Gaya: Centre for South East Asian Studies, 1989.

Mejia, Patricia Torres. *Philippine Virginia Tobacco: 30 Years of Increasing Dependency*. Quezon City: University of the Philippines Third World Studies Center, 1982.

Migdal, Joel S. *Strong Societies and Weak States: State-Society Relations and State Capabilities in the Third World*. Princeton: Princeton University Press, 1988.

Miller, Stuart Creighton. *Benevolent Assimilation: The American Conquest of the Philippines, 1899–1903*. New Haven: Yale University Press, 1982.

Miranda, Felipe and Ciron, Ruben F. 'The Philippines: Defence Expenditures'. In Chin Kin Wah (ed.), *Defence Spending in Southeast Asia*. Singapore: Institute of Southeast Asia Studies, 1987.

Mo, Timothy. *Renegade, or Halo²*. London: Paddleless Press, 1990.

Mo, Timothy. *Brownout on Breadfruit Boulevard*. London: Paddleless Press, 1995.

Mojares, Resil B. 'The Dream Goes On and On: Three Generations of the Osmeñas, 1906–1990'. In Alfred W. McCoy (ed.), *An Anarchy of Families: State and Family in the Philippines*. Madison: University of Wisconsin Center for Southeast Asian Studies, 1993.

Mojares, Resil B. *The Man Who Would Be President: Serging Osmeña and Philippine Politics*. Cebu City: Maria Cacao, 1986.

Mojares, Resil B. *Origins and Rise of the Filipino Novel: A Generic Study of the Novel Until 1940*. Manila: Islas Filipinas Publishing Company, 1985.

Mojica, Proculo L. *Terry's Hunters (The True Story of the Hunters ROTC Guerrillas)*. Manila: Benipayo Press, 1985.

Montes, Manuel F. 'The Politics of Liberalization: The Aquino Government's 1990 Tariff Reform Initiative'. In David G. Timberman (ed.), *The Politics of Economic Reform in Southeast Asia*. Makati: Asian Institute of Management, 1992.

Mulder, Niels. 'Philippine Textbooks and the National Self-Image'. *Philippine Studies* 38 (1990).

The NAMFREL Report on the February 7, 1986 Philippine Presidential Elections. Manila: National Citizens Movement for Free Elections, 1986.

Nemenzo, Francisco. 'A Season of Coups (Reflections on the Military in Politics)'. *Kasarinlan*, Volume 2, Number 4 (2nd Quarter 1987): 5–14.

Nemenzo, Francisco. 'An Irrepressible Revolution: The Decline and Resurgence of the Philippine Communist Movement'. Unpublished Manuscript, 1984.

Niksch, Larry A. and Niehaus, Marjorie. 'The Internal Situation in the Philippines: Current Trends and Future Prospects'. Washington, DC: Congressional Research Service Report, January 1981.

Noble, Lela G. 'The Moro National Liberation Front in the Philippines'. *Pacific Affairs*, Volume 49, Number 3 (1976): 405–424.

Nolledo, José N. *The Local Government Code of 1991*. Manila: National Book Store, 1992.

Nowak, Thomas C. and Snyder, Kay A. 'Clientelist Politics in the Philippines: Integration or Instability?' *American Political Science Review*, Volume 68, Number 3 (September 1974): 1147–1170.

Nowak, Thomas C. and Snyder, Kay A. 'Economic Concentration and Political Change in the Philippines'. In Benedict J. Kerkvliet (ed.), *Political Change in the Philippines: Studies of Local Politics Preceding Martial Law*. Honolulu: University of Hawaii Press, 1974.

Ocampo, Ambeth. *Makamisa: The Search for Rizal's Third Novel.* Pasig: Anvil Publishing, 1992.

Ocampo, Ambeth. *Rizal Without the Overcoat.* Pasig: Anvil Publishing, 1990.

Ockey, James Soren. 'Business Leaders, Gangsters, and the Middle Class: Societal Groups and Civilian Rule in Thailand'. Ph.D. dissertation, Cornell University, 1992.

O'Connor, Edwin. *The Last Hurrah.* New York: Bantam Books, 1956.

Orendain, Antonio E. II (ed.). *Zamboanga Hermosa: Memories of the Old Town.* Manila: Vera Reyes, 1984.

Palanca, Ellen H. 'An Analysis of the 1990 Top Corporations in the Philippines: Economic Position and Activities of the Ethnic Chinese, Filipino and Foreign Groups'. *Chinese Studies Journal,* Volume 5 (1995): 47–84.

Paredes, Ruby (ed.) *Philippine Colonial Democracy.* Quezon City: Ateneo de Manila University Press, 1989.

Paredes, Ruby. 'The Origins of National Politics: Taft and the Partido Federal'. In Ruby Paredes (ed.), *Philippine Colonial Democracy.* Quezon City: Ateneo de Manila University Press, 1989.

Pemberton, John. *On the Subject of 'Java'.* Ithaca: Cornell University Press, 1994.

Perez, Tony. *Mga Panibagong Kulam.* Pasig City: Anvil Publishing, 1996.

Pernia, Ernesto M., Paderanga, Cayetano W., Jr. and Hermano, Victoria P. *The Spatial and Urban Dimensions of Development in the Philippines.* Manila: Philippine Institute for Development Studies, 1983.

Phelan, John Leddy. *The Hispanization of the Philippines: Spanish Aims and Filipino Responses 1565–1700.* Madison: University of Wisconsin Press, 1959.

Pimentel, Benjamin Jr. *Edjop: The Unusual Journey of Edgar Jopson.* Quezon City: KEN, 1989.

Porter, Gareth. *The Politics of Counterinsurgency in the Philippines: Military and Political Options.* Honolulu: University of Hawaii Center for Philippine Studies, 1987.

Putzel, James. 'Democratization and Clan Politics: The 1992 Philippine Elections'. *South East Asia Research,* Volume 3, Number 1 (March 1995): 18–45.

Putzel, James. *A Captive Land: The Politics of Agrarian Reform in the Philippines.* Quezon City: Ateneo de Manila University Press, 1992.

Quigley, Kevin F.F. 'Towards Consolidating Democracy: The Role of Civil Society Organizations in Thailand'. Ph.D. dissertation, Georgetown University, 1995.

Quirino, Carlos. *History of the Philippine Sugar Industry.* Manila: Kalayaan Publishing Company, 1974.

Rafael, Vicente L. 'Taglish, or the Phantom Power of the Lingua Franca'. *Public Culture,* Volume 8 (1995).

Rafael, Vicente L. 'White Love: Surveillance and Nationalist Resistance in the U.S. Colonization of the Philippines'. In Amy Kaplan and Donald E. Pease (eds), *Cultures of United States Imperialism.* Durham: Duke University Press, 1993.

Rafael, Vicente L. 'Patronage and Pornography: Ideology and Spectatorship in the Early Marcos Years'. *Comparative Studies in Society and History,* Volume 32, Number 2 (April 1990): 282–304.

Rafael, Vicente L. *Contracting Colonialism: Translation and Christian Conversion in Tagalog Society under Early Spanish Rule.* Quezon City: Ateneo de Manila University Press, 1988.

Ramos, Elias T. *Philippine Labor Movement in Transition.* Quezon City: New Day Publishers, 1976.

Reyes, Emmanuel. *Notes on Philippine Cinema*. Manila: De La Salle University Press, 1989.

Riggs, Fred W. *Thailand: The Modernization of a Bureaucratic Polity*. Honolulu: East-West Center Press, 1966.

Rivera, Temario C. *Landlords and Capitalists: Class, Family, and State in Philippine Manufacturing*. Quezon City: University of the Philippines Center for Integrative and Development Studies and University of the Philippines Press, 1994.

Rivera, Temario C. 'Class, the State and Foreign Capital: The Politics of Philippine Industrialization 1950–1986'. Ph.D. dissertation, University of Wisconsin – Madison, 1991.

Rivera, Temario C. and Koike, Kenji. *Chinese-Filipino Business Families Under the Ramos Government*. Tokyo: Institute of Developing Economies Joint Research Program Series No. 114, 1995.

Rocamora, Joel. 'The Philippines under Cory Aquino'. In Barry Gills, Joel Rocamora and Richard Wilson (eds), *Low Intensity Democracy: Political Power in the New World Order*. London: Pluto Press, 1993.

Roces, Mina. 'Filipino Identity in Fiction, 1945–1972'. *Modern Asian Studies*, Volume 28, Number 2 (1994): 287–293.

Roff, William R. *The Origins of Malay Nationalism*. New Haven: Yale University Press, 1967.

Rosenbaum, Jon and Sederberg, Peter C. (eds). *Vigilante Politics*. Philadelphia: 1976.

Rosenberg, David A. (ed.). *Marcos and Martial Law in the Philippines*. Ithaca: Cornell University Press, 1979.

Roxas, Cynthia and Arevalo, Joaquin Jr. *A History of Komiks of the Philippines and Other Countries*. Manila: Islas Filipinas Publishing Company, 1985.

Ruland, Jurgen, 'Metropolitan Government under Martial Law: The Metro Manila Commission Experiment'. *Philippine Journal of Public Administration*, Volume 29, Number 1 (1985): 27–41.

Rutten, Rosanne. '"Mass Surrenders" in Negros Occidental: Ideology, Force and Accommodation in a Counterinsurgency Program'. Unpublished Paper presented at the 4th International Philippine Studies Conference, Australian National University, Canberra, July 1992.

Schumacher, John N., S.J. 'The Propagandists' Reconstruction of the Philippine Past'. In Anthony Reid and David Marr (eds), *Perceptions of the Past in Southeast Asia*. Singapore: Heinemann Educational Books, 1979.

Schwarz, Adam. *A Nation in Waiting: Indonesia in the 1990s*. Sydney: Allen & Unwin, 1994.

Scott, James C. *Comparative Political Corruption*. Englewood Cliffs: Prentice-Hall, 1972.

Scott, James C. 'Corruption, Machine Politics, and Political Change'. *American Political Science Review*, Volume 63, Number 3 (September 1969): 1142–1158.

Scott, William Henry. *Slavery in the Spanish Philippines*. Manila: De La Salle University Press, 1991.

See, Teresita Ang. *The Chinese in the Philippines: Problems and Perspectives*. Manila: Kaisa Para Sa Kaunlaran, 1997.

Senate Committee on Justice and Human Rights. *Report on Vigilante Groups*. Manila: Republic of the Philippines, 1988.

Shalom, Stephen R. *The United States and the Philippines: A Study of Neocolonialism*. Philadelphia: Institute for the Study of Human Issues, 1981.

Shantz, Arthur Alan. 'Political Parties: The Changing Foundations of Philippine Democracy'. Ph.D. dissertation, University of Michigan, 1972.

Siapno, Jacqueline. 'Alternative Filipina Heroines: Contested Tropes in Leftist Feminisms'. In Aihwa Ong and Michael G. Peletz (eds), *Bewitching Women, Pious Men: Gender and Body Politics in Southeast Asia*. Berkeley: University of California Press, 1995.

Sidel, John T. *Capital, Coercion, and Crime: Bossism in the Philippines*. Stanford: Stanford University Press, 1999.

Sidel, John T. 'Take the Money and Run?: "Personality" Politics in the Post-Marcos Era'. *Public Policy*, Volume II, Number 3 (July/September 1998): 27–38.

Sidel, John T. 'Siam and its Twin?: Democratization and Bossism in Contemporary Thailand and the Philippines'. *IDS Bulletin*, Volume 27, Number 2 (April 1996): 56–63.

Sidel, John T. 'On the Waterfront: Labour Racketeering in the Port of Cebu'. *South East Asia Research*, Volume 3, Number 1 (March 1995): 3–17.

Sidel, John T. 'Coercion, Capital, and the Post-Colonial State: Bossism in the Postwar Philippines'. Ph.D. dissertation, Cornell University, 1995.

Sidel, John T. 'Walking in the Shadow of the Big Man: Justiniano Montano and Failed Dynasty Building in Cavite, 1935–1972'. In Alfred W. McCoy (ed.), *An Anarchy of Families: State and Family in the Philippines*. Madison: University of Wisconsin Center for Southeast Asian Studies, 1993.

Siegel, James T. *Fetish, Recognition, Revolution*. Princeton: Princeton University Press, 1997.

Silliman, G. Sidney and Noble, Lela Garner (eds). *Organizing for Democracy: NGOs, Civil Society, and the Philippine State*. Honolulu: University of Hawaii Press, 1998.

Simbulan, Dante C. 'A Study of the Socio-Economic Elite in Philippine Politics and Government, 1946–1963'. Ph.D. dissertation, Australian National University, 1965.

Skinner, G. William. *Chinese Society in Thailand: An Analytical History*. Ithaca: Cornell University Press, 1957.

Skowronek, Stephen. *Building a New American State: The Expansion of National Administrative Capacities 1877–1920*. Cambridge: Cambridge University Press, 1982.

Sommer, Doris. *Foundational Fictions: The National Romances of Latin America*. Berkeley: University of California Press, 1991.

Soriano, J. Clark S. *Political Clans and Electoral Politics: A Primary Research*. Quezon City: Institute For Popular Democracy, 1987. *elim*

Stanley, Peter W. *A Nation in the Making: The Philippines and the United States, 1899–1921*. Cambridge: Harvard University Press, 1974.

Starner, Frances Lucille. *Magsaysay and the Peasantry: The Impact of Philippine Politics, 1953–1956*. Berkeley: University of California Press, 1961.

Startup, Patricia M.M. and Laird, Eileen M.M. (eds). *Truth Uncovered: Fact-Finding Mission Report – Cotabato-Zamboanga del Sur May 1985*. Quezon City: Claretian Publications, 1985.

Stauffer, Robert B. 'Congress in the Philippine Political System'. In Alan Kornsberg and Lloyd D. Musolf (eds), *Legislatures in Developmental Perspective*. Danton, NC: Duke University Press, 1970.

Stifel, Laurence Davis. *The Textile Industry: A Case Study of Industrial Development in the Philippines*. Ithaca: Cornell University Southeast Asia Program Data Papers Number 49, 1963.

Sturtevant, David R. *Popular Uprisings in the Philippines, 1840–1940*. Ithaca: Cornell University Press, 1976.

Suehiro, Akira. 'Capitalist Development in Postwar Thailand: Commercial Bankers, Industrial Elite, and Agribusiness Groups'. In Ruth McVey (ed.), *Southeast Asian Capitalists*. Ithaca: Cornell University Southeast Asia Program, 1992.

Tadiar, Neferti Xina M. 'Manila's New Metropolitan Form'. In Vicente L. Rafael (ed.), *Discrepant Histories: Translocal Essays on Filipino Culture*. Manila: Anvil Publishing, 1995.

Tambiah, Stanle. *World Conqueror and World Renouncer: A Study of Buddhism and Polity in Thailand Against a Historical Background*. Cambridge: Cambridge University Press, 1976.

Tancangco, Luzviminda. *The Anatomy of Electoral Fraud: Concrete Bases for Electoral Reforms*. Manila: MJAGM, 1992.

Tarling, Nicholas. 'Some Aspects of British Trade in the Philippines in the Nineteenth Century'. *Journal of History*, Volume XI, Numbers. 3 and 4 (September–December 1963): 287–327.

Tarrow, Sidney. *Struggle, Politics and Reform: Collective Action, Social Movements and Cycles of Protest*. Ithaca: Cornell University Western Society Paper No. 21, 1989.

Taussig, Michael. 'Culture of Terror – Space of Death: Roger Casement's Putumayo Report and the Explanation of Torture'. In Nicholas B. Dirks (ed.), *Colonialism and Culture*. Ann Arbor: University of Michigan Press, 1992.

Taussig, Michael. *The Nervous System*. London: Routledge, 1992.

Taussig, Michael. *Shamanism, Colonialism, and the Wild Man: A Study in Terror and Healing*. Chicago: University of Chicago Press, 1987.

Tesoro, Benjamin D. *The Rise and Fall of the Marcos Mafia*. Manila: JB Tesoro Publishing, 1986.

Thompson, Edward P. *The Making of the English Working Class*. New York: Vintage Books, 1963.

Thompson, Mark R. *The Anti-Marcos Struggle: Personalistic Rule and Democratic Transition in the Philippines*. New Haven: Yale University Press, 1995.

Thompson, Mark R. 'Searching for a Strategy: The Traditional Opposition to Marcos and the Transition to Democracy in the Philippines'. Ph.D. dissertation, Yale University, 1991.

Tiglao, Rigoberto. *Looking into Coconuts: The Philippine Coconut Industry*. Manila: ARC Publications, 1981.

Tilly, Charles. *Coercion, Capital, and European States, AD 990–1992*. Oxford Blackwell, 1992.

Tilly, Charles. 'War Making and State Making as Organized Crime'. In Peter B. Evans, Dietrich Rueschemeyer and Theda Skocpol (eds), *Bringing the State Back In*. Cambridge: Cambridge University Press, 1985.

Tsuchiya, Kenji. 'Javanology and the Age of Ranggawarsita: An Introduction to Nineteenth-Century Javanese Culture'. In *Reading Southeast Asia*. Ithaca: Cornell University Southeast Asia Program, 1990.

Ugarte, Edgardo. 'Muslims and Madness in the Southern Philippines'. *Pilipinas*, 19 (Fall 1992): 1–23.

Unger, Danny. *Building Social Capital in Thailand: Fibers, Finance, and Infrastructure*. Cambridge: Cambridge University Press, 1998.

Valdepeñas, Vicente B. Jr. *The Protection and Development of Philippine Manufacturing*. Manila: Ateneo de Manila University Press, 1970.

Van den Muijzenberg. 'Political Mobilization and Violence in Central Luzon (Philippines)'. *Modern Asian Studies*, Volume 7, Number 4 (1973): 691–705.

Van der Kroef, Justus M. 'The Philippine Vigilantes: Devotion and Disarray'. *Contemporary Southeast Asia*, Volume 10, Number 2 (September 1988): 163–181.

Van der Kroef, Justus M. 'The Philippines: Day of the Vigilantes'. *Asian Survey*, Volume 28, Number 6 (June 1988): 630–649.

Ventura, Rey. *Underground in Japan*. London: Jonathan Cape, 1992.

Vergara, Benito M, Jr. *Displaying Filipinos: Photography and Colonialism in Early 20th Century Philippines*. Quezon City: University of the Philippines Press, 1995.

Vidallon-Carino, Ledivina. *The Politics and Administration of the Pork Barrel*. Manila: University of the Philippines, College of Public Administration Local Government Center, 1966.

Villamor, Ignacio. *Criminality in the Philippine Islands 1903–1908*. Manila: Bureau of Printing, 1909.

Warren, James Francis. 'Trade, Slave Raiding and State Formation in the Sulu Sultanate in the Nineteenth Century'. In Jeyamalar Kathirithimby-Wells and John Villiers (eds), *The Southeast Asian Port and Polity: Rise and Demise*. Singapore: Singapore University Press, 1990.

Warren, James Francis. *The Sulu Zone 1768–1898: The Dynamics of External Trade, Slavery, and Ethnicity in the Transformation of a Southeast Asian Maritime State*. Quezon City: New Day Publishers, 1985.

Weightman, George H. 'The Chinese Community in the Philippines'. M.A. thesis, University of the Philippines, 1952.

Wickberg, Edgar. *The Chinese in Philippine Life 1850–1898*. New Haven: Yale University Press, 1965.

Wickberg, Edgar. 'The Chinese Mestizo In Philippine History', *Journal of Southeast Asian History*, Volume 5, Number 1 (March 1964): 62–100.

Willoughby, Charles A. *The Guerrilla Resistance Movement in the Philippines: 1941–1945*. New York: Vantage Press, 1972.

Winichakul, Thongchai. *Siam Mapped: A History of the Geo-Body of a Nation*. Honolulu: University of Hawaii Press, 1994.

Wolters, O.W. *History, Culture, and Region in Southeast Asian Perspectives*. Revised Edition. Ithaca: Cornell University Southeast Asia Program, 1999.

Wolters, Willem. 'Rise and Fall of Provincial Elites in the Philippines: Nueva Ecija from the 1880s to the Present Day'. *Sojourn*, Volume 4, Number 1 (February 1989): 54–74.

Wurfel, David. *Filipino Politics: Development and Decay*. Ithaca: Cornell University Press, 1988.

Wurfel, David. 'The Bell Report and After: A Study of the Political Problems of Social Reform Stimulated by Foreign Aid'. Ph.D. dissertation, Cornell University, 1960.

Yegar, Moshe. *Islam and Islamic Institutions in British Malaya: Policies and Implementation*. Jerusalem: The Magues Press, 1979.

Yengoyan, Aram A. 'Shaping and Reshaping the Tasaday: A Question of Cultural Identity – A Review Article'. *Journal of Asian Studies*, Volume 50, Number 3 (1991): 565–573.

Yoshihara, Kunio. *The Nation and Economic Growth: The Philippines and Thailand*. Kuala Lumpur: Oxford University Press, 1994.

Yoshihara, Kunio. *Philippine Industrialization: Foreign and Domestic Capital*. Singapore: Oxford University Press, 1985.

Zeitlin, Maurice and Ratcliff, Richard Earl. *Landlords and Capitalists: The Dominant Class in Chile*. Princeton: Princeton University Press, 1988.

Index

Rizal Without the Overcoat (Ocampo)
145–6
Rolex Twelve meeting 46

Sabah 171
Samal Balangingi: slave raiding and
piracy 167, 168, 169
San Juan, Metro Manila 140
Santa Cruz, Manila 119–20
Sarino, Cesar 98, 113 n54
savage war: doctrine 39; tactics 42
scholars: studying the Philippines 3–6
Scott, James C. 70, 81
Scott, William Henry 168
Scout Rangers 42
Senate (Philippine) 17
shipping 107
Shoemart (SM) 119, 124, 130–3, 138 n75
shopping malls 133–4, 139 n85; Manila
118, 122, 130–3, 135, 135 n1, n3, 139
n90
slave: raiders 168–9; trade 166–7
slum areas: Manila 1, 124, 129–30
SM *see* Shoemart
small-town bossism 92–4, 101, 103,
108–9
Smoky Mountain 1
smuggling 100, 170, 171
social injustice 3–4
social mobilisation 24
socio-demographic change 23
Southeast Asia: heroin trade 3; *see also*
Sulu zone
Spanish: attack on Balangingi (1848) 167;
colonial legacy 6–7, 70–1, 141;
colonial rule 71, 169; 'Forward
Movement' 169; presence 7
state: American nature of 6, 8, 39; formation 40, 173, 175; poorly insulated to
elected officials 108; resilience of 37–
8; role in the economy 78; structure
7, 16–17, 38, 178–9
street vendors: Manila 125
strikes: at Shoemart 132; suppression of
97
student: movements 159; protests 24, 27,
43, 126–7, 128–9
sub-contracting: of political violence 38
suburbs: Manila 123–4, 127, 128
suffrage: electoral 14, 15, 17, 21, 29 n11,
n12, 41
sugar: centrals 72–3; industry
involvement in politics 72–4, 75, 78;
plantations 3, 37, 72

'Sugar Bloc' 73, 75
Sulu 7, 9; Sultanate 166–7, 168, 169;
zone 167, 169, 170, 171, 172
Sy, Henry 119, 130, 131–3
Sy Quia 70–1
Sy, Teresita 131, 138 n75
Sycip Gorres Velayo (SGV) 67
Sydney Morning Herald 2
syndicates: criminal 91

Tagalog: films 152; literature 156
Tagalogs 142
taipans 66, 67, 79
Taluksangay 166, 168
Tasaday hoax 150
Taupan, Panglima 166–7
The Tesseract (Garland) 2–3
Thailand: bossism 176–7; centralised
bureaucracy 174; Chinese immigration and assimilation 174; civil society
177–8; comparison with Philippines
9, 10, 80–2, 172–8; corruption 173;
democratic institutions 174, 178;
economic performance 175; military
173; Muslim separatists 175–6
Thompson, Mark 3–4
Tiglao, Rigoberto 8
Tinio, Manuel 72
tobacco industry 74–5
Tondo 1
Total War 53, 64 n108
tourism 103
trade: with the English 167; in heroin 3;
regional 170, 172; in slaves 166–7; *see
also* retail trade
'transformist' mobilisation 13–14, 20, 25,
27, 28
trasformismo 13, 29

UNICOM *see* United Coconut Oil Mills
United Coconut Oil Mills (UNICOM)
76
United States: armed forces 38–9, 40;
assistance to the Philippines 44;
Central Intelligence Agency 3;
colonial legacy 6, 7–8, 16, 38–40, 58,
141; colonial rule 15, 39, 72, 120,
142; economic dependency on 8;
military assistance 47; military
presence 1, 8, 42, 58; role in shaping
Philippine military 41; state structure
39; support for counter-insurgency
campaigns 42, 51; support for military
coup plans 49; support for